RETRAINING THE UNEMPLOYED

# RETRAINING
# THE
# UNEMPLOYED

EDITED BY

GERALD G. SOMERS

1968

MADISON, MILWAUKEE, AND LONDON

THE UNIVERSITY OF WISCONSIN PRESS

JM

*Published by*
*The University of Wisconsin Press*
*Box 1379, Madison, Wisconsin 53701*
*The University of Wisconsin Press, Ltd.*
*27–29 Whitfield Street, London, W.1*
*Copyright © 1968 by*
*The Regents of the University of Wisconsin*
*All rights reserved*
*Printed in the United States of America by*
*The Colonial Press Inc., Clinton, Massachusetts*
*Library of Congress Catalog Card Number 68–19575*

# ACKNOWLEDGMENTS

The studies presented in this volume were financed in whole or part under the Ford Foundation Project for Evaluation of Retraining of Unemployed Workers, under the general direction of Gerald G. Somers. Many acknowledgments are included in the individual chapters.

We are all indebted to the Ford Foundation for making this volume possible, and to the Foundation staff, especially to Dr. Victor Fuchs, now with the National Bureau of Economic Research, for their assistance. We are grateful too for the counsel of the Advisory Committee established under the grant: Professor F. F. Foltman, New York State School of Industrial and Labor Relations, Cornell University, Ithaca, New York; Mr. David Francis, President, Princess Coals, Inc.; Professor Paul F. Lazarsfeld, Department of Sociology, Columbia University; Professor Albert Rees, Department of Economics, University of Chicago; Dr. Stewart Smith, President, Marshall University, Huntington, West Virginia; and Mrs. Aryness J. Wickens, Office of the Secretary, U.S. Department of Labor. Like the others named, they should not be held responsible for deficiencies in this report.

The various authors, research associates and graduate research assistants who cooperated in the overall Ford Foundation project have also published articles and papers elsewhere stemming from their work on this project. A current listing of these publications is included in the Bibliographical Appendix. Others are still forthcoming.

I am personally grateful to the authors of these chapters for their cooperation, and to those who submitted their manuscripts and revisions early for their patience in awaiting the final compilation of all. The editorial assistance of Barbara Dennis of the Industrial Relations Research Institute and the administrative aid of Pauline Fosdick are greatly appreciated.

GERALD G. SOMERS

*Madison, Wisconsin*
*December, 1967*

v

# CONTENTS

# RETRAINING THE UNEMPLOYED

I

## GERALD G. SOMERS

■

## INTRODUCTION

Can a displaced West Virginia coal miner be retrained to work as a welder in a Norfolk shipyard? Are illiterate welfare recipients in Chicago able to acquire attitudes and skills which will permit them to take their place in the world of work? Is retraining a good investment? Who should be retrained? Who should do the retraining?

These have become vital questions in the United States in the latter 1960's. Unemployment rates have persisted at excessively high levels for certain sub-groups and certain depressed areas in the economy in spite of generally "full employment." Additional millions of youngsters are entering the labor market at a time when employment opportunities in some major industries have been sharply reduced by automation and other technological change. Riots in urban ghettos threaten to expand, and burgeoning relief rolls strain municipal budgets. There is a recognized need to wage a war on the remaining pockets of American poverty. At the root of many of these current problems of unemployment, poverty, and unrest is a lack of skill and productivity, suffered by workers who are unable to command a living wage or, sometimes, any wage at all. When poverty and unemployment are found in the midst of affluence and emerging labor shortages, the interest in retraining is likely to increase.

### THE GROWTH OF RETRAINING

Efforts are being made to meet these problems through a variety of legislative attacks, and through manpower and welfare policies. Retraining is prominently featured in a number of recent federal enactments aimed at unemployment and low incomes. Beginning in 1961, the federal government launched the first large-scale training programs for the unemployed enacted since the depression of the 1930's. The Area Redevelopment Act provided up to sixteen weeks of training for unemployed and underemployed workers in depressed areas, and paid them an amount equal to average unemployment compensation during their government-sponsored courses. A much larger program was made possible by the Manpower Development and Training Act of 1962. Here, too, unemployed and underemployed workers were to receive a weekly allowance equivalent to unemployment compensation, but eligibility was to be open to workers in all areas and could be extended up to fifty-two weeks. Amendments to the MDTA adopted in the following years allowed for additional weeks of payments and a further amount per week when required by the trainee's educational background and financial position. Retraining was also accorded an important role in aiding displaced workers under the Trade Expansion Act of 1962; and training was stressed in the programs for the expansion of youth employment under the anti-poverty legislation enacted in 1964. At the end of 1967, the Social Security Act was being amended to include extensive retraining provisions for welfare recipients. Indeed, it has recently been estimated that there are currently twenty-nine different federally-supported job training programs in operation.

These federal courses supplement several state training and retraining programs designed primarily for unemployed workers. Encouragement has been provided for the retraining of the unemployed in California, Connecticut, Massachusetts, Michigan, Pennsylvania, West Virginia and a few other states, either through specific legislative provisions or by means of administrative procedures which permit eligible workers to receive unemployment compensation while enrolled in a training course. The state programs are being increasingly integrated with federal projects.

Retraining has also come to the fore in a number of large cities, such as Chicago, Detroit, New York, and Philadelphia, where municipal welfare departments have sought to reduce welfare rolls by insisting that employable relief recipients take suitable training courses. A number of these community projects for hard-core unemployed have been assisted through the experimental and demonstration projects division of the Manpower Administration, U.S. Department of Labor, as well as the work experience and training, and Community Action projects, of the Office of Economic Opportunity. They will undoubtedly be absorbed by the new welfare retraining provisions of the Social Security Act.

In addition to these government programs, a number of industrial firms, sometimes under union-management agreements, have recently initiated retraining projects for workers displaced by plant shutdown and technological change. The most extensive of these private schemes is that established under the Armour Automation Fund in a number of mid-western cities. However, a growing number of companies, such as IBM, Xerox, Chrysler, and Ford, have designed programs specifically for the disadvantaged. And at the end of 1967 President Johnson announced the formation of a formal consortium of corporations to help train and place youth from urban ghettos. The on-the-job training provisions of MDTA have also been greatly expanded so that they constituted almost one-half of all MDTA trainees by December, 1967.

## THE NEED FOR RESEARCH EVALUATION

The growth of retraining programs is indicative of their widespread support in the battery of current labor market policies. Proponents of retraining see it as an essential part of the general education process as well as a means for improving the functioning of the labor market. As national monetary-fiscal measures move the economy toward higher levels of employment, unemployed workers and new entrants into the labor force must acquire the skills which will permit them to fill the expanding jobs. A training program which successfully meets this objective will contribute to the welfare of the trainees; and, its supporters contend, it will also be a sound investment for society. The gains in production, earnings, and tax receipts are likely to outweigh the costs. Since many of the unemployed trainees will have been receiving unemployment compensation or relief payments in any case, the training allowances often constitute a small net addition to transfer payments. In short, the proponents of the recently instituted programs see much to gain and little to lose from the retraining of unemployed labor.

But the government-sponsored courses are not without their critics. Although the principle of retraining—like that of education—cannot be readily opposed in a democratic society, there are those who discount the need for extensive government intervention in this field. In a full-employment economy private employers can be expected to continue their traditional practice of training workers to fill job vacancies; in a depressed economy there is little point in training workers for non-existent jobs. The critics point out that the major job vacancies are at technical and professional levels that are beyond the reach of most of the hard-core unemployed even after an accelerated training course. In an effort to make a good showing the training officials are likely to concentrate on the cream of the unemployed, those who could most easily find work without government aid; and they are likely to bypass the hard core who will continue to have difficulties in the labor market even after retraining. The question is raised whether such new approaches as the concentrated Employment Program and Human Resource Development program in urban centers, emphasizing counseling and placement services rather than training, are not less costly than and just as effective as retraining in expanding employment for the disadvantaged. The opponents of the new programs see government subsidies for training as a costly, unnecessary, and unwise social investment.

These contending views call for careful research evaluations of the public retraining programs. Since the retraining legislation has been couched primarily in terms of expanding employment, two basic questions in the required research evaluation are, "Do the trainees find jobs?" and "How much of the post-training employment success can be attributed to the retraining?" An economic appraisal must also include the related issues of the cost of training, the income gain, and the estimated returns —for the individual and for society.

Beyond the basic economic questions of employment results, costs, and returns on the training investment, a thorough research evaluation should answer many detailed questions of special interest to educators, sociologists and psychologists. We wish to determine the best means for motivating unemployed workers toward retraining, for selecting trainees, for preventing dropouts, for inculcating proper work attitudes among trainees, and for providing them with needed literacy and skills. Instructional techniques, course length and content, training site, and other educational policies must also be evaluated in relationship to the characteristics of various groups of trainees. How can techniques and policies utilized in regular vocational or on-the-job training be best adapted to the special problems and needs of unemployed workers? In brief, we want to know whether the benefits to the trainees would be equally forthcoming in the absence of a government-subsidized program; we want to know the cost-effectiveness of training compared to other labor-market policies with the same goals, and the most effective techniques of training.

## LOCUS OF THE STUDIES

The studies described in this volume are among the first to evaluate the recent retraining programs for unemployed workers established under federal, state, municipal, and union-management auspices. Although scattered geographically and conducted by different research investigators, the studies were conceived, carried out, and reported in a coordinated framework; and they attempt to answer the same basic questions. At the same time each study makes a unique contribution because of differences in locale, type of training, and analytical approach. There are enough similarities and enough differences to give value to a comparative analysis.

The West Virginia surveys include trainees in federal ARA programs and in courses for unemployed workers established under state legislation. The trainees, located in five counties, are compared with control groups composed of dropouts from retraining courses, applicants who were not accepted for training, workers who did not report after acceptance, and unemployed workers who did not apply for retraining.

In Connecticut, trainees in ARA and state-supported courses were studied in four areas: Ansonia, Bridgeport, New London, and Norwich. The experiences of trainees who utilized their skill are compared with three control groups: trainees who completed training but who did not utilize their skill, dropouts, and those who qualified for training but failed to enter the program.

The Massachusetts study includes ARA trainees in New Bedford and Fall River. Comparisons are made between those who enrolled in the training courses and those who refused to take the selection tests or who failed to report for training after their selection.

ARA courses in Tennessee are studied in the chapters by Earl Williams and Richard Solie. Trainees from Campbell and Claiborne counties are compared with the following control groups: dropouts, those whose applications for training were rejected, those who did not report after acceptance, and a sample of unemployed who did not apply for training.

The Michigan study encompasses five training programs for the unemployed. Three are sponsored by private agencies and two by the government under the ARA and the MDTA. Analysis is made of the experience of all Michigan trainees in these two government programs in 1962, and comparisons are drawn between ARA and MDTA results.

Five retraining projects are investigated and compared by Arnold Weber in Chapter VIII. They include two union-management programs for displaced meatpacking workers in Omaha, Nebraska, and Fort Worth, Texas; two ARA programs in Carbondale and Murphysboro, Illinois; and the vocational training program of the Welfare Rehabilitation Service of the Cook County (Chicago) Department of Public Aid.

The final chapter presents a quantitative study of the gains and costs of government retraining of the unemployed. The data gathered in the West Virginia follow-up surveys are utilized to evaluate the investment in retraining in terms of a comparison between trainees and a sample of previously unemployed non-applicants for training.

The summary of findings presented below is only suggestive of the rich detail found in the case studies.

## THE GAINS OF RETRAINING

### EFFECTS ON EMPLOYMENT

The most significant conclusion to be derived from these studies is that the retraining of unemployed workers is a sound social investment. In almost all of the surveys at least 75 per cent of the trainees were employed after their training. With few exceptions, the post-training employment rates of those who completed their government-sponsored courses were substantially higher than the rates experienced by appropriately selected control groups of workers. Although there are obvious difficulties in choosing the ideal control group for such studies—workers identical to the trainees in every respect save their completion of the government-sponsored courses—a number of the studies came as close to the ideal as the practicalities of the research situation would permit. Comparisons with dropouts from the training courses, rejected applicants, those who did not report after acceptance, and/or unemployed workers who did not apply for training, indicate an employment advantage for workers who completed the government-sponsored courses. When additional efforts were made, as in the West Virginia study, to ensure comparability by analysis within similar age and education categories, trainees were found to have a significant employment advantage over non-trainees of the same age and the same education. These results were corroborated in a regression analysis of the West Virginia data, in which completion of a retraining course was found to be a more significant influence on employment success than such variables as age, education, sex, race, regular occupation and labor market area. Regression analysis of the Tennessee program led to similarly favorable results for the value of retraining.

Although the overall employment record of the trainees is a relatively good one, these studies raise some question about the factors associated with retraining which are the most significant in explaining the trainees' employment success. Did the jobs obtained by the trainees result primarily from the new skills acquired in their training or were other personal and labor-market considerations more important? One approach to this question adopted by government agencies is to determine the proportion of employed trainees who were placed in "training-related" jobs. Unfortunately, the concept of training-relatedness is an imprecise one. Differences in definition and methods of obtaining information on this point explain some of the marked variations in findings in the case studies. But much of the variation may also be attributed to differences in labor market area, types of training courses, and characteristics of the trainees.

The high rates of training-related employment (80–100 per cent) found under the training programs in Michigan, Omaha, and Chicago undoubtedly reflect the choice of specific courses, geared to specific employment opportunities available in these areas. Only half of the employed trainees in Tennessee and West Virginia were in training-related jobs, primarily because of the severely depressed state of the labor market in these areas.

Labor market conditions also explain the relatively low ratio of training-related placements in the Connecticut studies, and Fort Worth. Desperate workers will abandon their newly-acquired skills in pursuit of very scarce job opportunities.

Even within depressed labor-market areas, high rates of training-related placement can result when courses are geared to the needs of specific employers, as with the woodworking course in Tennessee, the riveter and welder courses in West Virginia, and the courses for nurse's aides in a number of localities. There is also some evidence in these studies that older trainees and those with other characteristics that make them "hard to place," are less likely to find employment in training-related occupations.

The fact that trainees are placed on jobs can be construed as an important contribution of the retraining courses even if the jobs are not directly related to the training occupation. Employers frequently used successful completion of a retraining course as a general screening device for selection of employees from the ranks of the unemployed. A significant proportion of the employers interviewed in West Virginia, Michigan, and Tennessee stressed the importance of the general characteristics of the trainees, rather than a particular newly-acquired skill, in prompting the decision to employ these workers. In Murphysboro, Illinois, McNair Metals used the ARA training program primarily as a means to screen applicants for permanent employment, often assigning a worker to a job which was only indirectly related to his formal course of instruction.

Whether the retraining programs imparted qualities which managements value in potential employees, or whether the programs merely provided an opportunity for the demonstration of such qualities, they apparently made a notable contribution to the employability of the trainees relative to other unemployed workers.

Given the fact that trainees, as a whole, enjoy higher employment rates than similarly situated nontrainees, the studies also throw light on the factors which explain why some trainees do better in the job market than other trainees. Such personal differences as sex, age, race, and education undoubtedly play a part, but these studies indicate that other factors may be equally important. These include the nature of the particular training course, the trainee's previous labor force experience, and the labor market in which his training and job search take place.

Because of a high rate of withdrawal from the labor force, the post-training employment level of women was significantly below that of male trainees in the West Virginia surveys. On the other hand, Arnold Weber found little male-female difference in the employment records of the Omaha, Fort Worth, and Illinois programs. The divergent results are partially explained by differences in the types of courses and the racial composition of trainees in the two studies, as well as by the shorter period of follow-up in Weber's surveys.

Race was not found to be a significant factor in the placement of trainees in Weber's surveys even though a relatively large proportion were non-white, especially among the Chicago welfare trainees. The number of non-white trainees was too small in the other programs to permit valid comparisons by race.

Age proved to be a serious job handicap for the West Virginia trainees only for those over 55. On the contrary, there is a consistent positive relationship between the educational level of the West Virginia trainees and their post-training employment success. In selecting older workers for the training courses, it is likely that officials sought to ensure that the age handicap was offset by such compensating factors as higher educational levels, thereby improving the job prospects of older trainees.

The previous labor force experience of the trainees appears to be a major predictor of post-training employment success. Workers with lengthy periods of unemployment prior to training are less likely to find post-training jobs than workers who are employed most of the time in the months before their training courses. Those who were in unskilled occupations prior to their retraining are also less likely to find post-training employment. These results are not surprising in that the worker's pretraining employment experience generally reflects a composite of his personal characteristics, attitudes, and skills; and these can be only partly modified by accelerated training courses such as those described in this volume.

Post-training employment success is also closely related to the particular course in which the trainee is enrolled and to the nature of the job opportunities in a specific firm or labor market. Understandably, those who are trained for work in a particular establishment enjoy higher initial employment rates—and usually in training-related occupations—than those who are trained for general opportunities anticipated in the labor market as a whole. Thus, placement rates were high in the courses specifically designed to fill openings in the Technical Tape Corporation and McNair Metals in southern Illinois and in Lockheed Corporation and the Food Machinery Corporation in West Virginia. On the other hand, workers in auto repair courses and other service occupations often found that expected job openings, based on earlier forecasts by numerous small firms in the area, had disappeared or were not available to particular trainees.

These practical considerations are apparently more important in determining post-training employment success than the skill level of the training occupation. On the whole, however, the workers trained for semi-skilled jobs fared better than the unskilled and those who aspired to relatively skilled occupations. It should be noted that few of the courses in these initial government and private programs were of sufficient duration to prepare unemployed workers for the highly skilled or technical occupations which are in greatest demand in the current economy.

## EARNINGS, COSTS, AND INVESTMENT

The earnings of the trainees provide further evidence of the advantages accruing from the retraining courses. Where these studies draw comparisons between the trainees' earnings and those of nontrainees, the margin enjoyed by the trainees is shown to be appreciable. In most cases the trainees' earnings also rose significantly over their own pretraining income. Exceptions are noted, however. Some of the women in West Virginia service occupations had post-training income below that of nontrainees in a comparable age-education category. The earnings of women, Negroes, and older workers in the Chicago and Fort Worth programs were also relatively low even after retraining.

Society also enjoyed monetary gains from the retraining, quite aside from the welfare of its citizens. In addition to the tax revenue resulting from increased employment and earnings, total social payments to the previously unemployed trainees were substantially reduced. Their training enabled Chicago welfare recipients to leave the relief rolls; considerable savings in unemployment compensation resulted from the retraining courses in Connecticut; and a variety of social payments were reduced for West Virginia trainees, relative to nontrainees and the trainees' own pretraining experience.

Although few detailed cost data are included in these studies, there is evidence that the costs of the retraining programs to society and to the individual trainees can be readily recovered on the basis of the employment, earnings, and social payment records described above. Assuming the continuance of their post-training increase in earnings, it is estimated that the individual trainee in West Virginia can recover the costs (including opportunity costs) of his training within four months, and the government can recover its costs within a year. As is indicated in the final chapter of this volume, government-sponsored retraining of the unemployed in West Virginia has been a sound monetary investment for the workers and for society. There is reason to believe that this conclusion can be generalized to include many similar retraining programs in other areas.

## NONECONOMIC GAINS

The studies in this volume go beyond a dollars-and-cents evaluation of the gains derived from the retraining programs. They recognize the importance of the quality of the training and the satisfactions derived from the trainee's increased productivity by the trainees and their employers. Inferences as to quality are derived from comments of the trainees, employers, and others concerning the value of the retraining.

In general these attitudinal responses accord overwhelmingly with the favorable objective evaluations described above. But exceptions are noted. There are some specific criticisms of trainee qualifications, course content, course length, inadequate preparation of instructors, inferior training equipment, and inadequate placement procedures. These are to be expected as "growing pains" of a new program; recommendations for improvement are outlined in these chapters, and many of these improvements have undoubtedly been forthcoming since our surveys were completed.

Changes in morale, social status, and self-esteem as a result of retraining are touched upon in a number of the studies. Mobility patterns receive special emphasis. In general, however, morale changes must be inferred from the data presented on improvements in employment and earnings. Many long-term unemployed have been returned to the world of work through their retraining; and even some of those who failed to find initial employment undoubtedly derived satisfaction from society's concern with their future welfare. But other unemployed trainees, and applicants who were rejected for training may well have suffered a loss of morale when their aspirations were disappointed.

## THE REDUCTION IN UNEMPLOYMENT

Are we to conclude, then, that the recently-instituted retraining programs present a major "solution" to the unemployment problems in the United States? It must be noted that the programs up to 1965 assisted the trainees in finding employment, but they did little to reduce the total volume of unemployment in particular areas or in the nation as a whole. The most obvious reason for this limited impact was the small scale of the retraining efforts relative to the size of the continuing unemployment problem.

### CHARACTERISTICS OF THE TRAINEES

Even if the resources devoted to retraining courses were vastly expanded, we cannot be certain that large sections of the unemployed work force would be in a position to benefit from them. The studies in this volume show, in considerable detail, that by and large the trainees in the initial government courses were a select group, the cream of the unemployed. Since the basic purpose of the program is to return workers to employment, it is natural that the most promising were the first to be chosen.

If the programs were greatly extended, digging much more deeply into the unemployment barrel, would the favorable employment-earnings results found in these studies continue to be achieved? Arnold Weber's findings about "disadvantaged" trainees in Omaha, Fort Worth, and Chicago are encouraging on this score; but the results in depressed areas of West Virginia provide fewer grounds for optimism. Only a follow-up of expanded training programs for the hard core of the unemployed can provide more definite answers to this question.

### MOTIVATION AND ATTITUDES

In assessing the impact on unemployment, one must also examine the motivation of the unemployed to enter and complete a retraining course. The hard-core unemployed may be underrepresented in the training programs because of their unwillingness to participate as well as because of their rejection by the Employment Service. A number of the studies in this volume discuss the attitudes of workers toward entry into retraining and analyze the reasons for early dropout from the courses. Chesler's study of the Massachusetts programs is especially valuable in comparing the characteristics of unemployed workers who do show an interest in retraining with those who do not. Youth and a rising personal trend of unemployment are found to be the principal correlates of a favorable motivation for retraining.

Thus these studies of the initial courses under the retraining programs are generally encouraging. They give evidence of current achievements and future promise; but they also point to the magnitude of the tasks still ahead, and they emphasize the problems that remain to be solved if retraining is to fulfill the labor-market role assigned to it.

## SUPPORTING EVIDENCE OF OTHER STUDIES

The favorable results derived from these studies of retraining are buttressed by a number of other evaluations which have been completed in recent years. They lend confidence to the interpretation made by the authors of these chapters.

The most comprehensive evaluations of training programs for the unemployed have stemmed from institutional MDTA programs and similar programs established earlier by state governments and by the federal government under the ARA. Reports based on operating data of the MDTA fall short of the methodological ideal, but they far surpass the data made available by the vocational education institutions or most OEO programs. A wealth of data on MDTA training appeared in a 1967 report issued by Senator Clark's Subcommittee on Employment, Manpower and Poverty. Included are follow-up data on employment status three months after training and income data for brief periods before and after training. These benefits are cross-classified by the trainees' demographic characteristics and previous employment experience.

The data present the benefits in a favorable light. In 1964 and 1965 the trainees had a post-training employment rate of 75 per cent, and 62.5 per cent were in training-related jobs. On-the-job trainees had an employment rate of over 90 per cent. The median earnings were 21 per cent higher after training than before, and through January 30, 1967, the median post-training earnings were $1.74; these results were cross-classified by trainee characteristics, and it was found that the level of post-training economic status of the disadvantaged was below average, but the improvement over their pretraining status was greater.

Although these "benefits" of retraining may be questioned because of the absence of a comparable control group (other than national changes in general employment and income), they are buttressed by a U.S. Department of Labor study of the post-training experience of 784 trainees and a comparable control group of 825, with significant similarities in pretraining employment. Those who completed training had significantly better employment rates, stability of employment, and improvement in income as compared with the control group.[1]

Although these officially-sponsored evaluations are somewhat rough and ready, the findings are supported by an impressive number of more sophisticated cost-benefit and regression analyses of specific MDTA and MDTA-type training programs for the unemployed. Studies by Borus in Connecticut, Page in Massachusetts, and Somers and Stromsdorfer in West Virginia found favorable benefit-cost relationships for trainees relative to control groups.[2] Regression analyses by Stromsdorfer found retraining to be a major explanatory variable in the improved income of formerly unemployed workers.[3]

In a nation-wide evaluation of 1,200 MDTA trainees and 1,060 other persons who were unemployed about the time the training courses started, Earl Main of the National Opinion Research Center found that the employment rate of "completers" was 78 per cent compared with 55 per cent for nontrainees and, when numerous other variables were controlled in a multiple regression analysis, that the net effect of completing retraining was about $10 per week in family income.[4]

These impressive results are even approached by evaluative studies of retraining programs for the seriously disadvantaged. Cain and Somers found that welfare trainees were more successful in leaving the relief rolls than a control group of nontrainee welfare recipients,[5] and, in another detailed evaluation, Cain found a positive benefit-cost ratio for the Job Corps.[6] Regis Walther has reported employment gains for those in New York City programs, relative to a control group.[7]

Vocational retraining fares well when related to other human resource programs. Ribich and Hansen, Weisbrod and Scanlon, have found that retraining may bring about greater improvements in income than general education, especially for the disadvantaged.[8] And McKechnie has found that retraining, when coupled with geographic mobility, enhances income beyond the level reached by retraining or mobility alone.[9]

### SOME UNANSWERED QUESTIONS

These benefits of retraining programs are impressive. Their worth would seem to be well established. But there are still some nagging questions. One unanswered question is whether on-the-job training would provide even better benefit-cost ratios and whether methods can be found for encouraging on-the-job training of the disadvantaged. Another is whether non-training job development and human resource programs might do as well for the disadvantaged unemployed, without the higher costs of vocational training courses. Finally, will the benefits of the trainees, relative to the nontrainees, hold up after the passage of many years? Work is now proceeding on questions such as these,[10] but the final answers await another volume.

## REFERENCES

1. 90 Cong., I Sess., U.S. Senate, Committee on Labor and Public Welfare, Subcommittee on Employment, Manpower and Poverty, *Examination of the War on Poverty* (Washington: GPO, 1967), Vol. II, 240.
2. See D. A. Page, "Retraining Under the Manpower Development Act: A Cost-Benefit Analysis," *Public Policy*, Vol. 13 (1964), 257–67 (Brookings Reprint No. 86), for Massachusetts; Gerald G. Somers and Ernst W. Stromsdorfer, "A Benefit-Cost Analysis of Manpower Retraining," *Proceedings of the Seventeenth Annual Meeting*, Industrial Relations Research Association, December, 1964 (Madison, Wisconsin: IRRA, 1965), pp. 172–85, for West Virginia; Michael E. Borus, "A Benefit-Cost Analysis of the Economic Effectiveness of Retraining the Unemployed," *Yale Economic Essays*, Vol. 4 (Fall, 1964), 371–430, for Connecticut.
3. Stromsdorfer's article, "Determinants of Economic Success in Retraining the Unemployed: The West Virginia Experience," appeared in the Winter, 1968, issue of *The Journal of Human Resources* (Vol. 3, No. 1).
4. Earl Main, "A Nationwide Evaluation of MDTA Institutional Job Training," appeared in the Winter, 1968, issue of *The Journal of Human Resources* (Vol. 3, No. 1). See also the favorable rates of return of MDTA trainees relative to other technical school students in "The Role of Technical Schools in Improving the Skills and Earning Capacity of Rural Manpower," U.S. Department of Labor, Office of Manpower Policy, Evaluation and Research, September, 1966, mimeo.
5. "Retraining the Disadvantaged Worker," in *Research in Vocational Education*, proceedings of a conference on research in vocational education, Center for Studies in Vocational and Technical Education, University of Wisconsin, 1967, 27–44.
6. Glen G. Cain, "Benefit-Cost Estimates for Job Corps," Institute for Research on Poverty, University of Wisconsin, September, 1967, mimeo.
7. "Retrospective Studies of the Effectiveness of NYC Out-of-School Programs in Four Urban Sites," November, 1967, mimeo.
8. Thomas Ribich, *Education and Poverty* (Washington, D.C.: The Brookings Institution, 1968); Burton A. Weisbrod, "Preventing High School Dropouts," in Robert Dorfman, ed., *Measuring Benefits of Government Investments* (Washington, D.C.: The Brookings Institution, 1965); and W. Lee Hansen, Burton A. Weisbrod, and William Scanlon, "Determinants of Earnings: Does Schooling Really Count?" Dept. of Economics, University of Wisconsin, December, 1967, mimeo.

9. Graeme McKechnie, "Retraining and Geographic Mobility: An Evaluation," unpublished Ph.D. dissertation, University of Wisconsin, 1966.
10. For a discussion of these questions, and some tentative answers, see Gerald G. Somers, "Government-Subsidized On-the-Job Training: Surveys of Employers' Attitudes," Center for Studies in Vocational and Technical Education, University of Wisconsin, Reprint Series, 1966; "Work Experience and Training," report prepared for 'he National Council on the Aging, 1967; (with Graeme McKechnie) "Vocational Retraining of the Unemployed;" Michael E. Borus, "Time Trends in the Benefits from Retraining in Connecticut," both in *Proceedings of the Twentieth Annual Meeting,* Industrial Relations Research Association, December 28–29, 1967 (Madison, Wisconsin: IRRA, May, 1968).

# II

## HAROLD A. GIBBARD
## AND
## GERALD G. SOMERS

■

## GOVERNMENT RETRAINING OF THE UNEMPLOYED

## IN WEST VIRGINIA

Government retraining of the unemployed in West Virginia began in 1959 in a state-assisted pilot program in McDowell county, deep in the southern coal fields. Beginning in 1960, retraining has been carried on, under state auspices, in most West Virginia counties. Federal government participation in retraining began with the passage of the Area Redevelopment Act in 1961. The state and federal programs were responses to stubbornly persistent unemployment, continuing at relatively high levels in 1962 and 1963 when our surveys of the trainees were conducted.*

* Harold A. Gibbard is currently (1967) at West Virginia University, Gerald G. Somers at the University of Wisconsin.

We are greatly indebted to S. D. McMillen, former State Director of Vocational Education, West Virginia, and his associates for their help and encouragement in this project. Special thanks are also due to Clement R. Bassett, Commissioner, Brumbach Stephens, Director of Employment Services, and Oscar A. Duff, Chief of Employer Services and Manpower Utilization, Department of Employment Security of West Virginia, for their generous assistance. The local school and Employment Security officers, the retraining instructors, trainees and other workers, and employers who suffered our prodding and probing deserve our special gratitude.

The research associates and assistants participating in this project deserve much for their worthy contributions to the research, without sharing the blame for deficiencies in our report. We are grateful to Wilbur Smith, West Virginia University, and Professor John Minick, Marshall University, for their supervision of portions of the field surveys, and to the many interviewers who tracked down the trainees and control groups.

For assistance with the processing and analysis of the data, as well as a myriad of

Nationally, a full year after the trough of the 1958 recession and at a time when most economic indicators were advancing, unemployment had fallen only to 5.3 per cent, a drop to be sure from the recession high of 7.4 per cent, but a fourth above the rate for the peak month before the recession. In 1960 and 1961, years in which there was a slight business downswing, unemployment averaged 5.6 and 6.7 per cent, respectively. In the next two years, the rate ranged between 5.5 and 6 per cent. While the overall level of business activity may have been less than optimal over much of this period, technological innovations were having an effect on unemployment. Semiskilled operatives had a persistently higher than average rate of joblessness.

## THE WEST VIRGINIA ECONOMY AND THE RETRAINING PROGRAMS

West Virginia is a severe testing ground for vocational retraining, for the state has been characterized by prolonged and acute unemployment, far above the national levels. At many times in recent years, one member of the civilian labor force out of every ten has been without work, and periodically the level of unemployment has been even higher. Within certain counties, the rate of joblessness has run at times to a third of all who are able and willing to work.

West Virginia lies wholly within Appalachia. The state is marked by a rugged terrain and is largely rural. In 1960, under 40 per cent of the population was urban. More than half of the total population was either in towns under 1,000 in population or in open country areas. No other state had so large a fraction of its population classed as rural-nonfarm. There were just four Standard Metropolitan Statistical Areas, three of them astride the western boundary of the state; the Charleston area alone lay wholly within it. Nationally, most of the economic and population growth is occurring within these highly urbanized areas.

Coal mining has dominated the economy of parts of the state for many years. The heaviest concentration of mining is in the southern counties, where Logan and McDowell are the production leaders. A second area of concentration is in the northern coal fields, especially Harrison, Marion, and Monongalia counties. Much of the depression which has marked

administrative functions, we are greatly indebted to Dr. Ernst Stromsdorfer, Pennsylvania State University. Graeme McKechnie, York University, ably assisted in data processing as did the programming and computation staff of the University of Wisconsin's Social Systems Research Institute. The numerous coders and keypunchers involved in this aspect of the project must go nameless, but they have our gratitude.

To the office staff goes our thanks for keeping the administrative wheels rolling and for the arduous task of typing the manuscript. In this regard, we are especially indebted to Pauline Fosdick, Project Supervisor. She was assisted in the typing chores by Conchita Jimenez, Caroline Nejedlo, and Rosalie Kaylor.

large parts of the state in recent years may be traced to this industry, for the coal industry was in decline from the peak years 1947 and 1948 until 1962. Over 173 million tons of coal were mined in West Virginia in 1947, the peak year. In 1960, production was 120 million tons, and in 1961 it was 111 million. At the same time as coal was losing markets to petroleum and natural gas, technological improvements, especially the spreading use of continuous mining machines, were cutting down still further on the need for miners. West Virginia miners averaged a little over six tons per man-shift in 1950 and about thirteen tons in 1961. In 1947, there were 116,421 men working in and around coal mines and coke ovens in the state, and in 1948 the number was reported as 125,669. But by 1960, only 48,696 were so employed, and in 1961, just 42,557. Some of the coal mining in the state is in out-of-the-way places, where alternative forms of employment are not available for displaced miners. Coal properties are not convertible to other economic uses which might open up new employment possibilities. Note that the heaviest concentration of coal mining, and hence of mining employment and unemployment, are in counties where other forms of economic activity are the most limited.

In 1963 manufacturing provided about three times as many jobs as mining. The West Virginia Department of Employment Security reported 122.4 thousand employed in manufacturing in April, 1963, as against 44.8 thousand in all forms of mining and 40.1 thousand in bituminous coal mining. Yet as recently as 1950 mining had employed the greater number.

Manufacturing has made modest gains in West Virginia in recent years, and in 1963 accounted for between 20 and 25 per cent of all employment in the state. The foremost manufacturing industry, from the point of view of employment, is chemicals. In 1963, it employed over 28,000, twice the 1940 figure. Characteristically, though, the industry is highly mechanized. It employs highly educated technical personnel, but relatively few production workers. Primary metals—iron, steel, and aluminum—rank second to chemicals both in value added by manufacture and in employment, and in 1963 employed between 23,000 and 24,000, about the same number as in 1950. Glass products rank third, with a labor force of under 15,000. It is not growing. No other industry employs as many as 10,000. The need is for greater diversification, and for growth industries.

Agriculture makes an important contribution to the state's economy in only a few areas. As elsewhere, it is the principal occupation of a dwindling population. It was the main occupation of nearly 80,000 in 1940, more than 60,000 in 1950, and just 23,847 in 1960.

The Area Redevelopment Act (Public Law 87–27, 87 Congress, S.1, May 1, 1961) set forth two sets of criteria by which areas (generally counties) were to be designated as "redevelopment areas." Identified as

5(a) areas, from the section of the Act which was so numbered, were territories marked by high and persistent unemployment.[1] Many of these areas were urban. The 5(b) areas were those which did not qualify through unemployment, but which the Secretary of Commerce determined to be among the highest in numbers and percentages of low-income families, and in which there existed a condition of substantial and persistent unemployment and underemployment. Virtually all 5(b) areas were rural and many were agricultural.

Except for Alaska, almost the whole of which is given a 5(b) classification, no other state had so large a proportion of its territory qualifying for redevelopment assistance as did West Virginia. Of the fifty-five counties, only four were excluded, two of them—Hancock and Brooke—lying at the top of the northern panhandle, the other two—Berkeley and Jefferson—at the end of the eastern panhandle. Twenty-nine counties, lying in the Upper Monongalia, the Ohio, and the Kanawha valleys, and in the southern coal fields, had a 5(a) classification in 1963. Twenty-two counties were classified as 5(b) redevelopment areas, most of them in a continuous territory lying in the central and eastern part of the state.

The unemployment and poverty of West Virginia would doubtless have been worse had there not been a substantial outmigration. The population of the state declined by 7.2 per cent during the 1950's. Forty of the fifty-five counties lost, two of them by more than 25 per cent. The counties along the Ohio River gained, as did two Kanawha Valley counties and three in the eastern panhandle, but a number of these did not hold their natural increase. The outmigration was especially high among very young adults. Unofficial estimates indicate that the state as a whole has continued to decline since 1960.

Outmigration is a private response to joblessness. The public response mainly consists of programs to help the unemployed meet their basic needs in absence of a job, and of efforts to help place people in jobs. Worker retraining is such a program.

## THE RETRAINING PROGRAMS

Beginning with a pilot program in 1959, West Virginia conducted a retraining effort that reached into 39 of its 55 counties, enrolled over 11,000 men and women by June, 1964, and led to about 4–5,000 known training-related job placements.

The pilot program was in McDowell county, a favorable testing ground from many points of view. Most of the county is wholly dependent on coal. In 1960, after a decade of precipitous decline in mining employment, almost half of all the employed persons in the county were still in mining. The average unemployment rate for the years 1958 through 1961 ranged from a low of 22.3 per cent to a high of 24.8. The rate of population shrinkage in the 1950's was in excess of 27 per cent, the highest in the state. The retraining program, sponsored jointly by the McDowell County School Board, the State Division of Vocational Education, the Department of Employment Security of West Virginia, and certain civic and business groups, offered courses in auto mechanics, carpentry, machine shop, mine machinery repair, and welding. The courses were conducted in the well-equipped vocational school in Welch in the late afternoon and early evening hours after the regular school day, and required six months for completion. By June, 1960, two sets of courses had been conducted, with 116 unemployed workers participating. Some of the trainees dropped out en route, a number of them to take jobs. A majority of the first group to complete training found work, in most cases out of the county.

Responding both to the persistent unemployment in the state and to the preliminary success of the McDowell county program, the West Virginia legislature in 1960 enacted the Area Vocational Educational Training Program (AVP) Bill to provide for state-wide retraining.

The bill provided $400,000 for the fiscal year 1960–61 to meet the costs of teachers' salaries, equipment and supplies, and trainees' travel costs. Residents of the state who were at least eighteen years of age and certified as not gainfully employed were eligible for retraining courses, provided they met the selection requirements. No subsistence payments were provided for the period of retraining. The program has been administered by the State Director of Vocational Education and carried out by county school officers.

Each year from 1960 to 1964 the state legislature appropriated $500,000 for the continuation of the program. In 1960, the minimum age was dropped from 18 to 16. A summary of enrollments, training locations and subjects, and training-related job placements appears in Appendix B.

A second broad program of worker retraining in West Virginia, and the first to be financed federally, was that of the Area Redevelopment Administration. The Area Redevelopment Act allowed a multipronged attack on the problems of depressed areas, including worker retraining. To receive assistance under the Act, a Redevelopment Area had first to prepare an Overall Economic Development Program (OEDP), which, when approved by the relevant state agency and the Area Redevelopment Administration, provided the basis for ARA support. The Act provided for low-cost loans to private industries, loans and grants to local governments for new or expanded public facilities such as access roads, water and sewage systems, and technical planning assistance to communities, as well as worker retraining.

Retraining could be offered to qualified unemployed and underemployed persons residing within the Redevelopment Area offering the retraining, providing there was a good prospect that such retraining would lead to gainful employment. Some of the retraining has prepared workers for jobs in plants erected or expanded with ARA assistance. Trainees under ARA received subsistence benefits equal to the average unemployment compensation payments within the state (about $23 in West Virginia) for a period not exceeding sixteen weeks, as long as they were also receiving unemployment compensation. In effect, retraining courses under ARA were limited to sixteen weeks' duration.

The first program in worker retraining under the Area Redevelopment Administration anywhere in the nation was in Huntington, West Virginia, in the fall of 1961, with the first class, for nurse's aides, graduating just before Christmas. From this beginning, ARA retraining courses enrolled over two thousand men and women in fourteen locations and more than twenty occupations. Some classes that were first given as a part of the state program were repeated under ARA sponsorship. A tabular summary of ARA retraining in West Virginia is in Appendix B.

A third public training program is provided by the federal Manpower Development and Training Act (MDTA), which became effective in July, 1962. The first retraining under MDTA in West Virginia was approved in December, 1962, and the first course completions were in the spring of 1963, too late to be included in the field surveys that make up the body of this report. ARA retraining was absorbed into the MDTA in 1965.

The Manpower Development and Training Act provides for retraining of greater scope and magnitude than was authorized under ARA. It is not confined to economically depressed areas. At the outset, it provided in the main for the retraining of unemployed heads of households who had at least three years' experience in gainful employment. Subsistence allowances could be paid for up to fifty-two weeks. Training has not been confined to the worker's home community, and provision has been made for travel costs and additional subsistence payments while the trainee is away from home. On-the-job training is permitted under the Act. During its initial period, 5 per cent of all training-allowance funds could go to young people aged 19 and under 22, who were to be compensated at a reduced rate. In the first years, the total cost of the program has been borne by the federal government. See Appendix B for a summary of MDTA retraining in West Virginia.

In its first years—those covered by this study—retraining was calculated to achieve a maximum flow of workers into post-training employment. New skills were to take the place of outmoded ones. Test-qualified workers, often the most advantaged of the unemployed, were trained to fill known job shortages. For the early phase of retraining, this may have been the best policy, but it did have shortcomings; it was not serving the hard-core unemployed, and it did relatively little for youth. A series of changes in MDTA have been designed to meet these limitations. Three innovations show the new pattern. First, trainees are no longer selected on the basis of fixed minimum aptitude-test scores or formal education. Second, the "basic education" amendment (December, 1963) now permits workers to receive instruction in basic language skills and arithmetic where needed, as a preliminary to vocational training. Subsistence support for up to twenty weeks was provided for this basic education. These changes are bringing the poorly schooled, more handicapped workers into retraining. The third change is the new emphasis given to the training of youth. The age-floor has been dropped back to 17 and training-allowance funds that may go to youth have been increased to 25 per cent of the total. In addition, MDTA supports a number of special youth programs. It is to be hoped that the newer programs prove helpful to the most disadvantaged among the unemployed.

## THE RESEARCH DESIGN

### OBJECTIVES OF THE STUDY

The objectives of the West Virginia study of retraining were to describe and to evaluate the effectiveness of training for selected occupations in five counties. The key facets of the study were:

1. An examination of the retraining courses themselves: their legislative basis, variables affecting the scope of retraining programs in different localities, the administrative procedures by which courses were set up and trainees selected, and the manner in which the retraining courses were conducted.

2. An analysis of the attitudes and characteristics of the men and women selected for training: comparisons with the men and women who applied for training and were not accepted, and with those who were unemployed when retraining courses were open yet did not apply for retraining. The personal variables include age, sex, race, family affiliations, formal education, previous skills, duration of previous unemployment, and willingness to move. Analyses were also made of the attitudes of rejected applicants and of dropouts from the training courses, and of the reasons for not applying for training.

3. A review of the outcome of retraining: the employment experiences, attitudes, mobility of men and women subsequent to retraining; the feelings of employers toward the retraining programs and toward the retrained workers whom they hired; a comparison of how retrained men and women fared against men and women who were unemployed when retraining courses were open but who did not get retraining.

4. The gains and costs of the retraining programs to the individuals and to society, including an appraisal of the impact of retraining programs

on the levels of unemployment in the areas where the retraining programs were conducted.

The four objectives were interrelated. The final tests of programs under review are found in their effects on the employment and outlook of the men and women who received training, and the dent they make in the total volume of unemployment. Yet the success of retraining is bound to be influenced by the manner in which the courses are set up and conducted and by the selection of men and women who enter them.

There can be no losing sight of the economic and social context of the retraining programs here reviewed. Each of the counties studied has its own characteristics. In the context of this study, the most important of these are the existing levels of unemployment, local job opportunities, and prevailing attitudes toward such aspects of employment as willingness to accept a change in occupation or willingness to move to another locality for work.

## THE SAMPLE AREAS

The research was limited to a small number of counties to permit the advantages that come from intensive study. The five selected are geographically scattered, each with distinctive economic characteristics, and a varied experience with retraining.

Monongalia and Harrison counties, both in the northern part of the state, are alike in that each has a central city of 20,000 to 30,000, and an economic base which includes manufacturing, mining, and some agriculture. Harrison had the more vigorous retraining programs. Kanawha county, like Charleston, the state's largest city and its capital, has a lively chemical industry and some other forms of manufacturing, as well as an active commerce. There is mining, with the consequent considerable economic hardship, in some of its outlying sections. Cabell county, like Huntington, and Kanawha county, is largely urban. It has perhaps the greatest industrial diversity of any area in West Virginia and was the scene of the nation's first ARA retraining program. McDowell county is in the heart of the southern coal fields. It has very little economic activity which is not related to the declining coal industry. Its rates of unemployment and population decline have been persistently high for a number of years. The site of the state's first retraining in 1959, it has conducted a distinctive program of retraining since that time.

The size of the civilian labor force and the extent and rate of unemployment in each of these counties during the period under review are given in Appendix C.

## THE FIELD SAMPLES

In the drawing of samples, the retraining class was selected as the unit in four of the five counties. In turn, the courses to be studied were selected purposely so as to assure the inclusion of a range of types of courses and to allow for the study of certain fields of retraining in depth.

The men and women who made up the samples of trainees were all those who were assigned to the sample courses in these four counties. Thus, the sample of trainees had an arbitrary character, and its composition should be kept in mind in interpreting the findings of the study. The choice of either a wholly random sample of men and women assigned to training, or of a stratified sample that would have allotted to each training class the same fraction of its enrollment, would have had advantages for certain kinds of statistical analysis. Either of these methods, however, would have precluded certain types of analysis. For example, they would have resulted in the inclusion of too few trainees from some of the classes to permit reliable analyses of results by training classes and occupations; and the class itself is considered to be a key variable.

In McDowell county, unlike the other four, all trainees who completed their retraining courses were included in the sample, provided they could be located and would agree to an interview.

The men and women assigned to retraining courses were classified with respect to training status at the time of the first field interviews. The training categories were (1) completed training, (2) dropped out of the training, (3) did not report for training, and (4) in training at the time of the field study. Each of these categories was treated as a separate population, for each had a different degree of involvement in retraining. The men and women in retraining at the time of the first field study were subsequently reclassified into "completions" or "dropouts." The combined samples of valid interviews for the five counties are as follows: of the total of 926 "trainee" interviews, 442 had completed training, 203 dropped out, 65 did not report, 127 were not accepted, and 89 were in training at the time the samples were drawn. Of these 89, 59 completed their course, and 30 dropped out. Thus 501 sample members eventually completed training, and 233 dropped out.

As an additional control group, interviews were also completed with 453 workers who had not applied for training. Ideally, we could have had the best evidence of the worth of retraining if we could somehow have compared the employment experiences of the men and women following training with the employment experiences the same people would have had if they had not been retrained. This patently was impossible. The next best would have been to compare the employment experiences of retrained people with those of people like them in every essential respect except for retraining. The procedure of drawing a carefully matched control group was practically impossible. It would have required finding a person whose education, skill, employment history, motivation, etc., was much like that of each retrained person. Even if the relevant kinds

of information had been known about the pool of workers who were unemployed at the time that men and women were being selected for training, it is unlikely that a close match could have been found for very many
of the trainees in a fairly small city and its rural environs. Even if a
matched population could have been found, it would not have had the
characteristics of an independent sample of the nonapplicant unemployed.
Also, there would have been interdependence among the observations
within such samples. Further, the men and women admitted to training
had a characteristic for which a true parallel would be out of reach: in
applying for retraining they showed a special kind of initiative.

Two comparison groups were included in this study. First, a sample of
*rejected* applicants for training were interviewed. Employment Service
officials prefer the term *nonreferred*. The reason given is that workers
may meet the normal qualifications but not be admitted for one reason
or another; for example, more have qualified than can be admitted to the
class, or the individual has personal traits that make it unlikely that he
will succeed in the course or in subsequent employment. The most common reason for rejection was inability to meet the entrance qualifications:
too little formal education or too low GATB (General Aptitude Test
Battery) scores. The rejected applicants, of course, were not a true control
group for the study of the trainees because of the lower qualifications of
the former. At best, they helped in providing a rock-bottom test of the
worth of retraining.

The second comparison group consisted of a sample of men and women
who were registered at the Employment Security Offices and had been unemployed at roughly the same time as the training courses in their county
were being organized, but who did not apply for retraining. The selection
of this sample of nonapplicants was governed by conditions laid down by
the West Virginia Department of Employment Security, which is required
to keep its files confidential. The Department agreed to make available,
through five Employment Security Offices in the counties under study,
sample lists of names of men and women who were registered for jobs.
The names were taken in equal numbers from the "active" and "inactive"
files. The former of these files listed unemployment compensation claim-
ants and other applicants for work who had validated their applications
within the previous thirty days. The "inactive" file contained the cards
of those who had failed to keep their applications validated, but had not
asked for their withdrawal. The cards were held in the inactive file for
about one year and then removed to storage. The names and addresses
for the sample of nonapplicants were selected at random from the two
files. To qualify for the sample, the job applicant had to be unemployed
at the time when a training course was being set up, and he was not to
have been a bona fide applicant for retraining. When a name was drawn

that was disqualified for either of these reasons, the next card in the file was substituted. Only names and addresses were taken from the files.

At the request of the Employment Security officials, all men and women drawn in the samples were offered $2.07 per mile for reporting to a central location—a vocational school, fraternal hall, or Salvation Army hall—for interview. Invitations to participate were sent out by the local Employment Security officers. The proportion responding was less than one-third in each of the five counties. The others were interviewed in their homes. It is unlikely that the procedures followed biased the sample in any way, since if the men and women who reported for interviews had not done so, they would have been sought out by the field staff.

The selection of a nonapplicant sample by the methods outlined above has both good and bad features. The principal advantage is that the trainees and the control samples are drawn from the same pool, i.e., the men and women who registered at the employment office and who thus met one qualification for retraining. A procedural advantage is that the Employment Security files could be sampled systematically, as no other assembled list of job seekers exists.

On the negative side, the nonapplicant samples cannot be treated as a cross-section of the unemployed in the five counties, for those who had not reported at the employment office for well over a year were excluded. This category doubtless included many of the hard-core unemployed. Moreover, the files include the names of some women who are marginal members of the labor force, willing to consider employment if an attractive job is offered, but not vigorously seeking work. The sample did include a few people still in school, who wanted only summer jobs. While they were interviewed, they were omitted from the final tabulations on the ground that they were not continuing members of the labor force.

With the exception of interviews for which the respondents came in and were paid, nearly all interviewing was done in homes. A very few interviews with men in training were taken at the training site in one county, and occasional interviews took place in other locations, including hospitals. The field procedure was to make at least four calls, if necessary, to locate each respondent. As in all field studies, some cases were lost. Refusals were rare. The principal source of loss was change of residence. Inquiry among neighbors and verification of address procedures in local post offices were used to locate some of the people who had moved. In many cases, though, the migrant had left no forwarding address.

A few interviews were completed with out-of-state migrants in the Norfolk-Newport News area, Baltimore, Washington, D.C., Columbus, Ohio, and Chicago; and several interviews were obtained with migrants home for a weekend. A few of these out-migrant respondents were assigned to the counties wherein the training occurred in the major county analyses, but most were studied separately in the section entitled, "Retraining and Relocation."

The final sample of valid interviews in the five areas is summarized in Tables II.1, II.2, and II.3.

TABLE II.1

WEST VIRGINIA SAMPLES BY TRAINING STATUS AND COURSE SPONSOR

| Training status | ARA[a] | | AVP[b] | | Not ascertained | | Total | |
|---|---|---|---|---|---|---|---|---|
|  | No. | % | No. | % | No. | % | No. | % |
| *Applicant* | | | | | | | | |
| Completed training | 198 | 44.8 | 240 | 54.3 | 4 | 0.9 | 442 | 100.0 |
| Dropped out of training | 45 | 22.2 | 156 | 76.4 | 2 | 1.0 | 203 | 100.0 |
| In training | 48 | 53.9 | 39 | 43.8 | 2 | 2.3 | 89 | 100.0 |
| Did not report | 19 | 29.2 | 46 | 70.8 | 0 | 0.0 | 65 | 100.0 |
| Not accepted for training | 59 | 46.5 | 57 | 44.9 | 11 | 8.6 | 127 | 100.0 |
| Total no. of applicants | 369 | | 538 | | 19 | | 926 | |
| *Nonapplicant* | | | | | | | 453 | |
| Total | | | | | | | 1,379 | |

[a] Area Redevelopment Act.
[b] Area Vocational Training Program (West Virginia State).

Several aspects of the sample merit further comment. First, note the large number of dropouts (DO) and the relatively small number of completions (COM) in McDowell county. In that county, all retraining was within the state AVP program. During the regular school year, retraining was after regular school hours, and each course was drawn out over several months. AVP trainees received no subsistence payments, only transportation costs. Many had been forced to drop out by economic necessity. Some of the withdrawals, however, had been after long and useful training. Another possible complicating factor in McDowell county was that much of its retraining was geared to out-of-town (and out-of-state) job prospects, and it is possible that COM's leave the area in relatively greater number than do the DO's.

Second, in all areas the dropouts are a heterogeneous population. Some left their courses to take a job. Some were dropped due to poor performance—for example, inability to learn to read blueprints—while others were discouraged by the difficulty of the work and left. A few felt themselves social misfits in their courses: examples may be found among the males who were enrolled in predominantly female nurse's aide courses.

## TABLE II.2
### West Virginia Samples by Training Status and Training Subject

| Training subject | Completed training[a] | | Dropped out of training[a] | | In training (Summer, 1962)[a] | | Did not report[a] | | Not accepted for training[b] | |
|---|---|---|---|---|---|---|---|---|---|---|
| | No. | % | No. | % | No. | % | No. | % | No. | % |
| Riveter | 88 | 19.9 | 15 | 7.4 | 0 | 0.0 | 1 | 1.5 | 6 | 4.7 |
| Clerical office | 68 | 15.4 | 23 | 11.3 | 5 | 5.6 | 8 | 12.3 | 32 | 25.2 |
| Auto repair | 27 | 6.1 | 35 | 17.2 | 19 | 21.3 | 6 | 9.2 | 14 | 11.0 |
| Nurse's aides & waitresses | 112 | 25.3 | 14 | 6.9 | 2 | 2.2 | 17 | 26.2 | 23 | 18.1 |
| Construction trades | 15 | 3.4 | 32 | 15.8 | 4 | 4.5 | 7 | 10.8 | 1 | 0.8 |
| Welding | 68 | 15.4 | 26 | 12.8 | 28 | 31.5 | 6 | 9.2 | 9 | 7.1 |
| Electrical & maintenance repair | 31 | 7.0 | 27 | 13.3 | 5 | 5.6 | 3 | 4.6 | 7 | 5.5 |
| Machine tool operator & inspector | 24 | 5.4 | 26 | 12.8 | 25 | 28.1 | 13 | 20.0 | 3 | 2.4 |
| Other | 7 | 1.6 | 3 | 1.5 | 1 | 1.1 | 1 | 1.5 | 6 | 4.7 |
| Not ascertained | 2 | 0.4 | 2 | 1.0 | 0 | 0.0 | 3 | 4.6 | 26 | 20.5 |
| Total | 442 | 100.0 | 203 | 100.0 | 89 | 100.0 | 65 | 100.0 | 127 | 100.0 |

[a] Courses in which respondents were enrolled.
[b] Courses for which respondents applied.

In like vein, DO's range all the way from those who attended for a day or two to others who, in McDowell county, attended for six months or more before letting their attendance lapse.

Third, the "did not report" (DNR) category includes some who did not care enough to bother, and some whose basic situation changed before their courses got under way. The members of this category may be viewed

TABLE II.3

WEST VIRGINIA SAMPLES BY TRAINING STATUS AND COUNTY

| Training status | Kanawha | | Cabell-Wayne | | McDowell | | Monongalia | | Harrison | | Total | |
|---|---|---|---|---|---|---|---|---|---|---|---|---|
| | No. | % | No. | % | No. | % | No. | % | No. | % | No. | % |
| Completed training | 27 | 6.1 | 109 | 24.7 | 82 | 18.5 | 50 | 11.3 | 174 | 39.4 | 442 | 100.0 |
| Dropped out of training | 6 | 3.0 | 41 | 20.1 | 112 | 55.2 | 16 | 7.9 | 28 | 13.8 | 203 | 100.0 |
| In training | 35 | 39.9 | 2 | 2.3 | 31 | 34.8 | 10 | 11.3 | 11 | 12.3 | 89 | 100.0 |
| Did not report | 0 | | 14 | 21.5 | 35 | 53.8 | 6 | 9.3 | 10 | 15.4 | 65 | 100.0 |
| Not accepted for training | 26 | 20.5 | 24 | 18.9 | 25 | 19.7 | 23 | 18.1 | 29 | 22.8 | 127 | 100.0 |
| Nonapplicant | 65 | 14.2 | 61 | 13.3 | 183 | 40.6 | 79 | 17.5 | 65 | 14.4 | 453 | 100.0 |
| Total | 159 | 11.5 | 251 | 18.2 | 468 | 33.9 | 184 | 13.3 | 317 | 23.0 | 1,379 | 100.0 |

as a control group rather than a trainee group, in that they all qualified for training but did not receive it. The small size of the sample of DNR's and its patent heterogeneity are limitations upon its use as a control group.

The men and women constituting the West Virginia samples were interviewed during the summer and fall of 1962. Typical interview time was about an hour. The interview instrument, forty pages long, contained several series of questions asked of all respondents, and some series asked only of persons of one or another training status.

Details of the interview instrument may be deduced from the analysis of the field data which appears later in this account. In outline, among the topics included were the following: personal characteristics of the respondent; the composition of the household of which he was a member, and the employment status of each of the members; retraining status and attitudes; educational attainments and attitudes toward schooling; work history since 1955; rootedness vs. willingness to migrate; social participation; and household income.

The worth of any program of worker training is not to be judged solely by the employment status of workers shortly after their training. The newly trained may need time to find jobs that will utilize their skills. They may have acquired a new incentive to move to places of higher employment opportunity. Some may have taken jobs that proved temporary. Women may have moved into or out of the labor force.

To test the outcome of retraining over a longer time-span, a follow-up study was made in 1963. A short questionnaire was used for this purpose. It probed into the current labor force status, work history since July 1, 1962, the relation of work experience to retraining, current views on retraining, changes of residence, and mobility attitudes.

The questionnaire was mailed to all the respondents in the basic samples in the spring of 1963. A second mailing was made to those who did not reply. In the early summer of that year, field interviewers sought out as many of those who did not respond as could be found. They either left questionnaires, which they picked up later, or gathered the information at the time of their call. As in the first field study, repeated calls were made where necessary.

In the end, 1,217 respondents, or 88.6 per cent of the people in the basic sample, were followed up in this round. A few refusals were encountered. The chief source of loss, however, was change of residence. It may be assumed that a large fraction—how large is not known—of the people who could not be found had left the state. Some were lost through illness, desertion from their families, imprisonment, and entry into the armed services. The follow-up sample, classed by geographic area and 1962 training status, is summarized in Table II.4.

TABLE II.4

FOLLOW-UP SAMPLES, SPRING-SUMMER 1963, BY COUNTY AND 1962 TRAINING STATUS

| Training status (1962) | Kanawha | | Cabell-Wayne | | McDowell | | Monongalia | | Harrison | | Total | |
|---|---|---|---|---|---|---|---|---|---|---|---|---|
| | No. | % | No. | % | No. | % | No. | % | No. | % | No. | % |
| Completed training | 25 | 6.1 | 103 | 24.9 | 75 | 18.2 | 49 | 11.9 | 161 | 39.0 | 413 | 100.0 |
| Dropped out of training | 5 | 2.9 | 35 | 20.5 | 101 | 59.1 | 12 | 7.0 | 18 | 10.5 | 171 | 100.0 |
| In training | 32 | 40.0 | 2 | 2.5 | 28 | 35.0 | 9 | 11.3 | 9 | 11.3 | 80 | 100.0 |
| Did not report | 0 | 0.0 | 13 | 22.8 | 32 | 56.1 | 4 | 7.0 | 8 | 14.0 | 57 | 100.0 |
| Not accepted for training | 24 | 21.2 | 21 | 18.6 | 24 | 21.2 | 20 | 17.7 | 24 | 21.2 | 113 | 100.0 |
| Nonapplicant | 51 | 13.3 | 54 | 14.1 | 159 | 41.5 | 68 | 17.8 | 51 | 13.3 | 383 | 100.0 |
| Total | 137 | 11.3 | 228 | 18.7 | 419 | 34.4 | 162 | 13.3 | 271 | 22.3 | 1,217 | 100.0 |

A comparison of the follow-up samples with the base samples indicates that the follow-ups do not differ significantly in composition from the originals. The distribution of the 1,217 follow-up cases by counties is almost identical with that of the original samples. Slightly more of the follow-up cases (33.9 per cent as against 32.0 per cent) had completed their retraining; slightly fewer (31.5 per cent to 32.8 per cent) were nonapplicant unemployed. Among the earlier respondents, 7.89 per cent were Negro; among the latter, the percentage was 7.90. Other personal characteristics, too, differed only by chance. The mid-1962 employment status of the later samples, by training-status groups, was almost identical with that of the earlier samples. Thus, contrary to our expectation, the loss of cases over the year did not change the relative composition of the study sample significantly.

Over three-quarters of the follow-up cases returned the mailed questionnaire, though some needed the prodding of second and even of third letters. The remainder were sought out and interviewed. Throughout the study, the questionnaire respondents and the field-interview respondents were treated as parts of the same population.

Three other phases of the study are to be noted in this statement on research design. First, out-of-town addresses were sought for all members of the sample classes who had moved from the state. The outmigration was highest from McDowell county. Fortunately, it was more frequently possible to obtain the addresses of men from this county than of outmigrants from the other sample areas. A very few outmigrants were interviewed. The others were sent an abbreviated mail questionnaire. Those who responded were treated in this study as a separate sample.

Second, since almost all retraining courses are designed to help men and women get jobs rather than become self-employed, the attitudes of actual and potential employers of the trainees are basic measures of the effectiveness of retraining. Interviews were sought with all known employers of retrained workers in the sample areas, as well as with a few outside the five counties but within commuting distance. A few additional interviews were held with relatively large employers who had not hired any trainees. An interview form was used which permitted the quantitative analysis of employer attitudes.

Third, inquiry was made into the manner in which the trainee courses themselves were conducted. Classrooms were visited and teachers interviewed. While an interview guide was used, the teacher interviews were generally informal and relatively unstructured. Topics included the manner in which the several courses were outlined, and the latitude given the teachers, the adequacy of quarters, equipment, and supplies, the ability and interest of the trainees, and others.

## ADMINISTRATIVE ARRANGEMENTS FOR THE ESTABLISHMENT OF TRAINING PROGRAMS

Retraining programs for adult workers are not mandatory in any West Virginia community, under either state or federal law. The laws permit qualifying communities, or administrative units, to establish retraining courses and provide financial support under terms laid down in the statutes. What sort of training program—and, indeed, whether there will be retraining at all—in any one locality rests in the first place on the eligibility of the local area for any specific program, and beyond that on local needs and local initiative.

In West Virginia, the administrative unit for retraining is the county. Since the programs are administered by the local school authorities and since in this state the school districts are counties, it is natural that the programs should be administered on a county basis.

## Legal Qualifications

The first factor determining if a county will carry on retraining is whether it qualifies under the law. In the state program (AVP), no county is disqualified, so that every part of West Virginia is technically able to apply for retraining courses under state auspices. Retraining under the Area Redevelopment Act is permissible, assuming the other qualifying procedures are followed and applications for retraining are approved, in any "redevelopment area." Only four counties are not classified as "redevelopment areas," namely Hancock and Brooke at the northern extremity of the state, and Berkeley and Jefferson at the eastern extremity; the other fifty-one all qualify for ARA retraining, subject of course to application and review procedures. The MDTA program is not limited by law to depressed areas. In summary, in West Virginia the law permits any county to qualify for either AVP or MDTA retraining, and permits all but four to qualify for ARA retraining. Until the advent of MDTA, however, many communities in other states were not eligible to offer retraining.

With all counties eligible to apply for retraining courses, what was the retraining picture in West Virginia in 1963–64? First, a majority, over two-thirds, of the counties carried on some training under the state AVP. Some had extensive programs, with a variety of offerings; others had limited and seemingly sporadic programs. Far more counties operated within the framework of AVP than ARA; indeed, by the summer of 1963, only fifteen counties had had ARA-sponsored retraining, and MDTA courses were still limited to a few locations. What were the conditions that accounted for these variations from county to county?

The analysis here presented of factors affecting the scope of retraining in any county is based in part on the observations of the five sample counties, in part on reports of experiences elsewhere in West Virginia. In turn, with only occasional exceptions, the variables are stated in general terms, and the counties whose experiences are drawn upon are not named. No meaningful purpose would be served by tying the variables to specific geographic locations.

## LOCAL PROMOTION

The most inclusive variable affecting the scope of retraining in a community or county is the quality of local promotion. With a few exceptions, all retraining on last analysis has resulted from local determination to take advantage of the state or federal programs. Among the exceptions are cases where regional or state officers have taken the initiative in setting up training as an enticement for the establishment of a new plant in one location or another. Even in these cases, there must be local cooperation, and the training is carried on under local administration.

The local promotion which underlies most retraining may be the work of public officers, such as managers of Employment Security Offices or vocational education coordinators. It may center in the Chamber of Commerce, through its executive secretary or its elected officers. The business leaders may provide the spark, either through an association to which they belong or simply through personal leadership. In some cases, the initiative comes from prospective employers of retrained workers. An important consideration is the basic power structure of the community. The men, and occasionally women, whose leads are often followed in a community may support economic growth of any promising sort and support as much and as varied retraining as the economic outlook justifies. Other community leaders may have narrower objectives; for example, they may stress the sort of plant recruitment that will find occupants for existing buildings and look on retraining as an instrument of that recruitment. It is alleged that in one small county seat in West Virginia the most forceful individual, an old-time businessman, accepted the status quo, and stood in the way of competing leadership or of further economic development of his community—a barrier to retraining.

The principal initiative for retraining may come from a single individual or a small group practiced in acting together. In some communities, though, support is more diffused. Tentatively, one may state that the combined leadership of different groups, including business and labor leaders and public officials, is the most effective.

A corollary of the thesis that the quality of community promotion affects the amount and variety of retraining in a community is that an effective training program needs the strong support of both the principal local officers of the West Virginia Department of Employment Security and the school officials under whom the actual retraining is conducted. Normally, the key individuals are managers of the local Employment Security Offices and the Trade and Industrial Education coordinators in the county school systems. They are inevitably involved in that it is they who together carry out the retraining. The local offices of the Department of Employment Security share in determining whether specific training courses are needed, draw up and forward applications for such courses to Charleston, recruit, screen, and select trainees, and later help place them in jobs. The school officials directly charged with the administration of the courses also have a voice in whether or not specific courses will be offered. With this authority, these officials more than any others influence the scope of training within their localities.

The readiness of these officials to work vigorously on behalf of retraining is affected in some instances by the press of other work. A mundane but real variable is the ability of the program administrators to muster the necessary time and energy to do the job well. The problem is most acute in the case of school officials charged with the administration of the retraining courses. In some counties, an assistant superintendent with an already heavy burden of duties has shouldered the tasks of administering retraining. It is neither surprising nor blameworthy that he has had too little time and only restrained enthusiasm for the program. A relatively small staff provides some of the county school administrations with but little choice, and the man who is already too busy may be the best training administrator available.

Some counties have Retraining Committees, while others do not. Such a committee was not mandatory under either AVP or ARA,[2] though one is expected as a condition of MDTA training. Where Retraining Committees do exist, they may review the need for skills in the community, weigh proposals for new courses, and serve as a general leavening for the whole retraining program. Retraining committees are established through local initiative. In a number of instances, the true driving spirit has been supplied by the manager of the local Employment Security Office.

A lively committee is to be found in Clarksburg, West Virginia. It consists of just three members: the local Employment Security manager, the acting coordinator of the trade and industrial program in the county schools who is also the administrator of retraining courses, and the regional representative of the Bureau of Apprenticeship and Training, U.S. Department of Labor. In close touch with this team is the field representative of the Area Redevelopment Administration. The three members meet together regularly in a spirit of cordiality and serious purpose. Their contributions to the active training program in their county cannot be precisely stated, for other influences have also been at work. It is plain, though, that these contributions have been considerable.

Retraining Committees may be both an effect and a cause of local concern about retraining. So long as they are active and the outlook of their members constructive, retraining opportunities are not likely to slip by for lack of local support. The presence or lack of a committee is a variable relating to the scope of retraining both because such a committee symbolizes local concern, and because it is a vehicle for the scrutinizing of community needs and opportunities for retraining.

The variables so far named—local promotion, the positive involvement of the local Employment Security manager and the school administration, the time and energy that officials can give to retraining, and the support of a Retraining Committee—all have to do with the promotion of retraining. Since retraining is intended to equip unemployed men and women with skills that will enable them to get jobs, local interest will not lead to the establishment of courses unless there is a reasonable assurance that those who complete them will find related employment. The next variables are tied to employment prospects.

### RELATIONSHIP TO EMPLOYMENT OPPORTUNITIES

Retraining is favored in a community where at least some segments of the local economy are expanding. The ARA training programs were widely understood to be tied to local employment opportunities, and were so conducted in most localities;[3] AVP and MDTA are not so restricted.

Some retraining has been for occupations in which there is a constant turnover and for which there is continual recruiting. Examples are waitresses and, in some communities, nurse's aides. While economic expansion may increase the need for service workers and make such positions more appealing because of its effects on wage rates, the larger demand results from turnover tied to the movement in and out of the labor force by married women.

Another set of retraining courses has met a backlog of demands for certain kinds of skills. An example is the automatic transmission course included in the series of ARA pilot courses in Huntington, West Virginia, in the winter of 1961–62.

Thus, some classes are intended to fill a need for trained workers that exists quite apart from the expansion of employment. In the whole picture of retraining, however, these are in the minority.

Training for *industrial* employment has depended largely on the creation of new jobs, either through the expansion of existing plants or the opening of new ones. Of the ARA courses in four of the sample counties (McDowell has kept to the AVP program) the ones most often repeated were those geared to giving men the special skills needed in the recently opened plant of the Food Machinery and Chemicals Corporation in Charleston and the new Lockheed-Georgia aircraft parts-assembly plant in Clarksburg. Though these particular plants were not established with ARA assistance, the state had ARA-assisted plants—e.g., in woodwork, glass, and apparel—for which workers were given training. (In the glass plant, ARA retraining was followed by an apprenticeship period.) This sort of training was part of the ARA package that included support for the improvement of community facilities to aid in attracting industries and loans to firms to help in establishing new plants or in expanding old ones, in addition to the training of workers. New plants to be manned, and hospitals to be staffed, provide men and women with a chance for jobs, and training courses may equip them with the skills to make them eligible.

New plants or service facilities have indeed led to government-supported vocational retraining. At the same time, some successful retraining has been based on dispersed employment opportunities, or even out-of-town jobs. Consider the sizable migration of welders from McDowell county to the shipyards at Norfolk and Newport News. While the presence or absence of new employment opportunities is a key variable affecting the amount of a community's retraining, it is not always the determining one.

Prospective employers may take the initiative in having certain classes offered specifically to meet their own need for workers. In at least some of these classes, the workers to be trained must meet the employer's hiring standards. The instructors may be drawn from the company and the skills taught may not be marketable anywhere else. The use by employers of government retraining courses as a main source of new workers is a major influence on the scope of a community's retraining. The new Union Protestant Hospital in Clarksburg was a case in point; it stood ready to hire all the nurse's aides graduated in certain training classes in the late spring of 1963.

The negative side of this condition exists when local institutional patterns preclude the use of public training programs as a source of new workers. In a large plant in one of the five counties, the union contract specified that new hirings were to be made at the lowest skill level. Any openings at higher grades were to be posted so that present employees might apply for them. There is no room in such an arrangement for the hiring of specifically trained workers.

In another community, a large hospital found that its need for nurse's aides outran the output of retraining courses offered in this field, and established a training program of its own sufficient in scope to provide a pool of qualified workers adequate both for its own needs and the needs of some smaller hospitals nearby.

Thus, among the central employment variables are general economic growth, the presence or absence of new or expanded plants or service facilities, the use or non-use of government-sponsored programs by new or expanded establishments in meeting their need for trained workers, the readiness of a community to train for out-of-town jobs, and local institutional practices in hiring, training, and upgrading that may preclude the employment of government-trained personnel.

## FACILITIES FOR RETRAINING

One remaining factor is to be noted, namely, the availability of physical facilities for retraining. While equipment may be purchased from retraining funds, it cannot be done without limit. A prime asset in McDowell county is its vocational high school, a superb facility with shops and instructors for woodwork, welding, sheet metal, machine shop, electricity, drafting, plumbing, radio and electronics, and auto mechanics. The pilot courses which preceded the establishment of the state AVP program were given in this school. There is every reason to believe that the equipment and staff of the school have been a persistent impetus to retraining in McDowell county, and at the same time have controlled the types of retraining to be given there.

At the other extreme are rural counties, outside our sample area, with so little vocational educational equipment that they could offer retraining only by leasing quarters and purchasing all the needed equipment. For single-time offerings to small enrollments, this cost is excessive. It is quite likely that counties of this sort have not received much encouragement to enter into retraining. Several of the smaller, primarily rural ones are among the counties with no retraining programs at all.

## THE RECIPIENTS OF RETRAINING

Retraining programs are intended to help the unemployed get jobs. The number of unemployed, however, far exceeds the number who will be retrained in any existing program. In 1962, the number of unemployed in the United States averaged about four million[4]; the West Virginia average during that year was in the range of 55,000 to 60,000.[5] Retraining programs can reach only a small fraction of these numbers. Through the end of 1962, retraining under the Area Redevelopment Administration was authorized for just 14,185 persons in forty states and American Samoa.[6] In the first year of its operation, the Manpower Development and Training Act was expected to provide training for just 60,000.[7] The West Virginia AVP, in its first two years, enrolled over 7,500, a substantial number, yet far short of the number of unemployed.[8]

The wide disparity between the number of unemployed and the number of men and women given training to help them in their search for employment demands an answer to the question: which of the unemployed have received training, and which have not? A prior question, however, is: what are the unemployed like?

The unemployed are neither a homogeneous population nor a true cross-section of the labor force. Disproportionately high rates of unemployment exist among five classes of workers.[9]

The first group is made up of the youngest members of the labor force. In 1962, the unemployment rate for boys 14–19 was 13 per cent; that for men 25 and over, 4 per cent. The rate is particularly high among young high-school dropouts. More than one-seventh of all the unemployed in the country in 1962 were high-school dropouts still under 25 years of age. The young unemployed now constitute a rising percentage of the long-term unemployed.

Older workers are also a high-unemployment group. Workers and those of the age group 55–69 have a lower unemployment rate than very young workers and those in the middle-age groups. However, because it is hard for displaced older workers to get new jobs, the proportion of long-term unemployed is higher among the older jobless than among those of middle age.

Negroes constitute a third group. In 1962, they constituted 11 per cent of the labor force and 22 per cent of the unemployed.

Fourth are unskilled workers. In the whole postwar period, laborers have had higher unemployment rates than any other major occupational group. These workers rank low in skill, training, and education.

The fifth category is made up of workers in industries which are declining or which are subject to wide employment fluctuations. The coal mining industry is a familiar example of the former, the construction industry of the latter.

The unemployed, then, are concentrated in certain population types, occupations, and industries. In turn, they are distributed unequally by geographic region. Another important basis of classification of the unemployed is by the duration of joblessness. Some people released from one job succeed in getting another very soon; others keep up the search for months and even years without finding work. In 1962, among all the unemployed, those who had been without work for fifteen weeks or more— the long-term unemployed—were more than a quarter of the total; one out of seven unemployed had been continuously without work for more than six months; and 6 per cent had had no work for a year or more.[10]

The hard-core unemployed are those whose occupational skills and personal circumstances combine to keep them out of work for long periods at a stretch. These are the most handicapped workers. So long as they must depend on their own resources, their prospect for employment is poor.

It may be assumed that the same classes of workers that experience a high rate of unemployment nationally also do so in West Virginia. In all likelihood, the average duration of unemployment has been higher in this state than throughout the country.

Are the men and women who are selected for retraining in West Virginia primarily those who face the heaviest handicap in their search for jobs, or are they rather the workers who would stand the best chance of getting a job even without retraining? This is a basic question, and any appraisal of retraining must take it into account. The policy issue that it raises is difficult, however. Is it better to offer retraining first to handicapped workers with the full awareness that retraining may not sufficiently offset their other disabilities in their quest for jobs? Or is it better to help those persons who, when trained, stand the best chance of being employed?

The basic hypothesis to be tested in this area is that the trainees are the best qualified members of the labor force. It is to be tested for age, race, education, and regular occupation.

## AGE

Since, in new hiring in almost all occupations, younger adults will usually be selected over older workers, retraining may be said to be serving the advantaged workers if it is concentrated among the younger adults, and to be serving the hard core if it enrolls a proportionate number of older workers.

The age composition of the respondents in the samples, given in Table II.5, indicates that the people who completed training are signifi-

TABLE II.5

TRAINING-STATUS GROUPS BY AGE, SUMMER, 1963

| Training status | 0–21 yrs. | | 22–34 yrs. | | 35–44 yrs. | | 45–54 yrs. | | 55+ yrs. | | Not ascertained | | Total | |
|---|---|---|---|---|---|---|---|---|---|---|---|---|---|---|
| | No. | % | No. | % | No. | % | No. | % | No. | % | No. | % | No. | % |
| Completed training | 61 | 12.2 | 226 | 45.1 | 130 | 25.9 | 65 | 13.0 | 14 | 2.8 | 5 | 1.0 | 501 | 100.0 |
| Dropped out of training | 23 | 9.9 | 111 | 47.6 | 59 | 25.3 | 33 | 14.2 | 5 | 2.1 | 2 | 0.9 | 233 | 100.0 |
| Did not report | 11 | 16.9 | 33 | 50.8 | 14 | 21.5 | 7 | 10.8 | 0 | 0.0 | 0 | 0.0 | 65 | 100.0 |
| Not accepted for training | 12 | 9.4 | 34 | 26.8 | 30 | 23.6 | 37 | 29.1 | 14 | 11.0 | 0 | 0.0 | 127 | 100.0 |
| Nonapplicant | 38 | 8.4 | 138 | 30.5 | 125 | 27.6 | 96 | 21.2 | 54 | 11.9 | 2 | 0.4 | 453 | 100.0 |
| Total | 145 | 10.5 | 542 | 39.3 | 358 | 26.0 | 238 | 17.3 | 87 | 6.3 | 9 | 0.6 | 1,379 | 100.0 |

cantly younger on the average than either those who applied for and were rejected for training or those who were uninvolved in training in any way but registered for employment at their Employment Security Office when trainees were being selected. The 1963 median age of the men and women who completed training was below 33, that of rejected or nonreferred applicants for retraining was just under 44, and that of the non-trainees unemployed was 39.

Of the respondents who completed training 15 per cent were 45 or over in 1963; just 3 per cent were over 55. In contrast, among the rejects, 40 per cent were 45 and over, and 11 per cent at least 55. The sample of nonapplicants registered for employment included 33 per cent 45 and over, and about 12 per cent 55 and over.

If those who completed their retraining courses are arranged in order of age, the middle half falls between 25.6 years and 41.5 years, and thus covers an age spread of 15.9 years. The middle half of the "rejects" falls between 29.6 and 50.2 years, for a spread of 20.6 years; while the comparable figures for the nonapplicant unemployed are 29.0 and 48.9 years, a span of 19.9 years. These figures, like the others given above, help substantiate that the retrained workers are younger on the average than the rejected or uninvolved, and also show less age spread within the middle half of the trainees as compared to the other two populations.

The age distribution of men and women who dropped out of training is strikingly like that of those who completed their training courses. A sixth of all who did not report for training after being assigned to a course were 21 or younger. Since the frequency of those not reporting in each age-category of the table is small, no statistical significance can be attached to the higher proportion of very young persons among them.

The retrained workers are thus a younger population than are either the men and women rejected for training or the members of the non-trainee unemployed. The age composition of all those assigned to training is essentially the same as the age of those who completed training. In other words, the age selection occurs before training begins. With respect to age, retraining is aiding the more readily employable workers and not serving many of the older workers.

It is alleged, and probably correctly, that in setting up selection standards for training courses, prospective employers place limits on the kind of people they are willing to hire. Some age selection may be so explained. It is also evident, however, that older workers as a class do less well on the qualifying tests given applicants; and it must be acknowledged that, in at least some kinds of retraining, the young workers learn better.

## RACE

Race is a significant variable in testing the hypothesis that the selection processes that sift people into retraining favor the least disadvantaged workers. National data indicate that Negroes are over-represented in those occupations which are most subject to low pay rates and irregular employment. They hold a large fraction of private household and other low-skilled service jobs. A slightly larger percentage of nonwhites than whites are operatives. The disparity is greater in unskilled labor jobs. While white-collar employment among Negroes is growing along with the move to white-collar jobs among whites, just 16.7 per cent of non-white employed persons were white-collar workers in 1962, as against 47.3 per cent of employed white persons.[11]

In recent years, the national unemployment rate among nonwhites has been higher than among whites. It has been higher in every age group and in all major occupational groups. Further, the gap between the races has been widening. From 1947 through 1954, the unemployment rate among nonwhites was less than twice that of whites, whereas from 1955 through 1962, it was persistently more than twice the white rate. In 1962, the nonwhite rate stood at 224 per cent of the white rate.[12]

The Negro population in West Virginia numbered just under 90,000 in 1960, and constituted 4.8 per cent of the population. All other non-whites together totalled under 1,000. Only in McDowell county, in the southernmost part of the state, is the Negro percentage higher than in the nation as a whole. The proportion of Negroes in the population of the five sample areas in 1960 was respectively: Cabell, 4.5 per cent, or Cabell-Wayne, 3.3 per cent; Harrison, 1.7 per cent; Kanawha, 5.8 per cent; McDowell, 22.3 per cent; and Monongalia, 2.1 per cent. The composite percentage was 6.2 per cent.

Within the civilian labor force, the 1960 census showed an unemployment rate of 8.3 per cent. The rate for whites was 8.2 per cent and non-whites 11.4 per cent. In the state as a whole, the counties with the largest proportion of nonwhites—the southern coal counties—were the same ones that had higher-than-average unemployment rates. In 1960, the higher unemployment rate among Negroes in the state was at least in part attributable to their concentration in the high unemployment areas. In McDowell county, located in the heart of the southern coal fields, the unemployment rate on the basis of the Census data was 11.0 per cent for the total civilian labor force and 12.7 per cent for nonwhites.

In 1960, 6.7 per cent of the unemployed in the five counties were non-whites. Since nonwhites other than Negroes were so few in number, the percentage may be applied to Negroes. In Table II.6, which gives the training status of the project samples by race, it can be seen that forty-seven Negroes were assigned to the sample courses. If the few trainees for which race was not reported are assumed to be white, then 5.9 per cent of all men and women assigned to those classes were Negro. Since the racial composition of the unemployed is not available on a month-by-month basis, there is no sure way of knowing whether a "chance proportion" of Negroes among trainees would be higher or lower than this. It appears probable that slightly fewer than a proportionate number of Negroes were assigned.

TABLE II.6

TRAINING-STATUS GROUPS, BY RACE

| Training status | White | | Negro | | Total | |
|---|---|---|---|---|---|---|
| | No. | % | No. | % | No. | % |
| Completed training | 474 | 94.6 | 27 | 5.4 | 501 | 100.0 |
| Dropped out of training | 225 | 96.6 | 8 | 3.4 | 233 | 100.0 |
| Did not report | 53 | 81.5 | 12 | 18.5 | 65 | 100.0 |
| Not accepted for training | 112 | 88.2 | 15 | 11.8 | 127 | 100.0 |
| Nonapplicant | 406 | 89.6 | 47 | 10.4 | 453 | 100.0 |
| Total | 1,270 | 92.1 | 109 | 7.9 | 1,379 | 100.0 |

If the numbers of whites and Negroes rejected for training are added in, Negroes then constitute 6.8 per cent. Since the number of "rejects" interviewed in the field surveys was arbitrarily determined, we cannot say that the sum of the numbers shown in Table II.6 as assigned to training and those shown as not accepted represents the total number of applicants for training. It is clear, though, that the proportion of Negroes among the pool of applicants for retraining is higher than is the proportion among those accepted for training; in other words, the rate of rejection is higher among Negroes.

It may be that the higher rate of rejection of Negro applicants is due to their poorer educational backgrounds and lower aptitude scores. Yet among the high-school graduates in the study samples, whites fared better than Negroes in the selection process: the percentage of high-school graduates was almost identical among whites and Negroes accepted for training, 47.1 and 47.8 per cent, respectively. Among the white applicants for training 94 per cent of the high-school graduates were accepted for training, while just 71 per cent of graduate Negro applicants were accepted. Among the applicants not accepted for training, 22 per cent of the whites and 60 per cent of the Negroes were high-school graduates. (The latter percentage is based on a total of just fifty-one cases, however.)

Since high-school graduates differ widely in both learning and ability, the above data do not prove that racial considerations entered directly into the acceptance or rejection of candidates for retraining. The allegation was heard in one of the five counties that qualified Negroes were not referred for training because their race would handicap them in their subsequent search for jobs, but this allegation was not proved. The firmer

conclusion is that the current difficulty Negroes face in seeking employment and the difficulty they have in meeting the qualifications for admission to retraining are both the results of pervasive discrimination
practices that have marked virtually every phase of their lives.

The percentage of Negroes in the sample of nontrainee unemployed is
significantly higher than the percentage of Negroes in the population assigned to training. The respective percentages are 10.5 and 5.9. Here is
further confirmation that disproportionately few Negroes enter into retraining.

A relatively large number of Negroes, on being assigned to training,
did not report for it. In the sample courses, a quarter of all Negroes admitted to training did not actually begin it. This is about twice the
fraction in the total sample. It may be that a few Negroes, having lived
with job discrimination, felt that there was no use. They could point to
others of their race who, after completing training, failed to get jobs.

### EDUCATION

Educational levels constitute a third measure of the relative qualifications of workers of different training statuses. The hypothesis that the
least handicapped workers are "over-represented" among trainees is supported if the men and women assigned to training went further in school
than either the rejected applicants or the nontrainee unemployed.

Some individuals in each training status had stopped school at or before the sixth grade, and some in each status had a year or more of college (see Table II.7). The table also shows, however, that as a class, the
trainees received more schooling than did any category of nontrainees.
Sixty per cent of all the men and women who completed their retraining
courses had finished high school, and a sixth of these had completed at
least one year of college. How do the members of other training-status
categories compare? Forty per cent of those who dropped out of training
had finished school, while a slightly lower per cent (37) of those who were
selected for training but did not report were high-school graduates.
Among the applicants who were not selected for training, just 31 per cent
had gone through high school, whereas 26 per cent of the sample of unemployed men and women not involved in any way with retraining had
gone this far.

The top half of those who completed training courses had twelve or
more grades of school; whereas the top half of the dropouts includes some
who finished only the eleventh grade, and the top half of those who did
not report for training includes some who went no higher than the tenth
grade. The upper half of both the sample of rejected applicants and the
sample of nontrainee unemployed includes individuals whose schooling
ended with the ninth grade. The finding is clear: within the combined

## TABLE II.7

### Highest School Grade Completed, by Training Status, Summer, 1962

Highest grade completed[a]

| Training status | 1-6 | | 7 | | 8 | | 9 | | 10 | | 11 | | 12 | | 13+ | | Total | |
|---|---|---|---|---|---|---|---|---|---|---|---|---|---|---|---|---|---|---|
| | No. | % | No. | % | No. | % | No. | % | No. | % | No. | % | No. | % | No. | % | No. | % |
| Completed training | 6 | 1.4 | 9 | 2.0 | 42 | 9.5 | 37 | 8.4 | 34 | 7.7 | 41 | 9.3 | 223 | 50.4 | 46 | 10.4 | 442 | 100.0 |
| Dropped out of training | 5 | 2.5 | 9 | 4.4 | 23 | 11.3 | 33 | 16.2 | 30 | 14.8 | 19 | 9.4 | 70 | 34.5 | 11 | 5.4 | 203 | 100.0 |
| In training | 6 | 6.7 | 5 | 5.6 | 10 | 11.2 | 16 | 18.0 | 13 | 14.6 | 6 | 6.7 | 23 | 25.8 | 10 | 11.2 | 89 | 100.0 |
| Did not report | 2 | 3.1 | 2 | 3.1 | 15 | 23.1 | 6 | 9.2 | 11 | 16.9 | 5 | 7.7 | 20 | 30.8 | 4 | 6.2 | 65 | 100.0 |
| Not accepted for training | 9 | 7.1 | 10 | 7.9 | 31 | 24.4 | 16 | 12.6 | 6 | 4.7 | 13 | 10.2 | 29 | 22.8 | 11 | 8.7 | 127 | 100.0 |
| Nonapplicant | 78 | 17.2 | 42 | 9.3 | 93 | 20.5 | 42 | 9.3 | 40 | 8.8 | 35 | 7.7 | 84 | 18.5 | 36 | 7.9 | 453 | 100.0 |

[a] Twelve cases for whom education was not learned are not shown in the body of the table, but are included in totals. Those twelve are distributed as follows: Completed training—4; dropped out of training—3; not accepted for training—2; nonapplicant—3.

samples those who completed training had the highest grade average; those who were assigned to training and either dropped out or did not report occupy a middle position; the men and women either rejected for training or wholly uninvolved in retraining held the lowest average.

Among the younger workers at least, a high-school diploma is a requirement for entry into a large number of jobs. The school dropout is very likely to find that he cannot get a job. In the United States as a whole, in October, 1962, school dropouts aged 16 to 24 in the civilian labor force had an unemployment rate of 29 per cent, or twice that of high-school graduates of these ages.[13] Further, they constitute a rising proportion of the long-term unemployed. It is known that during periods of labor surplus some firms require high-school graduation of men newly hired for unskilled jobs.

The survey data provide no firm clue whether the men and women with the most schooling are brighter than others. Since the main reason for rejecting applicants for training is their low General Aptitude Test Battery Scores, there exists at least a hint of a relationship between schooling and general ability.

High-school completion, besides providing an entry into certain jobs, equipping the graduate with useful knowledge, and possibly reflecting a measure of general ability, may also be an indicator of individual persistence. The point is speculative, but is supported by the evidence that, among those selected for training, the men and women who completed their courses had more regular schooling than did both those who dropped out en route and those who failed to report for training at all.

The trainees have both the higher mean level of education and what is generally considered to be a more favorable age distribution. Still, some men and women with a limited education, and some older workers, have been retrained. Do the trainees who are supposedly handicapped in one way have some compensating advantage? For example, are the older trainees relatively well educated? Or, are the trainees with only a grade-school education relatively young?

Of the sample populations 45 and over, the number completing twelve or more grades of school is as follows, by training-status groups:

| | |
|---|---|
| Completed training | 30 |
| Dropped out of training | 5 |
| Did not report | 3 |
| Not accepted for training | 13 |
| Nonapplicant | 18 |

An average of the percentages of all those accepted for training within this older age group reveals that 31 per cent of them were high-school graduates. This is the highest percentage of the three trainee-status groups. The smallest percentage is 12, among the nonapplicants, while those rejected fall in between. The difference between those accepted for training and those rejected is in the expected direction, but is not statistically significant. The difference between the proportion of high-school graduates among the applicants and the nonapplicants is significant. Among the older workers, education appears to be related to the readiness to seek retraining, but is not conclusively related to acceptance of applicants.

Among the men and women with no more than eight years of schooling, 32.1 per cent of the applicants for training and 32.4 per cent of the nonapplicants were under 35 years of age. There is but a chance difference. The applicants with less than eight years of school who were accepted for training tended to be a little younger than those not accepted; 34.4 per cent of the accepted and 26.0 of those rejected were under 35. This difference, again, is in the expected direction, but is not large enough to meet the test of statistical significance. The data give no more than tentative support to the hypothesis that among the poorly educated, those admitted to training have the more favorable age distribution.

While age and education do not consistently compensate for one another, the combination of youth and high education, or of age and limited education, is highly selective. Note the contrasts in Table II.8. More than

TABLE II.8

AGE AND EDUCATION

| Training status | I<br>Sample members aged 22–34,<br>with 12 or more yrs. of school | II<br>Sample members aged 45 +,<br>with 0–8 yrs. of school |
|---|---|---|
| Completed training | 158 | 22 |
| Dropped out of training | 51 | 16 |
| Did not report | 9 | 2 |
| Not accepted for training | 12 | 23 |
| Nonapplicant | 52 | 102 |

a quarter of all the men and women who were accepted for training had the age and educational traits represented by Column I, while only 5 per cent of those accepted had the traits represented by Column II. Among those rejected, fewer than a tenth had the first combination of traits, and 18 per cent had the second combination. The pattern of nonapplicants follows that of the rejected applicants. Age and education, in combination, have a strong bearing on the nature of workers' involvement in retraining.

## TABLE II.9

### Labor Force Status One Month Before Retraining, or Equivalent, by Training Status

| Training status | Employed | | Not in labor force | | Unemployed | | | | | | | | | | | Not ascertained | | Total | |
| --- | --- | --- | --- | --- | --- | --- | --- | --- | --- | --- | --- | --- | --- | --- | --- | --- | --- | --- | --- | --- |
| | | | | | 1–3 mo. | | 4–6 mo. | | 7–12 mo. | | 13–24 mo. | | 25+ mo. | | | | | | | |
| | No. | % | No. | % | No. | % | No. | % | No. | % | No. | % | No. | % | | | No. | % | No. | % |
| Completed training | 110 | 22.2 | 93 | 18.8 | 72 | 14.5 | 59 | 11.9 | 70 | 14.4 | 53 | 10.7 | 39 | 7.9 | | | 5 | —[a] | 501 | 100.0 |
| Dropped out of training | 70 | 30.6 | 34 | 14.8 | 32 | 14.0 | 22 | 9.6 | 23 | 10.0 | 29 | 12.7 | 19 | 8.3 | | | 4 | — | 233 | 100.0 |
| Did not report | 37 | 56.9 | 8 | 12.3 | 6 | 9.2 | 3 | 4.6 | 4 | 6.2 | 6 | 9.2 | 1 | 1.5 | | | 0 | — | 65 | 100.0 |
| Not accepted for training | 47 | 37.3 | 16 | 12.7 | 4 | 3.2 | 8 | 6.3 | 7 | 5.5 | 26 | 20.6 | 18 | 14.3 | | | 1 | — | 127 | 100.0 |
| Nonapplicant | 212 | 47.0 | 52 | 11.5 | 52 | 11.5 | 18 | 4.0 | 25 | 5.5 | 59 | 13.1 | 33 | 7.3 | | | 2 | — | 453 | 100.0 |
| Total | 476 | 34.8 | 203 | 14.9 | 166 | 12.1 | 110 | 8.0 | 129 | 9.4 | 173 | 12.7 | 110 | 8.0 | | | 12 | — | 1,379 | 100.0 |

[a] "Not ascertained" frequencies omitted in the calculation of percentages.

PRETRAINING LABOR FORCE STATUS

To qualify for retraining, a worker must be either unemployed or substantially underemployed. It may be assumed that the people who have been unemployed continuously over a long time are somehow handicapped in the job market. The length of unemployment of the members of the different training-status samples provides a further clue to whether the trainees are the best qualified workers among the unemployed. In Table II.9, the labor force status of the nonapplicants is given as of a single date when a number of courses were being organized. A number of persons in each training status were employed, either on a full-time or part-time basis, one month before retraining, while others were not in the labor force. Apparently, a number of workers became applicants for retraining shortly after turning to their local employment offices for jobs. The large number of nonapplicants listed as employed in Table II.9 may be influenced by the manner in which that sample was drawn; the only stipulation was that the worker be unemployed at a time when any retraining course was being established.

When only the men and women who were unemployed at the basedate are considered, a pattern emerges. First, a full third of those accepted for retraining had been unemployed for more than a year and 13 per cent for more than two years. (See Table II.10.) The long-term unemployed

TABLE II.10

LENGTH OF UNEMPLOYMENT OF THOSE UNEMPLOYED ONE MONTH
BEFORE RETRAINING OR EQUIVALENT

| Training status | Length of unemployment (in months) | | | | | |
| --- | --- | --- | --- | --- | --- | --- |
| | 1–3 | 4–6 | 7–12 | 13–24 | 25+ | Total |
| Completed training | 24.6% | 20.1% | 23.9% | 18.1% | 13.3% | 100.0% |
| Dropped out of training | 25.6 | 17.6 | 18.4 | 23.2 | 15.2 | 100.0 |
| Did not report | 30.0 | 15.0 | 20.0 | 30.0 | 5.0 | 100.0 |
| Not accepted for training | 6.3 | 12.7 | 11.1 | 41.3 | 28.6 | 100.0 |
| Nonapplicant | 27.8 | 9.6 | 13.4 | 31.6 | 17.6 | 100.0 |
| *Total % unemployed* | *24.1* | *16.0* | *18.8* | *25.1* | *16.0* | *100.0* |

were not excluded from retraining. The trainees' median duration of unemployment was about eight months. Second, among the rejected applicants, more than two-thirds had been unemployed for over a year, and 28 per cent for longer than two years. Their median duration was nearly eighteen months. The control group of nonapplicants fell between the accepted and rejected applicants; about half had been unemployed for over a year or more.

## TABLE II.11

### Regular Pretraining Occupations, by Training-Status Groups

| Regular occupation | Completed training | | Dropped out of training | | Did not report | | Not accepted for training | | Nonapplicant | | Total | |
|---|---|---|---|---|---|---|---|---|---|---|---|---|
| | No. | % | No. | % | No. | % | No. | % | No. | % | No. | % |
| Professional, farmer, manager | 13 | 2.6 | 7 | 3.0 | 1 | 1.5 | 3 | 2.4 | 11 | 2.4 | 35 | 2.5 |
| Clerical & kindred | 37 | 7.4 | 19 | 8.2 | 2 | 3.1 | 7 | 5.5 | 40 | 8.8 | 105 | 7.6 |
| Sales worker | 23 | 4.6 | 10 | 4.3 | 2 | 3.1 | 5 | 3.9 | 15 | 3.3 | 55 | 4.0 |
| Craftsman | 47 | 9.4 | 34 | 14.6 | 5 | 7.7 | 15 | 11.8 | 65 | 14.3 | 166 | 12.0 |
| Operative | 149 | 29.7 | 89 | 38.2 | 24 | 36.9 | 31 | 24.4 | 181 | 40.0 | 474 | 34.4 |
| Private & household service worker | 53 | 10.6 | 10 | 4.3 | 8 | 12.3 | 25 | 19.7 | 35 | 7.7 | 131 | 9.5 |
| Unskilled laborer | 55 | 11.0 | 34 | 14.6 | 10 | 15.4 | 18 | 14.2 | 60 | 13.2 | 177 | 12.8 |
| Not available or no regular occupation | 124 | 24.8 | 30 | 12.9 | 13 | 20.0 | 23 | 18.1 | 46 | 10.2 | 236 | 17.1 |
| Total | 501 | | 233 | | 65 | | 127 | | 453 | | 1,379 | |

In summary, while some long-term unemployed had been admitted to retraining, the trainees are characterized in the main by relatively short periods of prior unemployment. The rejects are, by and large, the long-term unemployed, the men and women who have had the most difficulty in getting jobs.

## PRETRAINING OCCUPATION

The thesis that workers selected for training are the best qualified by prevailing hiring standards may be tested further by an examination of their basic skill levels. All respondents in all training statuses were asked their "regular" occupation. Are the trainees from occupations of higher rank than either the unemployed not accepted for training or the non-applicant unemployed? The data from which the answer is to be drawn are summarized in Table II.11 (which combines the occupations of men and women).

In all training statuses, manual occupations far outnumbered white-collar ones. While the latter frequencies are too small to permit a systematic analysis, no difference among the training status groups is apparent. There are significantly more craftsmen and operatives among the nonapplicants than among those who completed training. The explanation lies in the nature of the study samples rather than in the kinds of workers attracted to training. McDowell county, with its heavy dependence on coal mining, accounts for a disproportionate number of workers with these occupations; it is also overrepresented in the nonapplicant sample, as it is in the sample of dropouts. No real difference exists between the proportion of craftsmen and operatives in the sample of dropouts and that of nonapplicants.

The only other significant contrast among the several training-status groups is the large number completing training for whom no regular occupation is reported. A part of the explanation is the relatively large number of women admitted to retraining who were not in the labor force shortly before retraining and who reported no regular occupation. It is quite unlikely that any remaining difference is significant; the rest of the trainees are just as likely as the nonapplicants to have identified themselves with a regular occupation.

When the location variable is controlled, no significant relation appears between training status and regular occupation. Unlike the data on age, race, and education, those on previous skill do not substantiate the basic hypothesis. Where does the explanation lie? There may be some dubious reporting of "regular" occupations, yet no obvious reason stands out for supposing that misjudgment would vary with training status. It is often conjectured that the more highly skilled workers, if unemployed, would be reluctant to enter into training that would equip them with a skill no higher than the one they already possess, even though their chance for a job would be increased. If this is so, it would lead us to expect a skill difference between applicants and nonapplicants, and nothing more. But even this relationship is not significant.

## CONCLUSION

Trainees are chosen from the applicants whose aptitude scores and other qualifications meet the required standards. They are a selected population. The thesis that they are the "cream" of the unemployed, the men and women who stand the best chance of getting jobs even without retraining, is supported by the study findings. More of the trainees are concentrated in the young-adult ages. A disproportionate number are whites. They have a higher mean level of education. Fewer are numbered among the really long-term unemployed. There is limited but inconclusive evidence that the trainees who are disadvantaged in one particular respect, such as age or education, are likely to have some compensating advantageous trait. Only with respect to previous regular occupation are the trainees not a specially selected group.

The early retraining in West Virginia, then, did not reach many of the hard-core unemployed. Bear in mind, however, that many of them could not meet the criteria for acceptance. A policy question remains: Is it better to give retraining to those men and women who are most likely to get jobs afterwards, even though many of them would find jobs anyway? Or is the public interest best served by retraining the more handicapped workers—those who will not learn the new skills so well and who will have more difficulty in getting post-training jobs, but who are most in need of help?

## RETRAINING: PERCEPTIONS AND ATTITUDES

The attitudes of men and women toward retraining both affect and reflect its successes. Retraining can succeed only if unemployed workers are ready to turn to new occupations, and if they have confidence in the government-sponsored programs as routes of entry to new kinds of work. Looking back at their retraining experiences, they can judge whether their confidence was justified, and the testimony of people who have experienced retraining, if spread through a community, can affect local support for it either positively or negatively.

### ATTITUDES TOWARD CHANGING JOBS

Workers who feel that they have settled into a life work are not going to be attracted to retraining, even if that work is interrupted from time to time by unemployment. On the other hand, workers who would like to be in some other kind of work may view retraining not merely as a way of getting a job, but as a means of gaining a new occupation. How do workers feel about their "regular" occupation, that is, the one with which they identified themselves prior to the field study? Do they feel that it is the right one for them? How many would like a change?

This question was put to each of the study subsamples in the following form: "Is there some line of work, different from any you have ever done, which you would like to do and feel you could handle if given a chance to learn the necessary skills?"

Of the 1,379 respondents in the total sample, 898, or 65 per cent, replied affirmatively and went on to name the new kind of work they would like to attempt. This particular population, then, contains a large number of men and women for whom a specific job change has some appeal. The range of hoped-for occupations was wide and, as was to be expected, many were named that could not be entered through retraining in the respondent's home community.

It is improper to generalize this finding to the whole labor force, for the reason that all the subsamples except one were constituted of workers who applied for retraining and thus accepted either the desirability or the necessity of entering some new kind of work. Even the subsample of nonapplicants was drawn from the job-applicant files of the Employment Service; and it may be conjectured that relatively more of them than of the nonregistered unemployed workers would accept a new kind of work.

A majority in each training status responded to the question affirmatively. But, whereas nearly 70 per cent of all applicants for training could point to another occupation that they would like to follow, just 56 per cent of the nonapplicants could do so. The difference is too great to be attributed to chance. The higher proportion of affirmative responses among the applicants for retraining, however, should not obscure the large number of nonapplicants who would have liked to try some other kind of work.

The right of a man to stay with his present occupation through a period of unemployment was probed by asking: "Do you think that after a man has been out of a job for six months he should take some other kind of work if he can get it?" Nearly everyone answered affirmatively. Over 96 per cent said yes, and just 2 per cent said no. The question may call for an affirmation of a basic American tradition, and thus be subject to response bias. For what it may be worth, it did not bring to light any general disposition to defend the man who prefers unemployment to a change of jobs.

## AWARENESS OF RETRAINING PROGRAMS

For the individual trainee, the starting point of participation in training is learning about it. Once the unemployed worker knows that retraining is offered in his community, he can then respond to it. Obviously, all applicants were at least enough informed about the program to take positive steps toward getting in. The 926 applicants for retraining were asked how they had heard about retraining. A large proportion of them, 406, or 43 per cent of the total, were approached through the Employment Service. The Employment Security Office itself was the largest single source of first information. Since these offices were charged with screening applicants and selecting trainees, this initiative on the part of these offices is to be commended. Had it been the only source, though, the unemployed men and women would not have been able to explore the possibility of retraining on their own initiative.

The second largest source was newspapers. Since about a third of all trainees who completed their courses and about a fifth of those in the other training statuses traced their awareness to the newspapers, it may be that the press stories and advertisements attract men and women with good personal initiative. If so, newspaper publicity for the programs can play the double role of building community support and attracting desirable applicants.

The third most common source was personal contacts. It provided the first information about retraining to between a fifth and a fourth of all the applicants.

How well were the nonapplicants for retraining informed about retraining possibilities? Of the 453 respondents in the nontrainee control group, 44 per cent indicated that they had not been aware of the existence of the program. Of those who had heard about it, almost 40 per cent had received their information in a rather casual manner from friends or relatives rather than through the more formal media of communication. About an equal number had first heard about the retraining opportunities through newspapers, radio, or television, and 15 per cent had received information about retraining at the Employment Security Office. Nearly all who had heard about retraining understood that the employment office was the place to ask about it.

In the smaller Employment Security Offices, the unemployed were approached selectively about retraining. Those who were judged to be good candidates were advised about retraining, while those whose education, aptitudes, and other personal traits would seem to disqualify them for retraining were not informed.

Even though few retraining classes were delayed or smaller than the allotted size for want of applicants, more might have been done to bring the program to the attention of the unemployed. If either a state or the national government is offering retraining, each unemployed man and woman has a right to try for a place in a course, even though an increase in the number of applicants would swell the number of rejections. It appears that many of the hard-core unemployed cannot be reached by means of the usual communication media. Rather than rely on newspaper accounts or radio and television announcements, it may be necessary to confront the potential trainees directly in their homes or clubs, or through the messages of ministers in the local churches. These means have been used successfully elsewhere in demonstration retraining projects designed for hard-core unemployed workers.

### Motivations for Retraining

Everywhere retraining has been voluntary. No one has been forced into it, and no immediate penalty, such as curtailment of unemployment benefits, was imposed on those who would not apply. Why, then, did men and women seek retraining? The obvious answer is that since in our society heads of households are expected to work, retraining is pursued as a way of getting a job. This is substantially the explanation given by most of the applicants for training regardless of their eventual training status.

A free-response question was: "What did you feel you would get out of the course?" The largest single response was, "a job." Of the 926 applicants included in the sample, 460, almost exactly half, gave this answer. Among those completing their course, 56 per cent felt that they would get a job out of the course; whereas among the dropouts just 40 per cent replied in this manner. Since disproportionately many of the dropouts were in McDowell county, where most of the training was for uncertain, out-of-town jobs, the difference between the two populations was not surprising.

The next-ranking response was "to learn a new skill." Nearly 24 per cent, 221, gave this answer. An additional 53 (6 per cent) expected to improve their skills.

The next largest response, given by 109 (12 per cent) pointed to a general enhancement of future opportunities.

Apart from a small number of ambiguous answers and negative replies, such as "not much of anything" or "nothing at all," the replies nearly all pointed either to the expectation of a job or to an improved chance for a job at the end of retraining. The proportion giving one of these two replies rather than the other is partly a function of the methodology of this study, and may not be the same as that which would be found in the total retraining population.

In replying to another question, 96 per cent of those who completed their course indicated that they had thought that the course would help them get a job. The percentages were barely lower for the other training statuses, ranging from 90.1 to 93.8. Yet two-thirds of all respondents could not name an anticipated employer, and fewer than 60 per cent were confident of a job in their immediate locality.

The men and women who were training for a job with a specific employer were more likely to complete their training course than those who were not. More than three-quarters of all those training in courses specifically designed to meet the needs of a single employer finished the course. Out of ninety-eight interviewed men who were assigned to training for jobs in an aircraft assembly plant, three did not report for their course, fifteen dropped out (some of them involuntarily), and eighty finished. Of the trainees who had a class of employers, e.g., hospitals, in mind, 60 per cent finished, as against just about half of those whose employment goals were less definite. Clearly, the more positive the employment prospect, the greater has been the motivation to stay through to the completion of the course.

### The Burden of the Rejected

Since the size of the sample of applicants who were not admitted to training was established arbitrarily, it is not a clue to the proportion of applicants who were turned down. The usual reason for nonacceptance was low General Aptitude Test Battery scores, though other qualifications, such as the health standards of specific employers, also barred some candidates. In some instances, applicants were turned away because the classes for which they applied could not accommodate all who met the technical qualifications for admission.

Bitterness was apparent in the responses of those who had not been accepted. Almost all of the 127 persons in the sample felt that they could have done the kind of work for which the course would have prepared them. Much of their bitterness was directed not at the testing procedures —most of them told the interviewers that they thought their tests were fair—but at the failure of the employment offices to inform them of their status. One-fourth of the "rejects" claimed that they had never heard from the Employment Security Office concerning their nonacceptance, and a number were first informed about the disposition of their application by the survey interviewer. About a third of the sample acknowledged that they had been informed about their failure to qualify for retraining, but complained that they were given no explanation of their failure.

Only a third of the rejected applicants appeared to accept the fact of their nonacceptance with good grace. The others expressed keen disappointment, discouragement, lack of confidence in the selection procedures of the Employment Service, dissatisfaction with the whole approach of the retraining program, racial discrimination, or simply a general sense of bewilderment and confusion.

The procedures for informing applicants of their failure to qualify were weak in the early period of retraining. The rejects, by and large, were hard-core unemployed. Their attitudes toward work and the world in general were likely to be further undermined by the rejection of their training application. The failure of the Employment Security Offices to notify some and to give any explanation to others undoubtedly stemmed from staff limitations in the offices. Funds for an expansion of the counseling services would appear to be one of the more fruitful areas for investment. Rejected applicants are more in need than ever of understanding and expert guidance as to their future course in the labor market and the world around them. After lengthy periods of unemployment, a rejection of their application for retraining must seem to many to be the end of their labor market hopes.

## ATTITUDES OF THOSE WHO DID NOT REPORT FOR TRAINING

A surprisingly large number of applicants for training did not show up for their first classes. Sixty-five men and women who were assigned to the same classes as were attended by the respondents in the study samples of trainees did not report for training. Thus, it is estimated that about 8 per cent did not enroll after being admitted. They are of interest because they qualified for training on the basis of their interviews and aptitude tests, and in this respect are like those who did enroll. In turn, they are similar to the "rejects" and the sample of nonapplicants in that they did not benefit from the training instruction.

This category includes relatively many young persons, women, and Negroes. When asked why they did not report for their classes, over one-third (36.5 per cent) indicated that they did not report because they got a job. An immediate goal of retraining was thus achieved without the retraining. It would take a long period of follow-up, however, to determine whether these workers acted in a short-sighted manner, taking advantage of the availability of opportunities, rather than seeking higher-level jobs which they might have obtained with the benefit of retraining.

A number of the respondents in this category stated that the scheduled hours of the classes conflicted with their other commitments. Some timely counseling might have prevented the loss of these people to retraining. It may be that in some classes a flexible schedule of instruction might have been attempted to provide for some part-time workers.

A few reported that they could not afford to undertake the retraining.

## REASONS FOR DROPPING OUT OF TRAINING

As is seen in the list below, similar reasons were given for dropping out of training as for not reporting at all:

| Respondent obtained job or was recalled to work | 65(32.8%) |
| Respondent became generally dissatisfied | 29(14.6%) |
| Respondent could not afford to take retraining | 21(10.6%) |
| Health reasons—respondent was ill | 13( 6.5%) |
| Health reasons—member of respondent's family was ill | 10( 5.0%) |
| Bad hours or hours conflicting with job | 15( 7.5%) |
| Respondent thought he couldn't learn the work | 4( 2.0%) |
| Respondent was dropped for cause | 2( 1.0%) |
| Other reasons | 5( 2.5%) |
| Not ascertained | 2( 1.0%) |

One-third of the dropouts withdrew from training in order to take a job or return to their previous employment, and over 10 per cent felt that they could not afford to stay with the retraining program. Only a lengthy study of their labor market experience would reveal whether those who might have continued in their retraining courses sacrificed some long-term benefit for short-run gain. At the same time, it is clear that training allowances play a very important part in the decisions of workers to enter into training courses once they have enrolled. The rate of dropout was much higher in the West Virginia Area Vocational Programs in which no training allowances were paid than in the ARA retraining which provided for subsistence payments during the period of training. A complicating factor, though, is that most of the AVP courses were of longer duration than the maximum sixteen weeks of ARA retraining courses.

While considerable emphasis must be placed on retraining allowances as a factor influencing dropouts, it should also be noted that over 14 per cent of the respondents quit because they became generally dissatisfied with the program. These dissatisfactions stemmed from the nature of the instruction and the trainee's assessment of future job prospects. Although some efforts are now being made to record the reasons for dropping out, a detailed exit interview might prove helpful. Suggestions from those who withdrew because of dissatisfaction might help bring about improvements in instruction, facilities, and the counseling process.

### EVALUATION OF THE RETRAINING COURSES

A number of retraining courses were given by the vocational high school teachers, using the vocational high school buildings and equipment. Some were offered in specially rented quarters, with new equipment provided. A few had instructors from the professional staffs of the prospective employing firms, while others were taught by teachers recruited in the community. Most courses followed a detailed course outline provided by the school system or the prospective employer. In some, however, the instructor was allowed initiative to improvise and experiment. It is natural that the courses were not of uniform quality, although by and large the trainees found them good.

The trainees were asked to evaluate the training courses in their own words by responding to a series of broad questions. The first concerned letting people know of the retraining program. Nearly half volunteered that more publicity would have been desirable. The usual sources—newspapers, radio, and television—were favored by most of them. A few proposed a mailed announcement to all the unemployed. Nearly all the other training applicants either found the publicity all right or had no comment. It is important to remember that these are the responses of men and women who know enough about retraining to apply for a place in a course.

A few had suggestions about the selection of trainees. Since the sample of applicants included 127 men and women not admitted to training, it is not surprising that there was some expression of dissatisfaction. There were suggestions for more thorough screening, lower entrance standards, the opening of courses to all comers, and so on. The following statements were offered by two women, the former trained as a typist but unemployed, the latter, an employed stenographer:

The tests that were given were of no value to no one. Putting nuts on a spindle and turn pegs upside down—What good does it do? For a person who works at a typewriter, a test on a typewriter should be given.

I think this program would have been better received in this area if the tests had not been so hard and quite so long. If the average person could pass the tests you all give them, they would not need training to find a job. . . . I also know of the girls that held office jobs prior to these exams and were told upon the completion of these tests that they were not qualified to do office work.

Another type of criticism was leveled at the selection of workers who for reasons of age or other personal handicaps would have difficulties in getting a job afterwards. Two men trained as welders made the same point, in effect, that the retraining of the hard-core unemployed is fruitless:

Why waste money to retrain men 40 years or older when factories or other places of employment will not hire them? If they are going to retrain men 40 years or older, they should have employment for them when they finish their course; then a lot of time and money would be saved.

I know some of the men that finished the training course and still not working because they are past 40 years of age. So I think the government is wasting money on us if we take the course and cannot get a job.

One trainee felt that in some cases workers had been assigned to courses for which they had but little aptitude. He foresaw that such individuals would not stay with their newly learned occupations.

I realize that there are many who train for certain jobs, then do not follow through. This is very unfortunate since it is a great waste of time for the instructors. Also, it is a great expense to the training program. I do feel that some of this could be avoided by doing a stricter job of canvassing the prospective trainees. . . . Little is gained when a man trains for a job he doesn't like. For he is not likely to stay with the trade even if he finds that type of employment.

Of more than 900 respondents, thirty-three thought that the whole selection procedure was wrong. The critics were but a small minority, however. Far and away, the largest response was one of approval, a not surprising outcome since most of the respondents had been selected for retraining by the existent methods.

The quality of instruction is as crucial in vocational training as in any other form of education. By and large, the trainees were satisfied with the performance of their teachers. A few were highly laudatory.

I think the training course was very good. And the instructor was the one who made it good. No one could have done better. And anyone who was priviledged to get to take the course and was interested in it and will leave their home and look for work can find it. I would have been a laborer the rest of my life if it hadn't been for R——B——, my instructor.

Of the 734 respondents who had attended classes, fewer than a hundred offered any critical evaluation. Fifty-six thought their instructors should have been better. Eighteen thought that their instructors were technically competent, but unable to "put it across." Seventeen spoke of variations in the quality of instruction. The large number of trainees who held favorable judgments of their instructors provides a basis for the opinion that, as a rule, the retraining was well taught. Since a majority of the instructors were regularly employed as high school vocational education teachers, this competence was to be expected, but it was gratifying.

There was somewhat more criticism of the equipment used in the retraining courses. Nearly all the courses instructed in manual skills which require the use of equipment of some sort or other. The adequacy of the equipment used in retraining had an obvious effect on the learning of the skills. Nearly three-quarters thought the equipment was all right, or had no comment to make about it. But 28 per cent were critical. Here are two of their statements:

The equipment we had was makeshift; appliances on which to practice were obtained, for the most part, by members of the class on their own initiative. The instructor was good but was hampered by lack of equipment, tools, etc. We waited nearly three weeks for books, for example, and never did have sufficient tools nor meters, etc. It might be explained that this was the first—the pioneer—retraining class in West Virginia.[14]

The training course was not interesting, because you read and study the books, and never get any action. Why read about generators and motors, and never have a generator or motor to work with? There's no use to have a training course like this; there's not any supplies to actually work with.

About 10 per cent thought there was too little equipment, and almost the same number were critical of its quality. A further 8 per cent made both these criticisms. In one course, the trainees felt that new equipment provided from retraining funds for their use was being held back rather than given full use. The explanation believed by the men was that it was being saved for use in the regular high-school vocational program.

From several parts of the state, men training in automobile mechanics' courses felt that they were being trained for a vocation for which they would be expected to have their own tools. The men felt stymied because they believed that they could not get jobs of the sort for which they were being trained without owning the tools, yet had no money with which to buy them. Some felt that as a part of the retraining package tools should have been given them, and one or two, at least, wrote their congressman about it.

A series of general questions was intended to uncover the trainees' basic feelings about their retraining courses. The first of these was: "How well did you like the course?" As might be expected, those who completed their course had more favorable reactions than those who dropped out. More than two-thirds of the men and women who completed their course liked it very much, and five-sixths of all the rest expressed general approval of it. Only five respondents out of 442 were ambivalent, and just three didn't like it. About half of the dropouts were recorded as liking their course very much, and two-thirds of the others expressed more restrained approval ("pretty well" or "it was o.k."). About 13 per cent of the dropouts expressed ambivalence or dislike of their course. Even if some response bias in favor of the courses is assumed, these reactions speak well of the courses.

The next question involved the matching of trainees and courses: "Would you say that you were in the right course for you?" More than three-quarters of all who finished their course gave an unequivocal yes answer, as did about 57 per cent of those who dropped out. An additional 10 per cent in each of the two training statuses made qualified affirmative replies. Over against these responses, nearly a third of all who dropped out thought that they had started the wrong course, as did nearly a tenth of those who stayed through to complete their course. When one remembers that the number of different courses offered at one time was never very large in any of the sample counties, and when one takes into account that the men who did not qualify for a course of their choice were sometimes admitted to a different one, those responses indicate a good degree of satisfaction with the training courses.

The trainees were all selected on the basis of ability and aptitude scores and thus were prejudged capable of mastering their respective courses. Most of the men and women assigned to courses found them not too difficult. Among both those who had completed their course and those who had dropped out, almost half found their retraining course pretty easy, and approximately a third said it was about right. Only a few in each training status found all of it or part of it hard.

The scope and depth of the training course affect the range of jobs for which the worker might qualify. There were three relevant questions asked of all who had either completed or dropped out of training:

"Does it now seem that the course covered too much, too many different skills?"

"Was it too narrow, not covering enough skills?"

"Do you think that you learned the skills well enough?"

There was broad agreement that the courses did not attempt to cover too much. Only about 6 per cent thought that their courses were too broad and around the same number gave a qualified or ambivalent answer. The remainder had no criticism on that score. A slightly larger fraction of those not at work (either unemployed or not in the labor force in summer, 1962) than those with jobs made this criticism.

More of the trainees thought their retraining course was too narrow and specialized. About three-eighths made this criticism. A welder put his own case thus: "The welding course was fine but much too short. Welders must have knowledge of all types and phases of welding and metals to be able to find jobs. Most employers want men who can start immediately on any type job they may have." Barely more than half thought their course was broad enough; the remaining eighth were unsure. Here, too, those not at work were a little more critical than the men and women with post-training jobs.

Almost half of those who attended the retraining courses would have preferred a longer course. Some favored more class hours per day; others would have extended the number of class days. A few would have assigned the extra time to more intensive training in the skills being taught. A somewhat larger number, however, wanted their course lengthened so that it could be broadened to provide a wider range of skills. Only a few trainees, chiefly from McDowell county where the AVP courses ran for several months, stated a preference for a shorter course.

While many were critical of the scope of their retraining courses, fewer were dissatisfied with their learning of the skills actually included. Three-quarters of all who had either finished or dropped out felt that they had learned the skills well enough. Seventeen per cent thought they had not. The other 8 per cent would not express a judgment.

## ATTITUDES TOWARD THE EMPLOYMENT SERVICE

Retraining courses are established on the basis of information about job opportunities assembled by the Employment Security Offices. The same offices screen and select the trainees. Later they serve as a job placement agency for those who have gone through training. How do men and women react to the help given them in their post-training search for a job? In response to the question: "What more might the Employment Service have done to help you find work after retraining?" 44 per cent of those employed at the time of the field interview thought that it had done all it could have under the existing labor market conditions, and an additional 26 per cent had no idea how it might have helped further. But about 20 per cent felt it should have made a greater effort on their behalf. Among those out of jobs (either unemployed or not in the labor force), the responses were barely more critical. Just 28 per cent were critical of the efforts of the Employment Service, feeling that it should have made a greater effort either to uncover jobs or to notify them about job openings. A majority of the others felt that it had done all it could.

A few trainees thought that they should have been given special letters of reference to present to employers. Others thought that the Employment Service should have made a special effort on their behalf, especially with respect to out-of-town job possibilities. But some of the dropouts absolved the Employment Service since they had not finished their courses.

The Employment Service cannot help people find jobs where none exists. Although a reasonable prospect of training-related employment is supposed to exist before a retraining course can be established, in some instances this provision was interpreted loosely during the early months of the retraining programs. The Employment Security officers note that it is difficult to get trainees to come in and register. By their own account, one-third of the trainees who were either unemployed or out of the labor force when interviewed in 1962 had not reported to the employment office since their retraining.

## THE OVERVIEW

The attitudes of participants to their retraining experience provide a measure of the program's success. While the crucial test of the usefulness of retraining is the number of men and women who get jobs as a result of it, the suggestion is made elsewhere in this report that its effect on the morale is significant. No attempt was made to measure the trainees' morale directly, but two summary questions were intended to elicit their general feelings toward their retraining. The first one asked: "If you could start over again, would you take a government retraining course?" Responses were overwhelmingly affirmative. By training status, the following percentages made yes replies: completed training—94 per cent; in training—94 per cent; dropped out of training—84 per cent; did not report—89 per cent; and rejected for training—78 per cent. Even acknowledging that the percentages may be inflated by some response bias, the declared approval of retraining by those who were attending their courses and by those who had completed them is impressively high. Three trainees expressed their reactions thus:

I think the welding course they had was the best thing West Virginia ever had for the unemployed people of this area.

I think the retraining program has helped many a man in this country to live again from the skill trade learned from this program. I was glad to have the chance to take part in it.

By all means I do hope training will not be discontinued! I feel that it has given me a new goal in life. I like the work. That is in my opinion the most necessary aim of the program, to train the man for something he wants to do.

But a Negro woman, apparently blocked by racial discrimination, felt differently:

My grades were among the highest if not the highest in the class in two retraining courses. Therefore, I feel that, as far as Negroes are concerned, these types of retraining are a waste of government money, and of people's time. I personally think the unemployment agencies are segregated and prejudiced.

Eleven or 12 per cent of the respondents in three training statuses—dropouts, did-not-reports, and rejecteds—would not enter retraining if they could start all over again, and a very few respondents would not venture an answer. The tally within the study samples is overwhelmingly for retraining.

The confirming question was: "Would you recommend it to a friend?" This item brought forth a slightly larger number of indefinite replies. Still in the combined samples, 88 per cent would recommend it, and among those who had completed their course and those who were still attending, the affirmative percentages were 92 and 94 respectively. Fewer than three-quarters of those rejected for training would recommend it to a friend, but 85 per cent of those who started and dropped out would recommend it. These variations by training status are in the expected direction.

Since the interviewers were probably identified with retraining in the minds of the respondents, it may have been difficult for the latter to express an outright rejection of retraining. To the extent that they are honest, however, answers to the whole set of attitude questions indicate a favorable outlook on retraining. This positive attitude is an asset both to retraining programs and to the men and women who have been unemployed members of the labor force.

## RETRAINING AND EMPLOYMENT

Behind all retraining programs is the single objective: to equip men and women with the skills with which they should be able to get jobs. In both the AVP and ARA programs analyzed in this report, training was limited to fields in which a demand for workers was shown to exist. Only applicants whose aptitudes and preparations were adequate were admitted to training and in some courses, at least, trainees not making satisfactory progress were dropped. Both these selective measures were intended to provide a fair probability that the retrained workers would be able to find training-related employment.

Some training courses were set up in cooperation with employers. In these cases, the courses were set up to train workers in the specific skills needed in the establishments, and enrollments were tied to anticipated staff needs. Examples were courses to prepare workers for jobs in the Food Machinery and Chemicals ordnance plant in Charleston, Lockheed-Georgia aircraft assembly plant in Clarksburg, and—more recently than our field studies—a hospital and a glass plant in Clarksburg. There was an orderly movement of trainees from such courses either to more on-the-job training or to regular employment. Other courses were intended to train workers for jobs with a diverse group of employers. Further, while most ARA retraining was geared largely to prospective local employment, some AVP courses prepared men for jobs for which they would have to migrate. The latter condition characterized much of McDowell county retraining. Throughout the five counties, courses were undertaken on the basis of a known demand for workers with specific competences, but without formal assurances from employers that they would hire any of the course graduates. There was some tightening up in this respect in 1963, when applications to offer training courses had to be supported by assurance from prospective employers of their intention to hire course graduates.

Employment data were gathered both in the first field interviews, most of which were completed in the summer and fall of 1962, and in the follow-up questionnaires and interviews in the spring and summer of 1963. These data provide a direct measure of the success of retraining. The basic questions to which they give answers are the following:

Do the retrained have a higher employment rate than the men and women who didn't enter a training course?

TABLE II.12

LABOR FORCE STATUS OF TRAINEES AND CONTROL GROUPS, SUMMER, 1962

| Training status | Employed | | Unemployed | | Not in labor force | | Not ascertained | | Total | |
|---|---|---|---|---|---|---|---|---|---|---|
| | No. | % | No. | % | No. | % | No. | % | No. | % |
| Completed training | 270 | 53.9 | 178 | 35.5 | 53 | 10.6 | 0 | —ᵃ | 501 | 100.0 |
| Dropped out of training | 120 | 51.7 | 96 | 41.4 | 16 | 6.9 | 1 | — | 233 | 100.0 |
| Did not report | 24 | 36.9 | 32 | 49.2 | 9 | 13.8 | 0 | — | 65 | 100.0 |
| Not accepted for training | 50 | 39.4 | 63 | 49.6 | 14 | 11.0 | 0 | — | 127 | 100.0 |
| Nonapplicant | 146 | 32.3 | 273 | 60.4 | 33 | 7.3 | 1 | — | 453 | 100.0 |
| Total | 610 | 44.3 | 642 | 46.6 | 125 | 9.1 | 2 | — | 1,379 | 100.0 |

ᵃ "Not ascertained" frequencies omitted in the calculation of percentages.

Has the passage of a year, from summer, 1962, to summer, 1963, altered both the employment rates and the relative employment standing of the men and women in the different training statuses?

Have personal traits such as age, sex, and education affected employment outcomes within retraining categories? Have the men and women in the five sample counties fared equally well or is locality a significant variable?

Tables II.12, II.13, II.18, II.19, II.20, and II.22 hold most of the an-

TABLE II.13

LABOR FORCE STATUS OF TRAINEES AND CONTROL GROUPS, SUMMER, 1963

| Training status | Employed | | Unemployed | | Not in labor force | | Not ascertained | | Total | |
|---|---|---|---|---|---|---|---|---|---|---|
| | No. | % | No. | % | No. | % | No. | % | No. | % |
| Completed training | 332 | 71.4 | 79 | 17.0 | 54 | 11.6 | 36 | —ᵃ | 501 | 100.0 |
| Dropped out of training | 139 | 70.9 | 47 | 24.0 | 10 | 5.1 | 37 | — | 233 | 100.0 |
| Did not report | 28 | 50.0 | 23 | 41.1 | 5 | 8.9 | 9 | — | 65 | 100.0 |
| Not accepted for training | 57 | 50.4 | 38 | 33.6 | 18 | 15.9 | 14 | — | 127 | 100.0 |
| Nonapplicant | 229 | 58.9 | 106 | 27.2 | 54 | 13.9 | 64 | — | 453 | 100.0 |
| Total | 785 | 64.4 | 293 | 24.0 | 141 | 11.6 | 160 | — | 1,379 | 100.0 |

ᵃ "Not ascertained" frequencies omitted in the calculation of percentages.

swers. In these tables, for summer, 1962 and summer, 1963, employment status and training status are persistent variables. A third dimension, age, sex, education, or locality, is included in some of them.

In tables summarizing the 1962 labor force status, eighty-nine trainees who were still attending their courses (classified elsewhere in this study as "in training") were assigned to their eventual status. Of these, fifty-nine were later to finish their courses and thirty were to drop out. The advantage of this procedure is that it places all trainees in the same categories in 1962 and 1963, and assures that any changes in rates occurring over the one-year period will result from changes in the employment status of the same individuals, not from the reclassifying of individuals. The disadvantage is that nearly all the men and women still in training at the time of the first field studies were otherwise unemployed —a total of eight reported some part-time work—and the unemployment rates for both those who are classed as having completed their courses and those who dropped out are thus exaggerated.

Table II.19, which reports the employment status for men and women classified by training status, indicates a significantly higher rate of employment for those who completed training and those who dropped out than for those who never entered training. The differences are too wide to be explained by chance. Retraining is clearly associated with a higher rate of employment shortly after the completion of training. If the respondents who had taken themselves out of the labor force are excluded and the "not ascertained" responses are dropped, the percentages employed in the summer of 1962 are as follows:

| | |
|---|---|
| Completed training | 60.3% |
| Dropped out of training | 55.6 |
| Did not report | 42.9 |
| Not accepted for training | 44.2 |
| Nonapplicant | 34.8 |

The effect of this step is to widen the difference between those who had completed their courses and those who had stopped en route. It also drops the nonapplicants down further below those who had applied for retraining but either were not accepted or did not report.[15]

When the workers who were in training during the summer of 1962 are excluded, the percentage employed among those who had completed training and were in the labor force was 67.68, while among the labor force members who had dropped out, the percentage was approximately 62. Thus when only bona fide labor force members at the end of their own retraining are considered, very nearly two-thirds were at work shortly after the completion of their training. This fraction is almost twice as high as that for the sample of nonapplicants.

A full third of the retrained persons who were in the labor force in the summer of 1962 were unemployed at the time. Since training was to be undertaken only in fields offering a reasonable expectation of employment, why was the rate so high? In interpreting the rate, several things must be kept in mind. First, except for a few who were grossly underemployed, all trainees were unemployed at the beginning of their training. Second, the documentary evidence needed to demonstrate employment opportunity before a course could be set up did not have to be so tight when retraining was first launched as it did later. Third, some trainees had only recently finished their courses by the summer of 1962, and had not had time to find suitable jobs. The rate of employment after a longer lapse of time is a better measure of the worth of retraining.

The relatively large number of retrained individuals who reported themselves out of the labor force points to a serious policy question: did so large a withdrawal of retrained workers from the work force constitute a failure for retraining? It is highly likely that many of the trainees who were not looking for work would have accepted a suitable job if it had been offered, and it may be that a number of the unemployed were not vigorously seeking jobs. The line separating the unemployed and those not in the labor force is not always clear in practice. Since many of the withdrawals from the labor force are women, further discussion of this topic will be withheld until the sex variable is treated.

In the first-round interviews, trainees (including dropouts) who were employed were asked: "Since leaving retraining, have you had a job of the kind for which you were retrained?" Of the 390 replying, 13 gave ambiguous or otherwise unsatisfactory replies; 185 said yes, while 192 said no. The difference between those completing their course and those dropping out was pronounced. Just over five-eighths of the former were in occupations for which they were trained, while just one-eighth of the latter were so employed. The field studies support the finding that those who stay to the end of their course are much more likely to find work in the field of their training than those who do not. But it is also clear that the people with the best chance of getting work in the field of their training are the most likely to complete their course.

When asked why they were employed outside their retraining occupation, those to whom the question applied offered a variety of reasons. The most frequent explanation among those who had completed their course was that no work of the type for which they had prepared themselves was available. Among the dropouts, inadequate training or experience ranked first. Some reported being called back to their old job; some got a better job; a few did not want the kind of job for which the training was to fit them.

## 1962 vs. 1963

The long-term effect of retraining can be established by drawing on tabulations of the follow-up which was made nine to twelve months after the first interviews.

The follow-up was taken by a combination of the mail-questionnaire and field-interview techniques. Some cases were lost to the sample over this period, most of them because they could not be located. A comparison of the 1962 employment status of the members of the original sample with that of the men and women who were also in the follow-up sample shows that the loss of cases did not distort the sample significantly, though a contrary outcome was anticipated. To illustrate the similarities of the two, the percentage employed in 1962 among those who had completed training was 60.3 in the first sample and 60.8 in the follow-up sample.[16] Among those who dropped out of training, the respective employment rates were 55.6 and 57.3. Among the nontrainee unemployed, the rates were respectively 34.8 and 32.9. These are insignificant differences.

In the 1963 tables, the cases lost from the original sample are tabulated as "not ascertained." All percentages shown are based on the remaining frequencies. The 1963 employment rate is above the 1962 rate for the total study sample and for every training status. Just 44 per cent of the 1962 population and 64 per cent of the 1963 population had jobs.

Some of this rise may be attributed to an improvement in economic conditions in West Virginia over this period. Although, in each of the five sample areas, both the size of the labor force and the rate of unemployment dropped during 1962–63, in three areas—Cabell-Wayne, Harrison, and Monongalia—there was an increase in the number employed. The employment gains were small, however, ranging downward from 4 per cent, far too little to account for much of the employment gain made by the study population. At least a part of the rise in their employment is perhaps attributable to the constantly shifting incidence of unemployment. As a result of the opening and closing of jobs and the movement of men and women in and out of existing jobs, some of the unemployed get work even while the general level of unemployment remains steady. Further, the lower the level of unemployment, the less the competition for the available jobs for which the unemployed can qualify.

The gain of employment between 1962 and 1963 varied by training status. The lowest 1963 rate, just 50 per cent, was held by the training applicants who did not report for training. The highest rates, 71.4 and 70.9 per cent, were among the trainees who completed their courses and the dropouts, respectively. The "not-in-the-labor-force" rate was a little higher in 1963. Only among the nonapplicants for training was the increase (from 7.3 per cent to 13.9 per cent) significant. When only members of the labor force are considered, the percentages employed in mid-1962 and in the summer of 1963 were as shown in Table II.14.

TABLE II.14

PERCENTAGES EMPLOYED, MID-1962 AND SUMMER, 1963

| Training status | 1962 | 1963 |
|---|---|---|
| Completed training | 60.3(68.0)%[a] | 80.8% |
| Dropped out of training | 55.6(62.0) | 74.7 |
| Did not report | 42.9 | 54.9 |
| Not accepted for training | 44.2 | 60.0 |
| Nonapplicant | 34.8 | 68.4 |

[a] The percentages in parentheses are for trainees including those still in training in the summer of 1962.

A reading of the figures will show that the employment gain, by training status, was roughly in inverse relation to the 1962 rate of employment. Whereas the gain for those who had completed training was nearly 20 per cent (with those in training in 1962 omitted), that for the nontrainee samples together was about 70 per cent, while that for the nonapplicants was close to 100 per cent. What hypotheses grow out of this contrast between the gains registered by the nontrainees and those made by the trainees? The lower rate of employment for the nontrainees in 1962, and thus the wider potential for gain, is surely relevant and may be the most important single consideration. Still, the striking gain of the nonapplicants, bringing them in 1963 to the level reached by the trainees a year earlier, stands out. May it be that the contribution of retraining is less that of giving its recipients a lasting advantage than it is of accelerating their return to gainful employment? Or will some gap between the employment rates of the retrained and the nontrainees persist in the years ahead? It is to answer these questions, among others, that further follow-ups were attempted.

Another aspect of the 1963 situation is that, despite the substantial improvement in the rate of employment, unemployment in the spring or summer of 1963 was higher for workers in every training-status category than for the labor force as a whole. The composite unemployment rate for the five labor market areas (two of them are larger than the territories included in this study) was 7.3 per cent in the summer of 1963, whereas the rates for the study population ranged from 19–45 per cent. But let it be repeated that virtually all individuals in the study samples were unemployed some time in 1961–62. The changed rates show movement toward those of the whole labor force.

## TABLE II.15

PERCENTAGE OF TIME EMPLOYED DURING FIRST TWELVE MONTHS AFTER RETRAINING (OR EQUIVALENT), BY TRAINING STATUS

| Percentage of time employed | Completed training | | Dropped out of training | | Did not report | | Not accepted | | Nonapplicant | | Total | |
|---|---|---|---|---|---|---|---|---|---|---|---|---|
| | No. | % | No. | % | No. | % | No. | % | No. | % | No. | % |
| 76–100 | 157 | 45.8 | 71 | 44.4 | 16 | 33.3 | 26 | 27.4 | 99 | 26.0 | 369 | 35.9 |
| 51–75 | 44 | 12.8 | 26 | 16.3 | 3 | 6.3 | 12 | 12.6 | 50 | 13.1 | 135 | 13.1 |
| 26–50 | 37 | 10.8 | 12 | 7.5 | 9 | 18.8 | 5 | 5.3 | 37 | 9.7 | 100 | 9.7 |
| 1–25 | 27 | 7.9 | 12 | 7.5 | 2 | 4.2 | 13 | 13.7 | 32 | 8.4 | 86 | 8.4 |
| Less than 1 | 78 | 22.7 | 39 | 24.4 | 18 | 37.5 | 39 | 41.1 | 163 | 42.8 | 337 | 32.8 |
| Not ascertained[a] | 158 | — | 73 | — | 17 | — | 32 | — | 72 | — | 352 | — |
| Total | 501 | 100.0 | 233 | 100.0 | 65 | 100.0 | 127 | 100.0 | 453 | 100.0 | 1,379 | 100.0 |

[a] "Not ascertained" frequencies omitted in the calculation of percentages.

TABLE II.16

PERCENTAGE USING RETRAINING SKILLS

|                            | Completed training | Dropped out |
|----------------------------|:------------------:|:-----------:|
| Riveter                    | 85                 | 0           |
| Welder                     | 72                 | 50          |
| Machine tool operator      | 77                 | 11          |
| Construction trades        | 40                 | 21          |
| Auto repair                | 48                 | 18          |
| Electrical maintenance     | 24                 | 18          |
| Clerical, office           | 57                 | 50          |
| Nurse's aide and waitress  | 71                 | 17          |

The analysis of employment rates at two dates approximately a year apart is useful in suggesting trends, but jumps over the intervening employment experience. A further comparison of the labor force status of men and women in the different training-status samples is provided by data on the percentage of time employed over an extended period. Table II.17 gives these data for the twelve-month period following training and for an equivalent time period for the nontrainees. This twelve-month period is not the same for all individuals. For most, it began earlier than the summer of 1962. Fewer than half of the trainees worked more than three-quarters of the first year after their retraining. But barely more than a quarter of the nonapplicants and of the rejected applicants worked this much. At the other extreme, more than a fifth of the trainees and over two-fifths of the nonapplicants and rejected applicants were without employment throughout the year. These latter fractions include individuals who had withdrawn from the labor force. The table makes clear that the employment status of trainees in the year-long period was much more favorable than that of nontrainees. Those who were admitted to retraining but did not attend were closer to the other nontrainees than to either those who had completed their courses or those who dropped out.

### EMPLOYMENT AND TRAINING OCCUPATION

The retrained workers had a better employment record in both 1962 and 1963 than the men and women who had not entered retraining. But they did not do equally well. One variable affecting employment outcomes is the training occupation.

The 1962 columns in Table II.17 are affected by the inclusion of workers who were still in training. Even so, it is clear that in that year the highest rate of employment was enjoyed by the workers trained specifically for jobs in a single aircraft assembly plant. Among those who complete a course which prepares workers for a job with a specific em-

## TABLE II.17

### LABOR FORCE STATUS, 1962 AND 1963, BY TRAINING OCCUPATION AND TRAINING STATUS

| Training status and training occupation | Employed | | | | Unemployed | | | | Not in labor force | | | | Not ascertained[a] | | | | Total |
|---|---|---|---|---|---|---|---|---|---|---|---|---|---|---|---|---|---|
| | 1962 | | 1963 | | 1962 | | 1963 | | 1962 | | 1963 | | 1962 | | 1963 | | |
| | No. | % | No. | % | No. | % | No. | % | No. | % | No. | % | No. | % | No. | % | |
| *Completed training* | 270 | 53.9 | 332 | 71.4 | 178 | 35.5 | 79 | 17.0 | 53 | 10.6 | 54 | 11.6 | 0 | — | 36 | — | 501 |
| Riveter | 73 | 83.0 | 71 | 86.6 | 11 | 12.5 | 7 | 8.5 | 4 | 4.5 | 4 | 4.9 | 0 | — | 6 | — | 88 |
| Welder | 49 | 59.8 | 58 | 79.5 | 30 | 36.6 | 15 | 20.5 | 3 | 3.7 | 0 | 0.0 | 0 | — | 9 | — | 82 |
| Machine tool operator | 18 | 39.1 | 34 | 77.3 | 26 | 56.5 | 9 | 20.5 | 2 | 4.3 | 1 | 2.3 | 0 | — | 2 | — | 46 |
| Construction trades | 6 | 37.5 | 10 | 71.4 | 8 | 50.0 | 1 | 7.1 | 2 | 12.5 | 3 | 21.4 | 0 | — | 2 | — | 16 |
| Auto repair | 18 | 45.0 | 28 | 75.7 | 20 | 50.0 | 7 | 18.9 | 2 | 5.0 | 2 | 5.4 | 0 | — | 3 | — | 40 |
| Electrical maintenance | 18 | 47.4 | 23 | 63.9 | 20 | 52.6 | 12 | 33.3 | 0 | 0.0 | 1 | 2.8 | 0 | — | 2 | — | 38 |
| Clerical, office | 24 | 35.8 | 39 | 57.4 | 36 | 49.3 | 13 | 19.1 | 13 | 17.8 | 16 | 23.5 | 0 | — | 5 | — | 73 |
| Nurse's aide & waitress | 62 | 54.4 | 67 | 62.6 | 25 | 21.9 | 13 | 12.1 | 27 | 23.7 | 27 | 25.2 | 0 | — | 7 | — | 114 |
| Other | 2 | 50.0 | 2 | 50.0 | 2 | 50.0 | 2 | 50.0 | 0 | 0.0 | 0 | 0.0 | 0 | — | 0 | — | 4 |
| *Dropped out of training* | 120 | 51.7 | 139 | 70.9 | 96 | 41.4 | 47 | 24.0 | 17 | 6.9 | 10 | 5.1 | 0 | — | 37 | — | 233 |
| Riveter | 6 | 40.0 | 6 | 60.0 | 7 | 46.7 | 4 | 40.0 | 2 | 13.3 | 0 | 0.0 | 0 | — | 5 | — | 15 |
| Welder | 19 | 47.5 | 30 | 85.7 | 21 | 52.5 | 5 | 14.3 | 0 | 0.0 | 0 | 0.0 | 0 | — | 5 | — | 40 |
| Machine tool operator | 19 | 63.3 | 20 | 74.1 | 9 | 30.0 | 4 | 14.8 | 2 | 6.7 | 3 | 11.1 | 0 | — | 3 | — | 30 |
| Construction trades | 18 | 51.4 | 22 | 75.9 | 15 | 42.9 | 7 | 24.1 | 2 | 5.7 | 0 | 0.0 | 0 | — | 6 | — | 35 |
| Auto repair | 21 | 51.2 | 23 | 65.7 | 17 | 41.5 | 11 | 31.4 | 3 | 7.3 | 1 | 2.9 | 0 | — | 6 | — | 41 |
| Electrical maintenance | 19 | 65.5 | 17 | 70.8 | 10 | 34.5 | 7 | 29.2 | 0 | 0.0 | 0 | 0.0 | 0 | — | 5 | — | 29 |
| Clerical, office | 10 | 41.7 | 10 | 50.0 | 10 | 41.7 | 5 | 25.0 | 4 | 16.7 | 5 | 25.0 | 0 | — | 4 | — | 24 |
| Nurse's aide & waitress | 5 | 35.7 | 8 | 61.5 | 5 | 35.7 | 4 | 30.7 | 4 | 28.6 | 1 | 7.7 | 0 | — | 1 | — | 14 |
| Other | 3 | 60.0 | 3 | 100.0 | 2 | 40.0 | 0 | 0.0 | 0 | 0.0 | 0 | 0.0 | 0 | — | 2 | — | 5 |

[a] "Not ascertained" frequencies omitted in the calculation of percentages.

ployer, employment tends to follow directly upon the completion of the course. This is the most successful sort of retraining.

It is also the sort in which the newly learned skills are the most likely to be put to use. The percentages of men and women using the skills they learned in retraining shows this. (The following percentages are based on "yes" and "no" answers. Indefinite responses, those persons not in the labor force, etc., are ignored.)

Even though the frequencies underlying some of these percentages are small and fine comparisons cannot be drawn, skills taught to fit workers for a specific known job, as riveter or nurse's aide, are the most likely to be used. In contrast, men and women who learn a craft in the construction trades, auto repair, or electrical appliance repair—occupations for jobs with scattered employers—are less successful in finding jobs in which they can use their new skills. Note that in all occupations the skill is more likely to be used if the training course is completed. When the course feeds men or women into a specific plant, only workers who stay to the end get training-related jobs.

The field data thus far presented give intuitive support to the thesis that retraining made a direct contribution to the employment of the trainees. Since we cannot know how many of those employed in either 1962 or 1963 would have had some jobs even if they had not been retrained, no precise measure of the contribution of retraining is possible. If outside variables were not present to mar the comparison, the differences between the employment rates of the retrained and the nonapplicants would stand as a measure of the value of retraining. It has already been shown, though, that the retrained men and women, as a class, were characterized by a favorable age distribution and relatively high educational attainment, and that a large number of them were white. Only with respect to previous skill level, among the variables measured, did they not bring a competitive advantage over other unemployed to the labor market. Further, enrollment in a training course may reflect a quality of initiative that would be useful in the search for jobs. Thus, some factors other than retraining itself may have contributed to the higher employment rate among the retrained. As a step toward isolating the effects of retraining per se, the relation of training status to subsequent labor force status, with age, sex, education, county, and pretraining labor force status successively controlled, is next examined.

## AGE

Young adults, in their twenties and early thirties, are generally thought to get jobs more readily than do either their still younger or their older competitors. Does the age variable operate in the same way among trainees as in the general population? Can the better employment record of the trainees be explained by their advantageous age distribution? These findings may be drawn from Table II.18.

1. In the summer of 1962, both the trainees who had completed training and those who had dropped out had a higher rate of employment than the nonapplicants in each of the five age categories shown in the table. Since the 1962 figures include men and women still in training, nearly all of whom were otherwise unemployed, the rate of employment among those who had ended their training was higher than the table shows, and the contrast with the nonapplicants is wider.

2. Again in 1963, those who had completed training had a higher employment rate than the nonapplicants in the same age category. At the later date, though, the spread was narrower at every age except 55 and over, where the observations are so few as to be meaningless. The dropouts, too, had a higher rate than the nonapplicants except at the age extremes, where the figures are too small to permit a sound comparison.

3. Above age 55, there is no consistent relationship between age and employment rate either in 1962 or 1963 in any of the three training statuses.

Since the trainees had a consistently higher employment rate than the nonapplicants of the same age levels, the more "favorable" age distribution of the trainees does not account for their better success in the labor market. Further, between ages 22 and 54, there is no evidence in the study data that the younger adults do have an advantage in the labor market. No explanation of this latter finding can be offered here.

## Sex

Of the 1,379 persons in the combined samples, 1,000 were men and 379 women. Women fit into the labor force differently from men: they move in and out of a labor force still preponderantly male, while men are expected to stay in until retirement; they are concentrated in a different set of occupations. The sex variable should be expected to affect the outcome of retraining.

Women constitute 33.5 per cent of the sample of those who completed their course and 13.3 per cent of the dropouts. When these two classes of trainees are combined, the female percentage is 27.1. Among the nonapplicants, 23.2 per cent are women. Since women have a lower employment rate than men, any overrepresentation of the former among the nonapplicants would depress its overall employment rate. But the proportion of women is higher among the trainees than among the nonapplicants. The sex variable does not help explain the higher employment rate among the trainees. Note also the following:

1. The male applicants had a much higher employment rate in 1962 than did the male nonapplicants. Both the male trainees and the male

TABLE II.18

LABOR FORCE STATUS BY TRAINING STATUS AND AGE, SUMMER, 1962 AND SUMMER, 1963

| Training status[a] and labor force status | 0–21 yrs. | | 22–34 yrs. | | 35–44 yrs. | |
|---|---|---|---|---|---|---|
| | 1962 | 1963 | 1962 | 1963 | 1962 | 1963 |
| *Completed training* | *61* | *61* | *226* | *226* | *130* | *130* |
| Employed | 52.5% | 69.6% | 58.4% | 73.1% | 50.8% | 70.2% |
| Unemployed | 39.3 | 10.7 | 33.2 | 18.3 | 35.4 | 14.5 |
| Not in labor force | 8.2 | 19.6 | 8.4 | 8.7 | 13.8 | 15.3 |
| Not ascertained | —[b] | — | — | — | — | — |
| *Dropped out of training* | *23* | *23* | *111* | *111* | *59* | *59* |
| Employed | 60.0% | 63.2% | 50.5% | 72.3% | 55.9% | 75.0% |
| Unemployed | 39.1 | 31.6 | 39.6 | 23.4 | 39.0 | 19.2 |
| Not in labor force | 0.0 | 5.3 | 9.9 | 4.3 | 5.1 | 5.8 |
| Not ascertained | — | — | — | — | — | — |
| *Nonapplicant* | *38* | *38* | *138* | *138* | *125* | *125* |
| Employed | 26.3% | 65.6% | 34.1% | 62.4% | 32.8% | 58.1% |
| Unemployed | 63.2 | 28.1 | 59.4 | 26.5 | 59.2 | 26.7 |
| Not in labor force | 10.5 | 6.3 | 6.5 | 11.1 | 8.0 | 15.2 |
| Not ascertained | — | — | — | — | — | — |
| *Total* | *122* | *122* | *475* | *475* | *314* | *314* |

[a] Training statuses "Did not report" and "Not accepted" omitted because frequencies were too small for analysis. Figures in italics indicate the number in the sample.

[b] "Not ascertained" frequencies omitted in the calculation of percentages.

nonapplicants made employment gains by mid-1963. While the latter made the greater relative advance in the one-year period, the trainees still had a significantly higher employment rate in 1963 than those who had not sought training.

2. Among the women, too, the employment rate was higher among trainees than among nonapplicants both in mid-1962 and in mid-1963. The contrast between the women dropouts and the nonapplicants was small at both times, and not statistically significant. Only a few women dropouts were included in the study, however, and they may not constitute a true sample.

3. The number of women in all three training statuses who were not in the labor force was high in both 1962 and 1963. Roughly a fourth of all retrained women were neither working nor looking for work at both dates.

So long as women move in and out of the labor force, the dividing line between being unemployed and being out of the labor force is often blurred. There are women who will work part-time during school hours,

TABLE II.18  (*continued*)

| 45–54 yrs. | | 55+ yrs. | | Not ascertained | | Total | |
|---|---|---|---|---|---|---|---|
| 1962 | 1963 | 1962 | 1963 | 1962 | 1963 | 1962 | 1963 |
| *65* | *65* | *14* | *14* | *5* | *5* | *501* | *501* |
| 52.3% | 72.9% | 35.7% | 53.8% | 20.0% | 80.0% | 53.9% | 71.4% |
| 32.3 | 22.0 | 57.1 | 30.8 | 80.0 | 0.0 | 35.5 | 17.0 |
| 15.4 | 5.1 | 7.1 | 15.4 | 0.0 | 20.0 | 10.6 | 11.6 |
| — | — | — | — | — | — | — | — |
| *33* | *33* | *5* | *5* | *2* | *2* | *233* | *233* |
| 45.5% | 69.2% | 40.0% | 25.0% | 0.0% | 100.0% | 51.7% | 70.9% |
| 48.5 | 23.1 | 60.0 | 75.0 | 100.0 | 0.0 | 41.4 | 24.0 |
| 6.0 | 7.7 | 0.0 | 0.0 | 0.0 | 0.0 | 6.9 | 5.1 |
| — | — | — | — | — | — | — | — |
| *96* | *96* | *54* | *54* | *2* | *2* | *453* | *453* |
| 34.4% | 64.0% | 25.9% | 35.6% | 100.0% | 100.0% | 32.3% | 58.9% |
| 58.3 | 21.3 | 68.5 | 42.2 | 0.0 | 0.0 | 60.4 | 27.2 |
| 7.3 | 14.6 | 5.6 | 22.2 | 0.0 | 0.0 | 7.3 | 13.9 |
| — | — | — | — | — | — | — | — |
| *194* | *194* | *73* | *73* | *9* | *9* | *1,187* | *1,187* |

but not full-time. The women in the samples of trainees were instructed in just three occupations: office work, waitress, and nurse's aide. The latter two, at least, are commonly characterized by high rates of turnover.

Since women constitute a large proportion of all withdrawals from the labor force, it must be asked whether these withdrawals signify a waste of retraining, or even misjudgment on the part of the Employment Security officers who selected the trainees. Is the whole story told when it is noted that the newly learned skills are not marketed immediately? Several considerations are relevant. First, there are many reasons why women move in or out of the labor force: marriage, pregnancy, the increase or lessening of home responsibilities, a change in the husband's employment, and others. It is to be expected that retrained women would follow a work pattern much like that of other women. Second, it is unreasonable to expect all young women to estimate their future availability for work correctly, for marriage, pregnancy, child care, and other home responsibilities cannot always be foreseen. Third, while many women leave the labor force, many in turn re-enter it. It may be assumed that at least some of the women who left the labor force after retraining would return to it and put their newly learned skills to use. In short, a shifting labor-force status for women reflects their position in American

## TABLE II.19

### Labor Force Status, Summer, 1962 and Summer, 1963, by Training Status and Sex

| Training status[a] and labor force status | Male 1962 No. | % | Male 1963 No. | % | Female 1962 No. | % | Female 1963 No. | % | Total 1962 No. | % | Total 1963 No. | % |
|---|---|---|---|---|---|---|---|---|---|---|---|---|
| *Completed training* | 333 | | 333 | | 168 | | 168 | | 501 | | 501 | |
| Employed | 197 | 59.2 | 237 | 76.9 | 73 | 43.5 | 95 | 60.5 | 270 | 53.9 | 332 | 71.4 |
| Unemployed | 119 | 35.7 | 59 | 19.2 | 59 | 35.1 | 20 | 12.7 | 178 | 35.5 | 79 | 17.0 |
| Not in labor force | 17 | 5.1 | 12 | 3.9 | 36 | 21.4 | 42 | 26.8 | 53 | 10.6 | 54 | 11.6 |
| Not ascertained | 0 | —[b] | 25 | — | 0 | — | 11 | — | 0 | — | 36 | — |
| *Dropped out of training* | 202 | | 202 | | 31 | | 31 | | 233 | | 233 | |
| Employed | 108 | 53.7 | 127 | 74.7 | 12 | 38.7 | 12 | 46.2 | 120 | 51.7 | 139 | 70.9 |
| Unemployed | 85 | 42.3 | 39 | 22.9 | 11 | 35.5 | 8 | 30.8 | 96 | 41.4 | 47 | 24.0 |
| Not in labor force | 8 | 4.0 | 4 | 2.4 | 8 | 25.8 | 6 | 23.1 | 16 | 6.9 | 10 | 5.1 |
| Not ascertained | 1 | — | 32 | — | 0 | — | 5 | — | 1 | — | 37 | — |
| *Nonapplicant* | 348 | | 348 | | 105 | | 105 | | 453 | | 453 | |
| Employed | 110 | 31.7 | 186 | 63.1 | 36 | 34.3 | 43 | 45.7 | 146 | 32.3 | 229 | 58.9 |
| Unemployed | 220 | 63.4 | 81 | 27.5 | 53 | 50.5 | 25 | 26.6 | 273 | 60.4 | 106 | 27.2 |
| Not in labor force | 17 | 4.9 | 28 | 9.5 | 16 | 15.2 | 26 | 27.7 | 33 | 7.3 | 54 | 13.9 |
| Not ascertained | 1 | — | 53 | — | 0 | — | 11 | — | 1 | — | 64 | — |
| Total | 883 | | 883 | | 304 | | 304 | | 1,187 | | 1,187 | |

[a] Training statuses "Did not report" and "Not accepted" omitted.
[b] "Not ascertained" frequencies omitted in the calculation of percentages.

society, and will not be overcome by retraining programs. In the case of women who withdrew from the labor force, retraining may be put to delayed use.

It may be argued that priority in retraining should be given to women who are most likely to stay in the labor force. This issue turns on value judgments. Retraining is intended to help both workers and employers. From the point of view of employers, labor turnover is costly and is best held to a minimum. Since retraining programs have been concentrated more in geographic areas of high unemployment than in regions with pronounced skill shortages, it may be inferred that the primary objective of the programs has been to aid the unemployed. From a social standpoint, may it be best to train those women whose income is most needed by their families? Many of these women are the very ones whose family obligations most interfere with their ability to work.

The large number of women withdrawing from the labor force raises another issue: Is it better to concentrate on the retraining of men? Certainly, more of them can be expected to stay at work. If the resources for training are to be allocated so as to yield the highest possible employment gain, it may be desirable to give priority to courses for men. But there are other considerations. Have any retraining courses for men been turned down because the needed funds have been committed to the retraining of women? And further, since retraining is tied to known jobs, may not the need for women workers in certain localities justify their training, even though some of them will not take jobs?

### EDUCATION

It is an axiom of the times that the uneducated face economic difficulty. Since the men and women selected for training had completed more years of school than the nonapplicants, their higher education may have contributed to their greater employment success. There are two questions raised here. First, does education affect, or at least relate, to employment rates within training status groups? Second, is training status related to employment rates among individuals with the same amount of formal schooling? The following findings apply to the study samples:

1. A majority of those who completed their retraining course had finished at least twelve years of school. Among the dropouts, the largest group stopped school after nine to eleven years. The largest group among the nonapplicants was that with no more than eight years of schooling.

2. When men and women of the same educational levels are compared, no consistent difference exists between the employment rates in either 1962 or 1963 of those who had completed their course and those who dropped out.

3. Within each of the three educational categories shown on Table

TABLE II.20

LABOR FORCE STATUS, SUMMER, 1962 AND SUMMER, 1963, BY TRAINING STATUS AND
YEARS OF SCHOOL COMPLETED

| Training status[a] and labor force status | 0–8 yrs. | | 9–11 yrs. | | 12+ yrs. | | Not available | | Total | |
|---|---|---|---|---|---|---|---|---|---|---|
| | 1962 | 1963 | 1962 | 1963 | 1962 | 1963 | 1962 | 1963 | 1962 | 1963 |
| *Completed training* | *64* | *64* | *136* | *136* | *297* | *297* | *4* | *4* | *501* | *501* |
| Employed | 40.6% | 65.0% | 47.8% | 70.2% | 59.3% | 73.2% | 75.0% | 75.0% | 53.9% | 71.4% |
| Unemployed | 45.3 | 23.3 | 40.4 | 16.5 | 31.3 | 15.7 | 25.0 | 25.0 | 35.5 | 17.0 |
| Not in labor force | 14.1 | 11.7 | 11.8 | 13.2 | 9.4 | 11.1 | 0.0 | 0.0 | 10.6 | 11.6 |
| Not ascertained | —[b] | — | — | — | — | — | — | — | — | — |
| *Dropped out of training* | *49* | *49* | *99* | *99* | *78* | *78* | *7* | *7* | *233* | *233* |
| Employed | 44.9% | 74.4% | 53.5% | 71.1% | 51.3% | 68.8% | 83.3% | 66.4% | 51.7% | 70.9% |
| Unemployed | 46.9 | 18.6 | 40.4 | 25.3 | 41.0 | 25.0 | 16.7 | 33.3 | 41.4 | 24.0 |
| Not in labor force | 8.2 | 7.0 | 6.1 | 3.6 | 7.7 | 6.2 | 0.0 | 0.0 | 6.9 | 5.1 |
| Not ascertained | — | — | — | — | — | — | — | — | — | — |
| *Nonapplicant* | *209* | *209* | *124* | *124* | *117* | *117* | *3* | *3* | *453* | *453* |
| Employed | 29.2% | 53.2% | 29.0% | 61.7% | 41.9% | 65.7% | 0.0% | 0.0% | 32.3% | 58.9% |
| Unemployed | 64.1 | 30.1 | 62.1 | 25.2 | 51.3 | 24.1 | 100.0 | 100.0 | 60.4 | 27.2 |
| Not in labor force | 6.7 | 16.8 | 8.9 | 13.1 | 6.8 | 10.2 | 0.0 | 0.0 | 7.3 | 13.9 |
| Not ascertained | — | — | — | — | — | — | — | — | — | — |
| *Total* | *322* | *322* | *359* | *359* | *492* | *492* | *14* | *14* | *1,187* | *1,187* |

[a] Training statuses "Did not report" and "Not accepted" omitted because frequencies were too small for analysis. Figures in italics indicate the number in the sample.

[b] "Not ascertained" frequencies omitted in the calculation of percentages.

II.20, trainees had a higher employment rate than the nontrainees both in mid-1962 and in mid-1963.

4. Only among those who completed their training course is there a consistent relationship between years of schooling and rate of employment. Among the nonapplicants, the two are positively related, though no difference existed in the summer of 1962 between those who had less than nine years of school and those who had nine to eleven years. The dropouts show no meaningful relationship between schooling and percentage employed.

5. Only among the high-school graduates did the spread between the employment rate of the trainees and that of the nonapplicants narrow significantly between the two successive time-readings. The higher employment rate among trainees within each educational category supports the theses that differences in educational background do not themselves explain the better employment record of the trainees, and that retraining helps its recipients to get jobs. These conclusions are reinforced by a second measure of employment in the percentage of time employed in the year following retraining (or its equivalent). As Table II.21 shows, the fraction of trainees who worked more than three-quarters of the time during the year was higher within each educational category than for nonapplicants, and the fraction not working at all was consistently lower for the trainees. The high-school graduates who had completed training had the highest proportion working over 75 per cent of the time and the lowest proportion not working at all. Among high-school graduates, the median fraction of time employed during the year was about three-quarters for those who completed their training, about half for those who had not applied for retraining, and in between for the dropouts.

COUNTY

Retraining has been undertaken in about three-quarters of West Virginia's counties. The present study is based on observations in five of them. The counties differ from one another with respect to the retraining offered in each and the employment opportunities that each affords.

The samples from Kanawha county in no way represent its trainees or its trainee courses. They were drawn in the main to yield information on training for a single manufacturing plant. Further, it must be borne in mind that all the samples are based on early retraining, with the disadvantages of retraining trial and error. These sample characteristics should enter into the interpretation of Table II.22. It points, however, to the following conclusions:

1. Those who completed their course and those who started but did not finish, when grouped together as "trainees," had higher rates of em-

TABLE II.21

Percentage of Time Employed During First Twelve Months after Retraining (or Equivalent), by Training Status and Years of School Completed

| Training status[a] and percentage of time employed | 0–8 yrs. | | 9–11 yrs. | | 12+ yrs. | | Not ascertained | | Total | |
|---|---|---|---|---|---|---|---|---|---|---|
| | No. | % | No. | % | No. | % | No. | % | No. | % |
| *Completed training* | *64* | | *136* | | *297* | | *4* | | *501* | |
| 76–100 | 16 | 36.4 | 33 | 39.3 | 107 | 50.7 | 1 | 25.0 | 157 | 45.8 |
| 51–75 | 3 | 6.8 | 10 | 11.9 | 29 | 13.7 | 2 | 50.0 | 44 | 12.8 |
| 26–50 | 6 | 13.6 | 10 | 11.9 | 21 | 10.0 | 0 | 0.0 | 37 | 10.8 |
| 1–25 | 1 | 2.3 | 13 | 15.5 | 12 | 5.7 | 1 | 25.0 | 27 | 7.9 |
| Less than 1 | 18 | 40.9 | 18 | 21.4 | 42 | 19.9 | 0 | 0.0 | 78 | 22.7 |
| Not ascertained | 20 | —[b] | 52 | — | 86 | — | 0 | — | 158 | — |
| *Dropped out of training* | *49* | | *99* | | *78* | | *7* | | *233* | |
| 76–100 | 14 | 37.8 | 30 | 45.8 | 23 | 45.1 | 4 | 66.7 | 71 | 44.4 |
| 51–75 | 6 | 16.2 | 13 | 19.7 | 6 | 11.8 | 1 | 16.7 | 26 | 16.3 |
| 26–50 | 1 | 2.7 | 5 | 7.6 | 5 | 9.8 | 1 | 16.7 | 12 | 7.5 |
| 1–25 | 4 | 10.8 | 3 | 4.5 | 5 | 9.8 | 0 | 0.0 | 12 | 7.5 |
| Less than 1 | 12 | 32.4 | 15 | 22.7 | 17 | 23.5 | 0 | 0.0 | 39 | 24.4 |
| Not ascertained | 12 | — | 33 | — | 27 | — | 1 | — | 73 | — |
| *Nonapplicant* | *209* | | *124* | | *117* | | *3* | | *453* | |
| 76–100 | 41 | 23.3 | 27 | 26.7 | 31 | 30.1 | 0 | 0.0 | 99 | 26.0 |
| 51–75 | 18 | 10.2 | 12 | 11.9 | 20 | 19.4 | 0 | 0.0 | 50 | 13.1 |
| 26–50 | 11 | 6.3 | 13 | 12.9 | 13 | 12.6 | 0 | 0.0 | 37 | 9.7 |
| 1–25 | 13 | 7.4 | 10 | 9.9 | 9 | 8.7 | 0 | 0.0 | 32 | 8.4 |
| Less than 1 | 93 | 52.8 | 39 | 38.6 | 30 | 29.1 | 1 | 100.0 | 163 | 42.8 |
| Not ascertained | 33 | — | 23 | — | 14 | — | 2 | — | 72 | — |
| Total | 322 | | 359 | | 492 | | 14 | | 1,187 | |

[a] Training statuses "Did not report" and "Not accepted" omitted because frequencies are too small for analysis.
[b] "Not ascertained" frequencies omitted in the calculation of percentages.

TABLE II.22

LABOR FORCE STATUS, SUMMER, 1962, AND SUMMER, 1963, BY TRAINING STATUS AND COUNTY

| Training status and labor force status | Kanawha | | Cabell-Wayne | | McDowell | | Monongalia | | Harrison | | Total | |
|---|---|---|---|---|---|---|---|---|---|---|---|---|
| | 1962 | 1963 | 1962 | 1963 | 1962 | 1963 | 1962 | 1963 | 1962 | 1963 | 1962 | 1963 |
| *Completed training* | *52* | *52* | *110* | *110* | *94* | *94* | *60* | *60* | *185* | *185* | *501* | *501* |
| Employed | 46.2% | 93.6% | 47.3% | 52.4% | 53.2% | 74.1% | 56.7% | 70.7% | 59.5% | 75.9% | 53.9% | 71.4% |
| Unemployed | 51.9 | 6.4 | 39.1 | 28.6 | 39.4 | 15.3 | 31.7 | 17.2 | 28.1 | 13.5 | 35.5 | 17.0 |
| Not in labor force | 1.9 | 0.0 | 13.6 | 19.0 | 7.4 | 10.6 | 11.7 | 12.1 | 12.4 | 10.6 | 10.6 | 11.6 |
| Not ascertained | —a | — | — | — | — | — | — | — | — | — | — | — |
| *Dropped out of training* | *16* | *16* | *42* | *42* | *130* | *130* | *16* | *16* | *29* | *29* | *233* | *233* |
| Employed | 18.3% | 85.7% | 73.8% | 75.0% | 50.0% | 70.0% | 62.5% | 50.0% | 39.3% | 66.7% | 51.7% | 70.9% |
| Unemployed | 81.3 | 14.3 | 23.8 | 19.4 | 43.8 | 24.1 | 12.5 | 41.7 | 50.0 | 27.8 | 41.4 | 24.0 |
| Not in labor force | 0.0 | 0.0 | 2.4 | 5.6 | 6.2 | 5.2 | 25.0 | 8.3 | 10.7 | 5.5 | 6.9 | 13.9 |
| Not ascertained | — | — | — | — | — | — | — | — | — | — | — | — |
| *Nonapplicant* | *64* | *64* | *59* | *59* | *185* | *185* | *78* | *78* | *67* | *67* | *453* | *453* |
| Employed | 21.9% | 55.5% | 18.6% | 53.7% | 34.1% | 61.0% | 37.2% | 55.2% | 43.9% | 66.0% | 32.3% | 58.9% |
| Unemployed | 68.8 | 33.3 | 76.3 | 33.3 | 58.4 | 26.8 | 59.0 | 22.4 | 45.5 | 22.0 | 60.4 | 27.2 |
| Not in labor force | 9.4 | 11.1 | 5.1 | 13.0 | 7.6 | 12.2 | 3.8 | 22.4 | 10.6 | 12.0 | 7.3 | 13.9 |
| Not ascertained | — | — | — | — | — | — | — | — | — | — | — | — |
| *Total* | *132* | *132* | *211* | *211* | *409* | *409* | *154* | *154* | *281* | *281* | *1,187* | *1,187* |

a "Not ascertained" frequencies omitted in the calculation of percentages.

ployment than the nonapplicants in each of the five areas in both 1962 and 1963.

2. The small Kanawha sample indicates that training for a specific employer results in a high rate of employment. The 1962 report on Kanawha county assigns "complete" status to a number of men who had not yet finished their course and were thus classed as unemployed.

3. The early retraining experience in the Cabell-Wayne area appears not to have yielded much sustained advantage to its recipients. The 1963 employment rate among those finishing retraining in that area was about the same as that of the sample of nonapplicants, and much below that of the dropouts.

4. The samples from McDowell county, in the heart of the coal fields, had employment rates close to the mean of the other counties both in mid-1962 and in mid-1963.

The contrast between the Cabell-Wayne (Huntington) and the Mc-Dowell employment outcomes for those completing training could not have been predicted from the unemployment rates in the two labor market areas. The McDowell unemployment rate (15 per cent in 1963) was about twice as high as that of the other counties together, while the Cabell-Wayne rate was about 7.7 per cent at the same time. How is the contrast to be explained? We can offer only hypotheses.

McDowell county, deep in the southern coal fields and heavily dependent on mining employment, had endured high rates of unemployment for several years. It also had the longest sustained program of retraining in the state, all of it under AVP auspices. The retraining was concentrated in fields for which the vocational high school in Welch had adequate facilities. McDowell county had high rates of outmigration after World War II; no other county in West Virginia lost so heavily in the 1950's, and tentative reports indicate that the exodus has continued since 1960. Much of the retraining in Welch was geared to out-of-state employment. It may be that the prevalence of outmigration from throughout the county and the retraining of men for out-of-state jobs have combined to heighten the readiness of trainees to move on and seek jobs elsewhere. This hypothesis is supported by the fact that there has been a considerable movement of retrained men from the area, particularly into the Norfolk-Newport News area. What would the rate of employment have been had more of the retrained men stayed in McDowell county? Almost certainly lower.

To the extent that outmigration to areas of higher employment opportunity was stimulated by retraining, one of the basic goals of retraining was achieved. Further detail on this point is presented in the following section.

The Cabell-Wayne area had high unemployment rates, about half those of McDowell county. Huntington had the pilot ARA retraining program in the United States. It had been suggested in a number of quarters that the first courses were hurriedly set up before an adequate canvass of job possibilities could be undertaken, so as to get the national program launched. Were the first courses chosen for ARA retraining such as to give the program a favorable reception in the community? The pilot courses included one for route salesmen and one for waitresses, and some weeks passed before a suitable number of qualified applicants enrolled. In the circumstances, were the trainees a favorable selection of people with respect to employability? In other words, may part of the responsibility lie with the problems of launching a new program?

It should be said on behalf of Cabell-Wayne retraining that some retraining courses given after the time of our first field studies had excellent placement results. A series of AVP power sewing machine courses in 1963 resulted in 100 per cent placement of those who completed the course, as did three arc welding classes. If the contention is valid, that the early programs were not as effectively carried out as might be wished, it may be that retraining later moved ahead on firmer footing.

### LABOR FORCE STATUS BEFORE RETRAINING

Labor force status one month before retraining, or at an equivalent time for nontrainees, is a highly significant variable. All members of all the study samples were either unemployed or grossly underemployed when the courses were being set up. Among those periodically out of work, some manage to avoid long periods of idleness while others do not. Shortly before the start of retraining, and at the same calendar time in the case of nonapplicants, some were employed, some were not in the labor force, and others had been unemployed for more than two years. These variables relate to mid-1962 and mid-1963 labor force status in the following ways:

1. In every one of the seven prior-labor-force-status categories included in Table II.23, the nonapplicants had a lower rate of employment than either class of trainees both in 1962 and in 1963. The contrast between the employment rates of trainees and applicants, either in 1962 or 1963, did not vary significantly among the different prior-labor-force-status categories. The differences were somewhat wider in 1962 than they were in 1963.

2. The 1963 employment rate was much the highest, among both trainees and nonapplicants, for those who had been employed one month before the time of retraining.

3. There is a negative relationship between the duration of pretraining unemployment and the post-training employment rate in both 1962 and 1963. The men and women who were unemployed only briefly before

## TABLE II.23

LABOR FORCE STATUS, SUMMER, 1962, AND SUMMER, 1963, BY TRAINING STATUS AND LABOR FORCE STATUS ONE MONTH BEFORE RETRAINING (OR EQUIVALENT)

| Training status[a] and labor force status | Employed | | Not in the labor force | | Unemployed | | | | | | | | | |
| --- | --- | --- | --- | --- | --- | --- | --- | --- | --- | --- | --- | --- | --- | --- |
| | | | | | 1–3 mo. | | 4–6 mo. | | 7–12 mo. | | 13–24 mo. | | 25 + mo. | |
| | 1962 | 1963 | 1962 | 1963 | 1962 | 1963 | 1962 | 1963 | 1962 | 1963 | 1962 | 1963 | 1962 | 1963 |
| *Completed training* | *110* | *96* | *93* | *89* | *72* | *66* | *59* | *57* | *70* | *64* | *53* | *50* | *89* | *38* |
| Employed | 72.7% | 81.2% | 43.0% | 65.1% | 55.6% | 83.3% | 50.8% | 66.7% | 58.6% | 65.6% | 47.2% | 74.0% | 28.2% | 55.3% |
| Unemployed | 23.6 | 9.4 | 21.5 | 10.1 | 44.4 | 10.6 | 40.7 | 22.8 | 27.1 | 29.7 | 45.3 | 22.0 | 64.1 | 26.3 |
| Not in labor force | 3.6 | 9.4 | 35.5 | 24.7 | 0.0 | 6.1 | 8.5 | 10.5 | 4.3 | 4.7 | 7.5 | 4.0 | 7.7 | 18.4 |
| *Dropped out of training* | *70* | *61* | *34* | *28* | *32* | *29* | *22* | *15* | *23* | *20* | *29* | *25* | *19* | *15* |
| Employed | 71.4% | 83.6% | 52.9% | 53.6% | 43.8% | 82.8% | 59.1% | 93.7% | 39.1% | 60.0% | 38.0% | 52.0% | 26.3% | 50.0% |
| Unemployed | 25.7 | 16.0 | 26.5 | 32.1 | 53.1 | 13.8 | 36.3 | 6.7 | 52.2 | 35.0 | 55.1 | 40.0 | 68.4 | 33.3 |
| Not in labor force | 2.9 | 0.0 | 20.6 | 14.3 | 3.1 | 3.4 | 4.5 | 0.0 | 8.7 | 5.0 | 6.9 | 8.0 | 5.3 | 6.7 |
| *Nonapplicant* | *212* | *183* | *52* | *45* | *52* | *42* | *18* | *15* | *25* | *23* | *59* | *53* | *33* | *27* |
| Employed | 45.8% | 72.1% | 25.0% | 48.9% | 17.3% | 57.1% | 27.8% | 60.0% | 16.0% | 39.1% | 18.6% | 37.7% | 21.2% | 48.1% |
| Unemployed | 50.0 | 20.2 | 44.2 | 15.6 | 78.9 | 35.7 | 61.1 | 33.3 | 84.0 | 43.5 | 79.9 | 43.4 | 72.7 | 33.3 |
| Not in labor force | 4.2 | 7.7 | 30.8 | 35.6 | 3.8 | 7.1 | 11.1 | 6.7 | 0.0 | 17.4 | 1.7 | 18.9 | 6.1 | 18.5 |

Labor force status one month before retraining (or equivalent)

[a] Training statuses "Did not report" and "Not accepted" omitted. "Not ascertained" responses not included in the percentages or in the number in the sample (ital. figures).

retraining were much more likely to be employed in 1962 and 1963 than those who had been unemployed for a long period.

4. The highest fraction of persons not in the labor force in both 1962 and 1963, in all training statuses, was among those who were also out of the labor force at the pretraining date. Of the people not in the labor force one month before the time of retraining, the proportion again out of the labor force dropped between 1962 and 1963 in the case of the trainees, but not in the case of the nonapplicants.

In a regression analysis of the variables which influence the employment success of trainees and control groups, it is found that the worker's employment experience prior to the training period and his training status are together the best single predictors of employment experience after the time of retraining.[17] Since previous employment and unemployment experience are affected by the worker's background and personal characteristics, it is not surprising that this variable emerges as a crucial one in determining current employment status. Let it be underlined, though, that among workers with the same pretraining labor force status, those who have been retrained fared substantially better in the post-training job market than those who did not enroll.

If the success of retraining is to be measured by the proportion of retrained people who get jobs afterwards, retraining of the short-term unemployed and the exclusion of persons recently out of the labor force from the programs would seem to be the most rewarding. But the same classes of people who have the best employment rate after retraining— the short-term unemployed—also have the best subsequent employment rate among the nonapplicants. Furthermore, retraining appears to make a positive difference among workers in every pretraining labor force status. If retraining is to be judged by employment gain, i.e., the contrast between the employment experience of the retrained and the nonretrained of similar backgrounds, an equally strong case can be made for retraining the less advantaged among the unemployed.

## THE RELATION OF RETRAINING TO EMPLOYMENT: A SUMMARY

Retraining appears to make a direct contribution to the employment of men and women. Those who have been in retraining classes have subsequently had higher employment rates than those who have not, and the differences in rates are of greater magnitude than can be explained by the advantages in age, education, and the like held by the trainees.

The individuals comprising the training-status samples that have been compared were all either unemployed or underemployed, at the time when training classes were being organized, as a condition for admission to retraining or as a condition for inclusion in the control sample of nonapplicants. Thus, any employment recorded for the members of any of the samples in either 1962 or 1963 represents a gain over the pretraining period.

The eighty-nine men and women who were still in training in the summer of 1962—mostly otherwise unemployed at the time—were placed in their eventual training-status categories in the tables on post-training employment. Thus fifty-nine individuals who were in training at the time were classed as "Completed training" in the 1962 columns of the tables, while thirty were classified as "Dropped out of training." The rates of unemployment shown in the 1962 columns are thus higher than those obtained for the trainees who had ended their training by that time, and the rates of employment are lower. The tables consistently understate the mid-1962 employment gains made by those who had actually either completed training or dropped out before that time and, in turn, understate the contrast between the employment rates of the trainees and those not receiving retraining. A correction has been possible but not when a third dimension such as age or education is introduced.

In the study findings on the relation of retraining to employment the following points stand out:

1. In the summer of 1962, more than half of the sample of trainees were employed. If the trainees who were still in training at that time are excluded, then 60 per cent of those who had completed training and 56 per cent of those who had dropped out of training had jobs. In contrast, only a third of the members of the control group of nonapplicants for training, and just slightly more of the applicants who did not enter training, were working.

2. One year later, in the spring of 1963, the employment rates were higher for workers in every training status. For both those who had completed their training course and those who had dropped out, the rate was about 71 per cent. Relatively greater gains were recorded for all three classes of nontrainees, and especially for the nonapplicants. The economic improvement in West Virginia and the shifting incidence of unemployment were probably contributing factors. While some gap remained between the employment rate of the trainees and that of each of the several classes of nontrainees, its narrowing over the year suggests the hypothesis that the contribution of retraining is less that of giving workers a long-term advantage than of speeding their return to work.

3. In 1962, about half of the trainees had had a job of the kind for which they were retrained. Those who completed their retraining course were much more likely to be working in the field of their training than were those who dropped out en route. But those who trained for known jobs with a specific employer were more likely to stay with their courses to the end.

4. A fairly large proportion of the trainees were not in the labor force

in either 1962 or 1963. About 12 per cent of those who had finished their training, and about 8 per cent of those who had dropped out, were not available for work in 1962. The rate of withdrawal from the labor force was about as high among trainees as among nontrainees. Women far outnumbered men in this population. They were most likely to drop from the labor force after training if they were also out of the labor force shortly before the beginning of their training.

5. The trainees are a selected population and may be expected to have had a higher employment rate, even without retraining, by virtue of their other personal traits. The study data do indicate that these traits do affect an individual's chance of getting a job, but are not a sufficient explanation of the higher employment levels among the retrained. The retrained outrank the nonapplicants with similar traits.

*Age.*—In both 1962 and 1963, the trainees had a higher rate of employment than the nonapplicants falling within the same age intervals. Below age 55, age was not closely related to employment in any of the training-status samples.

*Sex.*—Among the trainees, men had a higher rate of employment than women in both 1962 and 1963. The main male-female contrast, however, lies in the proportion of each not in the labor force. Since women are more heavily represented in the trainee sample than in the nonapplicant sample, differences in sex ratios do not contribute to the higher employment rate among trainees.

*Education.*—The men and women who entered retraining had more schooling, on the average, than those who did not. Among those who completed training, there was a consistent positive relationship between years of school completed and rates of employment. Among the other training statuses, the relationship was less uniform. When individuals of the same educational levels are compared, the trainees had the consistently higher employment rate both in 1962 and 1963. Educational differences, then, are not alone an adequate explanation of the higher employment rate among the retrained, though they are probably significant.

*Labor force status before retraining.*—The long-term unemployed before retraining do not do as well in the labor market after training as those whose previous period of unemployment had been brief. Technical analysis shows that prior labor force status is the most important single variable in determining post-training employment. The highest rates of employment were held by those either in jobs one month before retraining or unemployed not more than three months. But those who were long unemployed before retraining had as high an employment rate in 1962 and again in 1963 as did the nonapplicants who were either employed or briefly unemployed shortly before the retraining courses were opened.

When trainees and nontrainees with the same prior labor force status are compared, the former in every instance had relatively more jobs in 1962 and 1963.

6. The location of retraining had a bearing on employment outcomes. The early experimental programs in the Huntington, West Virginia, area did not result in a better long-term employment gain following retraining than was enjoyed by the nonapplicant sample from the same area. The later retraining in Huntington, according to reports, was more successful.

7. The greatest likelihood of post-training employment falls to the men and women in courses specifically tailored to fit them for job vacancies with a specific employer.

There is strong evidence that retraining itself makes a contribution to the subsequent employment of those who participate in it. A gain in employment is the most important goal of retraining. In some degree, at least, this goal was reached by the early retraining in West Virginia. There may be other goals, however. What effect did retraining have on the morale of the men and women in it, and indeed on the morale of the depressed community? Did it stimulate men and women to move to places where job prospects were better? Assuming that some of the trainees would have gotten jobs in any case, how many were helped to better jobs by their new learning experience? Were they earning more, and if so, was the increment adequate to justify the costs of their retraining? These and many other questions are still to be answered.

## RETRAINING AND RELOCATION

Relocation of unemployed workers has been linked with the attraction of new industrial facilities and the retraining of workers as part of the triumvirate of area redevelopment policies.[18] In practice, there have been serious political difficulties in providing for relocation allowances in legislation on area redevelopment. No such allowances were provided in the Area Redevelopment Act, nor in the original Manpower Development and Training Act. However, since that time there have been two significant breakthroughs in the inducement of migration. The Trade Expansion Act of 1962 provides for relocation allowances for workers displaced because of the liberalization of tariffs. And, more recently, the amendments to the Manpower Development and Training Act of December, 1963, taking cognizance of the widespread use of relocation allowances in some European countries, provide for an experimental fund of $4 million or 2 per cent of the total appropriation, whichever is less, to encourage relocation of unemployed workers. The detailed procedures for determining eligibility in the payment of relocation allowances under the Trade Expansion Act and the Manpower Development and Training Act had not yet been established in January, 1964.

In West Virginia, there has been a continuous net outward migration for at least three decades; and in recent years the outward migration has been so great as to exceed the rate of natural population increase, thereby resulting in an absolute decline of population. Such a decline is characteristic of other such areas of chronic labor surplus in the United States. It can be expected, however, that the rate of outmigration would be considerably heavier in McDowell county than in Harrison, Monongalia, Cabell, or Kanawha counties because of the lack of alternative opportunities following the sharp decline of employment in coal mining.

The Area Redevelopment Act has been utilized primarily to train workers for jobs in their home localities, preferably for jobs in new plants attracted under ARA provisions. In practice, however, it frequently has been necessary for ARA trainees to leave the county of their training for job opportunities elsewhere. The West Virginia Area Vocational Training Program was more deliberately designed to train workers for relocation to other areas where jobs were more plentiful.

Since a substantial number who had enrolled in the training program left their home county after their training, an effort was made to follow up these trainees in their new locations. If the trainee or dropout was not at the address to which the interviewer had been assigned by the Employment Service, neighbors and relatives still living in the house, or others in the locality, including the local post office, were questioned concerning the worker's current whereabouts. By these means it was frequently possible to obtain the outmigrant's address. Questionnaires were sent to these trainees and dropouts. In some cases, interviewers tracked them down in the few centers where they had gathered in larger numbers, such as Washington, D.C.; Baltimore, Maryland; Norfolk and Newport News, Virginia; Chicago; and Columbus, Ohio.

It was found that approximately two-thirds of the outmigrants were from McDowell county and no more than 10 per cent from each of the other counties in the West Virginia survey. Approximately one-third of all the trainees and dropouts had relocated by the time of our interviews in the summer of 1962. Only a relatively small percentage of the trainees and dropouts in the other West Virginia counties had relocated to other areas. As a result of the mail and interview questionnaires, 136 responses were obtained from outmigrant trainees (the term will be used to include both trainees and dropouts). Because of the preponderance of dropouts in the McDowell sample, the outmigrant sample has a slightly larger proportion of dropouts than of those who completed the training course.

CHARACTERISTICS AND TRAINING OCCUPATIONS
OF OUTMIGRANT TRAINEES

The outmigrants differed from the nonmobile trainees primarily on the basis of age. Like most geographically mobile workers, the outmigrant trainees were relatively young. Thirty-six per cent were under 25 years of age and only 3.7 per cent were over 50. The sex composition of the outmigrants also differed significantly from that of the nonmigrant trainees. Whereas 30 per cent of the trainees in the nonmigrant group were women, women represented only 20 per cent of the migrant trainees. There were more married persons among the outmigrants than among the nonmobile trainees (71 per cent as against 66 per cent). The racial composition of migrants and nonmigrants was approximately the same, with Negroes representing about 5 per cent of each group of trainees and dropouts.

Trainees and dropouts who had taken a course in welding represented an unusually large proportion of the outmigrants. Whereas one-fifth of the outmigrants had trained as welders prior to their relocation, only 14 per cent of the nonmobile trainees and dropouts were enrolled in this training occupation. Trainees in carpentry (entry occupations) and auto repair were also well represented among the outmigrants as well as among the migrant group. On the other hand, those trained as riveters represented only 2 per cent of the outmigrants even though they constituted one-fifth of all those who completed the training and 7.4 per cent of the dropouts. This contrast occurred because riveting courses were not included in McDowell county where most of the outmigrants originated, and the riveting course in Harrison county was designed primarily to fill the needs of the Lockheed Corporation which had located a new plant in that county. Similarly, women enrolled in courses for nurse's aides, waitresses, and office work were well represented among the nonmobile trainees, but played a very small role in outmigration. Here too, these courses for women were not given a prominent role in McDowell county.

THE DESTINATION OF THE OUTMIGRANTS

The destination of the outmigrant trainees was closely related to their training occupations as well as to the family ties. As in most studies of geographical mobility, it was found that the migrants tended to move to localities in close proximity to their point of departure. In spite of the depressed nature of economic conditions in most of West Virginia, one-third of the outmigrant trainees went to other West Virginia counties (see Table II.24). Over one-fifth of the outmigrants moved to the neighboring state of Virginia, primarily to work as welders in the shipyards of Newport News and Norfolk. The 11 per cent who went to Ohio, primarily Columbus, and the 7 per cent who went to Illinois, primarily Chicago, were trained in a diversity of occupations, but auto repairmen and carpenters were especially numerous. A significant number of the

TABLE II.24

AREAS TO WHICH TRAINEES MOVED

| Area | No. | Per cent |
|------|-----|----------|
| Elsewhere in West Virginia | 44 | 32.4 |
| Virginia | 31 | 22.8 |
| Ohio | 15 | 11.0 |
| Illinois | 10 | 7.4 |
| Pennsylvania | 7 | 5.1 |
| Maryland | 6 | 4.4 |
| Florida | 5 | 3.7 |
| California | 3 | 2.2 |
| North Carolina | 3 | 2.2 |
| New York | 2 | 1.5 |
| Washington, D.C. | 2 | 1.5 |
| Georgia | 1 | 0.7 |
| Maine | 1 | 0.7 |
| Missouri | 1 | 0.7 |
| Nebraska | 1 | 0.7 |
| New Jersey | 1 | 0.7 |
| Not ascertained | 3 | 2.2 |

outmigrants who went to Pennsylvania, Florida, and California also were welders; but the trainees destined for Baltimore, Maryland, and Washington, D.C., were more likely to have been trained in clerical occupations.

## MOTIVES FOR MIGRATION

The destination points of the outmigrants are also closely linked to the motives for their migration, which can be classified as follows:

| | |
|---|---|
| To obtain job | 95(67.7%) |
| Spouse was transferred or obtained job elsewhere | 11(8.1%) |
| Military service | 6(4.4%) |
| Had relatives or friends in other areas | 5(3.7%) |
| Health reasons | 1(0.7%) |
| Not ascertained | 18(13.2%) |

Thus, about 70 per cent indicated that their move was specifically-motivated by the desire to find a job. The remainder moved because their husbands were transferred or obtained jobs out of the area; some were transferred because of military service; and they had relatives or friends who attracted them to the new area.

It is not hard to understand why the outmigrants wished to leave their home area in search of employment. In their regular occupations before their retraining, well over half of the mobile workers had been in semiskilled and unskilled jobs. Most of the men in McDowell county had been attached to the coal mining industry.

Even more important than their lack of transferable skills, however, was the lengthy unemployment experience suffered by most of these workers. In the period from 1955 to the start of their training, 44 per cent had experienced at least six months of unemployment, one-fourth had suffered more than one year of unemployment, and 12 per cent had previously suffered more than two years of unemployment.

For many of these trainees, then, outmigration was an act of desperation, an effort to escape unemployment and insecurity. Even though many of the mobile trainees indicated that their migration was geared to the search for work, their desperation can be seen in the fact that only 15 per cent of the total had some assurance that a job was waiting for them in their city of destination. The remainder reported that no job was waiting for them.

Training and relocation were by no means unrelated. A sizable number of outmigrants, 37 per cent, reported that their decision to move had been influenced by the fact of their training. Only a little over half of the respondents indicated that there was definitely no such influence, and the remainder of the responses to this question could not be ascertained. The trainees who were induced to migrate as a result of their training indicated that they felt that the training would now permit them to obtain a job elsewhere. They stated that their employability in other areas had been improved, that the skill obtained through the retraining program was in demand in other areas but not in the home county.

The trainees' migration to a new locality was often motivated or influenced by the presence of relatives in the new area; but at the same time strong family ties were maintained in the county from which they moved. Over one-fifth of the migrants had one or more brothers in the new area and an equal number had one or more sisters in the locality of destination. A substantial number also had other relatives in the areas to which they moved. Even greater proportions, however, still had strong family ties in the areas they had left. For over half of the migrants, their mothers continued to live in the home county, while 42 per cent had fathers and 46 per cent had one or more brothers still living in the home area. Substantial proportions also had sisters, uncles, aunts, cousins, and grandparents who continued to reside in the area from which they had migrated.

These data indicate the importance of family ties as an influence on outward migration. It is generally agreed by students of labor mobility that migration of labor can be much more readily achieved if it occurs in family groups rather than with isolated individuals. At the same time, the continuing ties with the home areas presage the likelihood of return migration on the part of many of the trainees. Experience has indicated that workers who have migrated from their homes in search of work are prone to return to the friends and relatives they left behind when they become discouraged in the distant job market or when new opportunities open up in their home locality. It is probable that a lengthier period of follow-up will reveal a substantial return migration on the part of the trainees.

In an effort to get at this question of return migration, the outmigrants were asked what it would take to get them to return to their home locality. Only one-fifth stated that nothing could induce them to return. On the other hand, 22 per cent stated that they would return for any job in their home county; and an equal number stated that they could be induced to come back if there were a job opening in the occupation for which they had been trained. One-fourth felt that their return to their home locality could be induced if they were able to find a job in either their regular occupation (before their outmigration) or in the occupation in which they had obtained jobs in the area to which they had moved.

### The Costs and Gains of Outmigration

In the absence of relocation allowances, the mobile trainees were forced to undertake the costs of their own relocation. As is seen in Table II.25,

TABLE II.25

Moving Costs Incurred by Outmigrants

| Amount, in dollars | No. | Per cent |
|---|---|---|
| 10–19 | 9 | 6.6 |
| 20–29 | 17 | 12.5 |
| 30–39 | 9 | 6.6 |
| 40–49 | 12 | 8.8 |
| 50–74 | 17 | 12.5 |
| 75–99 | 10 | 7.4 |
| 100–49 | 10 | 7.4 |
| 150 and over | 31 | 22.8 |
| Not ascertained | 21 | 15.4 |

over one-fifth of the outmigrants spent $150 or more in moving costs. For many, however, the cost of relocating in another section of West Virginia, often without family, was not excessive. For 25 per cent, the costs did not exceed $40.

One of the major costs of moving from a depressed economic area is the sale of one's house, usually at a considerable loss. A little over one-fourth of the outmigrants (of those who responded to this question) had owned a home in the county in which they received their training. More than twice this number had been renting or living with their parents. As might be expected, an even smaller number owned homes in the area to which they had migrated. Almost 90 per cent of those who responded to this question were still renting in the new area at the time of the survey.

The major gain which many of the outmigrants hoped to achieve through their relocation was an opportunity for employment. However, many of the outmigrants were denied this goal, and their failure was partly in response to the "irrationality" of their movement. Only 50 per cent of the migrants replied that they were employed at the time of the interview survey in the spring of 1963; one-third were unemployed or not in the labor force, and the remainder did not respond to this question. However, the employment ratio is increased to 16 per cent if the non-responses are eliminated. Only one-third of the total outmigrant group, or 38 per cent of those who responded to this question, indicated that they had had a job in the occupation for which they had been retrained at some time or other since their retraining and migration. Almost all of these felt that they had obtained the job as a result of the training course, but only a little over 60 per cent were still working at that job at the time of the interview.

The Employment Service did not play a major role in obtaining the first job for the outmigrants following their training. Only 10 per cent of the respondents ascribed a major role to the employment office in their home county. Over half of the outmigrants had obtained their first post-training job after completion of the course in an informal manner through friends and relatives; and almost 25 per cent had obtained the first job by means of direct application at the company's personnel office. Nine per cent were referred by the vocational school in which their training had been undertaken. Thus, the Employment Service played a much more important role in the job placement of nonmobile trainees than it did in facilitating the employment of those trainees who showed a willingness to migrate in search of employment. This finding lends support to those who have urged improvement in the clearance procedure of the Employment Service—the procedure by which the unemployed workers in one area are matched with job opportunities in another.

## Conclusions on Relocation

There are strong impediments to geographic movement among workers. Even those who have experienced lengthy periods of unemployment in depressed economic areas are reluctant to move away from friends, family, and familiar surroundings. Their outmigration is often a last desperate act when all else fails.

But training and relocation are related to each other as well as possible substitutes for each other. The outmigrant respondents were almost equally divided between those who felt that it was harder to move geographically than retrain at home for a new occupation, and those who felt that it was harder to stay at home and retrain than to move elsewhere in their regular occupations.

The findings of this survey indicate that retraining can be an important inducement to relocation for workers in economically depressed areas. Some of the workers who had suffered long periods of unemployment were induced to relocate by means of skills acquired through government-sponsored retraining. It can be assumed that they were given a new sense of confidence, and, having invested in themselves, they were determined to make this investment pay off even if it required a change of residence.

It must also be noted, however, that the outward migration was not very "rational" from the standpoint of economic improvement or an enhancement of the labor market position. On the whole, the outmigrants fared no better in the labor market than their neighbors who stayed home. This could be explained in part by the proportion whose movement was not dictated by motives of job seeking. But a more important cause of failure in the job market could be found in the fact of a substantial migration to other economically depressed areas in West Virginia, apparently motivated more by proximity and the presence of relatives than by realistic expectation of improved employment conditions. And most of the trainees moved to new locations without any assurance that a job would be available.

There are lessons here for those implementing the experimental provisions for relocation allowances contained in the 1963 amendments in the Manpower and Training Act. The major role of government-subsidized relocation may not be to induce more geographic mobility; there already appears to be a substantial outmigration from many areas of West Virginia. Relocation allowances can perform a principal service in inducing a more rational relocation. If the government were to insist that those who were aided in location must move to areas where job opportunities are more plentiful and where the chances of employment are better, it is likely the placement ratio of outmigrant trainees would be substantially improved.

## EMPLOYERS' VIEWS OF TRAINING AND TRAINEES

The major economic test of the value of the retraining program is to be found in the job experience of the trainees following completion of their courses. We not only wish to know whether they remained in the labor force and whether they were able to obtain employment, but also how they performed on the job. In obtaining the answer to this latter question, it was necessary to solicit the views of employers who hired trainees.

Among the critical questions asked of employers were: How many trainees were hired? How many trainees separated from the company shortly after their initial employment? Why did the employer choose to hire the trainees? What type of training would the employer prefer, that is, is there a preference for institutional training in the vocational schools or on-the-job training in the employers' own establishment? Does government-subsidized training increase employment? Finally, what is the employers' general appraisal of the trainees who have been turned out under government-sponsored training and what are their views of the overall value of such training?

In order to obtain answers to these questions, a sample of employers drawn from the counties under study was interviewed on the basis of a structured questionnaire. Eighty-five employers were interviewed in West Virginia. Of these, 70 per cent had hired trainees. They were chosen on the basis of information provided by the local employment offices and the vocational schools. A number of employers who did not hire trainees were also included in order to obtain general appraisals of the government-sponsored training programs.

As part of the overall evaluation of the retraining, 47 employers located in other states were also interviewed, utilizing the same structured questionnaire. Because of the relatively small sample of employers questioned in West Virginia, the employers in other states are included in some of the analyses contained in this section. There appear to be no major distinctions between the West Virginia experience and the experience and views of the employers interviewed in other areas. The inclusion of employers in states other than West Virginia is especially useful in increasing the sample size in those analyses which cross-classify the findings by size of firm.

### THE REFERRAL AND HIRING OF TRAINEES

Over 450 trainees were hired by the employers included in the interview sample. A little over 60 per cent of these trainees were referred to the firms by the local employment office. This is notable in that the regular procedures established for both the ARA and state training programs provide that trainees are to be placed by the local office following their training in the vocational schools. Although no formal records were maintained of placement outside of the Employment Service, it is apparent that a fairly large number of trainees were actually placed by the instructors in the vocational schools. In some cases the instructors were merely responding to inquiries of employers who had heard of the training program and considered it to be a fruitful source of potential employees. In other cases, the instructors took special pains to canvass employers whom they considered to be good prospects.

Most of the employers in the interview sample hired only one trainee —especially those small firms whose total employment did not exceed fifty. However, there were a number of firms in the interview sample which hired more than ten trainees and three firms which hired over sixty ARA or AVP trainees.

It should be noted that some of the employers to whom we had been directed by the local employment office were unaware that they had hired trainees. In some cases the trainees had apparently been referred to companies without stipulation of their connection with the ARA and AVP programs. In other cases the trainee had applied for work at the firm without employment office referral and had not indicated his training status to the employer. In still other instances, the training connection of the applicant may have been established at the time he was hired; but no record of his training was maintained, and this information was not available at the time of the interview survey.

For those employers whose hiring of trainees was a deliberate and informed choice, the skill acquired by the worker in the training course was the major—but not the only—reason for his selection. When asked what they regarded as the most important factor influencing their choice of the retrained worker, two-thirds of the West Virginia employers stated that they were primarily influenced by the skill acquired by the worker as a result of his training. However, 37 per cent of the responding employers also stated that one of the most important factors in their hiring of trainees was the fact that they were more carefully screened by the Employment Service than the average referral. And 58 per cent felt that the trainees were simply better than the average unemployed worker because they had taken the selection tests and the retraining.

Thus, the motivation of employers in hiring trainees was complex. The newly acquired skills were important. But for many of the employers, it was enough that these workers had been specially screened and selected from among the other unemployed because of their above-average qualifications and potentialities for future employment. A number of employers felt that the trainees were better prospects than the average run of the unemployed because they had the ambition, stamina, and sense of discipline to enroll in a training course and to stay with it until their training was completed.

In some instances the employer was induced to hire trainees rather than other unemployed workers primarily because the employment office was more insistent and more enthusiastic in their referral. Because the training programs were new and well publicized, there was a natural tendency in some local employment offices to accord special attention to the referral and placement of trainees. This was an especially important factor in one of the West Virginia cities where the initial placement record of the trainees was widely criticized as being inadequate. In response to these criticisms the local employment office renewed its efforts at the placement of trainees and greatly increased its placement ratio.

It appears, therefore, that the job-placement value of training goes well beyond the actual skills acquired, and that other, more general considerations may often loom larger in the eyes of a prospective employer.

Approximately 22 per cent of the trainees had separated from the companies in which they had been hired at the time of our interview survey of employers. Of these, 85 per cent quit voluntarily; most of the others were discharged by the employer for unsatisfactory work. The voluntary quits were especially noticeable in some of the low-paying service occupations such as nurse's aides and waitresses. As noted above, many of those who voluntarily left their post-training employment were women who withdrew from the labor force.

### Qualifications of the Trainees

Even though the skill of the trainees was rated as a more important selection factor in large firms than in small, two-thirds of the large employers felt that the qualifications of the trainees should be rated "good" as compared with only 42 per cent of the medium-sized firms and 44 per cent of the small firms (see Table II.26). None of the large firms, and only a handful of the small and medium-sized firms, felt that the trainees were clearly "inadequate" in their qualifications. The remainder of the respondents to this question indicated that the workers were "adequately" trained.

Many of the most critical comments came from employers in small automobile service garages or service stations. There were complaints that the equipment for training workers as auto repairmen in the vocational schools was badly outmoded. Some employers also felt that the instructors were not well versed in the latest innovations in automobile repair. A few employers went so far as to state that the trainees' small-scale skill acquisition was a dangerous thing. Feeling they were qualified mechanics, the trainees often attempted tasks beyond their capabilities. Employers of waitresses in small restaurants were also frequently critical of the quality

TABLE II.26

EMPLOYER ESTIMATION OF QUALIFICATION OF RETRAINED WORKERS

| | Location of employer | | Size of firm | | | All employers |
|---|---|---|---|---|---|---|
| Estimate | West Va. areas | Other states | Small | Medium | Large | |
| **Good** | | | | | | |
| No. | 30 | 12 | 18 | 14 | 10 | 42 |
| % | 48.8 | 44.4 | 43.9 | 42.4 | 66.7 | 47.1 |
| **Adequate** | | | | | | |
| No. | 19 | 9 | 12 | 13 | 3 | 28 |
| % | 30.6 | 33.3 | 29.3 | 39.4 | 20.0 | 31.5 |
| **Inadequate** | | | | | | |
| No. | 3 | 1 | 3 | 1 | 0 | 4 |
| % | 4.8 | 3.7 | 7.3 | 3.0 | 0.0 | 4.5 |
| **Not ascertained** | | | | | | |
| No. | 10 | 5 | 8 | 5 | 2 | 15 |
| % | 16.1 | 18.5 | 19.5 | 15.2 | 13.3 | 16.8 |

of the trainees. Some might well have been embittered because a number quit shortly after having been hired.

The criticism by employers in small establishments often went beyond the trainees' lack of skill. They felt that many were inadequate in such personal characteristics as ambition, honesty, and conscientiousness. A significant proportion of these critical employers stated that the local employment office had been negligent in screening the unemployed for selection of trainees. While a number of evaluators of government-sponsored training programs have stressed the failure of selection officials to include a sufficient number of the hard-core unemployed, many employers feel that the Employment Service has already moved too close to the bottom of the barrel. Thus Employment Service officials are placed in a difficult position, in the crossfire between those concerned with the re-employment of the most disadvantaged and employers concerned with the qualifications of the workers they hire. Perhaps one solution to this dilemma could be provided through a more sensitive testing device than is now prevalent in the selection process for regular training courses. A testing instrument would be required to permit workers with little skill or education to demonstrate other personal qualities which would make them attractive to prospective employers. At the present time, those with very low levels of formal education are likely to be excluded on the basis of the aptitude and intelligence tests even though their ambition and drive, if discovered, might more than offset the educational disadvantage.

## Institutional vs. On-the-Job Training

A number of the employers, especially in the small establishments, expressed a preference for on-the-job training over training in the vocational schools. As is seen in Table II.27, however, the preference for govern-

TABLE II.27

Retraining Programs: Employer Preferences

|  | Location of employer | | Size of firm | | | All employers |
|---|---|---|---|---|---|---|
| Estimate | West Va. areas | Other states | Small | Medium | Large | |
| Government-sponsored training of the unemployed using vocational education | | | | | | |
| No. | 48 | 24 | 34 | 21 | 17 | 72 |
| % | 56.4 | 51.1 | 52.3 | 50.0 | 68.0 | 54.4 |
| Government subsidies to employers to encourage on-the-job training of unemployed workers | | | | | | |
| No. | 29 | 18 | 26 | 16 | 5 | 47 |
| % | 34.1 | 38.3 | 40.0 | 38.1 | 20.0 | 35.6 |
| No government aid for retraining unemployed workers | | | | | | |
| No. | 5 | 4 | 4 | 3 | 2 | 9 |
| % | 5.9 | 8.5 | 6.2 | 7.1 | 8.0 | 6.8 |
| Ranking not ascertained | | | | | | |
| No. | 3 | 1 | 1 | 2 | 1 | 4 |
| % | 3.5 | 2.1 | 1.5 | 4.8 | 4.0 | 3.0 |

ment-subsidized on-the-job training is by no means restricted to the small firms. Over one-third of the total sample of employers were in this category. They included two-fifths of the small firms, a slightly smaller percentage of the medium-sized firms, and one-fifth of the large firms. Employers in some of the small automobile service garages and in some other service establishments viewed subsidized on-the-job training not only as a means of acquiring employees specialized in the type of work in which they would engage, but also as a method of acquiring employees at relatively small cost during the training period.

Over half of the responding employers indicated a preference for a continuance of the vocational school training under government sponsorship. Many of the employers in small and medium-sized establishments stated that they had no facilities for on-the-job training and were forced to rely on trainees turned out by the vocational schools.

It is notable that only 6.8 per cent of the responding employers stated that they would prefer that the government provide no aid whatsoever for retraining unemployed workers; this proportion is approximately the same regardless of the size of the establishment. For establishments in depressed economic areas, government-sponsored retraining, of either the institutional or on-the-job variety, is apparently viewed as a necessary and desirable component of labor market policy.

### GOVERNMENT-SUBSIDIZED TRAINING FOR A SPECIFIC EMPLOYER

Even though no on-the-job retraining programs were included in the survey of West Virginia ARA and AVP retraining courses, as noted above there were two instances in which courses were specifically designed to meet the needs of a new industrial facility attracted under the provisions of the Area Redevelopment Act. Since the training specifications were established by the employers and since they sometimes provided instructors as well as some equipment to be used in the training program, these courses designed for a specific employer come close to the arrangements found in on-the-job training. As has already been indicated, these employers also exercised considerable influence over the selection of trainees, and for this reason, too, the training arrangement established on their behalf approached that under on-the-job training.

For these reasons, it is perhaps understandable that the employers interviewed in the two large establishments for whom specific courses had been arranged spoke of the retraining programs in the most laudable terms. Because of their intervention in the selection process, they were generally well pleased with the personal characteristics of the trainees whom they hired; and because many of the training specifications were established by the companies themselves, they were appreciative of the skill adaptation of the trainees to the needs of the jobs on which they were placed.

It is seen, then, that training programs designed for a specific employer, like on-the-job training, may have some definite advantages. However, as has been noted in a previous section, this type of specifically oriented training may also have disadvantages. Because the trainees are new employees with little seniority protection, they are vulnerable to further displacement. If a government contract should end, or be curtailed, or if any of the other ills which have traditionally beset labor-surplus areas become pressing, then the newly hired trainees may well find themselves without a job once again; and, then, their highly specific training for a particular job in a particular establishment would not always serve them well. It might then be necessary for them to undertake further, more general training which would qualify them for a wider variety of employment opportunities.

For long-term unemployed in an area of chronic labor surplus, however, the most pressing need is for an immediate job; and this is provided by on-the-job training and by courses designed for a specific employer. There is a natural tendency under these circumstances to place a premium on the short-run advantage and let the long-run take care of itself.

### Does Government-Sponsored Retraining Create Employment?

Labor market experts may argue, as they are apt to do, about the true value of retraining as a factor in increasing employment. The employers in our survey seem to be overwhelmingly convinced that retraining programs will result in additional jobs. Over 70 per cent of the West Virginia employers, and a similar proportion in other states, felt that the government retraining programs would result in additional jobs for workers in their area. As is seen in Table II.28, employers in small establishments

TABLE II.28

Effect of Government Retraining Programs on Jobs in Area:
Employer Opinions

| Estimate | Location of employer | | Size of firm | | | All employers |
|---|---|---|---|---|---|---|
| | West Va. areas | Other states | Small | Medium | Large | |
| Extra jobs will result | | | | | | |
| No. | 60 | 34 | 49 | 29 | 16 | 94 |
| % | 70.6 | 72.3 | 75.4 | 69.0 | 64.0 | 71.2 |
| Extra jobs will not result | | | | | | |
| No. | 22 | 12 | 14 | 12 | 8 | 34 |
| % | 25.9 | 25.5 | 21.5 | 28.6 | 32.0 | 25.8 |
| Not ascertained | | | | | | |
| No. | 3 | 1 | 2 | 1 | 1 | 4 |
| % | 3.5 | 2.1 | 3.1 | 2.4 | 4.0 | 3.0 |

are more convinced of the job-creating value of retraining than are employers in medium-sized and large firms. Whereas three-fourths of the employers in small firms expressed a favorable view on this question, less than two-thirds of employers in the large firms supported the retraining programs on these grounds.

Employers were also asked whether they would hire more workers if on-the-job training costs were absorbed by the government. Although only one-fourth of the respondents indicated that they would do so, this must still be construed as a significant potential contribution to the expansion of employment. Here, too, we find a difference in the views of employers in large and small establishments. Whereas one-third of the employers in small firms stated that they would hire workers if on-the-job training costs were absorbed by the government, only a little over 20 per cent of the medium-sized firms and 17 per cent of the large firms were willing to make such an optimistic prediction.

It should be reiterated that West Virginia employers and those in other development areas are generally in favor of government-sponsored retraining of the unemployed. Although they may have many specific criticisms, such as inadequacies in the screening process and in certain aspects of the instruction and equipment, they are generally convinced that the retraining programs create additional employment, and they could be expected to support an expansion of such retraining.

A number of the smaller firms would prefer subsidized on-the-job training, and those larger firms with training courses designed specifically to meet their occupational needs appear to be especially appreciative of the government programs. The large firms are happier with the trainees whom they have selected, but, on the whole, they are not as enthusiastic as the small firms about the basic principle of government subsidization of the retraining of the unemployed.

## A CONCLUDING BALANCE SHEET: THE GAINS AND COSTS OF RETRAINING

### TRAINING AND EMPLOYMENT

The findings of this study lead to the conclusions that the government-sponsored retraining courses in West Virginia improved the labor market position of the trainees. Following their training, a larger proportion of the trainees obtained employment than comparable groups of unemployed workers who had not applied for training, who did not report for training, or whose applications for training were rejected. In corroboration of the objective statistical data, an overwhelming majority of the trainees were personally convinced that their training furthered their opportunities for employment.

Like the trainees, most of the employers in our sample felt that the retraining programs increased employment opportunities in their area. Many employers were willing to hire trainees in preference to other unemployed workers even when they felt that the newly acquired skill was not a crucial consideration. They were convinced that the trainees were better employment prospects simply because they had had the training experience.

Completion of the retraining courses also helped to induce outmigration of workers who had previously suffered long periods of unemployment and underemployment in chronically depressed areas. Although the initial employment ratio of the outmigrants was not high, the failure may have stemmed primarily from lack of guidance in choice of area of relocation and the short period of adjustment in the new locality at the time of our survey.

The training programs were on too small a scale to make an appreciable dent in the serious unemployment problems of West Virginia. Although the employment position of the trainees was improved, they may simply have found jobs at the expense of the remaining untrained and unskilled among the unemployed. Whether an expansion of the training programs would substantially reduce total unemployment in West Virginia would depend on the extent of improvement in the overall economic conditions in the state, the success of other area redevelopment policies, and the emphasis placed on planned policies of relocation.

### THE GAINS IN EARNINGS

Because employment after retraining—like employment before retraining—may be intermittent, an analysis of earnings is required for a more complete picture of the gains to be attributed to the retraining of the unemployed. Earnings data also provide an implication of the quality of the jobs obtained as a supplement to information on quantitative employment rates.

Two approaches are adopted in the following discussion. First, the gains and losses in earnings before and after the training period are compared for trainees and nontrainees during a six-month period. This comparison is based on data gathered in 1962 and 1963. Second, the average monthly earnings, net of taxes and including taxes, are traced over an eighteen-month period following training, in comparisons between trainees and nontrainees. These analyses are based on data gathered in the 1964 follow-up.

In Table II.29 it is seen that some trainees suffered losses in average monthly earnings during the period six months after their training courses, compared with the six-month period preceding training. Since many of these workers were laid off from relatively high-wage coal mining occupations just prior to their training, it is not surprising to find that over one-fifth were forced to take lower-paying jobs (or remain unem-

TABLE II.29

Gains and Losses in Average Monthly Earnings
of Trainees and Nontrainees[a]

| Gains and losses | Completed training[b] | | Nonapplicant sample[c] | |
|---|---|---|---|---|
| | No. | % | No. | % |
| *Average net loss* | | | | |
| *in dollars per month* | | | | |
| 251+ | 17 | 8.7 | 55 | 19.6 |
| 250–201 | 2 | 1.0 | 11 | 3.9 |
| 200–151 | 5 | 2.5 | 11 | 3.9 |
| 150–101 | 5 | 2.5 | 9 | 3.2 |
| 100–51 | 5 | 2.5 | 12 | 4.3 |
| 50–1 | 6 | 3.0 | 9 | 3.2 |
| Total who lost | 40 | 21.3 | 107 | 38.1 |
| *Average net gain* | | | | |
| *in dollars per month* | | | | |
| 1–50 | 18 | 9.2 | 7 | 2.5 |
| 51–100 | 17 | 8.7 | 8 | 2.8 |
| 101–150 | 27 | 13.8 | 9 | 3.2 |
| 151–200 | 14 | 7.1 | 11 | 3.9 |
| 201–250 | 11 | 5.7 | 6 | 2.2 |
| 251+ | 30 | 15.5 | 12 | 4.3 |
| Total who gained | 117 | 59.8 | 53 | 18.9 |
| *No change* | 39 | 19.9 | 121 | 43.1 |

[a] Average monthly earnings six months before training were compared with average monthly earnings six months after training period.

[b] 196 persons.

[c] 281 persons.

ployed) in the period immediately following their training. Since almost all of the trainees were unemployed immediately prior to their courses, it can be presumed that their private income at the point of entering the training was close to zero. Almost one-fifth of the trainees experienced no significant change in earnings, and almost 60 per cent gained in the six months following their retraining. The gains ranged widely; 10 per cent added $50 or less to their post-training monthly earnings, while 15.5 per cent increased their average monthly earnings $250 or more.

Among the sample of workers who did not apply for training, some also experienced gains in earnings during the same post-training period. But the gainers numbered less than one-fifth of the total, and almost two-fifths suffered a loss of average earnings. For over 43 per cent of the nontrainees there was no significant change in average earnings during the two six-month periods. Unlike those who completed training, relatively large proportions of nontrainees suffered very substantial losses in earnings in the period following retraining.

The contrasts in earnings between trainees and nontrainees are generally confirmed by comparisons of net earnings during the eighteen months after the retraining period (Table II.30). With the exception of

TABLE II.30

AVERAGE MONTHLY NET EARNINGS OF MALE TRAINEES AND NONTRAINEES
IN EIGHTEEN-MONTH PERIOD FOLLOWING TRAINING,
BY AGE AND EDUCATION[a]

| Age and education | Completed training | Nonapplicant sample |
|---|---|---|
| *Less than 35 years of age* | | |
| Less than 12 years' education | $231 | $148 |
| | (n = 37) | (n = 61) |
| 12 years' education | 300 | 232 |
| | (n = 132) | (n = 34) |
| *35–54 years of age* | | |
| Less than 12 years' education | $251 | $160 |
| | (n = 33) | (n = 33) |
| 12 years' education | 268 | 261 |
| | (n = 24) | (n = 17) |

[a] Earnings are net of income taxes and other deductions. Workers who became unemployable are excluded.
Source: Ford Foundation Project in West Virginia.

one small group of workers (older and better educated), the average monthly earnings of male trainees in specific age-education categories substantially exceeded those of nontrainees. The greatest percentage differentials were found among less educated workers, again implying that retraining may be a major service in furthering the employability of those who have had limited formal education. Because of the relatively small numbers of trainees included in the older age cells, the comparisons within this category must be approached with caution.

When an imputed income tax is included in average monthly earnings (Table II.31), the magnitude of earnings for male trainees and nontrainees changes, but the relationship between the two groups is relatively constant.

Less contrast is found in the earnings of female trainees and nontrainees. Only in the category of older, less educated women is there a significant earnings advantage of trainees over nontrainees. The earnings comparison for women is beclouded by the very high rate of labor force withdrawal among trainees and nontrainees. Here too, however, the small

TABLE II.31

AVERAGE MONTHLY EARNINGS AND INCOME TAXES OF TRAINEES AND NONTRAINEES
IN EIGHTEEN-MONTH PERIOD FOLLOWING TRAINING,
BY AGE AND EDUCATION[a]

| Sex, age, and education | Completed training | Nonapplicant sample |
|---|---|---|
| MALE | | |
| *Less than 35 years of age* | | |
| Less than 12 years' education | $240 | $141 |
| | (n = 37) | (n = 61) |
| 12 years' education | 332 | 240 |
| | (n = 132) | (n = 34) |
| *35–54 years of age* | | |
| Less than 12 years' education | $256 | $158 |
| | (n = 33) | (n = 103) |
| 12 years' education | 276 | 281 |
| | (n = 24) | (n = 17) |
| FEMALE | | |
| *Less than 35 years of age* | | |
| Less than 12 years' education | $81 | $73 |
| | (n = 19) | (n = 11) |
| 12 years' education | 80 | 80 |
| | (n = 30) | (n = 23) |
| *35–54 years of age* | | |
| Less than 12 years' education | $111 | $63 |
| | (n = 28) | (n = 21) |
| 12 years' education | 114 | 105 |
| | (n = 38) | (n = 14) |

[a] Includes an imputation for income tax based on the average number of exemptions in each set. 1962 tax rates are used. Males who became unemployable are excluded.
Source: Ford Foundation Project in West Virginia.

number of respondents in some of the cells calls for a note of caution.

On the whole, the differential gains in post-training earnings relative to pretraining earnings and in the levels of earnings of West Virginia trainees compared to nontrainees provide further support for the view that government-sponsored retraining has raised the economic position of the trainees. Other studies conducted under the overall Ford Foundation project—in areas of Connecticut, Illinois, Massachusetts, Michigan, and Tennessee—also demonstrate the economic advantage accruing to the trainees.

## THE SOCIAL GAINS

The gains to society resulting from the retraining program are not so readily documented or evaluated. As has been noted, a reduction in unemployment for particular trainees does not necessarily imply that the retraining programs have reduced total unemployment. They may merely have contributed to a change of faces in the unemployment compensation and welfare queues. Nonetheless we can assume that the demonstration of government-induced improvement in the labor market position of any significant number of citizens makes a positive contribution to stability and welfare in our political economy. And for the successful trainees, at least, there is a reduction of social payments and an increase in income tax contributions.

The reduction in social payments made to trainees, compared to control groups of nontrainees, is indicated in Table II.32. Although the

TABLE II.32

Average Social Payments Received by Trainees and Nontrainees
Six Months before Training, during Training,
and after Training Period[a]

| | Average monthly payments | | |
|---|---|---|---|
| Training status | Six months before training period | During training period | Six months after training period |
| Completed training | $54.60 (n = 74) | $61.16 (n = 112) | $38.69 (n = 49) |
| Dropped out of training | 54.40 (n = 47) | 59.70 (n = 60) | 52.11 (n = 41) |
| Did not report | 29.50 (n = 4) | 31.12 (n = 8) | 45.60 (n = 8) |
| Not accepted for training | 36.92 (n = 13) | 50.31 (n = 16) | 43.93 (n = 15) |
| Nonapplicant[b] | 75.82 (n = 92) | 82.66 (n = 148) | 86.91 (n = 168) |

[a] Social payments include unemployment compensation, public assistance benefits, workmen's compensation, and similar transfer payments. Training allowances are included in the period during training.
[b] Post-training data for nonapplicants based on two-month period.
Source: Ford Foundation Project in West Virginia.

training allowances paid during the training period raised the government payments to the "completed training" group above their pretraining social income, there was a substantial reduction in these payments following the training period. The post-training payments to the "dropped out of training" group also declined slightly relative to pretraining social income. But for each of the nontrainee groups, social payments increased relative to the six-months' average before the beginning of the training period. The continued high rate of dependency among the nontrainee unemployed follows logically from the earlier finds on post-training employment comparisons between trainees and nontrainees.

Similar evidence of reduced social payments relative to nontrainees are found in other studies evaluating the social gains attributable to retraining. One such study of retrained workers in Massachusetts concludes:

Although the control group had similar compensation costs in 1959, its cost by 1962 had increased 28 percent. On this basis the retrainees' unemployment costs would probably have amounted to about $31,000 in 1962 in the absence of retraining. Actually unemployment payments to this group in 1962 were only $8,000. Thus, for that one year, a saving in unemployment compensation of $23,000 can be attributed to the retraining program.[20]

Some evidence of the government's gain in income tax payments can be deduced from the data on gross earnings in Table II.29. To the extent that the higher earnings of trainees result at least in part from their training (and this appears to be a reasonable conclusion), training serves to help fill the purse from which future retraining allowances must be paid.

## Costs and Returns

The exact governmental costs of ARA, MDTA, and state training programs for the unemployed are not readily determined. Training facilities and instructors are frequently utilized in part for regular vocational classes, and costs will differ considerably depending on the locale of the training and the training occupation. Problems frequently arise in determining the specific item which should be included in the costs attributable to particular training courses. For these reasons, even government estimates vary.

It has been reported that the average cost of MDTA institutional training per trainee is $1,300. On-the-job training costs are about one-third of this.[21] A careful study of the costs of training 12,696 MDTA trainees in ten occupations estimated that the cost per trainee would be $991. These include a training allowance (equal to average state unemployment compensation payments) of $35 for twenty-one weeks (average length of training programs), or $735 per trainee. A subsistence allowance not to exceed $35 per week and a travel allowance not to exceed 10 cents per mile can be paid. Only 7 per cent of the trainees under study were receiving such allowances. Educational costs could run as high as $630 for each trainee in the study group, but were estimated to be considerably lower than this.[22]

The costs per trainee in the West Virginia programs are estimated to run much lower than these national MDTA estimates. The lower cost is partly a result of the lower average ARA training allowance ($23 per week), and the absence of any training allowance under the state program. On the basis of data provided by state authorities, it has been estimated that the average cost per trainee in the courses and during the time span covered by this study was $545.

In assessing the cost of training allowances, it should be noted that many of the trainees were receiving other government transfer payments prior to training. These payments were generally supplanted by the training allowance. It has been estimated that approximately one-third of the MDTA trainees were eligible to receive unemployment compensation payments at the time they entered training, and 8 per cent of the trainees in the MDTA study were receiving public assistance benefits at the time of their referral to training.[23] As noted above, the West Virginia trainees were receiving a variety of social payments prior to their entry into the training courses. The total amount of social payments to trainees was increased only slightly during the training period (Table II.32).

It is an even more difficult task to arrive at the opportunity cost involved in foregone wage income during the worker's training period. Since almost all trainees enter the program because they are unemployed, and since the training allowance usually replaces most of the social payments which would have been received by the nontrainee unemployed, one is tempted to conclude that the opportunity costs for the trainee are close to zero, especially in a depressed area such as West Virginia. At most one might take the average earnings of nontrainees during and after the training period as a basis for calculating the alternative wage income foregone by trainees during their training period. Another possibility would be to use the average earnings of dropouts from the training courses as a basis for determination of the trainees' opportunity cost. Such calculations would be based on the assumption that the jobs which were to be held by nonapplicants for training, or the jobs which were made available to dropouts, would also be available to trainees during their training period.

Given a calculation of costs along lines suggested above and assumptions concerning the interest rates, subsequent trainee employment and earnings could be used as a basis for determining a rate of return on the trainee's investment and society's investment in the retraining programs. Such analyses, utilizing the data acquired in the 1964 follow-up of the West Virginia trainees, are included in Chapter IX of this volume, and they have been reported elsewhere. (See the references to the Introduction and the Bibliographical Appendix.)

In more general terms, if one were to accept the notion that the differentials in average monthly earnings between male trainees and nontrainees indicated in Table II.30 were wholly attributable to the retraining, it is likely that reasonable opportunity costs of the trainee already had been recovered in the eighteen-month period after the training ended. Moreover, if it were assumed that these differentials were to persist, it would take little more than the eighteen-month period to return a sufficient increase to the government in income tax revenue to cover fully the relatively low cost of the training programs in West Virginia. The post-training differentials in social payments between trainees and nontrainees indicated in Table II.32, if attributed to the retraining, would go further to defray the government costs of retraining and provide a considerable social bonus in little more than the eighteen-month period.

All of this assumes, of course, that the success of the trainees has not been at the expense of opportunities for other unemployed workers. Efforts to resolve complications introduced by an abandonment of this assumption go beyond the scope of this paper.

### A Concluding Balance Sheet

The analysis presented above points in directions which are favorable for government-sponsored training of the unemployed. The economic gains to the trainees, and perhaps to society, derived from the retraining would appear to outweigh the economic costs. If social-psychological benefits accruing from an unemployed worker's return to the active labor market are added, the scales are heavily weighted on the positive side.

But the analysis also raises questions concerning the future of the retraining programs. Can retraining provide many more employment opportunities without an accelerated expansion of the economy? Can the same placement success for male trainees be expected to continue when necessary efforts are made to enroll the very hard-core unemployed? And, if not, will Congress and the Employment Service be willing to accept a lower employment ratio? Are the courses for women likely to give as high a rate of return as those for men, and if not, should they be abandoned? Should employers receive tax subsidies to encourage the retraining investment in human resources? These questions should suffice for our discussion.

### Nonmonetary Considerations

Even if we should come to the unlikely conclusion that the economic costs of retraining outweigh the immediate gains, it would not necessarily follow that we should abandon the ARA and AVP retraining. Although there has been very little research on this question, there are already some indications that the real pay-off in retraining of unemployed workers may be a very long-run proposition. If we look for immediate gains in the job market and in wages, we may sometimes be disappointed, but it is possible that the retraining experience will regenerate members of the hard-core group of unemployed, restore their confidence, return them to a commitment to the life of work instead of one of hopeless idleness. There is some evidence that even if an immediate job is not provided, many of these hard-core unemployed workers have benefitted in changed attitudes and outlook. One can then hope that in more prosperous times the rejuvenated workers will find a place in the labor market.

On the other hand, bitterness may be created in trainees who are unable to find jobs immediately after their retraining, and special efforts will be necessary to reassure and aid such workers.

The following letter received from a trainee in McDowell county is instructive in this and with regard to a number of other aspects. A fifty-year-old former coal miner, he had one year of high-school education, and had successfully completed the auto repair retraining course under AVP. At the time of our initial interview survey he had moved to North Carolina in order to take a job in a nontraining occupation. After his new address was obtained from relatives, two outmigrant mail questionnaires were sent to him, without reply. Finally, the following reply, typed on the back of our covering letter, was returned from McDowell county, to which the trainee had returned. The letter is reproduced in full and without change:

Sir(s)

You are, indeed, wasting Time, and Effort . . . in trying to force me . . . ————, Gary, West Virginia . . . to give answers to your questionnaire forms . . . which you claim are survey questions . . . relating to the history of my own personal self . . . as a supposed "trainee" of a Government-sponsored-trade-school-course . . . however . . . whenever . . .

I shall go further to say: West Virginia is my home State; I still live here . . . and I don't need, or want the University of Wisconsin, nor the Government of the United States . . . to give me charity . . . nor sympathy . . . as a displaced coal miner . . . thus; you are to fully understand, here and now, that I shall NEVER give you any answers to your despisable questions pertaining to which is my own personal self . . . and, you are to consider this your final effort to bother me with your unwanted mail to my address . . . for NO professor of Economics . . . whomever . . . wherever . . . has my welfare in mind . . . nor, that of any West Virginian . . . as far as I believe . . . so, whatever is my present-day economic status . . . I owe nothing to nothing . . . for the bread that I consume is jellied with enough pride . . . and dignity . . . to sustain my life without any help from source's beyond my own will-power to labor . . . at honest work . . . for honest wages . . . and, as far as I'm concerned . . . retraining labor is a lost cause . . . when . . . the retrained is to find the ends to the means . . . with means that dont exist . . . which brings me to say, again, that I owe nothing to nothing . . . except . . . that I owe, and give "thanks" . . . to Almighty God . . . for my American birthright . . . and, for the fact that I have lived . . . in the good State of West Virginia . . . long enough, indeed, to gain an insight to the nature of it's problems . . . economic, and political . . . and, while dwelling on the thought . . . things are sure to change; West Virginia will rise from present-day dependence on others charity and sympathy . . . perhaps . . . never again to wallow in the mire of muddy shame . . . economic and political . . . therefore; your survey does not include ME . . . for I despise conformity beyond the true meaning of the Stars and Stripes . . . and no particular person, place, or thing, is bigger than the fact that I know my "rights" under this flag . . . today, tomorrow, and forever . . . so get lost with your survey of my soul and body . . . which is my own even if I must starve to death . . . I don't want Kennedy charity . . . nor promises that mean nothing . . . but red tape around the World.

This reply reflects the hopes as well as the problems of West Virginia. The prospective trainees are proud and stubborn and dedicated to their earlier occupations and traditional way of life. This does not bode well for the experiment in induced occupational mobility through retraining. But they are also independent, patriotic, and aggressive. And herein lies the hope for a successful adjustment to the exigencies of the changing labor market and socio-economic milieu in which they find themselves.

## REFERENCES

1. Areas given a 5(a) classification are those wherein unemployment is currently 6 per cent or more, and has both averaged at least 6 per cent or more and has stood at least 50 per cent above the national average for three of the preceding four calendar years, or 75 per cent above the national average for two of the three preceding calendar years, or 100 per cent above the national average for one of the two preceding years.
2. These committees are not the same as those assembled to draw up the overall Economic Development Plans which are necessary for local participation in any ARA program.
3. The wording of the retraining section of the Area Redevelopment Act indicates that its framers did not intend it to be so restrictive.
4. U.S. Department of Labor, "Mobility and Worker Adaption to Economic Change in the United States." *Manpower Research Bulletin No. 1,* July, 1963 (revised), p. 5.
5. West Virginia Department of Employment Security, *Labor Market Digest,* various issues, 1962.
6. U.S. Department of Labor, "Mobility and Worker Adaption . . . ," p. 41.
7. *Ibid.,* p. 41.
8. Data from Oscar A. Duff, Chief of Employers Services and Manpower Utilization, West Virginia Department of Employment Security.
9. The summary statement which follows is all based on U.S. Department of Labor, "Mobility and Worker Adaption . . . ," pp. 8–14.
10. U.S. Department of Labor, "Manpower and Training, Trends, Outlook, Programs," *Manpower Research Bulletin No. 2,* July, 1963, p. 25.
11. Mathew A. Kessler, "Economic Status of Nonwhite Workers, 1955–62," *Monthly Labor Review,* Vol. 86 (July, 1963), 781. The 1948 percentages were, respectively, 9.0 and 39.1.
12. *Ibid.,* pp. 782–83.
13. U.S. Department of Labor, "Mobility and Worker Adaption . . . ," p. 10.
14. This course was one of a group of pilot ARA courses, but was antedated by West Virginia AVP training courses elsewhere in the state.
15. The difference between the completions and the dropouts is not statistically significant, though in the expected direction. The difference between the other applicants

(did-not-reports and rejects together) and the nonapplicants is significant at the 5 per cent level.

16. Men and women in training in the summer of 1962 are not included in the determination of any of the percentages.

17. For a technical treatment of this topic see Appendix A. It shows that when a number of intuitively important independent variables are analyzed, previous employment experience is found to have the greatest impact on $R^2$, with a partial beta coefficient of 31.99; and the worker's training status is found to have the second greatest impact, with a partial beta coefficient of 28.75. Other variables, such as regular occupation, labor market area, education, age, race, sex, seasonal and cyclical factors, are seen to have progressively less significance.

18. We are especially indebted to Wilbur Smith for assistance with the material in this section.

19. We are especially indebted to our research associate, Dr. Ernst Stromsdorfer, for assistance in the analysis of data on earnings and social income.

20. "Retraining the Unemployed: Part III—Retraining, A Good Investment," *New England Business Review* (April, 1963), p. 2.

21. *Report of the Secretary of Labor on Manpower, Research and Training* (March, 1964), p. 16.

22. Leroy A. Cornelsen, "Economics of Training the Unemployed" (U.S. Office of Education, Division of Vocational and Technical Education, January, 1964, mimeo.).

23. *Ibid.*, p. 2.

# Appendix A

![black bar]

# Regression Analysis of Variables Influencing
# Employment Success

A regression analysis, controlling for the intervening influence of secondary variables, further substantiates the impression that retraining is a significant aid in increasing the employment of unemployed workers. When the percentage of time the worker is employed in the twelve months following the end of the retraining period is designated as the dependent variable, the independent variables having the greatest impact on the dependent variable are Training Status and Labor Force Experience one month prior to the start of retraining— here indicated as Previous Labor Force Experience or PLFE (see Appendix Table A.1) .[1]

PLFE has the largest F-statistic, 17.2942, and Training Status the next largest, 10.8531. In addition, the partial beta coefficients indicate that PLFE has the greatest impact on $R^2$, with the value of 31.99, while Training Status has the second greatest impact, its partial beta coefficient being 28.75. Next in order of their impact on $R^2$ are Regular Occupation and Labor Market Area, then Education and Age. Variables introduced to control for race, sex, and season and cycle have relatively small impacts on the dependent variable.[2]

Training Status, when introduced as the last variable in the regression, increases $R^2$ by 3.23, or 25 per cent, after the intervening influence of a variety

1. The independent variables in this study are all of a binary nature. That is, they assume a value of *one* or *zero*, depending on whether or not a respondent falls into a particular category in question. One must bear in mind this fact when interpreting the significant tests. The variable set PLFE was developed as follows: the labor force status of the respondent was ascertained one month prior to the start of the retraining period, and this status was traced back to ascertain its duration. The model date of training start for those involved in retraining was used as the starting date of the Nontrainee Unemployed.
2. See James N. Morgan *et al.*, *Income and Welfare in the United States* (New York: McGraw-Hill, 1962), Appendix E, pp. 508 ff., for a discussion of the technique used to develop partial beta coefficients for a dummy (binary) variable set.

*degree of Employment?*

## APPENDIX TABLE A.1

IMPACT OF SOCIO-ECONOMIC AND RETRAINING VARIABLES UPON THE PERCENTAGE OF TIME EMPLOYED IN THE TWELVE-MONTH PERIOD FOLLOWING THE END OF RETRAINING

n = 1065      $R^2$ = .1605†      Standard Error = 47.58      Constant = 62.88 (8.109)

| Variable | Partial regression coefficient | Standard deviation | Means[a] | Partial beta coefficient[b] | F-Statistic for variable set |
|---|---|---|---|---|---|
| *Age* | | | | | |
| 18–21 | 4.410 | 5.706 | .1015 | 0.093 | 2.1002 |
| 22–34 | | | .3946 | | |
| 35–44 | .04682 | 3.993 | .2632 | | |
| 45–54 | −2.930 | 4.605 | .1758 | | |
| 55+ | −18.23 | 6.921 | .0648 | | |
| *Sex* | | | | | |
| Male | | | .7227 | | |
| Female | −5.706 | 4.352 | .2773 | 0.081 | 1.7190 |
| *Race* | | | | | |
| White | | | .9107 | | |
| Nonwhite | −8.439 | 5.438 | .0893 | 0.046 | 2.4081 |
| *Education* | | | | | |
| 0–8 | | | .2866 | | |
| 9–11 | 2.527 | 4.206 | .2942 | 0.094 | 2.4435 |
| 12 | 11.15 | 4.628 | .3440 | | |
| 13+ | 10.29 | 6.796 | .0752 | | |
| *Marital status* | | | | | |
| Married | | | .6833 | | |
| Single | −.5766 | 4.234 | .2218 | 0.024 | 0.2383 |
| Widowed | 1.468 | 11.03 | .0197 | | |
| Separated, divorced | −4.724 | 5.747 | .0752 | | |
| *Labor force experience prior to retraining* | | | | | |
| Employed 1–6 mo. | 31.95 | 6.976 | .0564 | 0.292 | 17.2492† |
| Employed 7+ mo. | 35.41 | 4.037 | .2961 | | |
| Unemployed 1–6 mo. | 14.15 | 4.394 | .1974 | | |
| Unemployed 7+ mo. | | | .2932 | | |
| Not-in-labor force 1–6 mo. | 1.238 | 12.59 | .0150 | | |
| Not-in-labor force 7+ mo. | 2.683 | 5.341 | .1419 | | |
| *Regular occupations* | | | | | |
| Semiskilled | | | .3176 | | |
| Prof., technological & kindred | 4.124 | 9.044 | .0310 | 0.121 | 2.1061* |
| Farmers & farm managers | 62.76 | 48.2 | .0009 | | |
| Clerical | −3.781 | 7.049 | .0658 | | |
| Sales | −6.452 | 7.245 | .0573 | | |
| Skilled | −1.130 | 5.566 | .0968 | | |
| Service | 9.604 | 5.836 | .1043 | | |

APPENDIX TABLE A.1    (*continued*)

| Variable | Partial regression coefficient | Standard deviation | Means[a] | Partial beta coefficient[b] | F-Statistic for variable set[c] |
|---|---|---|---|---|---|
| *Regular occupations* (Cont.) | | | | | |
| Unskilled | −12.67 | 4.740 | .1551 | | |
| No regular occupation | −3.264 | 5.562 | .1711 | | |
| *Labor market area* | | | | | |
| Charleston | | | .0996 | | |
| McDowell | −10.05 | 5.943 | .3506 | 0.108 | 2.9457* |
| Harrison | −13.99 | 6.075 | .2274 | | |
| Monongalia | −12.28 | 6.485 | .1344 | | |
| Huntington | −20.93 | 6.279 | .1880 | | |
| *Previous training* | | | | | |
| No previous training | | | .7867 | 0.000 | 1.1792 |
| Previous training | 4.080 | 3.757 | .2133 | | |
| *Mobility of respondent*[d] | | | | | |
| No mobility | | | .9530 | | |
| Moved 0–499 miles | 18.06 | 7.673 | .0395 | 0.070 | 2.9509 |
| Moved 500+ miles | −9.017 | 17.50 | .0075 | | |
| *Year training ended* | | | | | |
| 1960 | 11.48 | 10.70 | .0235 | | |
| 1961 | −4.666 | 5.130 | .1617 | 0.062 | 1.4799 |
| 1962 | | | .8035 | | |
| 1963 | −19.80 | 14.63 | .0113 | | |
| *Quarter training ended* | | | | | |
| First | −1.049 | 4.635 | .2256 | | |
| Second | | | .5676 | 0.029 | 0.2978 |
| Third | −.7596 | 5.258 | .1410 | | |
| Fourth | 5.397 | 7.000 | .0658 | | |
| *Training status* | | | | | |
| Completed training | | | .3722 | 0.257 | 10.8531† |
| Dropped out of training | −5.103 | 4.937 | .1607 | | |
| Not accepted | −27.66 | 6.624 | .0658 | | |
| Did not report | −20.80 | 7.557 | .0460 | | |
| Nonapplicant | −28.83 | 4.903 | .3553 | | |

\* Significant at .05 level.

† Significant at .01 level.

[a] The mean values here indicate the proportion of respondents in the total sample size falling into a given category. Multiply the relevant figures by 100 to get the proportion.

[b] These partial beta coefficients establish a sample rank order of the relative importance of each set of categorical (dummy) variables such as sex or age. For a further discussion of their nature and statistical content see James N. Morgan, *et al.*, *Income and Welfare in the United States* (New York: McGraw-Hill, 1962), pp. 38–39 and Appendix E.

[c] The blank variable in each variable set represents that variable which is included in the constant term. For comparisons within a variable set, it may be assumed to have a value of zero for its partial regression coefficient.

[d] Distance between address in summer, 1962 and summer, 1963.

of socio-economic variables has been held constant. The independent variables explain about 16 per cent of the variance in the dependent variable. $R^2$ is significant at the .01 level.

The foregoing is further substantiated by an inspection of the components of the Training Status variable set. The status, Completed Training, which enters into the constant term, raises its height by about 50 per cent. Hence, completion of training has a positive effect on employment success. Further, the partial regression coefficients of the other components of the variable set all have *negative* signs, and their relative heights with respect to the Completed Training status and to each other is as expected. Thus, relative to the Completed Training, the Nontrainee Unemployed were the least successful in gaining employment, the value of their partial regression coefficient being −28.83. Those applying for but rejected for training did only a little better, having a coefficient of −27.66. Those accepted for but not reporting for retraining had somewhat better success, with a coefficient of −20.80; while those who dropped out of training before its completion, often in order to accept a job, were the most successful relative to those who completed training, having a partial regression coefficient of −5.103.

In summary, therefore, after controlling for the simultaneous influence of the major variables thought to influence employment success in the labor market, one sees that Training Status has a large and significant explanatory effect and that those respondents in our sample who completed training fared better than any other group in the Training Status variable set.

# Appendix B

███████████████

# Summary of Government Retraining Programs, West Virginia
## July 1, 1960, to June 30, 1964

AVP (STATE) TRAINING COURSES COMPLETED AND IN PROGRESS,
JULY 1, 1960–JUNE 30, 1964

| No. courses | | No. | No. in | No. completed training | | | Employed |
|---|---|---|---|---|---|---|---|
| Total | In progress | enrolled | training | Total | Male | Female | |
| 552 | 75 | 11,393 | 965 | 6,674 | . . . | . . . | 4,564 |

*Courses*

| | |
|---|---|
| Nurse's aide | Seamstress |
| Typist | Weaving |
| Stenographer | Aircraft riveter |
| Machine tool operator | Auto transmission repair |
| Welder | Auto body painter |
| Bookkeeper | Auto brake and tune-up specialist |
| Auto mechanic | Bricklayer's helper |
| Mill and cabinet work | Cook's assistant |
| Electrical wiring | Presser-dry cleaner |
| Carpenter's helper | Electronic operator |
| Appliance repair | Lens grinder |
| Sewing machine operator | Mine maintenance mechanic |
| Waitress | Plumber's helper |
| Auto body repair | Sheet metal worker |
| Drafting | Radio & TV repairman |

Areas: Thirty-nine counties and one state college.
Source: State of Virginia: *The Employment and Industrial Review*, No. 84,
Fourth Quarter, 1964, pp. 11, 12.

ARA Training Courses Completed and in Progress,
December 4, 1961–June 30, 1964

| No. courses | | | No. completed training | | | |
|---|---|---|---|---|---|---|
| Total | In progress | No. enrolled | Total | Male | Female | Employed |
| 130 | 3 | 2,213 | 1,842 | 1,409 | 433 | 1,491 |

*Courses*

Auto mechanic                    Psychiatric aide
Cook                             Aircraft riveter
Draftsman                        Routeman
Dry cleaner                      Seamstress
Appliance repairman              Sewing machine operator
Farm mechanic                    Spray painter
Fork lift operator               Typist
Machine shop occupations         Vehicle tester
Millman (wood)                   Waiter / waitress
Nurse's aide                     Welder
Plasterer's helper

*Areas (by county)*

Cabell & Wayne                   Mercer
Fayette                          Mingo
Grant                            Monongalia
Harrison                         Raleigh
Kanawha                          Taylor
Marion                           Webster
Marshall & Ohio                  Wood

MDTA Training Courses Completed and in Progress,
January 7, 1963–June 30, 1964

| No. courses | | | | No. completed training | | | |
|---|---|---|---|---|---|---|---|
| Total | In progress | No. enrolled | No. in training | Total | Male | Female | Employed |
| 82 | 32 | 1,007 | 367 | 459 | 363 | 96 | 337 |

*Courses*

| | |
|---|---|
| Auto service occupations | Male attendant (hospital) |
| Cabinet maker | Mason's helper |
| Carpenter's helper | Office machine service man |
| Stenographer | Office reproduction worker |
| Cook | Operating room technician |
| Custodian | Pipefitter's helper |
| Diesel mechanic | Practical nurse |
| Electrician's helper | Radio & TV repairman |
| Electronics assembler | Ward clerk (hospital) |
| Farm occupations | Welder |
| Glass finisher, glass blower | Millman (woodworking) OJT |
| Machine shop occupations | Draftsman |

*Areas (by county)*

| | |
|---|---|
| Berkeley | Mason |
| Greenbrier | Mercer |
| Hancock | Mingo |
| Harrison | Monroe |
| Jackson | Ohio |
| Jefferson | Raleigh |
| Kanawha | Summers |
| Logan | Taylor |
| Marion | Wood |

# Appendix C

## The Civilian Labor Force, and the Number and Percentage Unemployed, for the Sample West Virginia Counties, Various Dates

| County and date | Civilian labor force | Unemployed No. | Unemployed % |
|---|---|---|---|
| *Monongalia* | | | |
| June, 1961 | 18,250 | 1,960 | 10.8 |
| June, 1962 | 19,420 | 1,960 | 10.1 |
| June, 1963 | 18,920 | 1,250 | 6.6 |
| *Harrison*[a] | | | |
| June, 1961 | 34,150 | 4,260 | 12.5 |
| June, 1962 | 34,240 | 4,060 | 11.9 |
| June, 1963 | 33,860 | 2,170 | 6.4 |
| *Kanawha* | | | |
| July, 1959 | 114,350 | 10,499 | 9.1 |
| July, 1960 | 95,200 | 6,850 | 7.4 |
| July, 1961 | 93,400 | 7,000 | 7.5 |
| July, 1962 | 93,100 | 5,750 | 6.2 |
| July, 1963 | 91,250 | 5,500 | 6.0 |
| *Cabell*[b] | | | |
| July, 1960 | 92,000 | 10,900 | 11.7 |
| July, 1961 | 89,650 | 10,150 | 11.3 |
| July, 1962 | 89,200 | 8,950 | 10.0 |
| July, 1963 | 88,950 | 6,850 | 7.7 |
| *McDowell* | | | |
| June, 1961 | 17,210 | 4,040 | 23.5 |
| June, 1962 | 16,120 | 2,480 | 15.4 |
| June, 1963 | 15,420 | 2,310 | 15.0 |
| *Five-county totals* | | | |
| June–July, 1961 | 252,660 | 27,410 | 10.8 |
| June–July, 1962 | 252,080 | 23,200 | 9.2 |
| June–July, 1963 | 249,400 | 18,080 | 7.2 |

[a] Data are for Labor Market Area which includes Harrison, Doddridge, and Taylor counties.

[b] Data are for Labor Market Area which includes Cabell and Wayne counties, West Virginia, Lawrence county, Ohio and Boyd county, Ky.

Source: All data from West Virginia Department of Employment Security, various releases.

# III

## MICHAEL E. BORUS

■

# THE EFFECTS OF RETRAINING THE UNEMPLOYED

# IN CONNECTICUT

## INTRODUCTION

The persistence of high levels of unemployment among portions of the labor force is viewed as a major problem by almost everyone concerned with economic problems—members of the executive branch, congressmen, and economists. Such high unemployment seems paradoxical for, as an inspection of the classified advertisements in any newspaper will show, it has coincided with the existence of attractive job openings. The failure of the unemployed and underemployed to move into these vacancies has been ascribed largely to their lack of skills, i.e., the skill requirements for the occupations with job openings serve as effective barriers to labor force mobility.*

As a specific remedy for this aspect of unemployment, Congress has established retraining programs to train the unemployed and underemployed for occupations with labor shortages. Four objectives have been specified for these programs: (1) to increase the nation's output; (2) to

* Michael E. Borus is currently (1968) at Michigan State University. This study, taken from the author's doctoral dissertation submitted to Yale University, was supported by funds from the Ford Foundation Retraining and Relocation Project, the Cowles Foundation for Research in Economics, and the Yale University Department of Economics. The author owes a debt of gratitude to Mr. Joseph J. Gibbons and Mrs. Mary Dewey of the Connecticut State Labor Department; Messrs. Joseph Borus, Arthur Gernes, and Louis Levine of the United States Department of Labor; and Professors E. Wight Bakke, Merton J. Peck, and Peter Schran of Yale University for their assistance.

reduce the aggregate level of unemployment; (3) to reduce the costs of unemployment and public assistance; (4) to reduce the unemployment of specific groups of the unemployed.[1] This is a report evaluating how successfully early retraining courses in Connecticut met these objectives.

## THE RESEARCH QUESTIONS

The congressional objectives are rather grand statements which have to be translated into more precise questions for research purposes. Therefore, this chapter will discuss these three questions: (1) Do the employment records of the retrained workers evidence significant improvements as a result of the retraining program? This answer will be found by comparing the incomes, unemployment, and unemployment benefits of the retrained workers and of control groups. (2) What have been the effects of retraining on aggregate output, unemployment, and government unemployment payments? The occupations for which the workers were retrained will be compared with records of job openings to determine whether retraining reduced labor shortages or merely shifted unemployment to other workers. (3) What groups in the labor force have been retrained, and are these the workers Congress desired to retrain? We will compare the statements made by Congress and the administration in hearings on the retraining legislation with the characteristics of the workers actually retrained.

## RETRAINING IN CONNECTICUT

Connecticut's retraining programs were selected to answer these research questions because Connecticut was one of the first states to offer publicly supported classes specifically designed to retrain unemployed workers. Prior to the passage of any federal retraining programs, the Connecticut Departments of Labor and Education, at the direction of the governor, initiated courses in two areas of the state—Bridgeport and New London. The courses in Bridgeport, begun in May, 1961, provided training in basic machine shop operations, a skill determined to be in great demand by an area labor market survey. At the same time, the New London courses were begun to retrain workers for shipyard trades, since the Electric Boat Division of General Dynamics Corporation needed trained workers to expand its production of atomic submarines.

The courses in the two areas differed in one important respect. The retrainees in New London were told that they would be employed upon the successful completion of the course (assuming that they were able to pass security and health examinations). In Bridgeport, however, they could not be guaranteed employment by any single employer or group of employers, and they had to rely on their own initiative and the placement services of the Connecticut State Employment Service to locate a post-training job. Hence, retrainees in Bridgeport ran a greater risk that retraining would not result in a job.

The experience gained from the state's two pilot programs allowed the Connecticut towns of Ansonia, Bristol, and Danielson to be among the first in the country to qualify for retraining funds under the Area Redevelopment Act (ARA).[2] This act, passed in May, 1961, was the first federal venture into retraining the unemployed. It provided for retraining in areas of "substantial and persistent unemployment," a condition met by these three towns. The retraining courses begun under this act in October, 1961, differed from the earlier state programs in the amount of financial aid provided the retrainees. State-sponsored courses permitted unemployed workers to collect any unemployment compensation to which they would have been entitled had they not entered the course. Those unemployed workers who had used up their credits or who for another reason were not eligible to receive unemployment compensation received no government unemployment aid; they might have qualified for public assistance, however. The unemployed in the ARA courses, on the other hand, could choose between the unemployment compensation they would normally be qualified to receive, or a federal training allowance of $37.00 a week (an amount equal to the average unemployment compensation benefit in Connecticut). Thus, while all of the retrainees in the ARA courses received some government aid during retraining, some persons in the state program received no aid.

During the first half of 1962, the state-sponsored retraining programs were expanded. By June 1, 1962, courses had been established in seven areas of the state, and 981 workers were enrolled in a total of fifty-three classes.[3] Retraining in three areas was supported by the ARA and in the other four by the state. Following passage of the Manpower Development and Training Act of 1962 (MDTA), the state requested federal assistance for the courses it was supporting and proposed additional retraining courses. Connecticut, however, did not wait for the appropriation of federal funds, as did most other states. In July, 1962, the expanded program was put into effect under state auspices. As a result of its pilot program and its early start in retraining under the MDTA, Connecticut had enrolled more than 2,000 workers in retraining courses in the first two years of the program and, by July 1, 1963, had placed more graduates of MDTA programs than had any other state.[4]

## THE ECONOMIC EFFECTS OF RETRAINING ON THE TRAINEES

The first of the research questions enumerated above was, "Do the employment records of the retrained workers improve as a result of retraining?" The answer lies in the workers' experience upon completion of retraining as compared to their expected experience had they not been retrained. To estimate this difference a sample had to be selected which included both retrainees and other workers who were comparable except for retraining. (See Appendix A.) Differences between the incomes, unemployment experiences and unemployment benefits of these groups could then be assumed to reflect the benefits of retraining.

The approach used here, however, differs from that used in previous studies. In earlier studies the workers involved were divided into three categories: (1) workers who successfully completed the retraining courses, (2) workers who entered the retraining courses but withdrew before the course was completed, and (3) workers who qualified for the retraining courses by passing the aptitude tests and meeting any other entrance requirements, but chose not to enter. The three groups of workers were then compared, and the latter two served as control groups.

This trivariate classification system has two distinct advantages, which have led to its use in past studies.[5] First, the categories are clear-cut. Second, all required information can be secured from class registers or state employment service records. The workers need not be contacted. These advantages are offset by the limitations of an implied assumption: that each category is homogeneous in composition. Such homogeneity does not exist. There are two distinct groups of workers in each category, and their aggregation leads to the loss of relevant information.

More specifically, some workers who refuse retraining after meeting the requirements for the course do so because they have found employment in occupations which do not require them to be retrained. Similarly, some workers who withdraw from retraining prior to completing the course do so because they have found employment in occupations other than those taught. By definition, these workers have rejected retraining in favor of another type of employment which offers them a greater expected "net economic advantage." To be sure, some of them may miscalculate the relative advantages of retraining and the alternative type of employment. A degree of uncertainty was involved in retraining for some workers in the sample, especially for those in Bridgeport and Ansonia where there was no guarantee of placement on successful completion of the course. Others may have been forced by the financial constraints of low retraining allowances and a lack of capital to take jobs which offered them greater income in the short run, although in the long run retraining would have yielded greater advantages. However, such cases were relatively rare among the sample studied.

The average employment experience of workers who rejected retraining in favor of another type of employment should be better than that of workers who had not been offered employment with greater expected "net economic advantages." This latter group includes both workers who completed retraining and workers who did not have an offer of employment when they withdrew from or refused retraining. Thus, only those workers who withdrew from or refused retraining for reasons other than employment are fully comparable with the retrainees.

Even the retrainees are not a homogeneous group. Some of them were not placed in positions which made use of the skills learned in the course, so that retraining aided them only indirectly in finding employment. Their experience was not substantially changed by retraining and therefore should not be used to illustrate the benefits of retraining. Rather, these individuals should serve as a control group with which to compare the retrainees who made use of the skills learned in the course.

To compensate for the lack of homogeneity in the standard trivariate classification system, the following six-fold classification was used:

1. Utilized retraining—Those workers who, as a consequence of having taken the retraining course, were placed in jobs in which they used skills learned.

2. Completed retraining but did not utilize skills learned in the retraining course—Those workers who completed retraining but were placed in jobs in which they used skills other than those taught in the retraining course, or were placed in a job in which they used skills taught in the retraining course, but not as a consequence of having learned new skills.

3. Withdrew from retraining for employment—Those workers who entered, but did not complete, the retraining course because they found employment for which retraining was unnecessary.

4. Withdrew from retraining without employment—Those workers who entered, but did not complete, the retraining course for reasons other than an offer of employment.

5. Refused retraining because of employment—Those workers who qualified for, but did not enter retraining, because they found employment for which retraining was unnecessary.

6. Refused retraining without employment—Those workers who did not enter retraining for reasons other than an offer of employment.

### THE CONTROL GROUPS

The control groups chosen for this study were those who "Completed retraining but did not utilize skills learned in the retraining course," "Withdrew from retraining without employment," and "Refused retraining without employment." None of these groups, however, was fully comparable with those workers who utilized retraining, for differences existed in demographic characteristics,[6] motivation, and ability. The effects on the employment records of the differences in demographic characteristics of the four groups were recognized in intergroup comparisons by the use of multiple regression techniques (see Appendix B). The differences in motivation and ability were not quantifiable and, therefore, had to be handled in the following, less precise manner.

It was assumed that workers who did not enter or complete retraining and who had no offer of employment were not as able or as highly motivated as were workers who completed retraining, or they, too, would have completed the course. Consequently, the expected employment and earnings of these persons would have been less than those of workers who utilized retraining, even if the latter group had not participated in the retraining program. Therefore, comparisons between the employment records of workers who utilized retraining and those of workers who withdrew from or refused retraining without an offer of employment overstate the effects of retraining.

In contrast, comparisons of the employment records of workers who utilized retraining with those of workers who completed retraining but did not utilize skills learned are assumed to understate the effects of retraining. Some workers who completed a course did not utilize their retraining because they found or were called back to more attractive jobs than those offered in the occupations for which they were retrained. They were presumably the most able and motivated of the retrainees who would be expected to have better employment records than retrainees not offered such positions. In addition, workers who completed but did not utilize retraining were nevertheless aided indirectly by having completed a course, since the State Employment Service tended to give special attention to the placement of retrained workers. Their demonstrated occupational mobility and motivation also encouraged employers to hire them for jobs unrelated to the occupations for which they were retrained. Thus, the income and employment of workers completing but not utilizing their recently acquired skills were raised above what they would have been had they, the workers, not been retrained.

For these same reasons, the expected employment records, in the absence of retraining, of retrainees who utilized skills learned in the course would lie somewhere in the range between the actual employment records of the less able and less motivated workers who refused or withdrew from retraining without employment and the employment records of the more able or more motivated workers who completed and benefitted from retraining but did not utilize it. Where within this range the expected earnings and employment experience of this group of retrained workers actually fall cannot be ascertained. However, to obtain a conservative estimate of the benefits of retraining, the expected values were set close to the observed values for workers who completed but did not utilize their retraining.[7]

## INCOME EARNED FROM WAGES

There can be little doubt that retraining aided the workers who utilized the skills they had learned in the courses. The earnings of the retrainees who utilized their newly acquired skills were considerably higher than the earnings of each of the control groups.

Two measures were used to ascertain the earned wage income of the sample. The first measure, based on interview data, was the average income per week in the labor force. This income was computed by multiplying the gross hourly wage rate by the reported average number of hours worked for each week the worker was in the labor force, from the end of the retraining period to the date of the interview. No allowance was made for occasional days lost through illness or days lost because of strikes because they were not a function of the occupation. Time lost due to the nature of the job, such as launchings at the submarine works or seasonal layoffs in construction, was included in the calculations.

By use of linear multiple regression techniques that take into account the different demographic characteristics of the retrainees and the control groups (see Appendix B), the workers who utilized retraining averaged $7.44 more for each week in the labor force than did the workers who completed but did not utilize the retraining, $8.83 more per week than the workers who refused retraining without employment, and $15.06 more per week than the workers who withdrew from retraining without employment. Although not all of the earnings were greater by statistically significant amounts (i.e., a Student "t" significant at the .05 level would be 1.645), the increments were quite large in absolute terms in all cases (see Table III.1). Also, the expected value for the retrainees

TABLE III.1

THE AMOUNT BY WHICH THE AVERAGE COMPUTED WAGE INCOME PER WEEK
IN THE LABOR FORCE, OF THE WORKERS UTILIZING RETRAINING
EXCEEDED THAT OF EACH OF THE CONTROL GROUPS[a]

| Control group | Regression coefficients | Standard error | Student "t" |
|---|---|---|---|
| Completed but did not utilize retraining | $ 7.44 | 5.25 | 1.418 |
| Withdrew without employment | $15.06 | 6.01 | 2.504 |
| Refused training without employment | $ 8.83 | 6.19 | 1.425 |

[a] The effect of additional independent variables was determined for each control group by subtracting the regression coefficients of Regression Model Three from those of Regression Model Four. The impact of the additional variables was to increase the weekly differential by $1.18 for the workers who completed but did not utilize retraining, and $2.85 for the workers who refused retraining without employment. The differential for the workers who withdrew from retraining without employment was decreased by $.23.

should lie among the regression coefficients of the three control groups.

The second measure of earned income was taken from employers' reports to the Unemployment Insurance Division of the Connecticut Department of Labor. Earnings of the workers were gathered for four quarters during 1962 and 1963.[8] These data, which are presented in Table III.2, indicated that, for workers who utilized skills learned in re-

TABLE III.2

THE AMOUNT BY WHICH THE AVERAGE QUARTERLY EARNINGS OF THE WORKERS
UTILIZING RETRAINING AS REPORTED TO THE UNEMPLOYMENT INSURANCE DIVISION,
CONNECTICUT DEPARTMENT OF LABOR, EXCEEDED THAT OF EACH
OF THE CONTROL GROUPS[a]

| Control group | Quarter | Regression coefficients | Standard error | Student "t" |
|---|---|---|---|---|
| Completed but did not | 2nd 1962 | $ 61.07 | 84.77 | 0.720 |
| utilize retraining | 3rd 1962 | 156.30 | 90.48 | 1.727 |
| | 4th 1962 | 77.90 | 92.98 | 0.839 |
| | 1st 1963 | 129.13 | 150.80 | 0.856 |
| | Total | $424.40 | | |
| Withdrew without | 2nd 1962 | 283.63 | 90.57 | 3.131 |
| employment | 3rd 1962 | 352.55 | 96.66 | 3.647 |
| | 4th 1962 | 216.02 | 99.23 | 2.177 |
| | 1st 1963 | 323.50 | 161.11 | 2.008 |
| | Total | $1,175.70 | | |
| Refused training | 2nd 1962 | 314.33 | 103.51 | 3.037 |
| without employment | 3rd 1962 | 206.59 | 110.48 | 1.870 |
| | 4th 1962 | 205.04 | 113.41 | 1.808 |
| | 1st 1963 | 306.89 | 184.13 | 1.667 |
| | Total | $1,032.85 | | |

[a] The effect of additional independent variables was determined for each control group by subtracting the regression coefficients of Regression Model Three from those of Regression Model Four. The impact of the additional variables was to increase the total differential for the four quarters by $31.87 for the workers who completed but did not utilize retraining, and by $257.89 for the workers who refused retraining without employment. The differential for the workers who withdrew from retraining without employment was decreased by $41.43.

training, the average total earnings for the year exceeded by $424.40 the average income of the workers who completed retraining but did not utilize the skills.[9] The average yearly earnings of workers who utilized retraining exceeded those of the other two groups by even greater amounts: $1,032.85 more than the earnings of workers who refused retraining without employment and $1,175.70 more than the earnings of workers who withdrew from retraining without employment.

These figures indicate that retraining increased the annual earnings of the workers who utilized the skills learned by an amount ranging from $400 to $1,200 a year. The actual benefits probably lie closer to the lower value, since most of the workers who did not enter or complete the course probably were not as highly motivated or as able as the retrainees. On this basis it will be assumed that the average added income received by the worker who was retrained and made use of the skills learned was approximately $500 per year.

### UNEMPLOYMENT

The greater earnings of the workers making use of their retraining were not due to higher wage rates, as the average wage rates of the four groups were approximately the same (see Table III.3). But, as Table III.4 in-

### TABLE III.3
### AVERAGE HOURLY EARNINGS

|  | At time of first placement | Six months after retraining | One year after retraining |
|---|---|---|---|
| Completed and utilized retraining | $1.78 | $1.93 | $2.01 |
| Completed but did not utilize retraining | 1.88 | 1.97 | 1.97 |
| Withdrew without employment | 1.67 | 1.81 | 2.13 |
| Refused training without employment | 1.81 | 2.08 | 2.04 |

Source: Worker interviews.

dicates, they earned more because they had less unemployment than did workers in the control groups. Data gathered in the interviews showed that workers who utilized retraining were unemployed 4.6 per cent of the time they were in the labor force in the period from the end of retraining to the time of the interview, while workers who did not utilize retraining were unemployed 14.1 per cent of the time, workers who withdrew without employment were unemployed 17.1 per cent of the time, and workers who refused retraining without employment were unemployed 17.9 per cent of the time.[10] Thus the retraining increased the employment of the workers who made use of it by approximately 10 percentage points.

### GOVERNMENT UNEMPLOYMENT PAYMENTS RECEIVED

As would be expected, the ten-percentage-point reduction in unemployment led to significant reductions in the unemployment payments, in-

TABLE III.4

AMOUNT IN PERCENTAGE POINTS BY WHICH THE AVERAGE RATE OF EMPLOYMENT
WHILE IN THE LABOR FORCE FROM THE END OF THE RETRAINING UNTIL THE DATE
OF THE INTERVIEW OF THE WORKERS UTILIZING RETRAINING EXCEEDED
THE AVERAGE RATE OF EACH OF THE CONTROL GROUPS[a]

| Control group | Regression coefficients | Standard error | Student "t" |
|---|---|---|---|
| Completed but did not utilize retraining | 9.469 | 3.147 | 3.009 |
| Withdrew without employment | 12.484 | 3.603 | 3.465 |
| Refused training without employment | 13.305 | 3.710 | 3.586 |

[a] These calculations are based on Regression Model One.

*Note:* The effect of additional independent variables was determined for each control group by subtracting the regression coefficients of Regression Model Three from those of Regression Model Four. The impact of the additional variables was to increase the differential in the employment rates by .280 percentage points for the workers who completed but did not utilize retraining and .934 percentage points for the workers who refused retraining without employment. The differential was decreased by .464 percentage points for the workers who withdrew from retraining without employment.

cluding unemployment compensation, special veterans' benefits, food stamps, aid to dependent children, and relief, received by workers utilizing retraining. The average weekly benefits received by workers who completed but did not use their retraining were $1.16 higher than those received by the workers utilizing retraining. Similarly, workers who refused retraining without employment received $2.65 more per week, and the workers who withdrew from retraining without employment received

TABLE III.5

THE AMOUNT BY WHICH THE AVERAGE GOVERNMENT UNEMPLOYMENT PAYMENTS PAID
PER WEEK TO EACH OF THE CONTROL GROUPS EXCEEDED THE AVERAGE
WEEKLY BENEFITS PAID TO THE WORKERS UTILIZING RETRAINING[a]

| Control group | Regression coefficient | Standard error | Student "t" |
|---|---|---|---|
| Completed but did not utilize retraining | $1.16 | 0.876 | 1.328 |
| Withdrew without employment | $3.25 | 1.004 | 3.247 |
| Refused training without employment | $2.65 | 1.033 | 2.570 |

[a] These calculations are based on Regression Model One.

*Note:* The effect of additional independent variables was determined for each control group by subtracting the regression coefficients of Regression Model Three from those of Regression Model Four. The impact of the additional variables was to decrease the weekly differential by $.23 for workers who completed but did not utilize the retraining and by $.17 for workers who refused retraining without employment. The differential was increased by $.06 for the workers who withdrew from retraining without employment.

$3.25 more per week than did the workers utilizing retraining (Table III.5). Thus, the federal, state, and local governments paid approximately $100 a year less to the workers utilizing retraining than they would have paid in the absence of the retraining program.

Although the reduction of unemployment benefits was a gain to society, it represented a loss of income for the individual workers. The income gain of the average worker utilizing retraining was reduced by approximately $100 per year.

The findings discussed above indicate that retraining benefitted the workers who made use of it. They were effectively moved from occupations with labor surpluses to occupations with labor shortages, with the result that their unemployment fell sharply and their incomes increased considerably. In addition, the community now spends less to maintain these workers during their periods of unemployment.

## THE NET EFFECTS OF RETRAINING [11]

The first three congressional objectives for retraining, enumerated earlier, were directed toward changing *aggregate* levels of production, unemployment, and unemployment benefits paid by the government. The individual gains just cited do not necessarily reflect aggregate gains. Retraining must also meet three other criteria. First, the retrainees must not replace other workers, and thus merely shift the burden of unemployment from one group to another. Second, the retrainees must be placed in occupations where labor shortages would exist in the absence of retraining; there must not be other workers in the labor force who, without being retrained, are able and willing to fill the job vacancies. Third, the retrainees must be placed on the basis of their having been retrained. The retrainees must not have been able to find work in these occupations without the retraining.

Whether retraining has met these criteria is difficult to test conclusively. There is, however, much circumstantial evidence that indicates that retraining improved the aggregate level of productivity and reduced unemployment and governmental unemployment costs in Connecticut.

### Retraining for Occupations with Labor Shortages

The Manpower Development and Training Act (Section 202[e]) states: "the Secretary [of Labor] shall determine that there is a reasonable expectation of employment in the occupation for which the person is to be retrained." To meet this requirement, before retraining can be undertaken the state employment service must certify that an inadequate supply of labor exists in a particular occupation. The employment service bases its judgment of the labor market on its experience with job orders that have been difficult to fill over a long period of time, on specific requests from employers for retrained workers, and on labor force questionnaires sent to employers.

These are not perfect tools, of course. For instance, in Connecticut, employers were asked to estimate their employment needs in key occupations for the two following years. These estimates were rough since the businessmen had to predict their needs based on imperfect knowledge of the demand for their product two years in the future. The information did serve, however, as a useful supplement for the Connecticut Employment Service, since it alerted it to some jobs which normally would not be listed.

Moreover, if a state employment service misjudges the demand for labor, with the result that regular workers are being replaced by retrained workers, a feedback mechanism will inform the employment service of its error. Increased numbers of regular workers in the occupation for which people are being retrained will apply for unemployment compensation and for aid in finding new jobs. The displacement will be especially evident if it occurs in a situation where the retraining is designed to meet the needs of a single employer. For example, several of the workers interviewed mentioned one small company's practice of replacing retrainees with other retrainees once the first group began to approach higher wage levels. The Connecticut State Employment Service soon became aware of this practice and adjusted the retraining program accordingly.

In Connecticut, a further reason against the retrainees being used to displace other workers was that it would not be in the employer's interest. The Connecticut retraining courses were not intensive; their basic purpose was to familiarize workers with the occupational environment. The retrainees were not trained for a period long enough to enable them to move into the jobs of semiskilled or skilled workers. Most of them were placed as learners or apprentices. Thus, they were unlikely to be more productive than the employer's existing work force.

In conclusion, an assumption appears justified that the retrainees did not displace other workers.

### The Existence of an Inadequate Supply of Trained Workers

As shown previously, the workers who utilized retraining were placed in jobs that offered considerably higher earnings and more consistent employment than did the jobs they would have taken had they not been retrained. If workers trained in those occupations were available in the unemployed labor force or in the unskilled labor force, it is reasonable to assume that the jobs would not have remained unfilled. Yet, as mentioned above, a major criterion for determining the retraining occupations was the inability of the State Employment Service to fill long-existing vacancies in these occupations. Obviously, unless there was a complete breakdown of the market, a trained labor supply did not exist among the unemployed or the underemployed workers, or if it did exist there was a lack of communication between the trained workers and the employers with the job openings. In either case the openings would have remained vacant if no retraining courses were given.

The inadequacy of the existing labor force in Connecticut is further shown by the excellent placement record of the workers completing retraining courses. If trained workers had been available, it is doubtful that employers would have allowed their job openings to remain vacant for the many months between the preparatory surveys for the courses and their completion, and the retrainees would not have been able to find jobs in the occupations for which they had been retrained. Yet, 84 per cent of the workers in the sample who completed retraining were placed in jobs in which they used skills learned in the course.[12] In addition, many of the other 16 per cent were offered such jobs but did not accept them. Most of these workers sought or were called back to jobs that paid higher wages. A few decided, upon completion of the course, that they did not care to work in the occupation for which they had been trained. The one notable exception to the high placement rate in training-related employment was the sewing machine course in Ansonia. Two-thirds of the women were not placed in training-related occupations, partly because the courses were too short to train them adequately and partly because many of the women had taken the course only for its value in sewing at home.

Another indication that a labor shortage existed in these occupations was the great amount of overtime work offered to the retrainees. Following the course, 44 per cent of the workers who utilized retraining worked more than forty hours per week at least three-fourths of the time they were employed. Almost all of the men were offered some overtime work; only 7 per cent never worked more than forty hours after the end of the retraining courses. Overtime was particularly prevalent among the workers at Electric Boat, where all of the employees were encouraged to work six days a week.

THE OCCUPATIONS OF THE RETRAINEES IN THE ABSENCE OF RETRAINING

Not many of the 84 per cent of the retrainees who were placed in occupations in which they used skills learned in retraining would have been placed in these occupations had they not been retrained. In the interviews, 7 per cent of these workers claimed that they would have been placed in the same jobs even if they had not taken the course. This is quite possible, for 19 per cent of the workers who withdrew from retraining or refused retraining were placed in jobs that made use of skills taught in the retraining courses. Even if this latter figure is adopted, 68 per cent of the workers who completed retraining were placed in the training-related occupations as a result of acquiring the necessary skills in the course.

## Long-Run Net Effects

The effects examined above were short term. In the long run, even though the retrainees did not prevent other workers from filling the job vacancies existing at the time of the retraining, it would be a mistake to assume that these jobs would have remained unfilled indefinitely. Similarly, a retrainee who was placed in an occupation in which he used his training should not be expected to remain in this occupation for the remainder of his working life. Failure to take these two factors into account will result in greatly overestimating the value of retraining.

Unfortunately, it is impossible to predict with any authority how long a labor shortage would have continued in any given occupation. For the occupations examined in this study, despite the retraining program, labor shortages still existed three years after the courses began, as was demonstrated by the successful placement of graduates of courses identical to those studied here. Since these occupations had continuing labor shortages prior to the introduction of retraining, five years would appear to be a conservative estimate, and ten years a more realistic estimate, of the duration of retraining's effectiveness.

Movement out of the retraining occupation appears to place a much greater limitation on the length of retraining's effectiveness. Twenty-four per cent of the workers placed in the retraining occupations left these occupations within one year after completing the course. One-fourth of this 24 per cent moved to occupations that made use of some aspect of the retraining. Thus, only 18 per cent of the workers placed in retraining-related occupations left for non-retraining-related employment in the twelve months following their retraining. If this figure is projected for five years, however, 63 per cent of the workers utilizing retraining would not be in retraining-related jobs, and ten years after their retraining, only 14 per cent would still be utilizing skills learned in the course. This is an overly pessimistic estimate, though, for most workers who disliked or were ill-suited to their new occupations would move within the first year. In the absence of other data, however, this projection may serve as an upper limit on the losses due to turnover.

## Summary of Net Effects

The information presented above indicates that retraining has affected the aggregate levels of production, unemployment, and governmental unemployment costs. At least 68 per cent of the retrainees were employed as a result of having completed their courses, and the consequent increase in aggregate production could reasonably be expected to persist for five to ten years from the time that these workers completed the course. The size of the increased production, however, would become smaller each year, by as much as 18 per cent, because the retrainees moved from the retraining-related occupations.

## THE WORKERS BENEFITTING FROM RETRAINING

The materials presented above indicate that retraining leads to substantial improvements in the employment records of the workers who utilize skills learned in retraining courses. Thus, the first three objectives of retraining are being fulfilled. The fourth objective is to provide the benefits of retraining to specific groups of the unemployed. Retraining is desired for those workers who suffer disproportionately high levels of unemployment (youths, Negroes, and workers with less than twelve years of education), those workers who suffer the longest periods of unemployment (workers forty-five years of age and older), and those workers who have others dependent on their incomes (hereafter referred to as "the specified groups" or "the specified workers").[13]

For the courses examined, retraining did not benefit all of these groups. This can readily be seen if the characteristics of the male workers in the sample who utilized retraining are compared with the characteristics of the male unemployed labor force, or the male population.[14] Only 2.8 per cent of the men who utilized retraining were 45 years of age or older while 28.4 per cent of the male unemployed were in this age group. Similarly, 32.3 per cent of the workers in the sample utilizing retraining had not completed high school, while 59.8 per cent of the male population over 13 years of age had not.[15] Finally, only 54.4 per cent of the workers who used their retraining were married, while 81 per cent of the workers in the male civilian labor force were married.

### The Problem of Eligibility for Retraining

The characteristics of the sample members indicate that the workers in the specified groups did not even qualify for retraining. Comparisons of the characteristics of the men in the sample, all of whom qualified to enter retraining, and the characteristics of the unemployed labor force from which they came demonstrate significant differences in the two groups: Only 3.6 per cent of the sample were over 45 years of age, only 32.4 per cent of the men in the sample did not have a high-school education, and 54 per cent of the sample were single. Also, the percentage of entrants to the labor market was higher among the workers in the sample; among the experienced workers in the sample, 65.4 per cent were either unskilled or semiskilled, while only 46.1 per cent of the experienced unemployed were so classified; and the average income of the men in the sample for the twelve months preceding the start of retraining was $800 less than that of the total unemployed labor force. Finally, contrary to what is desired, the workers unemployed for more than fifteen weeks prior to the course were no larger a proportion of the sample than they were of the total unemployed labor force.

## Possible Explanations for the Failure of the Specified Groups to Qualify for Retraining

Three reasons may explain why the older and less educated workers did not qualify for retraining:

(1) A high level of educational attainment is necessary, or felt to be necessary by the workers, in order to meet the aptitude requirements for retraining. These requirements apparently were very important in determining eligibility for the courses. The percentage of the workers who took the test and passed it varied greatly with the different tests and requirements as indicated by Connecticut State Employment Service records. The percentages of those who passed the test for the courses and areas covered in this study were: Bridgeport machine shop course, 36 per cent; Ansonia machine shop course (where lower standards were used), 64 per cent; Norwich pipefitter course, 77 per cent; New London pipefitter course, 83 per cent; Norwich shipfitter course, 40 per cent; New London shipfitter course, 54 per cent; and Ansonia sewing machine course, 75 per cent. Since the average older worker often has a low level of educational attainment, he cannot qualify for retraining, either because he is unable to pass the aptitude tests or because he does not take the tests in the belief that he will not be able to pass them.

(2) Workers with few responsibilities are more inclined to take the risks both of lost income during retraining and of the possibility that employment will not result from the course. Older workers usually have families and must worry about supporting them; they feel that they are not able to accept the risks involved in retraining. Also, they may actually face a greater risk of not finding employment in which they can use the retraining, for many employers discriminate against older workers in their hiring.

(3) Since younger workers lack skills and experience prior to retraining and have significantly lower expected incomes in the immediate future, the possibility of their gaining an economic advantage from retraining is greater than that of older workers, especially if the older worker has some expectations of being called back to a former job.

## SUMMARY

The amendments to the MDTA[16] sought to correct the failure of retraining to attract the specified groups. They have accomplished this objective with limited success. On the basis of Connecticut's experience with the retraining program, however, it is clear that retraining has admirably accomplished its other objectives. Retraining has increased the nation's output by increasing the productivity of the retrained workers, has reduced the aggregate level of unemployment by moving unemployed and underemployed workers from occupations of labor surplus to occupations of labor shortage, and has lowered the costs of unemployment compensation and public assistance by increasing the annual employment of the retrained workers without decreasing the employment of other workers. Thus, even if the amendments fail to satisfy the fourth objective of the retraining program, the experience in Connecticut indicates that retraining can improve the nation's economy.

## REFERENCES

1. "Statement of Findings and Purpose," *Manpower Development and Training Act of 1962*, Public Law 87–415.
2. Public Law 87–27.
3. Connecticut Labor Department, *Monthly Bulletin*, Vol. 27, No. 7 (July, 1962), p. 9.
4. U.S. Bureau of Employment Security, "Employment Service Spurs Job Placements of MDTA Trainees," *The Labor Market and Employment Security* (August, 1963), p. 1.
5. See for examples: "Retraining the Unemployed: Part I—The New England Experience," *New England Business Review* (August, 1962), pp. 1–4; and U.S. Office of Manpower, Automation and Training, *Training for Jobs in Redevelopment Areas* (Washington: OMAT, 1962).
6. Differences existed in the workers' ages; education; labor force attachment and participation; and previous training, incomes, unemployment, and unemployment benefits.
7. Unless otherwise noted, all calculations are made only for the men in the sample as the distribution of women by training status did not yield control groups large enough to be meaningful.
8. From April 1, 1962, to March 31, 1963. Data beyond the first quarter of 1963 were not available when the information was collected, and data for periods before the second quarter of 1962 would have included earnings of some of the workers before they had completed retraining.
9. Regression Model Two was used to make these computations. Differences in the average computed earnings per week in the labor force and the earnings reported by employers may arise from any of the following considerations: the change in the size of the subsample used for Regression Models One and Two, gaps in the unemployment insurance data for part-time jobs which were reported in the interview but were not covered by the unemployment insurance program; incorrect reporting by the interviewees of their wages, hours, or overtime rates; slightly different time periods for the two sets of data; or the fact that the computed figures are per week in the labor force and the reported figures include time not in the labor force. There was also a definite downward bias in these comparisons that arose from the nature of the data. Many employers only reported the first $4,800 of earnings for a year. Thus, it was found that 12.7 per cent of the retrainees who utilized the acquired skills had their incomes understated while 7.4 per cent of the workers who completed but did not use the retraining, 9.5 per cent of the workers who withdrew without employment, and none of the workers who refused retraining without employment had their incomes underestimated.
10. The unemployment rates were calculated by adding the average differential between the control groups and the workers who utilized retraining to the average unemployment rate for the latter group.

11. The problems involved in determining whether the workers would be retrained by private programs, if no government retraining program existed, will not be discussed here. This section of the paper will deal with the net effects of any program of retraining regardless of its sponsor. For a discussion of the relative merits of governmental and private retraining programs see Michael E. Borus, "A Benefit-Cost Analysis of the Economic Effectiveness of Retraining the Unemployed," *Yale Economic Essays*, Vol. 4 (Fall, 1964), 419–22.

12. The national average for MDTA graduates through May 19, 1963, was 87 per cent. U.S. Bureau of Employment Security in *The Labor Market and Employment Security* (August, 1963), Table 1, p. 1.

13. Among workers unemployed fifteen weeks and over, the national unemployment rates of these groups in 1962 were: workers under twenty years of age—13 per cent, Negroes—11 per cent, workers over 44 years of age—40 per cent (*Manpower Report of the President and a Report on Manpower Requirements, Resources, Utilization and Training by the United States Department of Labor*, transmitted to Congress March, 1963 [Washington, D.C.: GPO, 1963], Tables A8, A10, A13, and B12, pp. 144–57); workers with less than four years of high school—8 per cent (adapted from Denis F. Johnston, "Educational Attainment of Workers, March 1962," *Monthly Labor Review*, Vol. 86 [May, 1963], Table 4, 507).

14. Statistics were not available for all characteristics of the unemployed labor force. Therefore, figures for the male labor force and male population were also used. These statistics were taken from U.S. Bureau of the Census, *Census of Population 1960: Detailed Characteristics Report*, Connecticut P.C. (1)–8D, Tables 103, 115, and 116; pp. 103, 240 and 246, respectively.

15. The educational attainment of the unemployed was probably less than that of the total population. In March, 1962, the median years of education in the male population for the United States as a whole were 11.6 while the figure for the unemployed was 10.0. Johnston, "Educational Attainment . . . ," Table 3, p. 506.

16. Public Law 88–214, Public Law 89–15, and Public Law 89–792.

# Appendix A

## The Sample Involved in the Study

Three hundred and seventy-three workers were interviewed for this study. These workers had been involved in Connecticut's retraining courses between May, 1961 and March, 1962. They lived in four labor market areas and were retrained for four occupations. The areas and courses were chosen on the basis of the following criteria:

1. The sample was limited to workers involved in the retraining program at its inception, because their work histories since retraining provided a longer time period over which to determine the effects of retraining.

2. The effects of retraining may depend greatly on the level of unemployment in the area, for retrained workers may be easier to place in areas of higher employment. Therefore, the courses and areas were chosen so that the same course was offered in areas of both relatively high and low unemployment. (Unemployment, not seasonally adjusted, between May, 1961 and May, 1963 was about 6 per cent in Bridgeport; 9–12 per cent in Ansonia, until late in 1962 when it fell sharply; 3–4 per cent in New London, and about 9 per cent in Norwich.)

3. Classes for women were included to enable judgment to be made of the effects of retraining on women as well as on men.

4. Both ARA courses and the state courses were included to examine the effects of providing subsistence allowances.

5. Both courses where the retrainees were guaranteed a job with a specific employer and courses where no such guarantee existed were included to examine the influence of having such job assurances.

The courses and areas selected were:

a. The first five classes in basic machine shop operations for workers from Bridgeport, held from May 15 to December 8, 1961.

b. The first two classes of the same course for workers from Ansonia, held between October 16, 1961, and February 28, 1962.

## TABLE A.1

PERCENTAGE DISTRIBUTION OF THE SAMPLE BY AREA, COURSE, AND TRAINING STATUS

| Area and course | No. | Utilized retraining | Completed but did not use retraining | Withdrew for employment | Withdrew without employment | Refused training for employment | Refused without employment |
|---|---|---|---|---|---|---|---|
| Bridgeport machine | 110 | 44.5% | 22.7% | 9.1% | 5.5% | 10.0% | 8.2% |
| Ansonia machine | 59 | 28.8 | 15.3 | 6.8 | 15.3 | 18.6 | 15.3 |
| New London pipefitter | 33 | 54.5 | 0.0 | 3.0 | 12.1 | 21.2 | 9.1 |
| Norwich pipefitter | 31 | 41.9 | 3.2 | 9.7 | 6.4 | 32.3 | 6.4 |
| New London shipfitter | 49 | 61.2 | 0.0 | 2.0 | 10.2 | 22.4 | 4.1 |
| Norwich shipfitter | 30 | 60.0 | 3.3 | 0.0 | 3.3 | 20.0 | 13.3 |
| Ansonia sewing | 61 | 11.5 | 23.0 | 0.0 | 3.3 | 19.7 | 42.6 |
| Total | 373 | 40.8 | 13.4 | 5.1 | 7.8 | 18.2 | 14.7 |

## TABLE A.2

### PERCENTAGE DISTRIBUTION OF MEN IN THE SAMPLE BY AREA, COURSE, AND TRAINING STATUS

| Area and course | No. | Utilized retraining | Completed but did not use retraining | Withdrew for employment | Withdrew without employment | Refused training for employment | Refused without employment | Total |
|---|---|---|---|---|---|---|---|---|
| *Area* | | | | | | | | |
| Bridgeport | 110 | 33.8% | 69.4% | 52.6% | 22.2% | 19.6% | 31.0% | 35.3% |
| Ansonia | 59 | 11.7 | 25.0 | 21.4 | 33.3 | 19.6 | 31.0 | 18.9 |
| New London | 82 | 33.1 | 0.0 | 10.5 | 33.3 | 32.1 | 17.2 | 26.3 |
| Norwich | 61 | 21.4 | 5.6 | 15.8 | 11.1 | 28.6 | 20.7 | 19.5 |
| Total[a] | 312 | 100.0 | 100.0 | 100.0 | 100.0 | 100.0 | 100.0 | 100.0 |
| *Course* | | | | | | | | |
| Machine | 169 | 45.5 | 94.4 | 73.7 | 55.6 | 39.3 | 62.1 | 54.2 |
| Shipfitter | 79 | 33.1 | 2.8 | 5.3 | 22.2 | 30.4 | 17.2 | 25.3 |
| Pipefitter | 64 | 21.4 | 2.8 | 21.1 | 22.2 | 30.4 | 20.7 | 20.5 |
| Total[a] | 312 | 100.0 | 100.0 | 100.0 | 100.0 | 100.0 | 100.0 | 100.0 |

[a] Totals have been rounded.

c. The first four classes in shipfitting for workers from New London and Norwich, held from September 6, 1961, to January 11, 1962.

d. The first three classes in pipefitting for workers from New London and Norwich, held from November 13, 1961, to January 12, 1962.

e. The two classes in power sewing machine operation for women from Ansonia, held from January 3 to March 16, 1962.

The distribution of the sample by area and course is shown in Tables A.1 and A.2.

# Appendix B

## The Regression Models

Many factors were found to be correlated with the training status of the men in the sample. Therefore, simple comparisons of average wage incomes, unemployment, and government unemployment benefits received for the workers in each training status would not properly indicate the effects of retraining. The influence of these characteristic differences among the different groups of workers would be included along with the actual effects of retraining. Multiple regression techniques using binary variables, however, permit the variables which are correlated with retraining to be taken into account, so that the actual effects of retraining can be determined. Such techniques were therefore used in this study.

Each interview did not yield complete information on every variable. Consequently, four subsamples of the total male sample were used. The regression models include the subsample which contained the greatest number of observations for which all information was available on each variable. Following is a list of the dependent and independent variables used in each of the regression models:

### REGRESSION MODEL ONE—285 OBSERVATIONS

*Dependent Variables:* Computed average weekly income from end of training to date of interview,[1] unemployment as a percentage of time in the labor force from the end of training to the date of interview, and government unemployment benefits received from the end of retraining to the date of the interview.

*Independent Variables:* Course, area, age, marital status, number of dependents including self, education, number of weeks from the end of training to the interview, and training status. The binary categories for the independent

---

1. Weekly income was computed on the basis of the average number of hours worked times the different wage rates for each week in the labor force. No allowance was made for days lost occasionally due to illness or strikes. Time unemployed due to nature of the job, such as launchings at the submarine works or seasonal layoffs in construction, was not included in the number of hours worked.

variables were: less than 20 years, 20–24 years, 25–34 years, and over 34 years of age; less than 10 years' education completed, 10 or 11 years completed, and 12 or more years completed; and less than 60, 60–70, and more than 70 weeks from the end of training to the interview. These personal variables were contemporary with the retraining.

### REGRESSION MODEL TWO—234 OBSERVATIONS[2]

*Dependent Variables:* Quarterly wages for the four quarters from the second quarter of 1962 through the first quarter of 1963 (as reported to the Connecticut State Labor Department Unemployment Insurance Division).

*Independent Variables:* All independent variables in Regression Model One.

### REGRESSION MODEL THREE—169 OBSERVATIONS

*Dependent Variables:* All dependent variables listed in Regression Models One and Two.

*Independent Variables:* All independent variables listed in Regression Models One and Two; plus the number of nonmilitary moves from 1951 to 1961; Connecticut State Employment Service labor force attachment classification in August, 1962; race; training lasting three months or more prior to retraining; employment status at the time of the aptitude test; and, for the twelve-month period preceding the beginning of training, unemployment, governmental unemployment benefits received, income earned, and labor force participation.

The binary categories, in addition to those mentioned in Regression Model One, were: C.S.E.S. Classification as entrant or nonentrant; unemployed, employed, not in the labor force at the time of the aptitude test; less than five weeks, more than five weeks but less than six months, and six months or more, unemployed; nothing, $1–$500, and over $500 received as unemployment benefits; less than $1,000, $1,000–$3,000, and more than $3,000 earned income; and four quarters or less than four quarters in the labor force.

### REGRESSION MODEL FOUR—169 OBSERVATIONS

*Dependent Variables:* All dependent variables listed in Regression Models One and Two.

*Independent Variables:* All independent variables listed in Regression Models One and Two.

(This regression model was constructed to allow a comparison to be made to determine how much of the change in the regression coefficients between the first two regression models and the third regression model was due to the addition of the new independent variables, and how much of the difference was due to the change in the size of the sample.)

2. The sample was reduced in size because complete wage records were not available on all workers. Also, if the worker had left the labor force for an extended period because of a service commitment or in order to return to school, his records were not included.

IV

## HERBERT A. CHESLER

■

# THE RETRAINING DECISION IN MASSACHUSETTS:

# THEORY AND PRACTICE

This exploratory study of worker response to the opportunity for participation in the retraining programs, established by state governments under the aegis of the Area Redevelopment Act of 1961, examines the relationship that exists between an individual's decision for or against
training and his selected personal characteristics and work history experiences. The principal concern is with the decisions of workers to
accept or reject given retraining offers.*

The data stem from personal interviews with residents of the New
Bedford and Fall River redevelopment areas—two major labor market
areas in southeastern Massachusetts with substantial and persistent problems of labor surplus. The two courses under investigation were the first
to be conducted within the Commonwealth of Massachusetts. They began in January, 1962, and were completed during the months of May and
June of the same year.

### THE INSTITUTIONAL SETTING

Each local office of the Commonwealth's Division of Employment Security
was responsible for recruiting, processing, and selecting the trainees. In

* Herbert A. Chesler is currently (1967) at the University of Pittsburgh. This study is
taken from the author's doctoral dissertation, "Worker Retraining Under the Area
Redevelopment Act: A Massachusetts Study," submitted to the Department of
Economics and Social Science at the Massachusetts Institute of Technology on
August 21, 1963. The author acknowledges a debt of gratitude to Professor Robert
Evans, Jr., his thesis supervisor, for assistance and encouragement.

accordance with this grant of autonomy, the New Bedford and the Fall River Employment Service Offices developed a set of preconditions for training-course eligibility to guide them in screening applicants. The purpose of the criteria was to assure that the men chosen would be both qualified for training and suitable for placement.[1]

Each office placed a very high premium upon the individual's desire to participate in the training program, and their interviews were directed toward ascertaining each person's interest and willingness to commit himself to the program from beginning to completion. Individuals who voluntarily sought information about the course, or who received an interview following the receipt of a call-in request, were not informed about the availability of subsidy payments during the initial interview. Only after they had satisfied the interest-criterion were they told about the system of benefit payments. This practice was applied consistently throughout the screening stages. Each office sought to turn the subsidy into an incentive payment for participation in the training course; each was determined to prevent abuse of the ARA opportunity on the part of persons who might have responded solely to collect the subsidy. Each was attempting to assure itself of the selection of self-motivated individuals. Furthermore, it should be noted that the mailed or telephoned call-in requests issued by each local Employment Service Office did not specify the purpose for which the individual was being asked to come to the office.

To the men who asked about post-training employment arrangements, the offices neither made direct promises about the availability of specific jobs nor mentioned anything about wages that the men might expect to receive when entering the labor market with their newly acquired training skills. However, each office did acknowledge a responsibility to exert efforts on behalf of the men who successfully completed the courses.

The aptitude tests enabled the local offices to separate the interested individuals into a group of qualified and a group of nonqualified persons, and each office allowed every eligible individual to take the examination in order to establish his qualifications for training. Those who agreed to sit for the aptitude test were classified as "interested in training" (hereafter, "IT") and those who were eligible but refused to take the test were considered as "not interested in training" (hereafter, "NIT").

The individual's decision, it is suggested, is made within an environmental complex composed of personal elements and institutional forces. The latter component, encompassing the elements of course design and administrative procedures, gives rise to a specific and unique retraining opportunity. More succinctly, the question before the individual is seldom merely a simple interrogative: "Are you willing to attend an occupational retraining program?"

The training opportunity presented to the men in New Bedford, phrased to describe the complex question with which the respondent was compelled to grapple, was essentially: "Are you interested in learning to become a machine operator by participating in a sixteen-week training course, without the guarantee that a job will be waiting for you upon the successful completion of the program?" The question posed for the Fall River men was similar but even more complex: "Are you interested in attending a twenty-week training course for machinists, knowing that prospects for utilizing this knowledge in gainful employment are negligible unless you are prepared to accept a job (or look for a job) that may be located at least twenty miles from the city?"

## THE DECISION RULE

The decision to accept or reject the training course offer may be regarded as a function of cost and net discounted value of the future income stream attributable to the training knowledge. Symbolically, this is described by the following equation, where $M$ represents the present discounted value of the future income stream from the start of training ($t = 0$) to the time of retirement from the labor force ($T$):

$$M = \sum_{t=0}^{T} P_t(Y_t^R - Y_t)\left(\frac{1}{(1 + r)^t}\right) - C_{t_0},$$

Where $Y^R$ represents income from work which is derived from the acquisition of the training course skill; $Y$ is the income from work performed by the individual, but not related to the knowledge gained from ARA training; $r$ is the individual's internal rate of discount. The symbol $P$ represents the probability of the individual's being capable of actually working in any given year or period of time, $t$; $C$ denotes the costs of training.[2]

On the assumption that persons confronted with the retraining offer, or giving it consideration, are capable of making and do actually make a rational economic calculation of the benefits to be derived from retraining, it follows that (1) if the value of $M$ is greater than zero, the rational economic decision is to undertake training; (2) if $M$ is negative, retraining is not a rational choice, and (3) should $M$ take the value of zero, the individual will be on the margin—he will be indifferent to the retraining opportunity.

This rule assumes a permanent job change and commitment to the new skill following completion of the course. However, retraining of persons with previous labor force experience will enlarge the set of opportunities for which they may qualify and, therefore, will possibly give rise to situations in which the retrained worker may change jobs (often and easily, perhaps) in response to wage differentials or personal preferences. When this prospect is perceived by the decision-maker, the appropriate evaluation of $M$ is determined by maximizing the future revenue stream among the set of added opportunities.

## HYPOTHESES AND FINDINGS

The preceding shows the decision for or against the retraining offer to be both a function of monetary and nonmonetary motives. The framework yields an understanding of the essential elements involved in the decision-making process, and provides a means for postulating about the relationship that exists between selected personal and economic variables of an individual and his decision.

The variables deemed to play an active role in the making of the decision were age, education, marital status, attitude toward governmental programs and subsidies, employment status at the moment of decision, and employment and unemployment experiences over a relatively recent period of time prior to the receipt of the retraining offer.

### AGE

The *a priori* expectation concerning the individual's age and his decision was similar to the generally established finding of an inverse relationship between age and labor market mobility.[3] Thus it was hypothesized that a willingness or interest in training would decline as the decision-maker's age increased. In terms of the data which were collected, it was anticipated that, given a group of workers confronted with the offer to be retrained, the younger members would emerge as the ones most likely to accept the opportunity to participate in the program.

Table IV.1 shows the age distribution. The hypothesis to be tested was that the mean age of both the New Bedford and Fall River IT groups was less than the average age of the individuals who were not interested in the retraining opportunity presented them by the local Employment Service office. The test selected for this purpose was the t-ratio based on "Students" distribution, and the null hypothesis (in each instance) was that the area's IT and NIT mean ages were equal at the .05 level of significance.

As computed from the unit observation, the mean age for each group was the following: 32.10 years for the New Bedford IT's and 35.17 years for the NIT's; 27.06 years for the Fall River IT's and 31.47 years of age for those who were not interested in the training course.[4]

The $t$ values were 1.67 and 1.90 for the New Bedford and Fall River areas, respectively. These values exceed the critical level of $t$ for a single-

TABLE IV.1

AGE DISTRIBUTION OF RESPONDENTS BY GROUP AND AREA

| Age group[a] | New Bedford | | Fall River | |
|---|---|---|---|---|
| | IT | NIT | IT | NIT |
| Under 20 years | 0 | 0 | 8 | 0 |
| 20 to 34 years | 107 | 13 | 18 | 13 |
| 35 to 44 years | 45 | 5 | 7 | 5 |
| 45 and over | 19 | 6 | 1 | 1 |
| Total | 171 | 24 | 34 | 19 |

[a] Age related to the highest birthday attained by the respondent at the completion of the training period (or which would have been attained by those not enrolled in the course). Determined from dates of birth and the date for scheduled completion of the program into which the respondent would have been assigned.

tailed test at the .05 level, and the null hypothesis is rejected. Specifically, the mean age of the persons interested in training is significantly lower than the mean age of the NIT's in the two labor markets.

In explanation of this predicted outcome, it seems reasonable to suggest that justification of the hypothesis is rooted in the propositions that (1) the number of years for concern with future income streams is smaller for the older worker than for the relatively young; (2) the opportunity costs incurred by the older worker exceed those incurred by the younger individual who participates in the retraining program; and (3) the probability of obtaining employment with the newly acquired training skill, this being the sole differentiating quality of the job applicant, is lower for the older worker than for the younger competitor; and, similarly, the probability of being advanced by progression through the levels of the new trade is apt to be lower for him than for the younger worker. Also, one must not overlook the distinct possibility that the older individual is likely to reject the opportunity to change his occupation for reasons associated with socio-psychological dimensions of his position and personality. In addition to inertia, it appears reasonable to propose that the older worker will refuse retraining more readily than his younger counterpart because of the higher risk coefficient he is apt to use in weighting the uncertainties of the retraining experiment. Furthermore, relatively older persons are expected to place a greater value upon present income and, consequently, to be more reluctant to forego income earning prospects in exchange for an uncertain, estimated income stream associated with the acquisition of the retraining skill.[5]

Without specifying a critical age that separates or distinguishes a younger worker from an older worker, it should be noted that the hypothesis does not preclude older workers from a display of interest or willingness to take retraining. For example, if retraining is perceived as a means of improving or upgrading their level of skill to qualify for promotions, for supervisory positions, or for bidding on job assignments in a period of layoff from employment within their companies, persons described as "older workers" may be expected to decide in favor of the retraining offer. Present findings do suggest, however, that, given any group of older workers, the youngest among them will emerge as the individuals with an interest in retraining.

### EDUCATION

Parnes' survey of the literature suggests (only inconclusively) that mobility is somewhat greater among persons with the relatively higher levels of educational attainment.[6] In the context of decision-making for retraining, however, the opposite conclusion appears as the more reasonable expectation. That is, above the minimum level of education necessary for effective training, the expectation is that educational attainment and the decision to take retraining are inversely related.

It is reasonable to contend that educational attainment and ability to learn how to perform a given task with a satisfactory level of competence are generally highly correlated. In fact, it may be safe to suggest that the former is cause and the latter is effect, while the ultimate consequence is higher income-earning capacity. In the first place, a more educated person may qualify sooner for a position at a higher skill level than the less educated, and secondly, he may experience less difficulty in obtaining employment (especially when ability is equal) than the less educated job seeker who competes with him at the personnel office.

The advantage of being able to obtain alternative employment in the immediate short run, and the longer-run advantages of being able to qualify for more types of jobs than the less educated individual, together with the higher income potential, explain the weak associative finding of the mobility studies. In terms of the retraining decision-making rule, however, the sum of the discounted value of $P_t Y_t^R + (1 - P_t)Y_t - Y_t$ is likely to be zero or close to zero (if not negative) for the relatively more educated decision-maker. Also, perception of a need to participate in an occupational retraining program is probably going to be less for the more educated person.

The data on educational attainment levels of the respondents appear in Table IV.2. An examination of the distribution reveals disparity between areas in the relationship between education and willingness to take training. In New Bedford, willingness declines as educational level increases; the opposite tendency is suggested by the Fall River data.

TABLE IV.2

HIGHEST LEVEL OF EDUCATIONAL ATTAINMENT, BY GROUP AND AREA

| Grade level[a] | New Bedford | | | | Fall River | | | |
| | IT | | NIT | | IT | | NIT | |
| | No. | % | No. | % | No. | % | No. | % |
|---|---|---|---|---|---|---|---|---|
| Below 8 | 36 | 21.05 | 5 | 20.83 | 0 | 0.0 | 1 | 5.26 |
| 8 | 34 | 19.88 | 1 | 4.17 | 0 | 0.0 | 2 | 10.53 |
| 9–11 | 63 | 36.84 | 7 | 29.17 | 11 | 32.35 | 9 | 47.37 |
| 12 | 33 | 19.30 | 9 | 37.50 | 22 | 64.71 | 6 | 31.58 |
| Over 12 | 5 | 2.92 | 2 | 8.33 | 1 | 2.94 | 1 | 5.26 |
| Total | 171 | 100.00 | 24 | 100.00 | 34 | 100.00 | 19 | 100.00 |

[a] Grade levels represent the last grade of formal schooling completed by the respondent plus any years of grade equivalents he may have acquired through extra-school programs such as extension, correspondence, or military service courses in education. A 12th grade level, therefore, does not necessarily imply a regular high-school diploma.

The evidence, therefore, does not support the *a priori* expectation of an inverse relationship between educational level and willingness or interest in training. In fact, a chi-square test of association performed by combining the data from the two areas reveals that the two variables are independent of each other at the .05 level of significance.

In explanation of the divergent finding and in the absence of a dependent relationship between the two variables, it is suggested that the absolute level of educational attainment is not a major influence on the decision for or against the retraining opportunity. However, additional data that were collected indicate that importance ought to be attached to the individual's perception of the adequacy of his education and the relationship it bears to his experience in the labor market.

First, from an examination of the pattern of responses obtained to the question, "Has not being a high-school graduate made any difference to you?", it is found that among the "yes" responses the New Bedford IT's constitute 94.3 per cent of the total. The data are shown in Table IV.3, where a "yes" answer reveals an individual's belief that his employment situation would have been better had he possessed the equivalent of a high-school education. Answers of this type were commonly illustrated by experiences that showed that the men strongly believed they were refused employment, and even denied application forms, because of their lack of a high-school diploma.

The result of a chi-square test, conducted for the New Bedford data, supports the suggestion that perception of a gap in educational qualifications may create a strong need for training. In Fall River, on the other

TABLE IV.3

RESPONDENTS' IMPRESSION OF WHETHER OR NOT THE LACK
OF A 12TH GRADE EDUCATION ADVERSELY AFFECTED THEIR
SEARCH TO OBTAIN EMPLOYMENT, BY GROUP AND AREA

|  | New Bedford | | Fall River | |
|---|---|---|---|---|
| Response | IT | NIT | IT | NIT |
| Yes | 83 | 5 | 2 | 5 |
| No | 42 | 10 | 6 | 7 |
| Total | 125 | 15 | 8 | 12 |

hand, there was no association between answers to the question and
willingness or lack of willingness to accept the offer of retraining. This is
not unexpected, however. The relatively higher educational level of the
Fall River respondents—a function of the preconditions for training
course eligibility established by the local office—is sufficient to suggest
they are persons who usually do not encounter employer refusals and
hiring frustrations for reasons attributable to inadequate education.

A similar conclusion, this time with respect to self-perceived deficiency
in marketable skills, is suggested by the data in Table IV.4, which presents

TABLE IV.4

EXPERIENCES OF JOB REFUSALS ATTRIBUTABLE
TO RESPONDENTS' INADEQUATE VOCATIONAL
PREPARATION PRIOR TO THE START OF
TRAINING COURSE, BY GROUP AND AREA

|  | New Bedford | | Fall River | |
|---|---|---|---|---|
| Response | IT | NIT | IT | NIT |
| Yes | 34 | 1 | 5 | 0 |
| No | 132 | 23 | 29 | 19 |
| Total | 166 | 24 | 34 | 19 |

the responses to the following question: "Were you ever refused a job,
for which you applied and knew the job was available, because the employer claimed you did not have the 'right' skills, training, or experience
to do the work?" An examination of the response pattern shows a greater
proportion of IT's to have acknowledged a refusal of employment because
of skill-related shortcomings than was the experience of the New Bedford
and the Fall River NIT's.

A chi-square test of association confirms the suspected relationship between perceived skill-deficiencies and willingness to take training.[7] An

important conclusion suggested by this finding, one that obtains in Fall River as well as in New Bedford, is that the relatively more educated workers will respond favorably to the opportunity for participation in a retraining course with almost the same probability as that for the less educated persons.

In the first instance, it may be said that the relatively more educated workers are the ones with a greater awareness (not need) of the advantages to be obtained from increasing their stock of education and adding or acquiring new training in a specific skill. Secondly, in the case of the less educated workers, the emphasis which employers place upon training and education (when two job seekers are otherwise similar) stimulates an individual's perception of the need to secure an improvement in his job qualifications.

### MARITAL STATUS

Studies investigating the relationship between mobility of workers and marital or family status show the two to be only slightly associated, but Parnes' examination of the evidence suggests married men are less mobile than single men.[8] This is reasonable on *a priori* grounds, for the obligations which the society imposes upon male heads of households may increase a decision-maker's opportunity costs associated with probable short-term decline in earnings and, thus, reduce his propensity to experiment with the uncertainties of change. One might, therefore, expect that married men would be less willing to participate in the training program than would the single men.

Among households which include a working wife, on the other hand, the declining marginal utility of money-income argument reduces the opportunity cost element of the decision-making individual. Thus, if one allows for some amount of social pressure (or direct pressure originating with the spouse) on the unemployed or underemployed husband of a working wife in a depressed economic community, the following emerges as a reasonable hypothesis: married men in households with a working wife are more willing to participate in training courses of the ARA type than are married men who are the sole wage earners in a household. The value which the family unit would attach to small and/or irregular increments to present income, in other words, is considered to be less than what it would be if the wife were not contributing to the consumption power of the spending unit.

The marital status of the decision-makers when they received the offer is presented in Table IV.5. An examination of the data reveals a strikingly similar distribution: 82.7 per cent of the married respondents and 82.9 per cent of the single were willing to enter the programs; 71.8 per cent of the IT respondents were married and 72.1 per cent of the

TABLE IV.5

MARITAL STATUS OF RESPONDENTS
BY GROUP

| Status | IT | NIT |
|--------|-----|-----|
| Single | 58 | 12 |
| Married | 148 | 31 |
| Total | 206 | 43 |

NIT's were married. This evidence suggests that both married and non-married persons are equally likely to enter training, for there is no relationship between the variables. The *a priori* expectations are not substantiated by the findings.

The data contained in Table IV.6 show that, contrary to the hypothesis

TABLE IV.6

LABOR FORCE STATUS OF MARRIED
RESPONDENTS' WIVES DURING 1961,
BY GROUP

| Status | IT | NIT |
|--------|-----|-----|
| Working | 80 | 17 |
| Nonworking | 68 | 14 |
| Total | 148 | 31 |

above, a working wife has, in fact, little or no effect upon the individual's decision: 82.5 per cent of the households with working wives are represented in the IT group, while 82.9 per cent of the NIT group are heads of a household with a working spouse. Similarly, among the men who decided in favor of training, the percentage with working wives was 54.1; while the figure for the men opposed to the retraining opportunity was 54.8 per cent.

The absence of a relationship between marital status and the decision for or against retraining is not really surprising. The influence of a wife is subtle, and an argument based upon a wife's participation in the labor force is contingent upon the nature of a highly private relationship between two persons whose union, in the eyes of an economist, gives rise to an economic unit. However, in the matter of the decision to accept or reject the opportunity for participation in a retraining program, it is quite possible that the focus ought to be largely upon the individual decision-maker and his perception of his relationship to the external realities of the labor market.

In other words, one should probably concede that marital status or the presence of a working spouse within the household unit is equally likely to exert a positive or a negative influence upon the decision for or against retraining. The ultimate decision, it is here suggested, is a personal one, made in response to the pressures and the exigencies of the individual's position in the labor market. The state of marriage, like the absolute level of educational attainment, is not an ultimate determinant of a man's willingness or unwillingness to take training.

### ATTITUDE TOWARD GOVERNMENT

It was suspected that individuals who rejected the retraining offer might have done so because of an inherent dislike of government-sponsored programs and subsidies. To test this assumption, the unwilling decision-makers were asked:

(1) Do you think that the state or federal government should provide retraining courses for people who are out of work?

(2) Do you think that the government should provide a person with money for living expenses while he is being retrained?

Twenty-four of the New Bedford men and 18 from Fall River (100 and 95 per cent, respectively) said "yes" to the first question. Twenty-one from New Bedford and 16 from Fall River (88 and 82 per cent, respectively) said "yes" to the question dealing with government subsidies during retraining. Only 3 men—2 from New Bedford and 1 from Fall River— were unequivocally opposed to government subsidies; one person from each area was uncertain about the role he believed the government should assume in subsidizing a trainee. One must therefore conclude that an unwillingness to take training is not the result of a negative attitude toward government activity and assistance.

### EMPLOYMENT STATUS

Table IV.7 shows the status of the respondents at the moment of their decision, and makes clear that there is no relationship between status

TABLE IV.7

EMPLOYMENT STATUS AT MOMENT OF DECISION-MAKING
BY AREA AND GROUP

| Status | New Bedford | | Fall River | |
|---|---|---|---|---|
| | IT | NIT | IT | NIT |
| Unemployed | 139 | 19 | 30 | 17 |
| Underemployed | 14 | 4 | 1 | 0 |
| Employed | 18 | 1 | 3 | 2 |
| Total | 171 | 24 | 34 | 19 |

and the choice made. The percentage distributions, by status class and interest group, are almost identical within each area. Furthermore, the evidence does not even permit one to infer that the unemployed individuals were more likely to want to take training than the employed.

This finding is to be qualified. It implies only that there is apt to be no difference in decisions reached by individuals who are unemployed or marginally employed (real or perceived); nothing conclusive may be said about the decision that would be made by the individual whose position with an employer is stable and secure. The data reveal that men who are eligible, under statute, will leave their jobs to enroll in the training courses.

The theoretical framework permits one to postulate that the employed individual may respond to the offer of retraining because of the expectation that his discounted income stream from a training-related job will exceed the earnings he can expect to make on his present job or in any future job he may acquire. He may also accept the training offer because of a taste for the family of training-related jobs, even if the anticipated difference in comparative income streams is zero or slightly negative. On an *a priori* basis, however, one must not forget that this does not apply without qualification to persons with security of employment and relatively high skill levels. These persons are in a different class of workers from the one the training courses are designed to assist.

The present finding, therefore, emphasizes that there does exist a pool of individuals in the depressed economic communities who, although employed, are as willing to take training as the unemployed. Also, it shows that the unemployed are as likely to accept the offer as they are to reject it.

### Duration of Unemployment

*A priori* expectations suggested that the willingness to take training might be influenced by the decision-makers' most recent period of unemployment—i.e., the longer the duration of unemployment (from the last job to the moment of decision), the greater the likelihood that the individuals would accept the retraining offer.

This hypothesis is not supported by the data of Table IV.8, which shows the number of weeks that the respondents were unemployed from full-time work. An examination of the data reveals no association between willingness and extent of current unemployment. This is underscored by the inconclusive trends that emerge from a comparison between areas. For example, among the respondents with less than five weeks of unemployment, the New Bedford data reveal 92.86 per cent of the men to have been willing to accept training, whereas only 27.27 per cent of the

TABLE IV.8

Duration of Unemployment from Full-Time Work,[a]
by Group and Area[b]

| Weeks[c] | New Bedford | | | | Fall River | | | |
| | IT | | NIT | | IT | | NIT | |
| | No. | % | No. | % | No. | % | No. | % |
| --- | --- | --- | --- | --- | --- | --- | --- | --- |
| <1 | 24 | 14.46 | 2 | 8.70 | 1 | 2.94 | 3 | 15.79 |
| 1 to under 5 | 15 | 9.04 | 1 | 4.35 | 2 | 5.88 | 5 | 26.32 |
| 5 to under 15 | 62 | 37.35 | 13 | 56.52 | 19 | 55.88 | 2 | 10.53 |
| 15 to under 27 | 37 | 22.29 | 5 | 21.74 | 6 | 17.65 | 7 | 36.84 |
| 27–52 | 23 | 13.86 | 1 | 4.35 | 3 | 8.82 | 2 | 10.53 |
| Over 52 | 5 | 3.01 | 1 | 4.35 | 3 | 8.82 | 0 | —— |
| Total | 166 | 100.00 | 23 | 100.00 | 34 | 100.00 | 19 | 100.00 |

[a] In computing the number of weeks of unemployment no deductions were made for any work performed on a part-time basis. Counting begins with the date of termination from full-time job to time of decision. The full-time job refers to the most recent job at which the individual worked at least one week, on a full-time basis, prior to the retraining offer.

[b] New Bedford data for the IT group are carried to the date of each man's aptitude test. The data for the NIT group are carried to the date of each man's interview with the Employment Service. The two terminal dates are equivalent, for tests were administered on the same day as the interview or no more than 2 days afterward. Fall River data, for both IT and NIT groups, are carried through to the date of the Employment Service interview.

[c] Three days of continuous unemployment from full-time work (on a Monday through Friday week) are counted as a complete week of unemployment; less than three days are entered as less than one week of unemployment.

Fall River respondents with less than five weeks of unemployment were willing.

In fact, the proportion of men willing to take training remains relatively constant as the length of unemployment increases from less than one week to more than one full year among the New Bedford respondents. Furthermore, going from interval through interval, the Fall River data show a substantial increase in willingness in the five to less than fifteen class (90.48 per cent), followed by a decline in the higher classes.[9]

This finding (or lack of it) is not too surprising. The evidence seems to indicate that it makes little difference whether an individual is unemployed for a brief period, a long period, or a very long time as concerns his decision to take or reject the training program. That long-term unemployed are no more likely to take the courses than are the short-term unemployed in a depressed labor market is understandable, however, since the decision rule is essentially a function of differences in the individual probabilities associated with prospects of alternative employment opportunities. There is no reason to believe that this should be different solely on the basis of the most immediate period of an individual's unemployment prior to the moment of his decision.

The emerging concept which links an individual's decision to his experiences in the labor market, and which assumes relevance in the analysis, is the individual's elasticity of expectations. This recognizes the person's past earnings and employment experiences and relates them to the prospects of obtaining post-training employment or any alternative types of employment that he might obtain if he does not attend the training course. In other words, it is assumed that events of the most recent past are relevant in shaping the individual's perspective of the future. Thus, it appears reasonable to expect the individual to decide in favor of training more readily when the trend of his unemployment has been increasing.

If it is assumed that there exists a minimum level of unemployment which is regarded as tolerable by an individual, any departure from this level is likely to increase his propensity to change. It seems likely that an individual will not perceive a need to effect a change in his labor market situation if the proportion of time spent in involuntary idleness levels off at or slightly below this minimum of acceptability. However, when it exceeds the level of toleration and/or is on the increase, an elasticity of expectations equal to unity or greater may generate the need and a willingness to experiment with change.

## Unemployment, 1959–1961

The following emerges as a reasonable hypothesis, given the preceding discussion: individuals with an absolutely greater amount of unemployment over a sustained period of time will probably view the retraining opportunity with favor; should their unemployment be increasing, they will evince a willingness to accept the retraining offer. Such people are apt to be relatively pessimistic about the future. The value which they may place on present income may be high, but their relatively lower expectations of securing a job or reducing the time spent in involuntary idleness—in the absence of participation in the retraining program—will undoubtedly cast an aura of profitability about the training course and its promises for employment and earnings in the future.

The year 1961 is designated the "decision-making" year, for it is the year which immediately precedes the introduction of ARA training in the New Bedford and Fall River communities. The two-year period, 1959–60, is designated as the "base" year against which the unemployment experiences of 1961 are compared.[10]

TABLE IV.9

Weeks of Unemployment from Full-Time Work during 1959–60 and 1961 Periods,[a] by Group and Area[b]

| | New Bedford | | | | Fall River | | | |
| | IT | | NIT | | IT | | NIT | |
| Weeks | Base | 1961 | Base | 1961 | Base | 1961 | Base | 1961 |
|---|---|---|---|---|---|---|---|---|
| <5 | 45 | 23 | 9 | 5 | 8 | 2 | 2 | 2 |
| 5–15 | 52 | 38 | 2 | 8 | 6 | 6 | 6 | 3 |
| 16–26 | 26 | 38 | 6 | 2 | 2 | 4 | 4 | 6 |
| 27–37 | 3 | 16 | 0 | 1 | 2 | 2 | 0 | 0 |
| 38–52 | 0 | 11 | 0 | 1 | 0 | 4 | 0 | 1 |
| Total | 126 | 126 | 17 | 17 | 18 | 18 | 12 | 12 |

[a] Base period data represent the average annual weeks of unemployment in the two-year period 1959–60.

[b] The table is limited to respondents who had three complete years of potentially productive labor force availability for full-time work in the 1959–61 period.

Table IV.9 shows the unemployment characteristics of the respondents in the two relevant periods. The average number of weeks spent in unemployment from full-time work by the groups, as derived from the unit observations, in the decision-making year was as follows:

1961

New Bedford

IT = 17.99 weeks
NIT = 11.59 weeks

Fall River

IT = 22.83 weeks
NIT = 16.00 weeks

An interpretation of these numbers reveals that (on the basis of a fifty-two-week year), the New Bedford IT's were unemployed on the average of 34.6 per cent of the year and the NIT's spent 22.3 per cent of their potentially productive labor force time in unemployment during 1961. The Fall River IT's were out of full-time work for 43.9 per cent of the year, and the NIT's were idle only 30.8 per cent of the time during the year.

The base period figures on weeks of unemployment from full-time work were the following:

1959–60

New Bedford

IT = 9.62 weeks
NIT = 8.50 weeks

Fall River

IT = 11.73 weeks
NIT = 9.84 weeks

A comparison of the data shows 1961 to be a relatively bad year for members of all groups. The increase in unemployment was substantially greater for the two IT groups. The New Bedford IT unemployment increased 87 per cent and the Fall River IT group experienced an increase of 95 per cent. The increase in 1961 unemployment relative to the base period for the NIT groups, on the other hand, was only 36 per cent in the New Bedford area and 63 per cent in Fall River.

The groups' experiences in the base period are essentially similar, and the intragroup difference in the mean weeks of unemployment is not statistically significant. However, the difference in the mean weeks of unemployment for 1961 is significant. That is, the finding of an average of 6.4 weeks of greater unemployment for the IT's of New Bedford as compared with the NIT's was a meaningful difference at the .05 level of significance; in Fall River, on the other hand, the results of the single-tailed t-test established the 6.8 week difference in average unemployment between the area's IT's and NIT's as meaningful in the .10–.05 range of significance.

The absolute and the relative increases in unemployment among the two IT groups, as compared with the experiences of the NIT's, suggests that 1961 was an atypical year for the men who decided in favor of the retraining course. The IT's were more adversely affected by the general economic recession of 1961 than were the NIT groups.

This supports the hypothesized relationship between the decision to take training and an increasing trend (or an abrupt change in the direction of severity) in the amount of involuntary unemployment, and makes it reasonable to contend that the IT's expectations of future employment prospects must have been more pessimistic than those of the men who refused the offer of retraining. More strongly, the men who were interested in training and willing to participate in the programs seemingly viewed the courses as the means by which they might secure an improvement in their labor market situation. It seems that a relatively long exposure to an undesired state is more likely to stimulate an interest in retraining than will obtain when the decision-maker experiences a constant, but short-term and possibly reversible, state of unpleasantness.

## CONCLUSION

The results of the New Bedford and Fall River investigations permit one to say that an individual's decision to undergo retraining expresses a willingness both to forego present income opportunities in return for a chance to enhance his future employment and earnings, and to assume the risks of uncertainty and change.

Every individual will not respond to the same stimulus in the same way, but the findings suggest that a pressure for change will be translated into effective action—in this case, retraining—when the individual perceives that the "unsatisfactory" or distasteful conditions are aggravated beyond the limits of toleration.

Employment Service specification of the retraining opportunity is one thing, but the individual's perception of the nature of the opportunity is another major factor which appears to influence the decision to take or reject the training offer. More emphatically, it is reasonable to expect the decision to be based on what he believes or is told the course *will* do for him more than on what the course *should* do for him. Given the measure of uncertainty surrounding the New Bedford and Fall River courses, it is therefore proposed that those who refused the retraining offer did so for one or more of the following reasons: (1) lack of interest (taste) for the particular skill; (2) the belief that earnings and employment opportunities would be less or no greater than they would be without the skills acquired through participation in the program; (3) a relatively high aversion for uncertainty; (4) a conviction that mastering the content of the course would be difficult; and (5) the failure to perceive a real need for effecting any change in one's general labor market situation.

It is to be expected that persons interested in one type of course might not be interested in another type and, similarly, that the qualifications for the successful completion of one course would differ from the qualifications essential for the other. In the context of a single-skilled, governmentally subsidized retraining course, the taste for training is an interest in learning and working in a specific job. Sometimes the strictures of the given program may embrace a particular employer or group of employers within the labor market area and the taste concept ought to be extended to include the place(s) of employment as well as the type of work. A positive value of $M$, in the decision-making rule, provides the economic motivation for training; but if the individual is to make himself available for consideration as a candidate for training, he must possess a minimum of taste for what he is about to do. Without this, he seldom has any alternative but to reject the given offer. He may hold himself available for different programs, but the probability of overcoming his reluctance to the given opportunity might be expected to increase as the scope of the course's preparation (in terms of a family of related jobs) is extended.

The type of course and the criteria established for the determination of eligibility limit the size of the pool that may qualify to benefit from the government retraining programs in a given labor market. However, the local Employment Service Office is in a position to influence the number of applicants for retraining. An explanation of the long-run prospects of employment and earnings for graduates of the programs—on the assumption they do exceed the present discounted value of the person's pretraining abilities and his attendant employment prospects—may succeed in persuading reluctant individuals to enter the program. Also, although the availability of subsistence payments was not a major determinant in the decisions of the respondents from New Bedford and Fall River, Employment Service efforts to refer trainees to part-time jobs to supplement the subsidy may serve to overcome a person's reluctance to accept training. Indirectly, this practice may strengthen the person's faith in the local office's ability and intentions to assist in effecting a post-training placement.

The Employment Service, however, cannot be expected to achieve much success with the individual who rejects the training offer because of a dislike for the course content. Similarly, the persuasive efforts of the office's interviewers and counselors cannot be expected to show much success when the person in question believes that he will obtain satisfactory employment or secure an alleviation of his distress through his own efforts in the not-too-distant future. Neither should it be expected that the retraining opportunity will be accepted by the individual who has accepted and adjusted himself to a given pattern of cyclical unemployment. This individual's freedom to show preference for the *status quo* must be respected; what he regards as subjectively satisfactory will impel no pressure for change.

In short, it is argued that the counseling, recruiting, and Employment Service interviewing of potential trainees is limited beyond the sphere of course design and the dissemination of information. When an individual initiates or responds to a retraining offer it is the result of his consciously determined decision to effect an "improvement" of his status in the labor market—either for the present or the future.

## REFERENCES

1. The New Bedford program was to train machine operators, over a period of sixteen weeks; the Fall River program was designed to train men in the fundamentals of the machinist trade, over a twenty-week period. In addition to the emphasis placed upon an applicant's interest in training, each office's preconditions of eligibility were functions of (1) the level of training skill, (2) the office's willingness to rely upon the aptitude test as the sole predictor of the individual's capabilities for learning, and (3) the extent to which each office sought to train men who would be most apt to satisfy the preferences and hiring standards of prospective employers.
2. The influence of $C$ in the decision-making equation is considered to be greatest in the short run. There are no direct costs for an individual connected with his participation in the ARA program, and C's value is a function of opportunity costs. The "taste" for the skill being offered is one variable in the opportunity cost equation; other important elements may be one or more of the following: (1) the surrender of leisure time for attendance in the classroom; (2) the scorn of relatives and peers directed at the adult who returns to school; (3) the difficulties inherent in getting mentally prepared for the homework-study-lecture-test cycle of the learning process; (4) the possible relinquishment of vested interests in seniority, vacation, insurance, and pension rights that may have been accumulated on previous jobs;

(5) the loss of earnings otherwise possible to obtain over the course of the training period, in excess of the direct money subsidy paid to participants; (6) the uncertainty and loss of potential earnings that may follow completion of the program when there is no guarantee of immediate post-training placement; and (7) the probability values one subjectively associates with the prospect of obtaining employment and earnings without training that would be at least equivalent to the prospects after the acquisition of the training course knowledge.

3. Herbert S. Parnes, *Research on Labor Mobility* (New York: Social Science Research Council, 1954), pp. 102–9.

4. Two respondents from the New Bedford IT group were excluded from the computation of the mean value. Their ages (59 and 61 years) exceeded the age limit fixed by the local Employment Service Office's preconditions of eligibility for participation in the course.

5. In the short run, in the immediate period which extends from the start of training to, for instance, five years following the course, the wage rates of older and presumably more experienced workers are apt to be higher than the rates of younger and less experienced workers.

6. Parnes, *Research on Labor Mobility*, pp. 122–23.

7. The chi-square value from New Bedford data was 3.891; it was computed at 3.074 for Fall River. One degree of freedom prevailed in both tests, and variables were found to be interdependent at the .95 probability level in New Bedford and the .90 to .95 range for Fall River.

8. Parnes, *Research on Labor Mobility*, pp. 118–21.

9. The mean duration of unemployment, from individual observations, was computed for each group: 14.62 weeks for New Bedford's IT's and 13.43 weeks for the NIT's; 15.50 weeks for Fall River IT's and 12.68 weeks for the NIT's. Neither of the differences in mean values for groups within an area was significant at the .05 level.

10. This particular base period was considered appropriate, in that it allowed for a variety of occurrences, establishing a reasonable pattern in the not-too-distant past, against which the individual might have been expected to compare his present situation. The respondents were asked to provide data beginning with the 1958 period, but it soon became apparent that they were unable to yield accurate details for the events of this year.

# Appendix

## Note on Methodology

In the ideal conceptualization of an IT group, the universe of interested persons should include persons who expressed a willingness to participate in the training courses but who were unable to satisfy the local offices' preconditions of eligibility. These persons were disallowed applicants; they were judged ineligible for consideration as participants in the particular courses for which applications were being accepted and were not given the opportunity to sit for the aptitude examination. Also, the ideal IT universe should include persons who failed to communicate their interest to the local offices, because of inertia or lack of information about the retraining opportunity.

Unfortunately, the record-keeping procedures of the local offices did not provide a means for the identification of either the individuals or the number of persons who might have fallen into one of these two sub-sets of interested men. The same limitation applies to the identification of those who were not interested in the retraining opportunity. However, the interviewers in each local office did enter notations on to the registration cards of individuals whom they processed to denote the men who, in their judgment, were qualified to take the aptitude tests but not interested in the retraining offer.

The New Bedford office scheduled 285 men for testing; 90 persons were scheduled for testing in Fall River. The IT groups for each labor market area were determined by subtracting both the men who reneged on taking the tests and the men who, after passing the aptitude tests, refused to accept a referral to the training school. In New Bedford, there were 21 persons who did not show up for the test and 2 men who refused to enroll in the course. Fall River had 6 men who backed out from the test and 3 men who refused the referral. The total IT populations, therefore, were 262 individuals in New Bedford and 81 individuals in Fall River.

An exhaustive search of the registration cards in each office disclosed 24 men who told the New Bedford office that they were not interested in the retraining course. The counterpart figure for Fall River was 32 men. To these numbers were added the persons who did not report for the aptitude test and the ones who did not accept the referral to training.

The first decision made concerning the collection of data was to avoid the selection of samples and to conduct interviews with all of the individuals whose interest status could be ascertained. The second decision was to give priority to interviewing the men who passed the aptitude test and the men who were not interested in training. It was expected that sufficient opportunity would remain for interviews with the men who failed to score the qualifying grades on the aptitude tests, but this had to be abandoned. This is not considered to have introduced any bias in the results, for a more than casual inspection of the data found on the registration cards in the Employment Service files suggested no reason to believe that the men who failed the tests possessed characteristics different from those who passed.

This reduced the size of the IT groups. The *effective* IT complements were 210 in New Bedford and 41 in Fall River. The size of the NIT groups remained unchanged. As a result, the total number of men with whom contact was sought was 336 in the two areas. The number of completed interviews totalled 248— a total response rate of 95 per cent. Fifty-two persons changed their place of residence without leaving a forwarding address; 4 persons were in institutions; and 19 were declared inaccessible following at least three visits to their homes. Thirteen men refused to participate in the survey.

# V

## J. EARL WILLIAMS

■

## RETRAINING IN TENNESSEE

The first retraining program in Tennessee is the subject for examination in this chapter. The trainees in the program, which was probably the first one in the South, were from Campbell and Claiborne counties. Campbell county is approximately forty miles north of Knoxville in east Tennessee and Claiborne is adjacent and to the northeast. Kentucky is adjacent to the north of the area, Virginia to the northeast.*

### GENERAL BACKGROUND

The region is typical of many Appalachian areas in that coal mining and agriculture, which once dominated, have been on the decline for years with a resulting net outmigration of the population. In 1960, the population of Campbell county was 27,936, down 18.7 per cent from 1950; in Claiborne county it was 19,067, down 23.1 per cent from 1950.[1] There are several small towns in the area, the largest of which is La Follette, with a population of a little over 7,000. While income from mining and agriculture has been declining, income from trades and services, construction, and manufacturing has been increasing. Income from trades and services was more than $12 million in 1960, double that of manufacturing which was in second place. Agriculture, mining, and construction round out a list of the major income sources.[2]

The largest of several small manufacturing plants in the area was the La Follette Shirt Company, which employed 1,200 in 1961; no other company in the area hired as many as 100 employees. The estimates of per capita income in 1958 showed Campbell county at $745 and Claiborne

* J. Earl Williams is currently (1967) at the University of Houston, Texas.

county at $675, substantially below the state average ($1,439) and the national average ($2,057).[3] It is not surprising that more than 12,000 people were receiving surplus commodities in Campbell county in 1961 and a comparable percentage was on the list in Claiborne. In the same year, there were more than 4,100 public assistance recipients in the two counties.[4]

According to the Overall Economic Development Program (OEDP) for the area, unemployment had been excessive for many years, running from a low of 11 per cent in 1960 to a high of 24.1 per cent in 1955. The latest figures in the OEDP showed a labor force of 16,900 and unemployment of 3,200 or 18.9 per cent. There are substantial differences shown in labor force statistics for the same year, both within the OEDP and between it and the Department of Commerce *Statistical Profile*. For example, the OEDP showed an unemployment rate of 11 per cent in April, 1960, and 13.8 per cent in October, 1960, while the *Profile* indicated only 8.3 per cent in April, 1960. The primary difference between the two in 1961 is that the OEDP shows approximately 1,300 more in agricultural employment and nearly 1,100 more in the unemployed category. Despite statistical problems, it was clear to the Area Development Committee that unemployment was excessive. Further, since a majority of employees in the area were semiskilled and unskilled, the Committee felt that retraining was vital in maintaining existing industry and attracting new industry.

## SELECTION OF COURSES

The selection of courses was partly the result of employment possibilities, as determined by the La Follette office of the Bureau of Employment Security, and partly by the availability of courses at Fulton Area Vocational Technical Training Center in Knoxville. For example, the two major manufacturing industries in the area were garment and woodworking. Openings for trained persons were generally available in both industries. Since the Fulton school was the only one in the area located within reasonable traveling distance, the courses were limited to those which the school was equipped to furnish. Facilities were not available for training for the garment industry; they were for woodworking. Thus, in the final analysis, it was necessary to determine the availability of training courses first and then attempt to determine the need for the skills. Seven courses were originally proposed; two were not approved by the U.S. Department of Labor due to the high cost and the small number of potential trainees. The training proposal for the area was quite optimistic about the prospects for placement of the trainees: "A review of the unfilled and cancelled job orders at the La Follette Employment Security office indicates that seventy-five per cent (75%) of the persons trained under this proposal will obtain employment in the county of their residence." While this optimism was based largely on the response of twenty employers to the training needs survey conducted by the Bureau of Employment Security, the justification varied from course to course. The general approach used for each course follows.

### AUTO MECHANICS (ENTRY OCCUPATION)

Approximately thirteen employer contacts in the area, mainly with automobile and equipment dealers and small garages, were made prior to establishing the course. Inasmuch as fifteen persons were to be trained, almost every possible employer would have had to hire a trainee to fulfill the prediction of 75 per cent employment in the area. This is improbable under normal circumstances and virtually impossible in a depressed area. It would appear that the possibility of most trainees remaining in the area depended largely on their ability to "pick up" jobs in the usually high-turnover service station business.

### MACHINE TOOL OPERATING (ENTRY OCCUPATION)

Four very small machine shops and one which employed approximately twenty-five persons were solicited in the hope that some of the trainees could get work as apprentices. It was also felt that the electronics plant in La Follette could take some apprentices. It doubtless was apparent from the beginning, however, that few of the twenty-two trainees would be able to obtain apprenticeships in the area and that their best opportunity would be to obtain jobs as machine operators outside the area, possibly in Ohio or other midwestern areas.

### RADIO AND TELEVISION SERVICE AND REPAIR (ENTRY OCCUPATION)

Although this job classification is listed on the approval sheet of the U.S. Department of Labor, the La Follette Employment Security manager had no illusions regarding the training of radio and television repairmen, even on an entry basis, in sixteen weeks. Three television repair shops were contacted in advance, but the principal job possibility for the twenty-five trainees appeared to be at the electronics plant in La Follette, which gave the only fairly definite advance agreement obtained by the Employment Security office. An electronics plant in Bristol, Tennessee, one hundred or more miles from the area, also was contacted in advance, but no prior commitment was received. Thus, it was known from the beginning that the jobs available to the trainees would be largely in simple electronic assembly work. The La Follette electronics plant closed just prior to the end of the training period, eliminating all possibilities of the trainees' obtaining training-related jobs in the area.

## WELDING

A trailer company in Claiborne county indicated a planned expansion of thirty-five to forty employees, including some welders. Otherwise, prior contacts consisted largely of the machine shops and construction companies in the area. It was clear from the beginning, however, that if the trailer company did not come through, the sixteen trainees would be forced to seek employment in construction, steel, and similar operations in cities such as Knoxville or Oak Ridge, or in other industrial districts outside the east Tennessee area.

## MILLMAN, WOODWORKING (ENTRY OCCUPATION)

In retrospect, it is apparent that the thirty-two trainees in this course had the most optimistic prospects for obtaining employment in the development area. The planned expansion of the house trailer company would require many woodworkers, and at least four other woodworking concerns which might hire one or more trainees were contacted. In addition, the city of Morristown, in a nearby county, was a furniture center and was within about twenty-five miles of the homes of most Claiborne county trainees. The high turnover rate in the industry and the fact that most workers hired by the industry had little or no training virtually assured the trainees of furniture jobs, if they wished them.

## THE SELECTION OF TRAINEES

A number of factors contributed to the selection of trainees. Some of the approaches used were as follows.

## CALL-IN

The La Follette Employment Security office reviewed their file records of a number of the unemployed. If such factors as test scores, periods of unemployment, counseling summaries, and repeated referrals and no hires indicated a need for and ability to achieve retraining, the individuals were called in for interviews. Thirty per cent of those offered training heard about the program in this manner.

## GENERAL PUBLICITY

Stories in area newspapers gave the details of the training program. In addition, spot radio announcements in the two counties were used, and the Superintendent of Schools of Claiborne county was asked to refer likely candidates to the Employment Security office. About 30 per cent of the trainees heard about the program through newspaper stories. Another 20 per cent learned about it from friends and relatives, and 17 per cent heard about it over radio or television. Significantly, 40 per cent of the nonapplicant group claimed not to have heard of the program. Of those who had heard about it, 45 per cent heard from friends and relatives, one-third through the papers, and 22 per cent over radio or television.

## SELECTION FACTORS

According to the employment office, constant selection factors included test results, physical capacity, interest, experience, education, and mobility. Of these, the test results and education were probably the most important. There was a strong motivation on the part of the employment office to achieve the greatest success possible in the first retraining program. It follows that a high education level and a high test score would probably result in a trainee being more successful than one who had a low ranking on these points but who was high in interest, mobility, etc.

## AGE

Prior contacts with employers indicated that only sixteen weeks of training would be insufficient and that many additional months of training at the place of employment would be necessary. Thus, even though the philosophical outlook of the Area Redevelopment Act Retraining Program was to train technologically displaced persons in their forties and early fifties, employers indicated they would not hire people of this age. Thus, other factors being equal, the younger applicant was selected for the training.

More than 500 applicants were considered for the 110 places in the training program. Approximately 300 applicants were rejected as a result of interviews without formal testing, largely because they did not meet the criteria listed above or simply because they had insufficient reading and writing ability to take the General Aptitude Test Battery (GATB). Some were turned down because they already had skills equal to or greater than those to be achieved in training. In only four cases was the test score not a major factor for selection; these particular selections were made immediately prior to the start of the training program.

## COMPARISON OF TRAINEE CHARACTERISTICS
## WITH OTHER SAMPLE GROUPS

Of the 110 trainees, twenty-three dropped out before completing their retraining. Both those who completed courses and those who dropped out were included in the total interview sample. In addition, samples were drawn from among those who rejected or did not report for training and from among the nonapplicants for training. A summary, to be used for purposes of comparison in the remainder of the chapter, is presented in Table V.1.

TABLE V.1

SAMPLE GROUPS

| Training status | No. | Total |
|---|---|---|
| Completed training | 87 | |
| Dropped out of training | 23 | |
| Total trainees | | 110 |
| Did not report for training | 12 | |
| Not accepted for training without testing | 15 | |
| Not accepted for training after testing | 13 | |
| Total rejected or did not report | | 40[a] |
| Nonapplicant sample | | 38[b] |
| Total interview sample | | 188 |

[a] A sample group of 40 was selected from the more than 400 additional unemployed who applied for retraining and were either accepted or rejected. Only 12 persons were offered training and either rejected it or failed to report when the course started; all 12 were included in the sample of 40. A second segment of the sample is composed of 15 persons out of 300 who were rejected without testing, all of whom were identified on a random basis from the files of the Employment Security office. The remaining 13 people in the sample were chosen from a group of 107 persons who were tested and rejected for training. However, data on some basic characteristics of all 107 were collected.

[b] Approximately 1,500 cards of unemployed who had not applied for retraining remained in the files of the employment office. Data on their basic characteristics were tallied from every third card, making a total of 490 cards reviewed. Every twelfth card from this group of 490 was selected, resulting in an interview sample of 40. All cards in the files were stratified according to occupation, giving a perfectly stratified sample for interview purposes. It was impossible to locate two people in the sample; consequently, the interview sample is composed of 38 individuals.

For example, the emphasis which the Bureau of Employment Security placed on youth is very apparent from Table V.2. It is quite significant that 70 per cent of the trainees and 75 per cent of those offered and not accepting training were under 25, whereas the percentage drops to 61 for those rejected for training after testing and to only 54 for those rejected without testing. Thus, it is obvious that age was a real factor in rejecting applicants without testing them. Finally, only 39 per cent of the nonapplicants were under 25, and 16 per cent of them were 45 or over. None of those offered training was 45 or older, and only one person who was over 45 was tested.

If, as the employment office indicated, the level of education was a significant selection factor only in the case of radio-television trainees, one must conclude from Table V.2 that there is a high correlation between GATB results (this was a significant selection factor) and education levels. Fifty per cent or more of the trainees and those offered training had a high-school education or better, whereas this was true for only

TABLE V.2

COMPARISON OF AGE, EDUCATION, AND MARITAL STATUS OF TRAINEES AND SAMPLE GROUPS

| Training status | Age | | | | | Education | | | | | Married |
|---|---|---|---|---|---|---|---|---|---|---|---|
| | Under 20 | 20–24 | Under 25 | 25–44 | 45+ | Less than 8 | 8 | 9–11 | 12 | 12+ | |
| Completed training | 23% | 46% | 69% | 31% | 0% | 7% | 20% | 20% | 49% | 4% | 46% |
| Dropped out of training | 9 | 65 | 74 | 26 | 0 | 8.5 | 21.5 | 30 | 40 | 0 | 48 |
| Total trainees | 20 | 50 | 70 | 30 | 0 | 7 | 20 | 22 | 47 | 4 | 46 |
| Did not report | 25 | 50 | 75 | 25 | 0 | 0 | 0 | 50 | 50 | 0 | 42 |
| Not accepted after testing, population | 25 | 36 | 61 | 38 | 1 | 24 | 35 | 25 | 15 | 1 | 40 |
| Not accepted without testing | 27 | 27 | 54 | 39 | 7 | 53 | 20 | 20 | 7 | 0 | 53 |
| Nonapplicant population | 15.5 | 23.5 | 39 | 45 | 16 | 25 | 27 | 23 | 22 | 3 | 64 |
| Total interview sample | 8.5 | 46.5 | 55.0 | 37.5 | 7.5 | 18 | 20 | 23.5 | 34.5 | 4 | 50 |

## TABLE V.3

COMPARISON OF LABOR FORCE STATUS AND PERIOD OF UNEMPLOYMENT OF TRAINEES AND SAMPLE GROUPS AS OF THE BEGINNING OF THE TRAINING PROGRAM

| Training status | Labor force status | | | | Weeks of unemployment | | | | | |
|---|---|---|---|---|---|---|---|---|---|---|
| | Employed | Under-employed | Not in labor force | Unemployed | Less than 5 | 5–14 | 15–26 | 27–39 | 40–52 | More than 52 |
| Completed training | 14% | 3 % | 0% | 83 % | 16.5% | 25 % | 30 % | 15 % | 0 % | 13.5% |
| Dropped out of training | 9 | 0 | 0 | 91 | 10 | 25 | 10 | 25 | 15 | 15 |
| Total trainees | 13 | 2.5 | 0 | 84.5 | 15 | 25 | 25 | 17.5 | 3.5 | 14 |
| Did not report | 25 | 0 | 0 | 75 | 22 | 22 | 22 | 22 | 0 | 12 |
| Not accepted for training | 10 | 0 | 8 | 84 | 18 | 27.5 | 18 | 9 | 0 | 27.5 |
| Nonapplicant sample | 0 | 3 | 0 | 97 | 5.5 | 30 | 16 | 24.5 | 8 | 16 |
| Total interview sample | 11 | 2 | 1 | 86 | 0 | 10.5 | 28.5 | 17.5 | 14 | 29.5 |

16 per cent of those rejected after testing and 7 per cent of those rejected without testing. Even the nonapplicant category, which constituted the best cross-section of most of the unemployed in the area, indicates that only 25 per cent had a high-school education or better. Conversely, there are roughly twice as many or more in the nontrainee groups with an eighth-grade education or less than is found in the trainee groups.

Some significance also could be attached to the fact that a substantially smaller percentage of the trainees than of the nonapplicants was married. The unmarried person, often living at home with fewer financial worries, apparently tends to be more willing than a married person to attempt a retraining course with a small subsistence allowance. Table V.3 represents some interesting comparisons of the labor force and unemployment status of the various groups. Despite the Bureau of Employment Security records, our investigation showed that only 84.5 per cent of the trainees were unemployed just prior to the start of the training program. Thirteen per cent were employed and 2.5 per cent were underemployed. One-fourth of those who did not report were employed, probably the reason why they failed to report after being selected for the program. Even in the case of nonapplicants, one person was found to be underemployed rather than unemployed. The remainder of Table V.3 gives a breakdown of the number of weeks of unemployment suffered by the various groups. Some of the possible conclusions which might be reached from these data are as follows:

1. Those unemployed for a year or more have a greater susceptibility to rejection for training than those unemployed for lesser periods.

2. Those with less than fifteen weeks of unemployment, conversely may stand a greater chance of being offered training.

3. Even within the group of trainees selected, it appears that there are a number of factors which cause those unemployed for six months or more to drop out in much larger numbers than those unemployed for less than six months.

4. Almost 50 per cent of those not applying for retraining had been unemployed for six months or more, which may be a reflection of their lower skill and educational level or a lack of interest and confidence due to the long period of unemployment. Also, a greater financial strain may cause them to feel that a regular job is much more important than several months of training.

## FACTORS RELATING TO POTENTIAL GEOGRAPHICAL MOBILITY

Based upon the comparison of characteristics in the previous section, it would appear that the trainees would be much more likely to be potentially mobile than the unemployed in the area generally. The fact that they are younger, better educated, and with fewer family responsibilities, and have generally been unemployed for much shorter periods of time would tend to support this supposition. However, a number of additional factors which might affect mobility existed for some time prior to the start of the training program, and although the data relate largely to the total interview sample, they give some indication of the environment from which the trainees were drawn. Since 60 per cent of the total interview sample is composed of trainees, the overall mobility factors should be important.

The financial status of an unemployed worker and his family can have important implications for mobility, inasmuch as the nearer the family is to poverty levels the more difficult it is for the worker to travel in search of employment. Table V.4, which gives the total family income

TABLE V.4

TOTAL FAMILY INCOME OF TOTAL INTERVIEW SAMPLE

| Income | 1958 | 1959 | 1960 | 1961 |
|--------|------|------|------|------|
| Less than $2,000 | 39 % | 33% | 33 % | 43% |
| $2,000–$2,999 | 19 | 26 | 29 | 20 |
| $3,000–$3,999 | 20 | 14 | 18 | 20 |
| $4,000–$4,999 | 12 | 17 | 15.5 | 10 |
| $5,000–$5,999 | 7 | 6 | 4 | 3 |
| $6,000–$6,999 | 0.5 | | 0.5 | |
| $7,000 or more | 2.5 | 4 | 4 | 4 |

for the total interview sample, not only indicates the low financial status of most families, but that it was becoming progressively worse. For example, the percentage of families with less than $3,000 income increased each year from 1958 through 1961. Given the size of the families in the area, the fact that 43 per cent of them had less than $2,000 total income is pathetic. Further, when 83 per cent had a total family income of less than $4,000, job-hunting trips were likely to be severely limited.

Thus, it is not surprising that two-thirds of the respondents indicated no family savings and that one-third were in debt; the debt level of 60 per cent of them was at $200 or more. Further, during the periods of unemployment just prior to the start of the training program, nearly three-fourths of the people in the total interview sample were not eligible to draw unemployment compensation. Of those who were eligible, a majority had exhausted their benefits by the time the training program started.

Table V.5 gives some interesting insights into the effect of unemployment compensation. Despite the fact that nearly three-fourths of the peo-

## TABLE V.5

### Comparisons of Sources of Income and Other Aid during Periods of Unemployment of Trainees and Sample Groups

| Training status | Drew unemployment compensation | Help from relatives | Money earned by other members | Surplus commodities | Home grown food | Odd jobs | Dwelling status | | |
|---|---|---|---|---|---|---|---|---|---|
| | | | | | | | Rent | Own | Live with parents or other relatives |
| Trainees | 16% | 60% | N.A.* | N.A. | N.A. | N.A. | 20% | 14% | 66% |
| Did not report for training | 45 | 66 | 11 | 22 | 45 | 56 | 33 | 8 | 59 |
| Not accepted for training | 18 | 60 | 25 | 54 | 46 | 70 | 12 | 25 | 63 |
| Nonapplicant sample | 54 | 50 | 53 | 35 | 46 | 40 | 16 | 47 | 37 |

* Not available.

ple in the total interview sample were not eligible to draw compensation, 45 per cent of the did-not-report group and 54 per cent of the nonapplicant sample drew compensation. On the other hand, only 16 per cent of the trainees and 18 per cent of those not accepted for training drew compensation. The obvious conclusion is that a worker who is not eligible for unemployment compensation is much more likely to apply for and accept retraining.

Unemployment compensation was not much of a cushion for most workers in the area, and Table V.5 sheds light on other sources of income for the sample groups during their periods of unemployment just prior to the start of the training program. For all groups combined, help from relatives in the form of food and money was the major source of income during unemployment, with about 60 per cent of the total group receiving this kind of aid. Odd jobs were a second major source of income and, even though data were not available for the trainees, it is known that a substantial proportion of them worked at odd jobs. It was not surprising to learn that about 50 per cent of all groups (and this would be a fair guess for trainees) raised much of their own food. Surplus commodities played a surprisingly large role during unemployment, particularly for the group rejected for training, and when this factor is added to the high percentage who derived income from odd jobs, the result is probably a rather good description of their normal environment. Finally, money earned by another member of the family was the least important of the income sources for all except the nonapplicant group. All of the women in the total interview sample were in the nonapplicant group and the fact that most of them had working husbands largely explains this abnormally high percentage.

Considering the income levels of the interview-sample families noted above, it is not surprising to find that more than two-thirds said it would take less than $4,000 a year to be as well off in Lexington, Kentucky, as they were in their home county. Most of the two-thirds also indicated they would move if a job in their occupation were available in Lexington or another town within 200 to 300 miles and if the cost of moving were paid. The fact that nearly 75 per cent of the total interview sample felt that young people should leave the area and 60 per cent even felt their sons should leave is a further indication of willingness to be mobile. Beyond this point, however, most of the factors related to mobility raise strong questions about the value of this statement and the willingness of most of the unemployed to become mobile. Some factors are as follows:

1. Most of the unemployed were born in the area where they were now living.

2. Almost two-thirds of them lived in rural areas or incorporated towns

with less than 2,500 population. Further, 75 per cent of them had lived or worked on a farm.

3. One-third of their fathers were miners when they were in their teens, and one-fourth were farmers. These families are notorious for immobility.

4. About 60 per cent of the total interview sample group lived with parents or relatives. Table V.5 data might lead to the conclusion that this was a major factor in applying for retraining, since a much smaller percentage of the nonapplicants was in this category. While this might indicate potential mobility for the trainees, it may be simply a reflection of financial status. Finally, about 50 per cent of nonapplicant respondents owned their own homes, which is always a deterrent to mobility.

5. Families in the area were large, and 42 per cent of the total interview sample group had five or more at home.

6. More than 90 per cent of the total interview sample had relatives living in the area in a different house, and half of them had five or more relatives in a different house. This compares with 87 per cent of the nonapplicant sample who had relatives in the area and 100 per cent of those not accepted for training and those who dropped out after beginning a retraining course. Well over 50 per cent of these three groups had five or more relatives in the area.

Thus, it is not surprising that 40 per cent of the unemployed had not made any geographical moves since 1950 and another 10 per cent had made only one. In fact, 40 per cent of the unemployed said they had not looked for jobs outside the area. However, it should be noted that most of the trainees claimed to have looked outside the area. It naturally follows that more than two-thirds of the unemployed would indicate that they expected to be living in the area five years in the future. The few who did not generally indicated that they might be forced to leave to get a job. They added, however, that it would be difficult to leave families and friends. Finally, more than 20 per cent responded that they would not leave the area for Lexington, Kentucky (only 100 miles away), even if they could obtain a job there, and 40 per cent of those who had not applied for retraining said they would not take a job out of the state.

7. The cultural habits, customs, and level of knowledge of the unemployed in the total interview sample would not whet an appetite for mobility. One-third read no magazines of any kind at any time. Sixty per cent watched mostly soap operas and westerns on television, with sports programs the only other significant television interest. Of those who belonged to some social group, 80 per cent were on a sports team, with a lodge being the only other organization to draw a few votes.

Finally, 60 per cent did not know the name of their congressman or either senator, and 25 per cent did not know the name of the governor. It is doubtful, then, that they were well informed on geographical labor markets.

## GENERAL ATTITUDE TOWARD RETRAINING

Almost everyone seemed to favor government-sponsored retraining, including trainees, their families, those who had not applied, and employers. Forty-four per cent of the total interview sample felt that retraining would result in a job locally, another one-third felt it would result in their finding a job in the state, and only 12 per cent felt that it might be necessary to go outside the state after retraining. All but one of the nonapplicant sample felt that the government should provide retraining and living expenses while training, and 80 per cent of them said they would like to enter a training program if it resulted in the achievement of a new skill. However, two-thirds of the nonapplicant respondents had not made any kind of inquiry about the program, for they felt that it was for younger, less educated, unskilled unemployed.

Virtually no comments were made by the total interview sample group on the methods used to publicize the program, and about the only comment regarding the selection of trainees was that it might be well to lower standards and open the courses to all applicants. Those who had been rejected for training were not critical of the testing, and 80 per cent of them accepted the fact that they did not qualify for retraining. The remaining 20 per cent were very disappointed and discouraged. The major complaint of all who had been rejected was that they were not informed of their test results. All of them felt that they could perform the job despite the fact that they were not accepted.

About 80 per cent of the employer sample felt that training programs would result in additional jobs in their areas,[5] and 54 per cent felt that their labor requirements could be met best by government-sponsored vocational training. Thirty-eight per cent felt that on-the-job training sponsored by the government would be best, and only 7.8 per cent (all very small companies) felt there should be no government retraining programs. One-third of the employers claimed that they would hire more workers, if the government would absorb the cost of on-the-job training.

## EVALUATION OF THE TRAINING PROGRAM

It should be noted in the beginning that the Fulton Vocational School in Knoxville, where the training was conducted, had had an outstanding reputation for years and doubtless was one of the best vocational schools in the South, with a placement rate of better than 85 per cent of its students immediately upon graduation. The entire staff of the school, which had class hours usually running from 8:00 a.m. to 2:30 p.m. for the regular school shift, took a short break and came back to teach another six hours starting at 3:00 p.m. The staff included the director, assistant director, and all five instructors, as well as office and janitorial help. The school was determined that the trainees would get the best possible training.

From the standpoint of such factors as space, equipment, safety, and lighting facilities, instruction in auto and radio-television repair ranked high, in that they were up-to-date in relation to industry needs. By these standards, the welding and machine shop was adequate; facilities for instruction in woodworking measured up to standard only to a limited degree. Students had no criticisms of these items. Employers were supposedly contacted about the equipment and course content, but most of those interviewed did not seem to know much about them. Nevertheless, all but one of the responding employers felt that these items were good or adequate; the one suggested that facilities were inadequate.

The instructors met the state standards for professional preparation and job experience. This observer's impression was that they did an excellent job, maintaining good rapport with the trainees and an unusually high level of student interest. The students were extremely enthusiastic about their teachers, with the exception of one instructor in the radio-television class. The illness of the original radio-television instructor forced a replacement for a period of time. Apparently the replacement did not give as much individual attention to students, had less classroom time, and covered subject matter more rapidly; it appears that dissatisfaction with the instruction combined with the complexity of the material motivated the high level of dropouts experienced by this class. Despite this one problem, employers, with one exception, thought the instruction was good, and only two felt that the trainees they hired did not know the fundamentals well enough.

Major criticisms related to the kind and length of course, established by law and government agencies, rather than to the school itself. For example, trainees and employers alike felt that skills should be taught in more depth and that more skills should be taught. The major criticism was of the legal limit of sixteen weeks for the course; almost everyone interviewed felt that sixteen weeks was far too short a period of training, even for entry skills in most occupations.

### EVALUATION OF TRAINEES

Seventy-three per cent of the employers who hired graduates of the training program considered them to be very good in the jobs for which they were hired. In fact, more than 50 per cent of the employers responded that the trainees were much better than the usual workers hired. Twenty per cent of the employer group (including some who did not hire any trainees) felt that the selection standards were too low. This response is significant, in view of the fact that most of those who were rejected for training felt they were too high, and it is doubtless true that the philosophical objectives of the ARA retraining program would include lower standards than the employment office maintained. The instructors were generally enthusiastic about the trainees. The instructor in the auto-repair course felt that their interest was generally higher and their classroom performance more highly motivated than that of the average day students. The machine shop instructor felt that his students were seriously interested in the course and that they learned much more than he had expected in so short a period. The welding instructor felt that the majority were high in interest when compared to regular day students. He stated that he wished all his classes were as good, from the standpoint of performance.

Slightly more than 80 per cent of the trainees in all classes graduated, with the exception of the radio-television course where the completion rate was 72 per cent. In view of the fact that it was probably more difficult to obtain a marketable skill in this course in sixteen weeks than in any of the others, and of its complexity and its instruction problem, this average could be considered relatively good. Further, it should be emphasized that lack of ability or interest was probably not the overriding reason for an individual's failing to finish a course. Of the twenty-three dropouts, eighteen obtained employment (several of them were called back to jobs from which they had been laid off), one was drafted, one became ill, two were terminated for violating school policy, and one was dropped for unknown reasons. It should be noted, however, that, in addition to the official reason of obtaining employment, other reasons for dropping out emerged from the data. For example, financial strain, lack of interest (particularly true in the radio-television class), and inability to keep up (particularly the person who was absent for some time due to illness) can be listed as secondary reasons. Only two of those obtaining employment found training-related jobs. Others went into a variety of occupations ranging from construction, painting, truck driving, and service station work to sales, co-op manager, and dance band and carnival work. One gets the distinct impression that many of the dropouts stopped going to class for some reason or other, and later found a job and reported it as the "official" reason.

Even so, the attendance record of the dropouts up to the time of their withdrawal was almost as good as the record of those who completed their courses. The latter were absent 10 per cent of the time, compared to 13 per cent for the dropouts. Those who completed training did show up better, however, in the individual instructor's rating. On classroom attitude, 36 per cent of the dropouts ranked as less than good compared to only 20 per cent of the graduates. Interestingly enough, however, the dropouts ranked slightly higher in the excellent category as it related to course interest. Further, all of the dropouts were considered by instructors to have measured up to their potential, whereas 7 per cent of those who completed training were not considered to have done so. The instructors did think that 22 per cent of the dropouts would have been better satisfied in another course. Finally, when the trainees were compared with others who normally spend 18 to 24 months in a course, the instructors rated 28 per cent of the dropouts below average compared to 23.5 per cent for those who completed training and 14 per cent above average compared to 11.5 per cent for the graduates.

## THE PLACEMENT PROCEDURE

Most of the employers in the sample group had no minimum educational requirements, and though most of them had unofficial age limits, such limitations were not a factor in placement as none of the trainees was in that age bracket. Further, most of the employers were in the habit of filling their labor force needs through the Employment Security office and felt that its staff and its knowledge of their needs were good.

In this kind of environment, the probability of placement was as good as could be expected, given the limited training of the graduates and the conditions of the area labor market. The employment office made a special case of the trainees, and undoubtedly they received more attention than any group of unemployed before or since. Even today, separate records of the progress of the trainees are kept. The names and addresses of all trainees and the courses they completed were published in county newspapers at the time of graduation, and all the employers in a three-county area who might hire workers with skills learned in the courses were visited by an employment service staff member and were given fact sheets on the trainees. In addition, dozens of lists were mailed to employers in Knoxville and other cities. With such an all-out effort to place the trainees, it is not surprising that most trainees and employers felt that the placement effort was very good. The major question, of course, is what results were achieved.

## THE POST-TRAINING EMPLOYMENT RECORD AND TRAINING ATTITUDES

In the following section are a few summary statements of the findings of a follow-up questionnaire, which was answered during June–July, 1963, by 70 per cent of those completing the training course and 48 per cent of the dropouts.

## Employment Experience

Seventy-six per cent of the graduates and 54 per cent of the dropouts held jobs. Eighteen per cent of the trainees were unemployed compared with 36 per cent of the dropouts. The record varies considerably by class, the woodworking graduates having the least unemployment (8 per cent), followed by machine shop with 16.5 per cent, auto repair with 25 per cent, radio-television repair with 27 per cent, and welding with 33 per cent. The employment record of the graduates at the time of the questionnaire was much better than the one for the nontrainee sample groups six months after the beginning of the training program.

## Occupations and Industries

Compared with the sample groups of nontrainees interviewed a year earlier, the trainees seem to have fared better. For example, more than twice as many nontrainees as trainees were in farmer classifications, 29 per cent of the trainees were in craft categories compared to 18 per cent for nontrainees, and 50 per cent of the trainees were in manufacturing compared to 22 per cent of the nontrainees.

## Geographical Location

The trainees had not been very mobile, in that 85 per cent of the graduates and 91 per cent of the dropouts still lived in Tennessee. The record of those who completed training varied considerably by class, with 100 per cent of the auto mechanic group still living in Tennessee, followed by 89 per cent of the welding trainees, 87.5 per cent of the woodworking class, 86.7 per cent of the radio-television repair class, and 75 per cent of the machine tool operating group. Those employed were slightly more mobile, with 70 per cent of the graduates and 84 per cent of the dropouts still in Tennessee. Interestingly, 57 per cent of the graduates and 50 per cent of the dropouts still lived at the same address they had when they started training.

## Earnings and Hours

Forty-seven per cent of those who completed training earned less than $60 a week and 26 per cent earned $80 or more. This is a far superior record to that of the dropouts or the nontrainees interviewed up to a year earlier. The graduates generally had jobs requiring much shorter hours, with only 18 per cent in jobs requiring more than fifty hours of work a week compared to 29 per cent of the dropouts and one-third of all nontrainees.

### TRAINING-RELATED VIEWS AND EXPERIENCE

(a) Thirty-six per cent of those who completed training had training-related jobs; the dropouts had none. It is interesting to note that the experience by class tends to show that those trained for skills in greatest demand in the area had the highest percentage of training-related jobs, whereas those with skills least in demand in the local area had the least number of training-related jobs. By class, they ran from 70 per cent training-related for woodworking to 44 per cent for welding, 33 per cent for machine shop, 25 per cent for auto mechanics, to zero per cent for radio-television repair.

(b) Almost 50 per cent of the graduates felt that the training course helped them get a job and that they had been able to use the skills learned.

(c) Virtually none of the trainees felt the course covered too much, but the majority of the graduates felt it was too narrow. Only 50 per cent of them felt they learned the skills well enough.

(d) While in school, virtually all trainees ranked their instructors as excellent, but later 17 per cent of the graduates and 10 per cent of the dropouts ranked them as fair.

(e) One-third of the graduates and two-thirds of the dropouts had decided the equipment was only fair.

(f) Virtually all would take retraining again and advise friends to do the same, but 40 per cent of those who completed a course and 70 per cent of the dropouts would have preferred another course.

### UNEMPLOYMENT EXPERIENCE

One-third of the graduates and 25 per cent of the dropouts had been unemployed at some time since 1962. However, two-thirds of unemployed graduates received unemployment compensation compared to virtually none of the dropouts. Finally, a substantial percentage of the trainees had been unemployed two or three times since the end of training, but two-thirds of the graduates had been unemployed less than fifteen weeks since the end of training. This was a much better record than the graduates had prior to training.

## CONCLUSIONS AND RECOMMENDATIONS

### ENVIRONMENT FOR TRAINING

1. If the Tennessee training experience is at all typical of retraining in depressed areas, there is no reason why there cannot be a real expansion of the program in all depressed areas.

2. The enthusiasm with which the program is received by the unemployed (including those not applying for retraining), the instructors in the school, and the employers is a factor which will determine the success of any program.

3. The fact that most trainees who graduated would be willing to try retraining again and would recommend it to their friends is a positive recommendation for such programs.

### SELECTION OF COURSES

1. It is likely that Area Development Committees in depressed areas will be limited in their selection of courses to what is available at the nearest vocational training school.

2. In an area similar to the one studied, it is farcical to attempt to justify training on the basis of the availability of jobs in the local area. Availability of jobs in the local area should be abandoned as a requisite, by law, for the establishment of retraining programs in these areas.

3. Greater emphasis should be placed on skills in great demand in other areas when setting up courses in depressed areas.

4. If successful placement in the local area is to be the criterion, course selection needs to be based on training in skills utilized by industries which are dominant in the local area.

5. Local vocational schools have a real obligation to establish courses in skills in short supply in local as well as outside areas.

### LENGTH OF THE COURSES

1. Perhaps the greatest single criticism of the ARA program, as it is administered, is the required maximum duration of sixteen weeks for all courses.

2. Employers, in general, will not hire workers past thirty-five years of age, if they will be required to give these people additional on-the-job training. This factor affects both the success of a course and the philosophical objectives of the act.

3. In the more complicated occupational skills, such as radio-television repair, it is virtually impossible for even young trainees to obtain employment in the occupation after only sixteen weeks of training.

### SELECTION OF TRAINEES

1. If the emphasis of the program is to be on successful placement, the call-in method of matching potential skills to the courses is very good, even though it may violate some of the philosophical objectives of the act.

2. The emphasis which the Bureau of Employment Security laid on placements as a measure of success of a program generally makes it very

difficult for local offices to select the older, less educated, and long-term unemployed for training.

3. It is possible that greater success with regard to dropouts could be achieved if a greater emphasis were placed on the desires and interests of the trainees. Many trainees felt that test scores largely determined the course in which they were placed. Further, 40 per cent of the trainees would have preferred to take a different course, and the instructors felt that a different course would have been better for 22 per cent of the trainees.

4. A greater emphasis on determining potential mobility prior to selection would be beneficial, particularly if it appears that trainees would have to leave their home counties to secure employment. There was a general feeling among potential trainees that retraining would result in local jobs, and many of them flatly stated that they would not leave the area under any circumstances.

5. Problems still exist in methods of contacting potential trainees and communicating to them information on who is eligible for retraining.

### APPLICATIONS FOR AND ACCEPTANCE OF TRAINING

1. It appears that individuals with few marital responsibilities, little eligibility for unemployment compensation, shorter periods of unemployment, and greater dependence on parents and relatives for living quarters are more likely to become trainees.

2. Many persons currently employed are interested in retraining.

3. The longer-term unemployed are less likely to apply for training and are more likely to drop out after beginning training than are other groups of unemployed.

4. Employment of a second member of a family unit is a factor which seems to deter a married person from applying for retraining.

### EVALUATION OF THE COURSES

1. A change of instructors during a course has an important effect on trainees' interest and potential employment.

2. Modern equipment in the classroom is not nearly as important as the availability of jobs in the area in placement success.

### POST-TRAINING RESULTS

1. Trainees appear to have a much better post-training employment record than dropouts and other sample groups.

2. Trainees tend to be employed in better occupations and industries, have better wages and hours, have greater eligibility for unemployment compensation, and have fewer weeks of unemployment than other groups.

3. Persons trained in skills utilized to a large degree in the local area tend to have a much higher percentage of training-related jobs. For example, the lack of potential radio-TV jobs in the area is directly related to the fact that not a single radio-TV trainee replying to the follow-up questionnaire was in a training-related job.

4. The more complex training course, particularly when coupled with instructor problems, tends to reduce the percentage of training-related jobs.

5. The importance of the mobility factor is shown by the fact that most trainees were still in Tennessee more than a year after retraining.

## REFERENCES

1. U.S. Department of Commerce, *Statistical Profile: La Follette-Jellico-Tazewell, Tennessee Redevelopment Area* (May, 1962), p. 2.
2. *Overall Economic Development Program for Campbell and Claiborne Counties, Tennessee,* Area Development Committee, 1961, p. 5.
3. *Overall Economic Development . . . ,* p. 6.
4. U.S. Department of Commerce, *Statistical Profile . . . ,* p. 5.
5. The employer sample consisted of 36 employers, 18 of whom hired trainees; 24 were employers in the two-county area; most of them were small and few hired any trainees. The remainder of the sample consisted of three companies in Middlesboro, Kentucky, just across the line from the area (the only one of the three hiring trainees was the Coca-Cola Bottling Company), four rather large furniture plants and two smaller manufacturing plants in Morristown, Tennessee (most of whom hired trainees), a lumber company in Knoxville which hired trainees, and Lockheed of Atlanta, Georgia, which hired several trainees.

# VI

## RICHARD J. SOLIE

■

## AN EVALUATION OF THE EFFECTS OF

## RETRAINING IN TENNESSEE

### INTRODUCTION

The effect of government-sponsored retraining programs on the labor market experience of the unemployed in depressed rural areas is examined in this chapter.* The empirical findings derive from a study of an early Area Redevelopment Administration (ARA) training program which ran from February 19 to June 8, 1962, in two Appalachian counties of northeast Tennessee. Personal interviews, which provided information on a number of socio-demographic characteristics and labor market experience for the period from 1956 through June of 1964, were completed on a sample of 217 workers divided into four subgroups.[1]

The first of these subgroups included eighty-five workers who completed the sixteen-week training program in one of the five courses offered: welding, machine tool operating, auto mechanics, radio-television repair, and woodworking. The experience of these people, the "Completes," provides the basic information on the impact of training on unemployed workers for this study.

* Richard J. Solie is currently (1968) at the University of North Dakota. This study comes from the author's doctoral dissertation, accepted by the University of Tennessee in August, 1965. The author is indebted to a number of persons who gave advice and assistance during the study, including Dr. J. Fred Holly, Dr. Ernst Stromsdorfer, and Dr. J. Earl Williams, all of whom served on the thesis committee, and Dr. Gerald G. Somers. The chapter is reprinted from the *Industrial and Labor Relations Review*, Vol. 21, No. 2 (January, 1968). Copyright © 1968 by Cornell University. All rights reserved.

The second subgroup included thirty-three workers who applied for and were accepted into the program, but who either did not report for any of the classes or else entered the course but dropped out before its completion. This subgroup, the "Noncompletes," represents one of the three control groups against whose experience that of the "Completes" is compared. Since the socio-demographic characteristics of the "Completes" and "Noncompletes" are very similar (see Table VI.1), it is

TABLE VI.1

Summary of Important Characteristics of Analysis Sample by Major Subgroup

| Characteristic | Completes | | Non-completes | | Rejects | | Non-applicants | |
|---|---|---|---|---|---|---|---|---|
| | No. | % | No. | % | No. | % | No. | % |
| Total sample | 85 | — | 33 | — | 22 | — | 77 | — |
| *Age* | | | | | | | | |
| 21 and under | 36 | 42.4 | 14 | 42.4 | 8 | 36.4 | 13 | 16.9 |
| 22–25 | 26 | 30.6 | 11 | 33.3 | 5 | 22.7 | 10 | 13.0 |
| 26–34 | 17 | 20.0 | 6 | 18.2 | 3 | 13.6 | 16 | 20.8 |
| 35+ | 6 | 7.1 | 2 | 6.1 | 6 | 27.3 | 38 | 49.4 |
| Mean age | 23.8 | — | 24.1 | — | 27.8 | — | 36.0 | — |
| *Education* | | | | | | | | |
| 0–7 yrs. | 7 | 8.2 | 2 | 6.1 | 9 | 40.9 | 36 | 46.8 |
| 8 yrs. | 14 | 16.5 | 6 | 18.2 | 6 | 27.3 | 18 | 23.4 |
| 9–11 yrs. | 17 | 20.0 | 11 | 33.3 | 3 | 13.6 | 16 | 20.8 |
| 12 yrs. or more | 47 | 55.3 | 14 | 42.4 | 4 | 18.2 | 7 | 9.1 |
| Mean education (yrs.) | 10.5 | — | 10.3 | — | 8.4 | — | 7.2 | — |
| *Marital status* | | | | | | | | |
| Single | 40 | 47.1 | 17 | 51.5 | 10 | 45.5 | 14 | 18.2 |
| Married | 42 | 49.4 | 16 | 48.5 | 11 | 50.0 | 58 | 75.3 |
| Other | 3 | 3.5 | 0 | 0.0 | 1 | 4.5 | 5 | 6.5 |
| *Prior labor force experience 1/1/62* | | | | | | | | |
| Emp. less than 6 mo. | 9 | 10.6 | 3 | 9.1 | 1 | 4.5 | 3 | 3.9 |
| Emp. 6 mo. or more | 15 | 17.6 | 7 | 21.2 | 3 | 13.6 | 16 | 20.8 |
| Unemp. less than 6 mo. | 42 | 49.4 | 9 | 27.3 | 7 | 31.8 | 32 | 41.6 |
| Unemp. 6 mo. or more | 17 | 20.0 | 13 | 39.4 | 9 | 40.9 | 26 | 33.8 |
| Not in labor force less than 6 mo. | 0 | 0.0 | 0 | 0.0 | 0 | 0.0 | 0 | 0.0 |
| Not in labor force 6 mo. or more | 2 | 2.4 | 1 | 3.0 | 2 | 9.1 | 0 | 0.0 |
| *County of residence on 2/1/62* | | | | | | | | |
| Campbell | 49 | 57.6 | 20 | 60.6 | 21 | 95.5 | 60 | 77.9 |
| Claiborne | 36 | 42.4 | 13 | 39.4 | 1 | 4.5 | 17 | 22.1 |

reasonable to assume that their employment experience would have been comparable except for the training.[2] The difference in post-training employment experience between these two groups might, therefore, be expected to be a reasonable estimate of the benefits from training.

The third subgroup included twenty-two workers who applied for but were not accepted for training. These "Rejects" possessed characteristics which could generally be expected to make them less employable than the "Completes" were prior to training, and thus a measure of benefits based on the post-training difference in employment experience between them and the "Completes" would probably have an upward bias. The use of multiple regression techniques in part of the analysis should have reduced or eliminated that bias; but the small size of the sample and its possible nonrepresentative character might have introduced a high degree of sampling error.

The fourth subgroup consisted of seventy-seven workers who were unemployed in the two-county area at the time when selections were made but who did not apply for entrance into the program. Since this group of "Nonapplicants" is a random sample of the total population of unemployed individuals who could be identified through the records of the Bureau of Employment Security and those of the Surplus Foods Office, and since it is also the largest group other than the "Completes," it serves as the principal control group in the study. A summary of certain important socio-demographic characteristics for this and the other three subgroups appears in Table VI.1.

## PLACEMENT IN TRAINING-RELATED JOBS

One indication of the impact of retraining is the percentage of trainees who subsequently obtain jobs which make significant use of the acquired skills. Such a measure, by itself, is a relatively poor indicator of training success since it provides no basis for determining the degree of improvement in labor market experience resulting from the retraining. Nevertheless, this measure is important for at least three reasons. First, unless the newly trained workers use their training quickly, its value will probably be lost through a deterioration of the newly acquired skills. Second, information on placement in training-related jobs may serve to corroborate or qualify the results of other measures, since a high percentage placement in training-related jobs would suggest that training is at least affecting the occupational pattern of employment, whereas a low percentage would suggest the opposite and would cast doubt on the extent to which the training per se is affecting labor market success. Third, in those cases where the "Completes" accepted jobs which were not training-related, it would be reasonable to assume that the positions could have been filled just as well by nontrainees. Thus, a low percentage of training-related job placement might well be an indication of a high degree of displacement of nontrainees by trainees in the competition for the available jobs, particularly when the jobs were located in areas of generally high unemployment. Such a condition would not, of course, reduce the benefit of training to the "Completes" themselves, but it would certainly reduce the impact of retraining on the overall level of unemployment.

In the Tennessee program, 65 per cent of the "Completes" who had obtained civilian jobs by June 30, 1964, had held a training-related job at some time in the period following training.[3] This figure, however, somewhat overstates the percentage of training-related jobs since only 42 per cent of the total jobs held by the "Completes" during that period were training-related. Furthermore, the percentage of trainees who were holding training-related jobs declined slightly over time—from 50 per cent of the first jobs obtained by the trainees to 45 per cent of those held on June 8, 1964 (two years after the end of the program)—and, in the opinion of the "Completes," only 39 per cent of the first jobs and 31 per cent of the total jobs could not have been obtained without the training.[4] Even these percentages, however, suggest that the training did have a significant impact on the employment experience of the "Completes." On the other hand, they also suggest that there may have been a significant amount of displacement of nontrainees by trainees from the available jobs.

There was a large difference in training-related job placement among the different courses of study, with the percentage who obtained at least one such job ranging from 33 per cent for the radio-TV repair class to 92 per cent for those in auto mechanics.[5] These differences probably largely reflected two basic factors: (1) the adequacy of the training program in meeting the minimal skill requirements of employers for entering the occupation for which the workers were trained, and (2) the shortage of workers with the particular skills relative to the demand for those skills. Both of these factors, therefore, merit careful consideration in planning courses for future programs.

Although 35 per cent of those who obtained jobs did not make direct use of their training, it cannot be concluded that they did not benefit from the training program. For one thing, the "Completes" did receive the benefit of special placement efforts by the Bureau of Employment Security. In addition, many employers, even though they had no need for workers with the specific skills acquired in training, probably viewed the training program as a good screening device since by completing the program the "Completes" had exhibited both ability and motivation.[6] Finally, in what could be one of the most important effects of relatively short training programs such as those under ARA, many of the trainees experienced a restoration of their self-confidence as a result of completing the program. Thus, some who had previously given up all but half-hearted attempts to find jobs, once again began an aggressive, active search for employment—a search which was rewarded in almost every case.

## EFFECT OF RETRAINING ON LABOR MARKET STATUS

A rough measure of the advantage imparted by retraining can be obtained by comparing the labor force status of the "Completes" with that of the various control groups as of selected dates both before and after the training. Such information is presented in Table VI.2, and Table VI.3 translates the information of Table VI.2 into unemployment rates as of the same dates.[7] It should be noted that such data present only a *gross* estimate of the effect of retraining since they provide no basis for eliminating that portion of the advantage arising from differences in socio-demographic characteristics among the sample groups.

The relatively small difference in pretraining unemployment rates for the "Completes" and "Nonapplicants" should not be interpreted as meaning that the two groups were equally disadvantaged prior to the training. Rather, as indicated in Table VI.1, the "Completes" were significantly younger and better educated than the "Nonapplicants." Thus much of the unemployment experienced by the "Completes" was probably of a short-term or frictional nature as the younger workers searched for their first jobs or moved from job to job in an attempt to find their niche in life. On the other hand, much of the unemployment experienced by the "Nonapplicants" was the result of permanent layoffs, and the prospects for the older, less educated "Nonapplicants" finding new jobs were certainly poorer.

In the two-year period following retraining, all of the sample groups experienced significant improvements in their employment situation. These improvements resulted partly from the shifting incidence of existing unemployment and also from a general improvement in the employment situation both locally and nationally during the period.[8] For the "Completes," however, a significant portion of the improvement may have resulted from the training program.

Once the training program ended, the "Completes" gained an almost immediate advantage over the other sample groups. One month after the end of the program, only the "Noncompletes" had a lower unemployment rate than the "Completes"—a situation relatively easy to understand since they had characteristics very similar to those of the "Completes" (see Table VI.1), and their principal reason for refusing training or for dropping out had been to accept employment or to look for work. Thus the "Noncompletes" had a head-start on the "Completes" in the job search which probably accounts for their early advantage.

TABLE VI.2

LABOR FORCE STATUS AS OF SELECTED DATES FROM 1961–64, BY TRAINING STATUS

| Labor force status | Completes | | Rejects | | Noncompletes | | Nonapplicants | |
|---|---|---|---|---|---|---|---|---|
| | No. | % | No. | % | No. | % | No. | % |
| *As of 6/1/61:* | | | | | | | | |
| Unemployed | 22 | 25.9 | 12 | 54.5 | 13 | 39.4 | 25 | 32.5 |
| Employed | 44 | 51.8 | 8 | 36.4 | 16 | 48.5 | 49 | 63.6 |
| Not in labor force—not in service | 13 | 15.3 | 2 | 9.1 | 2 | 6.1 | 1 | 1.3 |
| Not in labor force—in service | 6 | 7.1 | 0 | 0.0 | 2 | 6.1 | 2 | 2.6 |
| *As of 1/1/62:* | | | | | | | | |
| Unemployed | 59 | 69.4 | 16 | 72.7 | 22 | 66.7 | 58 | 75.3 |
| Employed | 24 | 28.2 | 4 | 18.2 | 10 | 30.3 | 19 | 24.7 |
| Not in labor force—not in service | 2 | 2.4 | 2 | 9.1 | 1 | 3.0 | 0 | 0.0 |
| Not in labor force—in service | 0 | 0.0 | 0 | 0.0 | 0 | 0.0 | 0 | 0.0 |
| *As of 7/8/62:* | | | | | | | | |
| Unemployed | 28 | 32.9 | 7 | 31.8 | 8 | 24.2 | 31 | 40.3 |
| Employed | 56 | 65.9 | 13 | 59.1 | 23 | 69.7 | 42 | 54.5 |
| Not in labor force—not in service | 0 | 0.0 | 1 | 4.5 | 1 | 3.0 | 2 | 2.6 |
| Not in labor force—in service | 1 | 1.2 | 1 | 4.5 | 1 | 3.0 | 2 | 2.6 |
| *As of 8/8/62:* | | | | | | | | |
| Unemployed | 21 | 24.7 | 6 | 27.3 | 7 | 21.2 | 25 | 32.5 |
| Employed | 63 | 74.1 | 14 | 63.6 | 24 | 72.7 | 47 | 61.0 |
| Not in labor force—not in service | 0 | 0.0 | 1 | 4.5 | 1 | 3.0 | 3 | 3.9 |
| Not in labor force—in service | 1 | 1.2 | 1 | 4.5 | 1 | 3.0 | 2 | 2.6 |
| *As of 9/8/62:* | | | | | | | | |
| Unemployed | 18 | 21.2 | 6 | 27.3 | 9 | 27.3 | 22 | 28.6 |
| Employed | 66 | 77.6 | 14 | 63.6 | 21 | 63.6 | 49 | 63.6 |
| Not in labor force—not in service | 0 | 0.0 | 1 | 4.5 | 2 | 6.1 | 4 | 5.2 |
| Not in labor force—in service | 1 | 1.2 | 1 | 4.5 | 1 | 3.0 | 2 | 2.6 |
| *As of 12/8/62:* | | | | | | | | |
| Unemployed | 13 | 15.3 | 7 | 31.8 | 9 | 27.3 | 27 | 35.1 |
| Employed | 67 | 78.8 | 12 | 54.5 | 21 | 63.6 | 44 | 57.1 |
| Not in labor force—not in service | 2 | 2.4 | 2 | 9.1 | 2 | 6.1 | 4 | 5.2 |
| Not in labor force—in service | 3 | 3.5 | 1 | 4.5 | 1 | 3.0 | 2 | 2.6 |
| *As of 6/8/63:* | | | | | | | | |
| Unemployed | 4 | 4.7 | 6 | 27.3 | 4 | 12.1 | 16 | 20.8 |
| Employed | 71 | 83.5 | 14 | 63.6 | 23 | 69.7 | 51 | 66.2 |
| Not in labor force—not in service | 4 | 4.7 | 1 | 4.5 | 3 | 9.1 | 8 | 10.4 |
| Not in labor force—in service | 6 | 7.1 | 1 | 4.5 | 3 | 9.1 | 2 | 2.6 |
| *As of 12/8/63:* | | | | | | | | |
| Unemployed | 2 | 2.4 | 4 | 18.2 | 4 | 12.1 | 17 | 22.1 |
| Employed | 68 | 80.0 | 16 | 72.7 | 20 | 60.6 | 50 | 64.9 |
| Not in labor force—not in service | 5 | 5.9 | 1 | 4.5 | 5 | 15.2 | 8 | 10.4 |
| Not in labor force—in service | 10 | 11.8 | 1 | 4.5 | 4 | 12.1 | 2 | 2.6 |
| *As of 6/8/64:* | | | | | | | | |
| Unemployed | 4 | 4.7 | 3 | 13.6 | 4 | 12.1 | 11 | 14.3 |
| Employed | 67 | 78.8 | 17 | 77.3 | 23 | 69.7 | 56 | 72.7 |
| Not in labor force—not in service | 2 | 2.4 | 1 | 4.5 | 3 | 9.1 | 8 | 10.4 |
| Not in labor force—in service | 12 | 14.1 | 1 | 4.5 | 3 | 9.1 | 2 | 2.6 |

Three months after the end of the training program the unemployment rate of the "Completes" was below that of all the other sample groups, and this advantage widened during the winter of 1962 as the situation of the "Completes" continued to improve while that of the other groups either stabilized or worsened. Thus, in December, 1962, six months after the completion of the program, 78.8 per cent of the "Completes" were employed as compared with 54.5, 63.6, and 57.1 per cent of the "Rejects," "Noncompletes," and "Nonapplicants," respectively. In terms of unemployment rates, that of the "Completes" ranged from approximately 14 to almost 22 percentage points below those of the control groups.

TABLE VI.3

UNEMPLOYMENT RATES AS OF SELECTED DATES FROM 1961–64, BY TRAINING STATUS

| Date | Completes | Rejects | Noncompletes | Nonapplicants |
|------|-----------|---------|--------------|---------------|
| 6/1/61 | 33.3% | 60.0% | 44.8% | 33.8% |
| 1/1/62 | 71.1 | 80.0 | 68.8 | 75.3 |
| 7/8/62 | 33.3 | 35.0 | 25.8 | 42.5 |
| 8/8/62 | 25.0 | 30.0 | 22.6 | 34.7 |
| 9/8/62 | 21.4 | 30.0 | 30.0 | 31.0 |
| 12/8/62 | 16.3 | 36.8 | 30.0 | 38.0 |
| 6/8/63 | 5.3 | 30.0 | 14.8 | 23.9 |
| 12/8/63 | 2.9 | 20.0 | 16.7 | 25.4 |
| 6/8/64 | 5.6 | 15.0 | 14.8 | 16.4 |

During the next year all of the groups experienced approximately equivalent reductions in percentage points of unemployment, and on December 8, 1963, the unemployment rate for the "Completes" stood at only 2.9 per cent—well below both the local and national rates at that time. Thus, the unemployment rate advantage of the "Completes" was almost identical to what it had been a year earlier; but in employment terms the advantage of the "Completes" had declined slightly throughout the year 1963. Whereas in December, 1962, the percentage of "Completes" employed had ranged from 15 to 24 percentage points above the other groups, by December, 1963, this advantage had fallen to a range between 7 and 19 percentage points. This drop, however, was largely the result of the relatively large proportion of the "Completes" who were no longer classified as being in the civilian labor force because of their entrance into the armed forces.

Between December, 1963 and June, 1964, the advantage enjoyed by the "Completes" declined as their unemployment rate rose slightly (from 2.9 to 5.6 per cent) while those of other sample groups were falling. Thus, on June 8, 1964, the unemployment rate of the "Completes" was only 9 to 11 percentage points below those of the other groups, and the number employed ranged from only 1.5 to 9 percentage points above the other groups. More will be said later about this decline in the advantage of the "Completes."

## THE EFFECT OF RETRAINING ON EMPLOYMENT
## OVER PERIODS OF TIME

A somewhat more comprehensive measure of the differences in employment or unemployment experience between the "Completes" and the
control groups can be obtained by measuring that experience over periods
of time rather than as of moments of time. Measurements were thus obtained which indicate weeks employed or unemployed for each of the
subgroups over the full twenty-four-month post-training period.

Not all of the post-training employment advantage indicated for the
"Completes" in the previous section can be attributed to the training
program itself, since the more favorable socio-demographic characteristics
of the "Completes," as compared with those of the "Nonapplicants" and
"Rejects" (see Table VI.1), might have been expected to make them more
successful in the labor market even without training. Multiple regression
techniques were thus used in connection with the "period" measures in
an attempt to eliminate the effect of these differences in characteristics.
Since a number of the dependent variables in the regressions were qualitative rather than quantitative (for example, county of residence), sets of
dummy variables were used instead of scaled variables for those characteristics.[9] In such cases, one level or value of each such characteristic enters
into the constant term, and the regression coefficients for the variables
representing each of the other levels indicate the mean difference in the
effect on the independent variable of those levels as compared with that
of the level entering into the constant term.

The multiple regressions presented in Tables VI.4 and VI.5 controlled
for differences in training status and for eight other socio-demographic
characteristics.[10] Since, in the training status variable set, the status of
"Completes" entered into the constant term, the regression coefficients
of the three control groups as compared with the "Completes" indicate
their employment (or unemployment) disadvantage after eliminating the
effect of differences in the eight socio-demographic characteristics. Thus,
if the regression equations adequately controlled for differences among
the sample groups not arising from the training, the regression coefficient
of the control groups should represent a reasonable estimate of the effect
of the retraining on the labor market success of the "Completes." [11]

Examination of Table VI.4 (in which the weeks unemployed from
July 1, 1962, to June 30, 1964, constitute the dependent variable) shows
the coefficient of the "Nonapplicants" variable to be significantly different from zero (that is, from the value of the estimated mean of the
"Completes") at the 10 per cent level. The coefficients of the "Rejects"
and the "Noncompletes" are not, however, significantly greater than
zero. This, of course, does not indicate that the true mean of the "Com-

pletes" is not smaller than the true means of these two control groups (indeed, it is much more likely that it is smaller than that the means are all equal); rather it shows that the hypothesis that they are equal cannot be rejected with a high degree of confidence (90 per cent probability or better).

TABLE VI.4

MULTIPLE REGRESSION OF TRAINING STATUS AND SELECTED SOCIO-DEMOGRAPHIC CHARACTERISTICS ON WEEKS UNEMPLOYED FROM 7/1/62–6/30/64

n = 217           $R^2$ = 0.2130
Std. Error = 26.65        F = 3.38

| Variable | Coefficient | Standard error | "t" Statistic |
|---|---|---|---|
| Constant[a] | 36.49 | — | — |
| 1. Age | 0.29 | 0.25 | 1.18 |
| 2. Education | −1.11 | 0.87 | 1.28* |
| 3. Claiborne county | −0.87 | 4.35 | 0.20 |
| 4. Semiskilled | −2.08 | 4.43 | 0.47 |
| 5. Skilled | −4.02 | 6.82 | 0.60 |
| 6. Other[b] | −11.06 | 8.64 | 1.28* |
| 7. Unemp. less than 6 mo.[c] | −16.27 | 4.46 | 3.65‡ |
| 8. Emp. less than 6 mo. | −15.52 | 7.80 | 1.99† |
| 9. Emp. 6 mo. plus | −26.23 | 5.34 | 4.91‡ |
| 10. Mobile before 6/30/64 | 7.48 | 5.98 | 1.25 |
| 11. Mobile on 6/30/64 | 0.25 | 4.17 | 0.06 |
| 12. Married | 6.16 | 4.16 | 1.48* |
| 13. Prev. training | 3.15 | 6.06 | 0.52 |
| 14. Rejects | 6.52 | 6.94 | 0.94 |
| 15. Noncompletes | 4.95 | 5.82 | 0.85 |
| 16. Nonapplicants | 8.29 | 5.42 | 1.53* |

* Significant at 0.10 level.
† Significant at 0.05 level.
‡ Significant at 0.01 level.
[a] Constant term includes Campbell county, unskilled laborers, unemployed more than 6 months, no mobility, no previous training, not married (single, widowed, divorced, separated), and "Completes" statuses.
[b] Includes professional, managerial, clerical, sales, and service.
[c] Includes NLF less than 6 months.

The training status regression coefficients indicate that during the twenty-four-month period from July 1, 1962, to June 30, 1964, the "Completes" experienced approximately 8.3, 6.5, and 5.0 fewer weeks of unemployment than the "Nonapplicants," "Rejects," and "Noncompletes," respectively. This advantage compares with a "gross" advantage of 15.2, 15.5, and 6.8 weeks over the same twenty-four-month period.[12] Thus, separating out the effect of the eight socio-demographic characteristics reduced the unemployment advantage of the "Completes" by anything from 27 to 58 per cent.

Table VI.5 presents the results of the regression of training status and the eight socio-demographic variables upon weeks employed from July

TABLE VI.5

Multiple Regression of Training Status and Selected Socio-Demographic Characteristics on Weeks Employed from 7/1/62–6/30/64

n = 217                R² = .2545
Std. Error = 32.63        F = 4.268‡

| Variable | Coefficient | Standard error | "t" Statistic |
|---|---|---|---|
| Constant[a] | 77.28 | | |
| 1. Age | −0.76 | 0.30 | 2.55‡ |
| 2. Education | 0.00 | 1.08 | 0.00 |
| 3. Claiborne county | −1.10 | 5.24 | 0.21 |
| 4. Semiskilled | 6.19 | 5.48 | 1.13 |
| 5. Skilled | 15.93 | 8.21 | 1.94† |
| 6. Other[b] | 13.97 | 10.58 | 1.32* |
| 7. Unemp. less than 6 mo.[c] | 21.10 | 5.45 | 3.87‡ |
| 8. Emp. less than 6 mo. | 18.12 | 9.54 | 1.90† |
| 9. Emp. 6 mo. plus | 33.36 | 6.54 | 5.10‡ |
| 10. Mobile before 6/30/64 | −13.30 | 7.35 | 1.81† |
| 11. Mobile on 6/30/64 | −11.02 | 5.27 | 2.09† |
| 12. Married | 15.00 | 5.08 | 2.95‡ |
| 13. Prev. training | 1.37 | 7.61 | 0.18 |
| 14. Rejects | −7.85 | 8.53 | 0.92 |
| 15. Noncompletes | −12.49 | 7.14 | 1.75† |
| 16. Nonapplicants | −12.99 | 6.63 | 1.96† |

* Significant at 0.10 level.
† Significant at 0.05 level.
‡ Significant at 0.01 level.

[a] Constant term includes Campbell county, unskilled laborers, unemployed more than 6 months, no mobility, no previous training, not married (single, widowed, divorced, separated), and "Completes" statuses.

[b] Includes professional, managerial, clerical, sales, and service.

[c] Includes NLF less than 6 months.

1, 1962, to June 30, 1964. It will be noted that the employment advantage of the "Completes" is greater than the earlier indicated advantage in terms of unemployment. Furthermore, the regression coefficients of both the "Nonapplicants" and the "Noncompletes" are significant at the 5 per cent level. This greater employment advantage suggests that the retraining may have caused both lower unemployment rates and higher labor force participation rates.

In terms of weeks employed during the twenty-four month period, the advantage of the "Completes" was approximately 13.0, 7.9, and 12.5 weeks over the "Nonapplicants," "Rejects," and "Noncompletes," respectively. This employment advantage is less than half that reported in the West Virginia study, which is the only one providing a comparable measure.[13] There are several possible explanations for this difference. Sampling variation, of course, may account for some of the difference, but it is unlikely that this would explain more than a relatively small portion of it. Furthermore, it is equally likely that sampling variation may have decreased rather than increased the difference between the two estimates. A second factor which very likely did cause some of the difference is the fact that the West Virginia regressions were based on the twelve-month period immediately following training and, as indicated earlier, the advantage in the present study declined from the first to the second period. This too, however, would explain only a part of the indicated difference. A third factor which might appear to have caused some difference in the results is the inclusion in the West Virginia regressions of four characteristics which were not included in the regressions of the present study.[14] Those four additional characteristics—sex, race, year training ended, and quarter training ended—were not relevant in the present study, however, since all of the sample members were white males, and all of the trainees completed their courses at the same time. It would appear, therefore, that factors other than differences in methods of measurement and analysis were involved.

One factor which may have caused a substantial increase in the advantage of the trainees in West Virginia was the fact that in at least some of the cases the training programs were geared to the needs of specific employers, and some of these employers had given advance indication (if not advance commitment) of their willingness to hire all or a large number of the graduates from certain courses.[15] No such arrangements were made in the Tennessee program.

Interestingly enough, placement figures from the two studies indicate that, at least in the spring and summer of 1963, the gross advantage of the "Completes" may have been greater in the Tennessee program.[16] In West Virginia, for example, 17.0 per cent of the "Completes" and 27.2 per cent of the "Nonapplicants" were still unemployed in the spring and summer of 1963, and both of these rates were above that prevailing in the local labor market area as a whole at that time.[17] On the other hand, in the Tennessee program, on June 8, 1963, only 4.7 per cent of the "Completes" and 20.8 per cent of the "Nonapplicants" were unemployed, and that rate for the former group was appreciably below the rate prevailing in the local labor market. Thus the smaller net advantage in the Tennessee program appears to reflect the fact that more of the gross advantage was caused by socio-demographic differences than was true in West Virginia. This suggests that the pretraining advantage of the Tennessee "Completes" over the control groups was greater than that of the trainees in West Virginia. It follows, therefore, that part of the reason for the reduced benefit in the Tennessee program was probably the smaller amount of "room for improvement" in the experience of those selected for retraining.

## SOURCES OF RETRAINING PROGRAM BENEFITS

Although the "Completes" experienced a net advantage over the "Nonapplicants" which, during the twenty-four-month period, was equal to approximately 8.3 weeks in terms of unemployment and 13.0 weeks in terms of employment, it would probably not be correct to say that this entire advantage derived from the vocational training per se. It is possible, of course, that even some of the net advantage resulted from a failure to control adequately for differences in characteristics not included in the present analysis. The fact that in the multiple regressions none of the three control groups experienced an unemployment or employment level significantly different from those of the other control groups suggests, however, that unmeasured differences in characteristics were not too important. Within the program itself, though, as indicated previously, the "Completes" received special placement assistance from the Bureau of Employment Security in the period immediately following training. In addition, some employers gave preference to the "Completes," even for non-training-related jobs, because they considered the training program to be a good screening device. Additionally, some of the trainees (and possibly some of the "Noncompletes" also) regained their self-confidence as the result of the program, and this may have played an important role in their improved employment experience. Finally, of course, there was undoubtedly some direct benefit of the training—the benefit which arose from the improved employability of the workers because of their increased level of skill.

At least the first of these sources of benefit (that arising from the special placement efforts) could be created without the considerable expense of a training program. It is possible, of course, that, in sales parlance, "the advertising campaign is more effective if it is accompanied by an improvement in the product to be sold," but the importance of the training complemented by the special Employment Service placement help remains to be tested.

It is also likely that an intensive program of interviews and testing could provide at least as satisfactory (from the employers' standpoint) a basis for screening prospective employees as the training programs.

Whether the benefits of such special efforts would be as great per dollar expended as when they are a part of an overall training program is a question which cannot be answered without further research.

The third and fourth sources of benefit from training are probably more uniquely the benefits of retraining per se. Even in their case, however, alternatives exist for imparting basically the same effect. It might be possible, for example, to restore the self-confidence of the worker through a series of counseling sessions (a rather natural complement to a program of improved placement services), and it is certainly possible to teach new skills to workers through means other than formal training courses. Additional research on such alternative programs is thus needed in order that the proper role of formal classroom training in an overall manpower program can be determined.

## THE PERMANENCE OF THE BENEFITS FROM RETRAINING

The possibility that the advantage imparted by retraining may decline over time—a possibility suggested by information presented earlier in this study—has important implications in the determination of the profitability of retraining programs. As indicated by the data in Table VI.6 (which translates the employment and unemployment data from Table VI.2 into terms of the advantage of the "Completes" over the control groups on each of the dates), a continuation of the type of decline such as occurred between December, 1963 and June, 1964, would mean the rapid disappearance of all the advantage enjoyed by the "Completes." It should be noted, of course, that this decline only manifested itself clearly in the last six months of the twenty-four-month period covered by the study. Whether this did, in fact, represent the beginning of a continuing decline in the advantage of the "Completes" cannot be determined without further follow-ups of the various groups. The West Virginia study, however (which also obtained data ranging from approximately eighteen to twenty-four months following training), reported a similar narrowing of the advantage of the trainees in the latter portion of the period and led Professors Gibbard and Somers to pose the question: "May it be that the contribution of retraining is less that of giving its recipients a lasting advantage than it is that of accelerating their return to gainful employment?" [18]

A second factor that should be noted is that the findings in the present study and also those in the West Virginia study are based primarily on short-term ARA-type training programs.[19] Admittedly, only a limited amount of training can be imparted in a sixteen-week period, and thus in every case the courses covered by the present study were designed only to permit entry into the particular occupation. It seems likely, how-

## TABLE VI.6

### Employment and Unemployment Advantage of Completes as of Selected Dates from 1962–64

| | Rejects | | Noncompletes | | Nonapplicants | |
|---|---|---|---|---|---|---|
| Status | % Advantage[a] | Direction of change[b] | % Advantage[a] | Direction of change[b] | % Advantage[a] | Direction of change[b] |
| *July 8, 1962:* | | | | | | |
| Unemployment | −1.1 | | −8.7 | | 7.4 | |
| Employment | 6.8 | | −3.8 | | 11.4 | |
| *August 8, 1962:* | | | | | | |
| Unemployment | 2.6 | ↑ | −3.5 | ↑ | 7.8 | ↑ |
| Employment | 10.5 | ↑ | 1.4 | ↑ | 1.4 | ↑ |
| *September 8, 1962:* | | | | | | |
| Unemployment | 6.1 | ↑ | 6.1 | ↑ | 7.4 | ↓ |
| Employment | 14.0 | ↑ | 14.0 | ↑ | 14.0 | ↑ |
| *December 8, 1962:* | | | | | | |
| Unemployment | 16.5 | ↑ | 12.0 | ↑ | 19.8 | ↑ |
| Employment | 24.3 | ↑ | 15.2 | ↑ | 21.7 | ↑ |
| *June 8, 1963:* | | | | | | |
| Unemployment | 22.6 | ↑ | 7.4 | ↓ | 16.1 | ↓ |
| Employment | 19.9 | ↓ | 13.8 | ↓ | 17.3 | ↓ |
| *December 8, 1963:* | | | | | | |
| Unemployment | 15.8 | ↓ | 9.7 | ↑ | 19.7 | ↑ |
| Employment | 7.3 | ↓ | 19.4 | ↑ | 15.1 | ↓ |
| *June 8, 1964:* | | | | | | |
| Unemployment | 8.9 | ↓ | 7.4 | ↓ | 9.6 | ↓ |
| Employment | 1.5 | ↓ | 9.1 | ↓ | 6.1 | ↓ |

[a] Percentage advantage of "Completes" over the training status indicated.

[b] Direction of change of "Completes" advantage since immediately preceding period.

ever, that under the longer-term programs now possible under MDTA, the advantage resulting from training will be both larger and more permanent.

Finally, it should be recognized that even if the smaller advantage indicated by the June, 1964, data does persist or even narrow somewhat, the advantage in terms of unemployment on that date, although lower than in some of the previous periods, was still substantial. Furthermore, the reduced advantage in civilian employment of the "Completes" was partly the result of the relatively high percentage of that group who were in the armed forces in 1964, and the consequent inability of these individuals to obtain civilian employment because of their service attachment should not be interpreted as an indication of lessened effectiveness of vocational training in general. At the same time, however, this factor, in all likelihood, reduced the long-run effectiveness of this particular program since a two- to four-year period in the armed forces will result in the loss of much of the skill acquired in the training program unless there is a reinforcement of those skills through practice or similar training in the service. The question might be raised, therefore, as to the desirability of continuing to accept individuals with an imminent service obligation into retraining programs.

An alternative to the hypothesis of a continuing decline in the advantage of the "Completes" may be that the advantage decreases during periods when general employment conditions improve and increases when employment conditions in general deteriorate. The implication of such a hypothesis is that retraining makes workers more immune to fluctuations in the overall level of employment. A relatively high degree of immunity to such fluctuations does tend to characterize the more highly skilled and educated workers in general, of course, and such a hypothesis certainly appears reasonable on its face.

Although the information contained in the present study is quite limited, it does contain some basis for testing this hypothesis. Two distinct changes in employment conditions occurred during the twenty-four-month period covered by this study. First, there was a general decline in seasonally adjusted unemployment rates from the beginning to the end of the period. Second, there was the normal seasonal change each year which saw unemployment rise during the winter months and fall during the summer months. A downward trend in the advantage of the "Completes" from an initial, high level (which, according to most of the measures, occurred in December, 1962) would thus be consistent with both of the hypotheses suggested. A seasonal fluctuation which was inversely related to the seasonal change in employment would, however, tend to substantiate the second hypothesis.

An examination of the data in Table VI.6 does indeed suggest a seasonal variation in the benefits which was inversely related to the employment level. Considering the measures of advantage in terms of both employment and unemployment for the three control groups on June 8, 1963, December 8, 1964, and June 8, 1964, the changes in fourteen out of the eighteen cases revealed such an inverse relationship. Only in the case of the "Rejects" (which accounted for three of the four exceptions) was there a sizable deviation from the hypothesized pattern of action, and this might well have been caused by sampling error resulting from the small size of the group of "Rejects" or by the possible nonrepresentative composition of the group (see fn. 2).

Training benefits which are inversely related to the level of employment would, of course, tend to make retraining programs less profitable during periods of prosperity. Indeed the possibility exists that such programs would not continue to show a high enough rate of return under such conditions as to justify their continued existence. In any event, in view of the relatively high levels of employment recently attained by the United States' economy, further research into the question is certainly justified.

It must be emphasized that the data presented in this study are insufficient to prove or disprove any hypothesis relating to the long-term trend of training benefits even for this one training program. It should also be noted that the two hypotheses advanced here are not necessarily mutually exclusive. That is, it is possible that the benefits may both decline over time and also fluctuate in inverse relationship to changes in the level of employment. It is also possible that the long-run behavior may be completely different from that suggested by either of these hypotheses. In any event, it seems clear that present knowledge is insufficient to permit any degree of confidence in long-range projections of retraining benefits.

## CONCLUSIONS

1. Evidence of this and other studies strongly suggests that retraining programs do improve the employment experience of unemployed workers. The improvement attributable to the programs is normally overstated by data which only measure gross differences in post-training labor market experience of "Completes" as compared with that of randomly selected control groups of unemployed workers, however, since part of the advantage of the "Completes" is the result of their more favorable socio-demographic characteristics. Nevertheless, multiple regression equations used in this and other similar studies to eliminate the effect of these differences in socio-demographic characteristics still indicate a substantial benefit of training to the "Completes."

2. It is not clear that retraining reduces the overall level of unemployment for the economy as a whole in the same way that it reduces unemployment for the "Completes." The evidence on training-related job placement in this study, for example, suggests that at least part of the improvement experienced by the "Completes" may have come at the expense of other nontrained workers. While such a condition would not reduce the training benefit for the individual trainee, it would certainly reduce the benefit for the economy as a whole. Additional research is thus needed to determine the degree of such displacements.

3. There is some evidence in the present study and also in the West Virginia study which suggests that the benefits of training are rather short-lived and consist principally of facilitating a rapid return to gainful employment for unemployed workers. An alternative hypothesis, which

would appear to fit the data of this study equally well, suggests that the benefits of training vary directly with changes in the general level of unemployment. Since the rate of return from investment in retraining is so dependent upon the long-run behavior of the level of benefits, the question of their permanence certainly merits further study.

4. Not all of the benefits of the training programs are the result of the training per se. As noted in this and several other studies, the benefits actually derive from a multitude of causes, including the special placement efforts extended to the trainees by the Bureau of Employment Security, the encouragement which the trainees receive as the result of their ability to complete the program, etc. Since there are alternative methods for imparting these same benefits—alternatives which may be more efficient than retraining—additional research should be undertaken to determine the proper role of retraining and the other alternatives in the nation's overall program of manpower development.

## REFERENCES

1. An initial sample of 239 individuals including 87 "Completes," 36 "Noncompletes," 26 "Rejects," and 90 "Nonapplicants" was selected for field interviews. Since no women were accepted into the training program, all 239 sample members were males. Inability to contact all of the individuals reduced the sample to 217. In designing the initial sample, all 87 who completed training and all of the 36 who were accepted for but did not complete the training were included. The 90 "Nonapplicants" were selected from an estimated population of 1,600 unemployed males by the use of random techniques. Selection of the sample of "Rejects" posed problems since records were available on all 107 workers who were tested and rejected, but they could be located on only 15 of an estimated 250 to 300 workers who were rejected without being tested. As a consequence, the sample of 26 "Rejects" included all 15 nontested rejects for whom records were available and one of ten of the tested rejects. For further information on the composition of the samples, see Richard J. Solie, "Job Retraining Under the Area Redevelopment Act: The Campbell-Claiborne Counties (Tennessee) Case" (unpublished Ph.D. dissertation, The University of Tennessee, 1965), pp. 52–61.

    The four-group classification used here is similar to the five-group classification employed by Somers and Stromsdorfer in their West Virginia study. The difference lies in the category of "Noncompletes" used here, which includes the "Dropouts" and "Did-not-reports" of their classification (see Gerald G. Somers and Ernst W. Stromsdorfer, "A Benefit-Cost Analysis of Manpower Retraining," in *Proceedings of the Seventeenth Annual Meeting*, Industrial Relations Research Association, December, 1964 [Madison, Wisconsin: IRRA, 1965], p. 3); these two groups were combined in the present study because of the small size of each and the similarity of their socio-demographic characteristics.

2. It is true, of course, that there was one major difference between the two groups: the "Completes" had whatever it took to finish the program whereas the "Noncompletes" evidently did not. This may thus have meant that the "Noncompletes" had less ability or less persistence than the "Completes." On the other hand, since the majority of those who failed to report or who dropped out did so to accept or to look for work, it may have signified merely a more urgent need for a higher income than was provided in the training program. It may, in some cases, even have signified a greater degree of employability for the "Noncompletes" who obtained

work than was true of the "Completes" since some of the latter may have desired employment but could not find it.

3. This percentage compares favorably with the figures reported by Gibbard and Somers in their West Virginia study (approximately 47 per cent at the end of one year) and the overall figures reported in the early period of ARA (56 per cent). It is somewhat lower than the 84 per cent reported by Borus in his Connecticut study and the overall 87 to 88 per cent reported for the MDTA programs and for the later ARA programs. The higher rates reported for the latter are probably largely a result of longer training periods and/or pretraining hiring agreements with employers. See Harold A. Gibbard and Gerald G. Somers, "Government Retraining of the Unemployed in West Virginia," Chapter II of this volume; Michael E. Borus, "A Benefit-Cost Analysis of the Economic Effectiveness of Retraining the Unemployed," *Yale Economic Essays,* Vol. 4 (Fall, 1964), 389–90; "Eight Months' Training Experience Under the Area Redevelopment Act," *Monthly Labor Review,* Vol. 85 (December, 1962), 1,377; U.S. Department of Labor, *Manpower Research and Training Under the Manpower Development and Training Act, A Report by the Secretary of Labor* (Washington: GPO, March, 1964), p. 33; and U.S. Department of Labor, Manpower Administration, Bureau of Employment Security, *Manpower Training Operations Under the ARA* (Washington: GPO, September, 1963), pp. 5–8.

4. The relatively large difference between the percentage placement in training-related jobs and the percentage which (in the trainees' opinion) could not have been obtained without training reflects the minimal skill requirements of some of the jobs (although what skill was required was in the area of the training). Thus employers were willing to hire untrained workers and train them themselves if the more desirable trainees were not available.

5. The percentages for the other classes were: welding—67 per cent, machine-tool operating—61 per cent, and woodworking—68 per cent. Some of these figures are slightly misleading, however, since those for auto mechanics include a number of trainees who obtained work in service stations where they worked primarily as attendants but did some mechanical work. In the case of the radio-TV class, placement was strongly affected by the closing (on the day the program ended) of a relatively large electronics plant in the immediate labor market area which had been expected to hire a number of trainees.

6. See, for example, Somers and Stromsdorfer, "A Benefit-Cost Analysis . . . ," p. 175; and Borus, "A Benefit-Cost Analysis of the Economic Effectiveness . . . ," pp. 375–76.

7. That is, Table VI.2 indicates the percentage of the total sample who were unemployed, whereas Table VI.3 indicates the percentage of those in the civilian labor force on the particular date who were unemployed. The rapid rise in unemployment rates from June 1, 1961, to January 1, 1962, reflects the fact that (with a very few exceptions in the case of the trainees) only those who were unemployed on February 1, 1962, were included in the sample groups.

8. In February, 1962, unemployment rates in Campbell and Claiborne counties, respectively, stood at 18.6 and 8.4 per cent, and for the year 1962 the annual averages were 16.3 and 7.0 per cent. By 1964 the respective annual rates had fallen to 10.4 and 5.5 per cent. (Source: Tennessee Department of Employment Security). Nationally the unemployment rate averaged 5.6 per cent in 1962 and 5.2 per cent in 1964.

9. The dichotomous variable for county of residence was thus represented by one dummy variable in which

$$x = 0 \text{ if Campbell county}$$
$$x = 1 \text{ if Claiborne county.}$$

More generally, a characteristic which had $r$ different levels or values required $r - 1$ dummy variables. For a discussion of the use of dummy variables, see Daniel B. Suits, "Use of Dummy Variables in Regression Equations," *Journal of the American Statistical Association,* Vol. 52 (1957), 548–51; and J. Johnston, *Econometric Methods* (New York: McGraw-Hill, 1963), pp. 221–28.

10. The eight socio-demographic characteristics are: previous labor force experience as of January 1, 1962 (PLFE—1/1/62); age, education, previous occupation, county of residence, marital status, and previous vocational training completed, all as of February 1, 1962; and post-training mobility from February 1, 1962, to June 30, 1964. The PLFE variable has four classifications according to the individual's status and the length of time in that status on January 1, 1962. The four PLFE classifications are: (1) unemployed or not in labor force for six months or more, (2) unemployed or not in labor force for less than six months, (3) employed for less than six months, and (4) employed for six months or more. The previous occupation variable is based on the individual's "regular occupation" as of February 1, 1962, and it too is divided into four classes: (1) unskilled, farm laborer, or new entrant; (2) semiskilled; (3) skilled; and (4) other (includes professional, managerial, clerical, sales, and service). County of residence is either Campbell or Claiborne county. Marital status is divided into two groups: married and not married (single, widowed, divorced, and separated) and previous training is split into those who have had and those who have not had previous vocational training. Post-training mobility includes several different types of mobility: the individual may have moved away from the labor market area (either Campbell or Claiborne county), he may have commuted to a job which was outside the labor market area, or he may have worked and lived away from the labor market area during the week but returned home on weekends. Based on these types of mobility, three classifications of post-training mobility are established: (1) no mobility following February 1, 1962; (2) mobility following February 1, 1962, which had ceased by June 30, 1964; and (3) mobility on June 30, 1964 (that is, the individual either lived outside or held a job outside the labor market area on June 30, 1964).
11. The use of only eight socio-demographic variables in the equations would imply an inadequate control for the nontraining differences. The fact that the regression coefficients for the "Rejects," "Noncompletes" and "Nonapplicants" are not significantly different from each other, however, suggests otherwise.
12. Solie, "Job Retraining . . . ," pp. 98–103.
13. In that study in the twelve-month period following the end of training the trainees fared 29, 28, 21, and 5 per cent better than the "Nonapplicants," "Rejects," "Did-Not-Reports," and "Dropouts," respectively. Somers and Stromsdorfer, "A Benefit-Cost Analysis . . . ," p. 178, fn. 7.
14. *Ibid.,* p. 177.
15. Gibbard and Somers, "Government Retraining . . . ," p. 56.
16. The data from the two studies are not strictly comparable, however, since those in the West Virginia study reflect the labor force status as of the day of the interview in the spring or summer of 1963, whereas the Tennessee figures indicate the status of all the "Completes" as of June 8, 1963.
17. Gibbard and Somers, "Government Retraining . . . ," p. 66.
18. *Ibid.,* p. 70.
19. Some of the training in the West Virginia study was carried out under the Area Vocational Training Program (AVP), a course set up under West Virginia state legislation. Somers and Stromsdorfer, "A Benefit-Cost Analysis . . . ," p. 173.

# VII

## LOUIS A. FERMAN
## AND
## SCOTT HARVEY

■

## JOB RETRAINING IN MICHIGAN

### INTRODUCTION

This chapter represents a stocktaking of Michigan's experience between 1960 and 1965 with the vocational training and retraining of workers.* It examines critically a number of training and retraining efforts to see what contributions they made to the functioning of the state economy as well as to the adjustment of workers to the changing world of work. In a broader sense, we are interested in seeing what lessons can be learned from the Michigan experience with retraining programs that can be applied to national economic problems.

There are two kinds of training and retraining programs in Michigan. There are, first, a number of permanent, well-established programs designed to meet the normal job mobility needs of the Michigan economy. Many of the large automobile companies and their supplier firms have company-based retraining programs designed to facilitate work transfers from one job to another or to acquaint new workers with the technical details of their jobs. All of the major craft unions conduct apprenticeship training, using either their own facilities or those of the local school board. The Adult Education Division of the State Education Service

* The authors, both at the University of Michigan, would like to express their appreciation to the Institute of Labor and Industrial Relations of The University of Michigan–Wayne State University, and especially to its co-directors, Ronald W. Haughton and Charles M. Rehmus, whose encouragement and support contributed substantially to the development of this paper.

gives a number of special vocational classes, usually for beginners but sometimes for workers who desire to increase their skill at a given occupation. All of these programs have a long history in Michigan.

The second kind of training and retraining programs was specifically developed as a response to economic and social problems—job displacement, "hard-core" unemployment, high-school dropouts, and surpluses in youth labor. These programs were designed to provide training for certain groups of disadvantaged workers in order that they might be useful participants in the economy. The training and retraining opportunities of these programs are not geared to the job mobility needs of a normal economy but, rather, to the needs of an economy where marked changes are occurring in the patterns of utilization and participation of workers in the labor market. These latter programs, unlike those previously described, are new in Michigan as well as in the nation.

These new programs represent a significant departure from the traditional philosophy of job-placement aid to the unemployed. Only a decade ago the vocational placement agencies, both public and private, were prone to limit their placement efforts to their view of the capacities and abilities of the unemployed. Little or no attention was given to the possibility of enlarging the job possibilities of the unemployed through training and retraining programs. Today we find more and more acceptance of the principle of preparing the unemployed worker for new jobs through enlarging his abilities and skills through retraining. One primary reason for this change of attitude has undoubtedly been the rapidity of technological change in the last two decades and the general recognition that new jobs in the economy require new skills. Another influence has been the shocks of economic recession in the 1950's and 1960's, which left larger and larger surpluses of unwanted workers. The impact of this new philosophy on policies of manpower utilization and on the functioning of the labor market will be profound. It marks the beginning of an active effort toward helping disadvantaged workers adjust to an industrial society characterized by increasing changes in skill and occupational demands.

In this report we will limit ourselves to a discussion of the training and retraining programs that were necessitated by special circumstances and problems in the Michigan economy. The report will begin by reviewing the problems and needs of the Michigan economy which have made special programs of training and retraining necessary, and will then turn to the operation of the two major retraining programs sponsored by the federal government: the Area Redevelopment Administration (ARA) and the Manpower Development and Training Act (MDTA).[1] In reviewing the operation of these programs we will be concerned with the following questions: Who were selected for training and how did they fare?

What differences were there in results between ARA and MDTA programs? What changes occurred in the operation and the structure of the programs over time, especially as the labor market changed? Finally, we will consider the future of retraining in Michigan, with particular emphasis to new directions and structure of programs.

### DATA SOURCES

The observations reported on retraining in Michigan do not come from a single set of data but are drawn from data made available from three separate sources.

1. The first set of data was derived from a series of tabulations prepared by the Research and Statistics Staff of the Michigan Employment Security Commission. These tabulations contain aggregate data on MDTA and ARA courses which were completed or in progress during a given fiscal year, and include such information as: the number of courses; the number of trainees enrolled; the number of trainees who completed the course or dropped out; employment and placement data following the completion of the course.

2. The second set of data was drawn from special tabulations on course and trainee characteristics prepared by the research staff of the Office of Manpower, Automation and Training. These data included characteristics of the trainee (e.g., sex, education, primary occupation, and race), course performance, and subsequent placement status.

3. Another source of data was a special study conducted by the author in February, 1963. In cooperation with the research staff of the Michigan Employment Security Commission, a study of MDTA and ARA trainees in Michigan—their characteristics, course performances, and adjustment in the labor market—was undertaken. Trainees who had attended courses in Michigan on or before December 31, 1962, were selected for study. The number of workers who fitted this criterion was 1,405, but complete data were available only for 1,273 trainees. The observations to be reported are based on this sample.[2]

In the presentation of data on retraining in Michigan, selective findings and observations from these three sources will be used.

### THE STATUS OF THE MICHIGAN ECONOMY, 1963

In 1963 Michigan was the seventh most populous state in the nation, comprising 4.4 per cent of the national population. It is a heavily industrialized state: at that time about 6.6 per cent of the nation's manufacturing payrolls were paid out to 5.5 per cent of the nation's manufacturing employees who work in Michigan. Its major city, Detroit, is one of the largest industrial centers in the United States and in 1963 was the fifth ranking metropolitan area in population. The state has always been regarded as a vital cog in the functioning of the American economy and as a barometer of the economic health of the nation.

Yet, between 1953 and 1962, Michigan and Detroit came to be regarded as soft spots in the American economy. A number of national, regional, and state economic trends tended to have an adverse effect on the patterns of manpower utilization in Michigan. As a result, the state had to contend with a serious problem of persistent unemployment. Every year between 1957 and 1962, the unemployment rate for Michigan was higher than that for the nation as a whole. In the recession year of 1958, national unemployment reached 6.8 per cent. The rate in Michigan was 13.6 per cent and in Detroit it was 15.3 per cent. In 1962, the Michigan unemployment rate was a full percentage point above that of the nation.

It would be difficult to attribute this high rate of persistent unemployment to any one factor. Undoubtedly, part of the problem has resulted from productivity increases in manufacturing through laborsaving devices. These productivity gains have been at the expense of manpower and have resulted in manpower surpluses in states which have a heavy concentration in manufacturing. Manpower needs in wartime also accelerated the movement of rural workers from farm areas to jobs in the industrial cities of the North. The result has been the concentration in industrial cities of aggregates of workers who are unskilled, undereducated, and strangers to the needs of an industrial society. Workers could find employment during periods of labor shortage (e.g., World War II and the Korean War), but find it difficult to compete for jobs in a surplus labor market. Workers are also hurt by the national shift away from blue-collar to white-collar employment and the national trend in the educational upgrading of jobs. These changes further reduced the demand for a large number of workers. Without some compensatory education and training, many found few good jobs open to them.

Finally, the labor force in the United States today is also being swelled to an unprecedented size by the entry into the labor market of young high-school graduates or dropouts and married women who desire some job to supplement family income or as a relief from the housewife role. At a time when surplus labor is being created by labor-saving machines, automation, and the movement of industry, these new patterns in labor force participation aggravate an already serious problem. The task, then, is not only to create new jobs, but to fit and prepare workers for job opportunities.

Although these national trends have been felt by a number of states, Michigan's problem has been made more acute by economic changes within the state. The Michigan economy has been built around industries which show the most marked cyclical fluctuation—the durable goods manufacturing sector. Further, these are industries where labor-saving devices are particularly applicable. For example, 20 per cent of Michigan's nonfarm employment is concentrated in the production of motor vehicles. It is the motor vehicle industry that has experienced the sharpest decline in defense contracts, largely as a result of the shift in defense technology from wheeled vehicles to electrical and missile production. The motor vehicle industry has also shown a marked tendency toward geographical decentralization of factories, which have moved closer to expanding markets. Additionally, in the motor vehicle industry consolidation and merger have been proceeding at a rapid rate and the larger companies have been purchasing supplier firms and incorporating their operations into the larger economic unit. These factors, together with mechanization and automation, contributed to a decline in Michigan automobile employment from a high of 411,700 workers in 1956 to 299,200 workers in 1962. Thus Michigan has been faced both with cyclical instability and a declining employment trend in the most important sector of its economy.

Michigan has also been marked by a shift in employment opportunities from commodity employment to noncommodity employment. There has been a decline in agricultural, mining, and manufacturing employment and an increase in employment opportunities in services, finance, utilities, and government. In 1947, about 48 per cent of Michigan's employment was in noncommodity industries, but by 1957 about 56 per cent of Michigan's employment was in these industries. There is every indication that this proportion will increase throughout the 1960's.

During the period 1940–50, Michigan's labor force increased by 26.3 per cent, in contrast to a 15.1 per cent increase for the nation, creating additional manpower problems. There was a heavy influx of migrants from the rural southern areas seeking high-paying jobs. These workers acquired jobs on production lines where the simple repetitive tasks required little education or training. The decline in these jobs through mechanization or decentralization meant unemployment for many of these workers. Their lack of skill, education, and knowledge of job opportunities invariably resulted in long-term unemployment for many of them. Detroit has by far the greatest concentration of these unwanted workers. Undoubtedly this group represents a sizable proportion of the hard-core unemployed.

Mention should also be made of the unprecedented number of new workers entering the Michigan labor market. Nearly one and a half million persons in Michigan will reach the age of 18 years during the 1960's, about 600,000 more than in the 1950's.[3] This marked increase is a result of the sharp rise in the birth rate which occurred early in World War II and continued into the postwar period. Not all of these young people will seek jobs; some will go on to higher education and some will either not enter the labor market or retire after a few years of unemployment. The majority, however—about 1,200,000 young people—will enter the labor market. With other additions to the Michigan labor force—adult women and others returning to work—a labor force of 3,600,000 workers in 1970 is quite possible. This represents a sizable increase over the 1960 labor force, which numbered 2,980,000 workers. Training and providing jobs for these new entrants is the central problem which Michigan must face in this decade.

The unemployment which has resulted from structural changes in the durable goods sector is concentrated in southeastern Michigan, and especially in Detroit. The other area of persistent unemployment is in the Upper Peninsula. Manufacturing plays a much smaller role in the Upper Peninsula than in the rest of the state. In a labor force of 95,000 workers, only 14,200 workers are employed in manufacturing, in contrast to 40,000 workers in nonmanufacturing concerns.[4] The high unemployment rate in the Upper Peninsula—9.2 per cent as compared to 4.9 per cent for the state in June, 1963—is probably due to the shut-downs of copper and iron mines and the failure to replace these lost economic activities with new employment possibilities. Many of the communities are economically depressed, and the solution would seem to be the attraction of new industry or the provision of incentives for outmigration from these areas. Tourism may emerge as a major growth industry, but its potential for re-employment of displaced mine workers cannot be gauged at this time.

The rest of the state has a smaller unemployment problem. The state-wide unemployment rate has been consistently lower than in Detroit or the Upper Peninsula. It is worth noting that the unemployment problem in Detroit differs from that in the Upper Peninsula, where the unemployed are more skilled and better educated than the Detroit unemployed. Sixty per cent of the latter are semiskilled or unskilled workers and 68 per cent do not have a high-school education. In contrast, 51 per cent of the unemployed in the Upper Peninsula are semiskilled and unskilled workers while 54 per cent do not have a high-school education. The Detroit unemployed are predominantly Negroes who migrated to the area from the rural South. The unemployed in the Upper Peninsula are white, native-born, and usually have had long residence in the area.

The economic problems and retraining needs, then, vary from area to area within the state. The case for structural unemployment is much stronger in Detroit and southeastern Michigan than in other areas of the state. In this section of the state, the trend of expanding economic activity and concurrent growth in the number of unemployed is most marked. The Upper Peninsula problem provides an interesting contrast in terms of the demands that are placed on economic recovery projects.

### THE STRUCTURE OF THE MICHIGAN ECONOMY AND RETRAINING

An understanding of retraining in Michigan must take into account some unique properties of its economy and labor market. First, employment and unemployment patterns in Michigan are subject to greater fluctuations than national patterns (see Figure VII.1). Part of the explanation for this lies in the industry mix of the state—a heavy reliance on the automotive industry and collateral supplier firms. Model changeover layoffs are reflected in lost employment in a broad sector of the labor market and the same is true of strikes in the automotive industry. The Michigan labor market is probably the most volatile of the large markets in the country, showing a high unemployment rate when automobile demand softens and a low unemployment rate when demand increases. This is illustrated by the abnormally low unemployment rates in the late months of 1965, a year in which automobile production exceeded 9.3 million units. In September, 1965, the state unemployment rate was 3.2 per cent and in October, 1965, the rate was 2.6 per cent. By way of contrast, the state unemployment rate in March, 1961, at the height of the recession, was 14.2 per cent. This volatility of the labor market suggests that the demand for retraining will vary, generating particular problems when automobile demand is low and others when demand is high.[5]

There is another feature of the Michigan labor market that should be noted. There has been a long-term tendency in Detroit for the city to move away from its traditional industrial base of manufacturing toward a more normal large metropolitan base, namely, services to an extended hinterland. Thompson suggests that this trend will radically alter the need for blue-collar workers and create a heavy demand for white-collar workers—professionals, technicians, and clerical personnel.[6] The shift from a commodity-producing center to one dominated by services will undoubtedly be one of the most significant changes in the Detroit labor market and will have a considerable impact on the structure and direction of future retraining.

### RETRAINING UNDER THE AREA REDEVELOPMENT ADMINISTRATION (ARA) AND MANPOWER DEVELOPMENT AND TRAINING ACT (MDTA)

The federal government in 1961 attempted to supplement local approaches to manpower training with federally financed programs in certain areas and occupations. The legislation which developed the structure of federal training in Michigan was the Area Redevelopment

## U.S. – Michigan Non - Farm Employment, Seasonally Adjusted

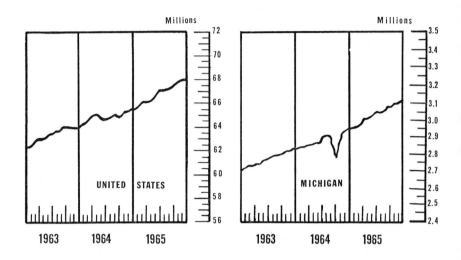

## U. S.- Michigan Unemployment Rate, Seasonally Adjusted ( Inverted )

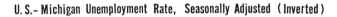

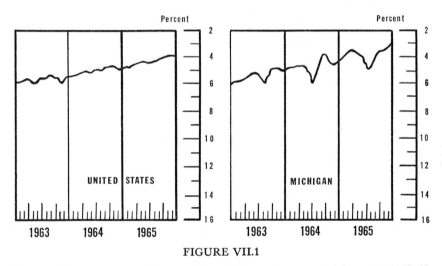

FIGURE VII.1

TRENDS IN EMPLOYMENT AND UNEMPLOYMENT, UNITED STATES AND MICHIGAN, 1963–65.
SOURCE: MICHIGAN EMPLOYMENT SECURITY COMMISSION.

Act (ARA) in 1961 and the Manpower Development and Training Act (MDTA) in 1962. Both programs provided uniform training opportunities for various counties and cities. The ARA provisions were designed to meet three objectives: (1) redevelopment of a given land area by providing loans for new industrial development; (2) encouragement of labor mobility in the form of outmigration from economically depressed areas; and (3) training and placement of unemployed workers in areas of substantial labor surpluses. The ARA program had area restrictions. Only communities that were characterized by a high rate of persistent unemployment, determined by certain criteria established under the act, could receive aid.[7] In Michigan, the two major redevelopment sectors were the Detroit area and the Upper Peninsula. Although both were characterized as economically depressed areas, the problems of these sectors were different. The Detroit area emphasized the need for retraining to fill new job openings, while the Upper Peninsula posed the need for retraining to encourage outmigration from an economically depressed area and to attract new industry. Any unemployed person who resided in these areas was eligible for ARA retraining.

The MDTA program, which did not have any area limitations, initially offered a longer training period with benefits, and included transportation and subsistence allowances. Training under MDTA was initially limited to unemployed heads of households who had accumulated at least three years of employment experience, but training was extended to other than household heads in December, 1963. Another provision of the act provided for on-the-job training to be financed by regular training allowances, although little use was made of this provision in Michigan.[8]

The actual operation of the ARA and MDTA programs was a cooperative effort between the state employment services and the local school authority. Typically, the need for a particular training course was determined by a survey which was conducted by the state employment office. The need for the training course was communicated to the state vocational service officers, who prepared a curriculum and a budget and arranged for space and teaching personnel in the area. Under MDTA, the course was then submitted for approval to a local advisory committee composed of business, labor, and civic leaders. Supervision of training was the responsibility of local agency officers and the designated teaching personnel.

### Comparison of ARA and MDTA Trainee Characteristics

By September 1, 1965, there were 15,546 individuals in Michigan who had been registered at one time or another either in an ARA or MDTA training course; 11,699 had registered in MDTA courses, while 3,847 had been registered in ARA courses.[9] What differences, if any, were to be

TABLE VII.1
COMPARISON OF ARA AND MDTA TRAINEE CHARACTERISTICS[a]

| Trainee characteristics | ARA[b] | MDTA |
|---|---|---|
| *Sex* | | |
| Male | 39.2% | 55.6% |
| Female | 59.1 | 43.7 |
| *Age* | | |
| Under 19 | 12.1 | 12.9 |
| 19–21 | 22.7 | 25.9 |
| 22–34 | 36.8 | 35.1 |
| 35–44 | 17.7 | 16.9 |
| 45 and over | 10.8 | 9.2 |
| *Education (grade)* | | |
| <8 | .9 | 5.5 |
| 8 | 4.8 | 7.7 |
| 9–11 | 33.1 | 34.3 |
| 12 | 54.1 | 47.1 |
| >12 | 6.6 | 4.2 |
| *Primary wage earners* | 46.2 | 60.5 |
| *Family heads* | 39.2 | 55.6 |
| *Nonwhite* | 52.4 | 40.0 |
| *Number of dependents* | | |
| 0 | 58.3 | 41.1 |
| 1 | 13.2 | 14.0 |
| 2 | 9.7 | 12.9 |
| 3 | 7.2 | 10.4 |
| 4 | 4.1 | 7.6 |
| 5 and more | 4.8 | 12.4 |
| *Prior employment status* | | |
| Unemployed <5 weeks | 19.6 | 23.3 |
| Unemployed 5–14 weeks | 16.0 | 16.4 |
| 15–26 weeks | 10.3 | 9.6 |
| 27–52 weeks | 8.7 | 7.9 |
| Unemployed >52 weeks | 28.0 | 22.5 |
| Family farm worker | .0 | 0.3 |
| Reentrant into labor force | 1.4 | 0.8 |
| Underemployed | 13.2 | 15.9 |
| *Years of gainful employment* | | |
| <3 | 48.3 | 39.2 |
| 3–9 | 31.7 | 37.5 |
| 10 or more | 18.5 | 21.3 |
| Total number of trainees | 3,847 | 11,699 |

[a] All trainees as of September 1, 1965.

[b] Differences in percentages due to "not ascertained" responses are insignificant. Where groups do not add up to 100 per cent, the difference is explained by "not ascertained" responses.

Source: Office of Manpower, Automation and Training.

found between these ARA and MDTA trainees? Which one of the two programs reached the most disadvantaged in the labor force? The data in Table VII.1 show the necessary information.

*Sex.*—ARA courses had a higher proportion of women, while men were more likely to be in MDTA courses. About 44 per cent of the MDTA trainees were women, compared to 59 per cent of ARA trainees. There are several reasons for these large proportions of women in training. First, employment opportunities have been most pronounced in the service sector with an increasing demand for clerical and medical personnel, occupations that are female-oriented. Second, in the early days of the ARA program, statutory restrictions limited the length of the course and considerable emphasis was placed on courses that were short in duration. Refresher clerical and medical aide courses fit this criterion, and women were attracted to these courses. Finally, as the labor market picture improved in Michigan, men were more likely to find employment in the automobile factories and refrain from training. The problem became one of training surplus female workers.

Closely associated with the number of female trainees is the family and wage status of the trainees. The high proportion of females in ARA courses contributed to the lower percentage of family heads and primary wage-earners among ARA trainees; 56 per cent of the MDTA trainees were heads of households, in contrast to 39 per cent of the ARA trainees.

*Dependents.*—The MDTA trainees had more dependents than did ARA trainees, a reflection of wage-earner role differences. Fifty-eight per cent of ARA trainees listed no dependents, while 41 per cent of the MDTA trainees had no dependents. In addition, about 12 per cent of the MDTA trainees had five or more dependents, while the proportion among ARA trainees was lower—about 5 per cent.

*Age.*—The trainees in MDTA courses appeared to be slightly younger than ARA trainees; about 39 per cent of MDTA trainees were under 22 years of age compared to 35 per cent of the ARA trainees. The greater proportion of youth in MDTA courses was undoubtedly a reflection of increased emphasis on youth programs under the new MDTA guidelines incorporated into the law in December, 1963.

*Education.*—The ARA trainees were better educated; 61 per cent had at least a high-school diploma, in contrast to 51 per cent of the MDTA trainees. It is apparent that, in both programs, a greater emphasis was placed on recruiting the better educated rather than the hard-core unemployed. What about the high-school dropouts? Among trainees under nineteen years of age, about the same proportion in both programs had high-school diplomas (63 per cent). The high-school dropouts were not represented in any great proportion in either program.

*Race.*—Negroes were represented in greater proportions among ARA trainees than among MDTA trainees. Fifty-two per cent of ARA trainees were nonwhite, compared to 40 per cent of the MDTA trainees. This statistic would seem to be a reflection of region, since the ARA courses were concentrated in the section of the state with the greatest number of Negroes, the Detroit area, while MDTA courses were not limited to locality.

*Length of unemployment and years of gainful employment.*—The ARA trainees had longer durations of unemployment and fewer years of gainful employment, statistics that undoubtedly reflected the economic conditions within certain depressed areas of the state.

### CHANGES IN THE STRUCTURE OF MDTA RETRAINING BETWEEN 1963 AND 1965

What changes in ARA and MDTA training occur when there are significant changes in the structure of the labor market? The Michigan labor market provides a convenient framework to examine this question, since the labor market changed appreciably between 1963 and 1965. In February, 1963, a key employment month, 197,000 workers were unemployed in Michigan and the unemployment rate was 6.8 per cent. In February, 1965, unemployment had decreased to 131,000 and the unemployment rate was 4.3 per cent. The comparable unemployment rates for Detroit were 6.7 per cent in February, 1963, and 3.7 per cent in February, 1965. Between these two years, there was a considerable improvement in the employment picture. What effect did this have on MDTA retraining?[10]

Such an improvement might be reflected in two ways: (1) a change in the composition of the trainee group, and (2) shifts in the kinds of courses initiated as a response to new labor market needs. Let us examine each one of these propositions in turn.

*Changes in the composition of the MDTA trainee group.*—It is apparent from an examination of Table VII.2 that there was a marked alteration in the composition of the MDTA trainee group between the 1963 fiscal year period and the 1965 fiscal year period. Part of the change was undoubtedly a result of a more favorable employment picture:

1. There were more women in training in 1965 than in 1963.

2. There was a decrease of older people in the courses and an increase of younger people.

3. There were fewer heads of households in 1965 than in 1963 and, thus, a sizable increase of trainees who had no dependents or who were secondary wage earners.

4. There was a significant decrease in the proportion of trainees who had completed high school but, even in 1965, slightly more than one-half of the trainees had a high-school education.

TABLE VII.2

CHARACTERISTICS OF MDTA TRAINEES IN MICHIGAN,
FISCAL YEARS 1963 & 1965

| Trainee characteristics | 1963 | 1965 |
|---|---|---|
| *Male* | 81.0% | 62.6% |
| *Age* | | |
| 45 and over | 11.5 | 9.2 |
| 21 and under | 25.3 | 38.8 |
| *Head of household* | 69.2 | 55.6 |
| *Education* | | |
| High school completed | 63.4 | 51.4 |
| *No dependents* | 26.8 | 41.1 |
| *Primary wage earner* | 76.8 | 60.5 |
| *Duration of unemployment* | | |
| 52 weeks or more | 13.6 | 22.5 |
| *Years in labor force* | | |
| <3 | 21.6 | 39.2 |
| 10 or more | 32.0 | 21.3 |

Source: Special tabulations from the Office of Manpower,
Automation and Training.

5. There was an increase in the proportion of trainees with both over fifty-two weeks of unemployment and less than three years of labor force participation, indicating that in the relatively prosperous economy of the mid-1960's, more attention in retraining was directed to training the new arrival in the labor market who had not managed to find steady employment.

The improvement in the economic climate in Michigan significantly refocused training. More emphasis was placed on training the worker who was less directly involved in the labor market. The full employment period permitted many primary wage-earners to return to work and forego training, thus opening training opportunities for women and new labor market entrants who held secondary wage-earning roles in the economy. There was also a determined effort to enlarge training for youths, as evidenced by the fact that 25 per cent of the trainees in 1963 were under twenty-two years of age and, by 1965, this proportion had increased to 39 per cent. Training opportunities also shifted to the more disadvantaged workers in the labor market, as the proportion of trainees with fifty-two weeks of unemployment increased and there was a decrease in the proportion of workers who had completed high school. It could be argued that this latter group was more highly disadvantaged than other groups in the labor market, since these people could not find jobs in this period of high employment when qualifications for work were lowered.

*Changes in MDTA courses.*—In the fiscal year of 1963, MDTA training had barely begun in the state and the total trainee group was 719. By the fiscal year 1965, MDTA training was well established and 4,871 trainees were attending or had completed courses. There were some significant shifts in courses, as can be seen in Tables VII.3 and VII.4.

TABLE VII.3

DISTRIBUTION OF MDTA TRAINEES BY COURSE SPECIALTY, FISCAL YEAR 1963

| Course | Detroit | | Lower Peninsula[a] | | Upper Peninsula | | Total trainees | |
|---|---|---|---|---|---|---|---|---|
| | % | No.* | % | No.* | % | No.* | % | No.* |
| Professional, semi-professional, technical | — | 0 | — | 0 | — | 0 | — | 0 |
| Clerical | — | 0 | 3 | 15 | — | 0 | 2 | 15 |
| Sales | — | 0 | — | 0 | — | 0 | — | 0 |
| Personal services | — | 0 | — | 0 | — | 0 | — | 0 |
| Agricultural | — | 0 | — | 0 | — | 0 | — | 0 |
| Manufacturing | 22 | 20 | 39 | 204 | 57 | 61 | 40 | 285 |
| *Trade & services* | | | | | | | | |
| Auto repair | 78 | 69 | 7 | 37 | — | 0 | 15 | 106 |
| Hospital | — | 0 | 44 | 230 | — | 0 | 32 | 230 |
| Other | — | 0 | 7 | 38 | 20 | 21 | 8 | 59 |
| Special | — | 0 | — | 0 | 23 | 24 | 3 | 24 |
| Total | 100 | 89 | 100 | 524 | 100 | 106 | 100 | 719 |

* Base on which percentages were calculated.

[a] Lower Peninsula includes all territory outside the Detroit Standard Metropolitan Area and the counties of the Upper Peninsula.

1. For the state as a whole, the proportion of trainees in manufacturing-oriented training courses decreased. In 1963, 40 per cent of the trainees were in these courses but in 1965 the proportion had declined to 32 per cent. The full employment market in 1965 was undoubtedly a factor in this, since many of the manufacturing firms, either in or marginal to the automobile industry, lowered their skill requirements and arranged on-the-job training opportunities for many of the newly hired men. However, in spite of this percentage decline, about five times *more* trainees were in manufacturing courses in 1965 than in 1963.

There was a percentage decline of trainees in the major trade and

TABLE VII.4

DISTRIBUTION OF MDTA TRAINEES BY COURSE SPECIALTY, FISCAL YEAR 1965

| Course | Detroit | | Lower Peninsula[a] | | Upper Peninsula | | Total trainees | |
|---|---|---|---|---|---|---|---|---|
| | % | No.* | % | No.* | % | No.* | % | No.* |
| Professional, semi-professional, technical | 8 | 152 | 3 | 76 | 16 | 102 | 7 | 330 |
| Clerical | 6 | 127 | 15 | 321 | 6 | 41 | 10 | 489 |
| Sales | 8 | 164 | — | 0 | — | 0 | 4 | 164 |
| Personal services | — | 0 | — | 0 | — | 0 | — | 0 |
| Agricultural | — | 0 | 3 | 57 | — | 0 | 1 | 57 |
| Manufacturing | 28 | 566 | 31 | 689 | 47 | 298 | 32 | 1,553 |
| *Trade & services* | | | | | | | | |
| Auto repair | 15 | 302 | 6 | 123 | 13 | 80 | 10 | 505 |
| Hospital | 24 | 484 | 35 | 772 | 4 | 24 | 26 | 1,280 |
| Other | 10 | 212 | 2 | 49 | 14 | 91 | 7 | 352 |
| Special | 1 | 23 | 5 | 118 | — | 0 | 3 | 141 |
| Total | 100 | 2,030 | 100 | 2,205 | 100 | 636 | 100 | 4,871 |

* Base on which percentages were calculated.

[a] Lower Peninsula includes all territory outside the Detroit Standard Metropolitan Area and the counties of the Upper Peninsula.

service courses—auto repair and hospital service—but there were five and one-half times more trainees in hospital service courses in 1963 and about five times more trainees in auto repair courses in 1965 than in 1963.

There was a major shift in course training emphasis from manufacturing and trades-services to the white-collar-oriented courses—technical, clerical, and sales training. In 1963, about nine out of every ten trainees were in the first group of courses—manufacturing and trades-services. In 1965, the ratio had changed to four out of ten trainees, with one out of every five trainees in white-collar-oriented courses (sales, technical, and clerical). This reversal can be explained by a number of factors. First, the 1963 amendments to the Manpower Development and Training Act extended training to non-heads of households. Many of the secondary wage-earners who became eligible were women, creating a demand for training in female-oriented jobs, largely white-collar employment. Second, many of the new job openings that were being created were in the white-collar employment sector, creating a demand for courses in the sales, clerical, and technical specialties. Finally, as has been mentioned, the character of the city of Detroit is changing, with a greater emphasis on white-collar employment as opposed to blue-collar employment.[11]

Since the city is a pacemaker for the state economy, its employment demands will be reflected in the profile of MDTA courses offered in the state.

2. The profile of retraining also changed within sections of the state. Within the Detroit area, there was a twenty-fold increase in the number of trainees between the two years. In 1963, there were eighty-nine trainees in the Detroit area in manufacturing and auto repair training. By 1965, the profile of course offerings was quite diffuse: one-fifth of the trainees were in white-collar-oriented training; one-quarter were in manufacturing; one-half were in trade and service courses. The most significant trend was the development of courses in which 70 per cent of the trainees were in nonmanufacturing training—a remarkable statistic, considering the industrial and manufacturing character of the city.

3. In the two other sections of the state, shifts also occurred. In the Upper Peninsula area, considerable emphasis was placed on manufacturing-oriented training. Forty-seven per cent of the trainees in 1965 were in such training in contrast to the Detroit figure. The difference in emphasis was a reflection of the need to develop a labor force with manufacturing skills in one case (Upper Peninsula) and technical-service skills in the second case.

TABLE VII.5

DISTRIBUTION OF ARA RETRAINING ACTIVITIES BY COURSE SPECIALTY,
FISCAL YEAR 1963

| Course | Detroit | | Lower Peninsula[a] | | Upper Peninsula | | Total trainees | |
|---|---|---|---|---|---|---|---|---|
| | % | No.* | % | No.* | % | No.* | % | No.* |
| Professional, semi-professional, technical | — | 0 | — | 0 | — | 0 | — | 0 |
| Clerical | 46 | 254 | 52 | 135 | 46 | 148 | 47 | 537 |
| Sales | 4 | 26 | — | 0 | — | 0 | 2 | 26 |
| Personal services | — | 0 | — | 0 | — | 0 | — | 0 |
| Agricultural | — | 0 | — | 0 | — | 0 | — | 0 |
| Manufacturing | — | 0 | 29 | 75 | 39 | 124 | 18 | 199 |
| *Trade & services* | | | | | | | | |
| Auto repair | 13 | 72 | 6 | 15 | — | 0 | 8 | 87 |
| Hospital | 37 | 205 | 5 | 12 | — | 0 | 19 | 217 |
| Other | — | 0 | 8 | 21 | 15 | 49 | 6 | 70 |
| Special | — | 0 | — | 0 | — | 0 | — | 0 |
| Total | 100 | 557 | 100 | 258 | 100 | 321 | 100 | 1,136 |

* Base on which percentages were calculated.

[a] Lower Peninsula includes all territory outside the Detroit Standard Metropolitan Area and the counties of the Upper Peninsula.

*Changes in ARA courses.*—There were also shifts in the ARA course profile over time (Tables VII.5, VII.6). In 1963, about 49 per cent of the ARA trainees were in clerical or sales courses. By 1965, this proportion had declined to 15 per cent, while 41 per cent of the trainees were in trade and service courses and 32 per cent were in manufacturing-oriented courses. Undoubtedly, part of this shift resulted from changes in ARA legislation, which permitted longer periods of time for training. Another factor was the restricted geographical location of ARA training, which meant that the course selections were largely oriented toward the labor market needs of depressed economies. In such areas, the pool of applicants available for training was limited to workers who had had poor prepara-

TABLE VII.6

DISTRIBUTION OF ARA RETRAINING ACTIVITIES BY COURSE SPECIALTY, FISCAL YEAR 1965

| Course | Detroit % | Detroit No.* | Lower Peninsula[a] % | Lower Peninsula[a] No.* | Upper Peninsula % | Upper Peninsula No.* | Total trainees % | Total trainees No.* |
|---|---|---|---|---|---|---|---|---|
| Professional, semi-professional, technical | 11 | 179 | — | 0 | — | 0 | 9 | 179 |
| Clerical | 8 | 117 | 38 | 57 | 8 | 31 | 10 | 205 |
| Sales | 4 | 62 | — | 0 | 14 | 54 | 5 | 116 |
| Personal services | — | 0 | — | 0 | — | 0 | — | 0 |
| Agricultural | — | 0 | — | 0 | — | 0 | — | 0 |
| Manufacturing | 41 | 639 | 21 | 31 | — | 0 | 32 | 670 |
| *Trade & services* | | | | | | | | |
| Auto repair | 15 | 240 | 15 | 22 | 3 | 13 | 13 | 275 |
| Hospital | 17 | 266 | — | 0 | 61 | 229 | 24 | 495 |
| Domestic | 2 | 25 | — | 0 | — | 0 | 1 | 25 |
| Other | — | 0 | 26 | 40 | 14 | 51 | 4 | 91 |
| Special youth program | 2 | 37 | — | 0 | — | 0 | 2 | 37 |
| Total | 100 | 1,565 | 100 | 150 | 100 | 378 | 100 | 2,093 |

* Base on which percentages were calculated.

[a] Lower Peninsula includes all territory outside the Detroit Standard Metropolitan Area and the counties of the Upper Peninsula.

tion for the labor market and negative labor market experiences. Undoubtedly, both of these factors contributed to the course profile of ARA trainees in 1965.

Both programs shifted in course profile over time, although in different directions. The MDTA courses were directed more toward white-collar employment, while ARA courses were linked to preparation for service-trade and manufacturing jobs. This may partly explain why the more disadvantaged in the labor force were to be found in ARA courses.

## THE MICHIGAN EXPERIENCE WITH ARA AND MDTA RETRAINING COURSES, 1960–62

The ARA and MDTA retraining programs were the first statewide efforts in Michigan to aid the unemployed by improving their skills for the labor market.[12] A study of the trainees—their characteristics, course performances, and adjustment in the labor market after training—was undertaken by us in February, 1963. In cooperation with the research staff of the Michigan Employment Security Commission, all ARA and MDTA trainees who had attended courses in Michigan on or before December 31, 1962, were selected for study. The number of workers who fitted this criterion was 1,405, and complete data were available for 1,273 trainees.

### CHARACTERISTICS OF THE TRAINEES AND THE MICHIGAN UNEMPLOYED

In Michigan, the rationale for the retraining programs was that they aided the unemployed by giving them new skills by which they could compete in the labor market. To what extent is this true? One way to answer this question is to compare the characteristics of the retrainees in our sample with the Michigan unemployed in 1963 to see if the trainees were representative of the unemployed population.

*Age.*—The median age of the sample members was 28 years with 81 per cent of the trainees under 40 years of age. In contrast, the median age of the Michigan unemployed was about 34 years. Seventy per cent of the Michigan unemployed were under 44 years of age. The trainees, then, were generally younger than the main body of the unemployed. This would seem to be a reflection of the demands of industry for younger workers and the higher educational attainment found among younger workers. The data emphasize the difficulties involved in solving the problems of the older unemployed workers.

*Sex.*—A significantly larger percentage of women were enrolled in the programs than would be expected on the basis of the sex distribution among the Michigan unemployed. Fifty-four per cent of the trainees were women while only 32 per cent of the Michigan unemployed were women. How can this emphasis on training for women be explained?

One explanation can be seen in the comparison of MDTA and ARA trainees. Sixty-one per cent of the ARA trainees were women in comparison with 33 per cent of the MDTA trainees. This difference in sex distribution is probably due to the predominance of clerical and nurse's aide courses in the early ARA experience; thirty-five courses involving 635 trainees were offered under the ARA program in the clerical and nurse's aide fields.

The ARA's early emphasis on training women can easily be explained. First, the ARA program was not, as in the case of the MDTA program, oriented toward heads of households. The primary goal of the program was to rehabilitate economically depressed areas, and this called for utilization of whatever human resources were to be found in the area. Insofar as women represented good possibilities for retraining in the area, they were singled out. Another reason for the stress on women in the ARA program is to be found in the emphasis which was placed on short courses of twelve to sixteen weeks. This limitation favored a program with the courses in areas where skills could be learned quickly, and training in nurse's aide and clerical work fulfilled this requirement. Finally, we must consider the demands of the labor market for jobs which traditionally involved training for women. The shortages of manpower seem to be in the service and clerical sectors where the pay is low, but suited to the income requirements of secondary wage-earners. The longer training period under the MDTA program—fifty-two weeks in some cases—would permit training for well-paid technical jobs which emphasize a higher level of skill. In these cases, we would naturally expect to find more men than women interested in the training.

*Education.*—The median education of the trainees was 11.34 years with 61 per cent of the trainees having had a high-school education and 9 per cent of the trainees having had some post-high-school training. In contrast, only 45 per cent of the Michigan unemployed were high-school graduates.[13] It seems obvious that there was a definite bias in favor of the educated person for training. The unemployed who were selected for training represented an educational elite among the Michigan unemployed.

There is also a difference in the educational distribution between ARA and MDTA trainees. The ARA trainees were significantly better educated than the MDTA trainees. Seventy-eight per cent of the ARA trainees were high-school graduates, in comparison with 53 per cent of the MDTA trainees. The length and type of course which was offered by the ARA program explains this difference. Because of the short period of training given, nurse's aide and clerical courses required that the trainees have a more extensive educational background. In addition, the high-school diploma was required by employers who had indicated an intention of hiring the trainees. The MDTA program, on the other hand, had greater flexibility in accepting trainees since its courses of instruction were longer and could be designed to remedy gaps in educational background by course instruction. It appears, then, that the MDTA program was better equipped to work with the main body of the Michigan unemployed.

*Primary occupation.*—We have already indicated that education makes a difference in being accepted for training. We can also assume that the work experience of the unemployed (i.e., the primary occupation) will be related to an individual's opportunities for training in the MDTA and ARA programs. This is indeed the case, as we see in Table VII.7.

TABLE VII.7

PRIMARY OCCUPATION OF ARA AND MDTA RETRAINEES COMPARED
WITH THE PRIMARY OCCUPATION OF THE MICHIGAN UNEMPLOYED

| Primary occupation | ARA and MDTA retrainees | Michigan unemployed |
|---|---|---|
| Professional and technical | 0.9% | 4.8% |
| Clerical and sales | 39.0 | 15.8 |
| Service | 12.3 | 8.7 |
| Skilled | 14.8 | 19.5 |
| Semiskilled | 24.6 | 31.5 |
| Unskilled | 10.0 | 19.7 |

Source: Michigan Employment Security Commission, July, 1963.

The data in Table VII.7 show that retraining opportunities were not geared to the needs of the Michigan unemployed. The most striking observation is that about half of the Michigan unemployed had previously worked in semiskilled and unskilled jobs; yet only about one-third of the trainees had this type of work experience in their backgrounds. On the other hand, about 24 per cent of the Michigan unemployed had previously been in clerical, sales, and service jobs, but more than half of the trainees came from this kind of work experience. The programs for retraining apparently did not reach to a great extent the unemployed who most needed the training. There was a definite tendency, dictated by the demands of the market and course requirements, to recruit the more skilled workers into the programs.

Another point should be noted. If we compare the work backgrounds of the ARA trainees with the MDTA trainees, we can clearly see that the MDTA program was better geared to the needs of the Michigan unemployed. While only 17 per cent of ARA trainees were from unskilled and semiskilled jobs, almost 37 per cent of the MDTA trainees formerly held such jobs. Again, it is apparent that the longer course of training and extensive range of courses under the MDTA program permitted greater flexibility in working with the unemployed of lower skills and education.

*Number of weeks unemployed.*—The median number of weeks of unemployment for the trainees was 24.4 weeks. One-third of the trainees had been unemployed for one year or more. Forty-six per cent had been unemployed twenty-six weeks or more. It would appear, then, that a substantial number of the trainees were without employment for a long period of time. This does not mean, however, that their families were financially without resources for this period. Forty-one per cent of the trainees were secondary wage earners in their households, and their families did not depend upon them for complete financial support. In almost one-half of the cases, the effect of training would be to supplement the income of the family rather than to provide an income to a family that was completely impoverished.

These observations about the characteristics of the trainees and the Michigan unemployed in 1963 suggest the following conclusions:

1. The structure of the programs in 1963 emphasized educational requirements and training for the service, clerical, and sales jobs, thus raising a barrier against training opportunities for the semiskilled and unskilled unemployed—the groups that probably needed training the most.

2. The differences which arose between ARA and MDTA retrainees in 1963 were related more to the length and types of courses which each program offered rather than to any other single factor. The longer period of training in MDTA courses permitted a greater flexibility in working with the unemployed than was possible in the shorter ARA courses. In these, the trainees must have possessed significant verbal abilities before entry into training, while in the longer MDTA courses some of these abilities could be developed during the training period. The differences in the length of courses also explained the greater involvement with clerical training in the ARA program. Typically, clerical training, building on existing verbal skills, could be accomplished in a short period of time.

### The Disadvantaged Worker in the ARA and MDTA Programs in Michigan

We have already shown that the ARA and MDTA trainees in the sample differed in several significant respects from the population of unemployed in Michigan. The trainees were, as a group, better educated and more skilled than the general population of the unemployed. This raises a question of great importance: how disadvantaged were the workers who were recruited into the two programs? The disadvantaged worker may be described by a combination of characteristics that could influence his chances of finding a job. We recognize that age, education, and skill level are factors that facilitate or impede finding a job. Workers who are old in terms of the demands of the job market and lack adequate education and training are certainly more disadvantaged than other workers. When described in this context, how disadvantaged were the trainees who were selected for training?

*Age, education, and skill level.*—In Table VII.8 we have grouped various combinations of age, education, and skill level among ARA and

TABLE VII.8

DISTRIBUTION OF AGE, EDUCATION, AND SKILL LEVEL COMBINATIONS
AMONG ARA AND MDTA TRAINEES

| Category | No. | % |
|---|---|---|
| Under 40, with a high-school education and skilled[a] | 494 | 36 |
| Under 40, with a high-school education and no skill | 300 | 21 |
| Under 40, with less than a high-school education and skilled | 78 | 6 |
| Under 40, with less than a high-school education and no skill | 236 | 17 |
| Over 40, with a high-school education and skilled | 118 | 9 |
| Over 40, with a high-school education and no skill | 50 | 4 |
| Over 40, with less than a high-school education and skilled | 42 | 3 |
| Over 40, with less than a high-school education and no skill | 50 | 4 |
| Total | 1,368 | 100 |

[a] "Skilled" designation means that regular employment before training was classified as skilled, sales, clerical, professional, or managerial. "No skill" means that regular employment before training was classified as semiskilled or unskilled.

MDTA trainees. These data reinforce our earlier finding that the most disadvantaged of the unemployed workers were not in the ARA and MDTA training programs. More than one-half of the trainees—57 per cent—were under 40 years of age and had completed high school. One trainee out of three was under 40 years of age and had both a high-school education and some previous experience in a skilled specialty. By way of contrast, only 4 per cent of the trainees were over 40 years of age and had neither a high-school education nor some past experience with a skilled specialty. The most striking observation about the table is the preponderance of trainees who were under 40 years of age; about four-fifths of the trainees were in this category. Even in cases where the effects of age could be offset by adequate education or training, the proportion of trainees is relatively low. Only 9 per cent of the trainees had both a high-school education and some skilled specialty and were over 40 years of age.

These observations about the selectivity of trainees become even more striking if we focus on the *most* disadvantaged of the unemployed. These would be the workers most in need of training to aid them in the labor market: youths and older workers who are both undereducated and underskilled. We can distinguish types as shown in Table VII.9.

These unemployed workers constituted a small minority of the ARA and MDTA trainees—about 7 per cent. Two factors may account for this. First, ARA and MDTA trainees were recruited on the assumption that they were trainable and that reasonable prospects existed for their employment. These workers might be considered doubtful prospects in view of their educational and employment backgrounds. Second, the se-

TABLE VII.9

YOUTHS AND OLDER WORKERS, BY AGE, EDUCATION, AND
SKILL LEVEL, AMONG ARA AND MDTA TRAINEES

| Category | No. |
|---|---|
| Youths, under 20 yrs of age; 8 yrs or less of education, no record of any skill | 2 |
| Youths, under 20 yrs of age, high-school dropouts, no record of any skill | 42 |
| Older workers, over 40 yrs of age; 8 yrs or less of education, no record of any skill | 15 |
| Older workers, over 40 yrs of age; high-school dropouts, no record of any skill | 35 |
| Total | 94 |

lection process for most training courses placed a strong emphasis on verbal testing which these workers would find difficult to master. The selection procedures of both programs were not geared to workers who were the most disadvantaged in terms of age, education, and past experience with skilled employment.

## FACTORS IN COURSE COMPLETION

The completion of the course by the trainee is essential if the state's economy is to reap the full benefits from the ARA and MDTA retraining programs. What factors were related to course completion? Eighty-eight per cent of the 1,273 retrainees completed the course in which they were registered.[14] The completion rate was higher in the ARA program than in the MDTA program—about 10 per cent of the ARA trainees failed to complete the course of training while 20 per cent of the MDTA trainees did not complete their training. It should be noted, then, that in both programs, the majority of trainees who began training managed to finish.

The higher completion rate in ARA courses as against MDTA courses can be explained by (1) the composition of the trainee groups in both programs and (2) the length of the courses in both programs. It has already been pointed out that the ARA courses had a much higher proportion of female trainees than the MDTA courses. These female trainees were more likely to be secondary wage earners and therefore did not feel the loss of income from a job as much as the male, primary-wage-earner trainees. In addition, trainees in the MDTA courses, mostly men who were primary wage earners, were committed to a longer period of training than under the ARA program. The point to be noted is that the training situation involved a loss in income for the trainee for a period of time. The trainee who had greater financial responsibilities—the primary or sole wage earner in the family—was under more pressure during the course to leave training and look for work or accept the greater aid afforded by the public welfare dole. We would expect, then, that the pressure to leave training would vary with the number of responsibilities of the trainee and the length of the training period, since both of these factors would influence his willingness to complete this course.

*Sex and course sponsorship.*—The data in Table VII.10 show the rela-

TABLE VII.10

COMPLETION RECORD OF TRAINEES BY COURSE SPONSOR AND SEX

| Course sponsor and sex | Completed | Dropped | No. |
|---|---|---|---|
| *ARA* | | | |
| Male | 84.2% | 15.8% | 366 |
| Female | 93.5 | 6.5 | 567 |
| All ARA | 90.7 | 9.3 | 933 |
| *MDTA* | | | |
| Male | 72.9 | 27.1 | 210 |
| Female | 92.4 | 7.6 | 105 |
| All MDTA | 79.4 | 20.6 | 315 |
| All respondents | 87.8 | 12.2 | 1,248[a] |

[a] Data were incomplete for 25 respondents.

tive effect of sex and course sponsorship—ARA program or MDTA program—on course completion.[15] Women had a lower dropout rate than men. About 6 per cent of the female trainees dropped out in contrast to 20 per cent of the male trainees. These sex differences also persisted within each age grouping and within each type of program, although the overall proportion of dropouts was lower in the ARA program than in the MDTA program. Sex and the type of program were important determinants of course completion.

*Sex, education, and course sponsorship.*—In Table VII.11 the relative effect of sex, education, and course sponsorship on course completion is examined. Sex differences within each educational grouping are related to the dropout rate—men discontinue their course work more frequently than women. The educational variable, however, is important. In general, the higher the educational level of the trainee, the more likely he was to finish the course. The exception to this finding was the small group of trainees whose education was limited to eight or fewer years. In these cases, the completion rate was high. Two factors probably explain this high level of performance by trainees who had a low level of education. First, the quality of these trainees must have been exceptionally high to overcome the lack of education which would operate against the trainee in the selection process. Secondly, it is possible that the labor market experiences of these trainees with low educational achievement had made a

TABLE VII.11

COMPLETION RECORD BY COURSE SPONSOR, SEX, AND EDUCATION OF TRAINEES

| Sponsor and sex | Education | Completed | Dropped | No. |
|---|---|---|---|---|
| *ARA* | | | | |
| Male | 1–8 | 94.3% | 5.7% | 36 |
| | 9–11 | 77.8 | 22.2 | 117 |
| | 12 | 86.8 | 13.2 | 182 |
| | Post-high-school | 82.4 | 17.6 | 34 |
| All males | | 84.3 | 15.7 | 369 |
| Female | 1–8 | * | * | (3) |
| | 9–11 | 87.5 | 12.5 | 48 |
| | 12 | 94.8 | 5.2 | 447 |
| | Post-high-school | 96.3 | 3.7 | 81 |
| All females | | 94.5 | 5.5 | 579 |
| Total ARA | | 90.6 | 9.4 | 948 |
| *MDTA* | | | | |
| Male | 1–8 | * | * | (9) |
| | 9–11 | 64.0 | 36.0 | 89 |
| | 12 | 75.9 | 24.1 | 108 |
| | Post-high-school | * | * | (6) |
| All males | | 72.2 | 27.8 | 212 |
| Female | 1–8 | * | * | (3) |
| | 9–11 | 89.6 | 10.4 | 48 |
| | 12 | 94.2 | 5.8 | 52 |
| | Post-high-school | * | * | (3) |
| All females | | 92.4 | 7.6 | 106 |
| Total MDTA | | 78.9 | 21.1 | 318 |
| All respondents | | 87.7 | 12.3 | 1,266 |

* Insufficient number of cases.

vivid impression on them of the necessity for training to achieve employ-ment. The latter might manifest itself by a high level of motivation in the course.

*Financial pressures and family obligations.*—These observations on the relationship between characteristics of the trainees and course completion suggest that financial pressures and family obligations in the training period may be basic considerations in explaining why trainees drop out. The wage-earner role, whether primary or secondary, and the length of the course tend to exert different pressures on the trainee, and leaving training might be one way to resolve these pressures. In order to test this possibility, we selected two variables: number of dependents and wage-earner status. We reasoned that these variables would be indicators of

financial pressures which might affect the trainees' decision to leave training before the course ended.

The data in Table VII.12 show a tendency for the dropout rate to

TABLE VII.12

| No. of dependents | Completed course | Dropped course | No. |
|---|---|---|---|
| None | 92% | 8% | 604 |
| 1 or 2 | 85 | 15 | 309 |
| 3 or more | 83 | 17 | 301 |
| Total no. | | | 1,214[a] |

[a] Data were not available on 59 trainees.

$x^2 = 30.929$

$df = 9$

$p = <.001$

increase with the number of dependents. In other words, the trainees who
were under the most financial pressure, as evidenced by family responsibilities, were the least likely to complete the course. This finding may
also explain why there was a higher dropout rate among the MDTA
trainees than among the ARA trainees. Not only were MDTA courses
longer, but the MDTA trainees also had a significantly higher number of
dependents.

Table VII.13 indicates that 57 per cent of the ARA trainees had no

TABLE VII.13

NUMBER OF DEPENDENTS BY ARA AND MDTA TRAINEE STATUS

| No. of dependents | ARA trainees | MDTA trainees |
|---|---|---|
| None | 57% | 30% |
| 1–2 | 24 | 29 |
| 3 or more | 19 | 41 |
| Total % | 100 | 100 |
| Total no. | 855 | 315 |

dependents while only 30 per cent of the MDTA trainees were without
dependents. On the other hand, 19 per cent of the ARA trainees had
three or more dependents in contrast to 41 per cent of the MDTA
trainees. The MDTA trainees, then, might have been under more pres-

sure to quit their course of training and seek jobs. The promise of future employment as a result of training may have paled in the light of immediate financial obligations and the long investment in training under the MDTA program.

Another indication of financial responsibilities is the wage-earner status. If we are correct that extensive financial pressures and obligations make it difficult for the trainee to complete training, then we would expect to find that sole and primary wage earners would be more likely to drop out than secondary wage earners. The data in Table VII.14 show the

TABLE VII.14

RELATIONSHIP BETWEEN COURSE COMPLETION AND WAGE-EARNER
STATUS OF THE TRAINEE

| Wage-earner status | Completed course | Dropped course | No. |
|---|---|---|---|
| *ARA* | | | |
| Sole and primary | 90% | 10% | 449 |
| Secondary and other | 91 | 9 | 406 |
| *MDTA* | | | |
| Sole and primary | 73 | 27 | 241 |
| Secondary and other | 97 | 3 | 74 |

$x^2 = 13.813$
$df = 3$
$p = <.01$

dropout rates for MDTA and ARA courses by the wage-earner status of the trainees.

Two observations of interest can be made about the data in Table VII.14. First, there is a much higher proportion of secondary wage earners in ARA courses than in MDTA courses; 47 per cent of the ARA trainees are secondary wage earners in contrast to 23 per cent of the MDTA trainees. Since the secondary wage earners are less likely than primary or sole wage earners to be subject to pressures from financial responsibilities, we would expect that there would be fewer dropouts among the ARA trainees. This was indeed the case.

The second point to be made is that there is no significant difference in dropout rate between primary and secondary wage earners in the ARA courses. At first, this finding appears to repudiate our hypothesis regarding the role of financial pressures in determining the dropout rate. It must be pointed out, however, that the short courses—twelve or sixteen weeks—in the ARA program might make it possible even for a trainee with financial obligations to withstand the pressures and finish the course.

When we examine the trainees in the MDTA courses—thirty-six to fifty-two weeks—we find that wage-earner status is related to the dropout rate. In the MDTA trainee groups, about three-quarters of the primary wage earners completed the course in contrast to 97 per cent of the secondary wage earners. The MDTA trainees who were sole or primary wage earners were subject to a double pressure, namely, financial obligations and prospective lack of income from a job for a considerable period of time. It is likely that some of the trainees gave in to these pressures and did not complete training.

### The Re-employment Experiences of ARA and MDTA Trainees

How well did the trainees fare in the labor market after training? How many of the trainees were employed in jobs that were training-related? How many trainees found full-time rather than part-time employment? The answers to these questions are important, since they would give some indication of the value of the ARA and MDTA programs to the state economy. In this assessment, we are dealing with a short-run rather than a long-run adjustment to the labor market. The data in the present study are restricted to the two-month period following the end of training.

*Post-training employment.*—We can begin by asking what proportion of the trainees were employed within a two-month period after the end of their retraining. The data tabulated in Table VII.15 show that 65

TABLE VII.15

PROPORTION OF TRAINEES EMPLOYED DURING TWO-MONTH PERIOD FOLLOWING
TRAINING BY COURSE SPONSORSHIP AND COURSE SPECIALTY[a]

| Course | ARA trainees % | ARA trainees No.[a] | MDTA trainees % | MDTA trainees No.[a] | Total % | Total No.[a] |
|---|---|---|---|---|---|---|
| Clerical | 75 | 420 | —[b] | — | 75 | 420 |
| Service | 59 | 121 | 30 | 88 | 50 | 209 |
| Metal and machine | 63 | 157 | 66 | 84 | 63 | 241 |
| Automobile repair | 74 | 50 | 74 | 38 | 74 | 88 |
| Other | 74 | 11 | —[b] | — | 74 | 11 |
| Total no. of trainees | | 759 | | 210 | | 969[c] |
| Total % employed | 70 | | 52 | | 65 | |

[a] The base on which percentage was computed.

[b] No cases available in that course for comparison.

[c] Based on 969 cases; no employment information was available for 143 respondents.

per cent of the trainees on whom employment information exists found jobs in the two-month period following the training.[16] This compares with a nationwide placement record of approximately 70 per cent.[17] We do not know, however, *how long* the trainees managed to keep these jobs or the nature of job changes following initial employment.

The best placement records were found in the clerical and automobile repair courses; about three-quarters of the trainees in these courses were placed in jobs. The second best placement record was in the metal and machine courses with 63 per cent of these trainees placed in jobs. The trainees in the service courses, predominantly nurse's aides in four- to six-week courses, had the poorest placement record. In this last group about 50 per cent of the trainees became employed. It is difficult to explain the low employment rate among the service trainees in light of strong current demand for their services. One answer may be the fact that the trainees in these courses were predominantly women with secondary wage-earner status, and their attachment to the labor market varied with circumstances. It should also be noted that many of the service jobs paid poorly and thus resulted in a low incentive to take employment.

Where comparisons are possible between ARA and MDTA trainees in the same course specialty (e.g., automobile repair and metal and machine trades), we find no significant difference in employment except in the service courses. Fifty-nine per cent of the service trainees in ARA courses became employed in comparison with 30 per cent of the trainees in MDTA courses. This discrepancy, along with the high placement rate in clerical courses, resulted in a higher placement rate for ARA trainees as a group (70 per cent) than for the MDTA trainees as a group (52 per cent). The difference in placement may also result from the longer experience with the ARA training program. It does not seem likely that the characteristics of the trainees were a factor in placement, since there was no significant difference in sex, age, education, or previous employment experience between ARA and MDTA trainees enrolled in the same course specialty. Automobile repair men in the ARA course, for example, were indistinguishable in background characteristics from automobile repair men in the MDTA course. Chances for employment were related more to the type of course than to the program under which the course was offered.

*Full-time and training-related employment.*—Besides the rate of employment, there are two other measures of how the trainees fared in the labor market: (1) how many trainees obtained full-time employment against part-time employment and (2) how many trainees obtained employment that was related to their training? Let us consider each of these measures in turn.

The data in Table VII.16 indicate that there was no significant difference between the two programs in the proportion of trainees who found full-time employment. About 88 per cent of the trainees in each program

TABLE VII.16

PROPORTION OF RE-EMPLOYED TRAINEES WITH FULL-TIME AND TRAINING-RELATED
JOBS, BY COURSE SPONSOR AND COURSE SPECIALTY

| Courses | % of re-employed trainees with full-time jobs | No.[a] | % of re-employed trainees with training-related jobs |
|---|---|---|---|
| *ARA* | | | |
| Clerical | 82 | 307 | 79 |
| Service | 100 | 70 | 99 |
| Metal and machine | 98 | 98 | 93 |
| Automobile repair | 92 | 37 | 60 |
| Other | 81 | 9 | 100 |
| Total % | 88 | | 83.2 |
| Total no. | | 521 | |
| *MDTA* | | | |
| Clerical | — | 0 | — |
| Service | 81 | 26 | 96 |
| Metal and machine | 95 | 55 | 89 |
| Automobile repair | 82 | 28 | 79 |
| Other | — | 0 | — |
| Total % | 88.1 | | 87.9 |
| Total no. | | 109 | |
| % for all trainees | 88 | | 84 |
| No. for all trainees | | 630 | |

[a] The base on which percentages on the line were computed.

were employed full-time. Only in the service courses was there a clear difference in full-time employment between ARA and MDTA trainees; all of the re-employed ARA trainees were in full-time jobs, while about 81 per cent of the re-employed MDTA trainees had full-time employment. ARA trainees in service courses, then, had both a high employment rate and a higher proportion of trainees in full-time employment. The main point, however, is that the overwhelming proportion of trainees from both programs obtained full-time rather than part-time employment.[18]

Looking at the data on training-related employment, we see that four out of five re-employed trainees had jobs that were related to the training in their courses, and this proportion is about the same for ARA or MDTA trainees. Where comparisons are possible in course specialties between the two programs, a difference is apparent only in the auto repair courses: ARA trainees in auto repair courses found fewer training-related jobs than MDTA trainees in auto repair courses. One explanation is that the auto repair courses in the ARA program were shorter in length than comparable MDTA courses and thus offered less preparation for the job market.

## THE OCCUPATIONAL MOBILITY OF ARA AND MDTA TRAINEES

What patterns in occupational mobility were found among the trainees in the sample? Were the trainees re-employed at jobs that differed in skill or status from their usual employment in the labor market? One way to answer these questions is to compare the pretraining employment of the trainee with his subsequent employment. Table VII.17 makes this com-

TABLE VII.17

RELATIONSHIP BETWEEN TRAINEE'S USUAL EMPLOYMENT IN THE LABOR MARKET
BEFORE TRAINING AND TRAINEE'S SUBSEQUENT EMPLOYMENT AFTER TRAINING
(Re-employed ARA trainees only)

| Pretraining usual employment | Post-training employment | | | | | Total pretraining jobs |
| --- | --- | --- | --- | --- | --- | --- |
| | Professional and technical | Clerical and sales | Skilled | Semi-skilled | Unskilled and service | |
| Professional and technical | 0 | 0 | 0 | 3 | 0 | 3 |
| Clerical and sales | 4 | 225 | 1 | 13 | 30 | 273 |
| Skilled | 0 | 2 | 2 | 9 | 0 | 13 |
| Semiskilled | 2 | 1 | 21 | 43 | 13 | 80 |
| Unskilled and service | 0 | 8 | 5 | 10 | 35 | 58 |
| Total post-training jobs | 6 | 236 | 29 | 78 | 78 | 427[a] |

[a] Complete information available on 426 ARA trainees.

parison for 427 ARA trainees. The number of MDTA trainees for whom this information was available—44 in all—was too small to make this analysis.

The data from Table VII.18 indicate that about 70 per cent of the trainees found jobs after training at the same skill level as their usual employment before training. This suggests that training for these trainees resulted in horizontal rather than vertical movement in the skill hierarchy. In other words, for the majority of these ARA trainees, new employment was in the same broad skill categories as their usual employment before training. The degree of mobility into higher skill levels was slight. This suggests that training, if it had an effect, resulted in upgraded skills within the same occupational category rather than new or different skills.

Re-employed trainees with previous clerical or sales employment were the most likely to have post-training employment in clerical and sales jobs (83 per cent). Fifty-four per cent of the trainees with semiskilled backgrounds and 60 per cent of the trainees with unskilled or service backgrounds found employment in these same occupational categories. The only exception to this finding is the trainee group with skilled specialties. Only 2 out of 13 of these trainees found skilled employment while 9 out of the 13 found semiskilled jobs. This is, of course, a small group and their presence in the training program may indicate that their skilled specialties have become obsolete. Perhaps no amount of training could help them to retain this skill level, and certainly the relatively short ARA courses would be less likely to do this.

One further observation about Table VII.17 deserves comment. The net effect of the training has been to decrease the number of clerical and sales workers in the group, from 273 before training to 236 after training. The number of skilled workers has increased, as has the number of unskilled workers and service workers. Only the number of semiskilled workers remains about the same. Altogether, 69 trainees "moved downward" in their new jobs while 53 trainees "moved upward" in their new jobs. Most of the downgrading occurred in movement from clerical jobs to semiskilled jobs. Most of the upgrading is explained by (1) movement from semiskilled to skilled jobs (about 20 per cent of the trainees with a semiskilled background made this move), and (2) movement by trainees with no known skill or service background to better jobs (e.g., semiskilled, skilled, clerical or sales). It should be noted, then, that for the group of ARA trainees, about as many found less desirable jobs as found more desirable jobs.

*Changes in the prestige and social standing of employment.*—In the previous section we compared the usual skill classification of the trainee before training with the skill classification of his post-training employment. The result indicated a high degree of stability in the skill classification. It should be noted, however, that the use of such broad skill categories (e.g., "clerical" and "skilled") [19] masks changes that occur within the skill category. It is possible that a more refined set of categories would show considerably more change.

One alternative would be to use the NORC socioeconomic ratings as the basis of comparing pretraining employment with post-training employment.[20] The NORC ratings of occupations emphasize the prestige or social standing attributed to a particular job by a cross-sectional sample of the public. The ratings range from 0 through 100. The higher the rating, the greater the prestige and social standing attributed to the job. Jobs that are ranked high are usually more desirable from the viewpoint of social standing and involve a higher degree of skill. What patterns of job mobility are to be noted using the NORC ratings? This information is tabulated in Table VII.18.

TABLE VII.18

RELATIONSHIP BETWEEN TRAINEES' USUAL NORC RATING IN THE LABOR MARKET BEFORE TRAINING AND TRAINEE'S SUBSEQUENT NORC RATING AFTER TRAINING
(Re-employed ARA trainees only)

| Pretraining NORC rating | Post-training NORC rating | | | | Total no. |
|---|---|---|---|---|---|
| | 0–20 | 21–40 | 40–60 | 61 and over | |
| 0–20 | 50 | 58 | 10 | 2 | 120 |
| 21–40 | 21 | 33 | 15 | 3 | 72 |
| 41–60 | 18 | 17 | 108 | 41 | 184 |
| 61+ | 2 | 2 | 21 | 42 | 67 |
| Total no. | 91 | 110 | 154 | 88 | 443[a] |

[a] Complete information available on 443 ARA trainees.

The data in Table VII.18 indicate that 53 per cent of the ARA trainees were employed in post-training jobs that were in the same range of NORC ratings as their usual pretraining employment. For this group, training did not have the effect of increasing the prestige or social standing of their employment. It is possible, however, that training did permit them to acquire new or upgraded skills to perform types of jobs that were not greatly different in prestige from their usual employment. Twenty-nine per cent of the trainees obtained jobs that were higher in the NORC ratings, while 18 per cent of the trainees became employed in jobs that were lower in NORC ratings. About one-half of the re-employed ARA trainees, then, experienced a change in the prestige and status of their employment.

The greatest proportion of the "stables" was in the clerical group. Four out of every five trainees in the clerical courses found new jobs that were about equal in prestige and status to their usual pretraining jobs. This would indicate that these ARA courses served to refresh existing skills rather than to develop new and different skills. Trainees who obtained more prestigious employment were either (1) service workers who had moved into the metal trades, or (2) semiskilled workers who had found more prestigious employment in the metal trades or auto repair work. The "skidders"—those trainees who found less prestigious jobs—were older than other trainees and generally had moved from clerical jobs to service or semiskilled employment. Workers who had at least a high-school education, particularly if they were in the 25 to 30 age group, obtained better jobs than any other group of trainees. Undoubtedly, this is a group that would probably do well in the labor market even without specialized training. To what extent the ARA training increased their advantage cannot be answered by the present data.

### Summary Remarks on Michigan's Experience with Federal Retraining Programs

In reviewing Michigan's experience with the ARA and MDTA training programs, it is necessary to note that only 6,335 trainees had been involved in programs—either started or approved—before November, 1963. This is, of course, a very small number of the total unemployed in the state and only about 0.2 per cent of the labor force. Viewed in this perspective, the program's impact on the unemployment problem has been limited. The programs, however, were relatively new and the initial training courses should be viewed as pioneering efforts to aid the unemployed. This fact must certainly color any evaluation.

*The trainees.*—The survey of trainees who were enrolled in courses prior to December 31, 1962, revealed certain tentative conclusions about the operation of the ARA and MDTA programs *in their early stages.* We have already noted that the trainees were not typical of unemployed workers in Michigan. Female workers who were secondary wage earners were over-represented among the trainees, as were younger and better educated workers. These criticisms of the programs should not be limited to Michigan. Despite efforts by federal and state agencies to develop special programs for the hard-core unemployed, the majority of trainees in the nationwide ARA and MDTA programs were atypical of the general population of the unemployed.[21]

These differences are probably explained by the selection procedures for these programs and the job openings for which training was given. In the early stages of the programs, there were few attempts to develop course offerings that would broaden the base of recruitment.

*Administration of the programs.*—There is no doubt that one of the benefits of the programs has been to coordinate the resources of a number of state agencies in manpower development and training. The programs have emphasized the interdependence between the vocational education activities of the State Board of Education and the counseling and placement activities of the State Employment Service. The programs may well serve as a basis for agency reappraisal of their manpower activities and result in a more integrated state manpower plan. It might well be that the significance of these programs for Michigan will be in this area rather than in the number of workers who are given training.

*Job placement.*—The job placement rate for trainees in Michigan is comparable to the national job placement rate. Future rates of placement will be the result of two opposing factors. On the one hand, it is likely that the placement rate may decrease when trainees are selected from "deeper" levels within the hard-core unemployed. Some of these trainees will be difficult to place because their education and skill backgrounds may not be compatible with market demands. On the other hand, job placement efforts under the programs have been improving steadily with experience, and a higher placement rate is a good possibility.

*Impact of the programs.*—The experience with the ARA and MDTA programs has undoubtedly been beneficial to the state. More public concern with manpower problems is evident in Michigan today than at any time since the Great Depression of the 1930's. There is activity both on the state and local levels to examine vocational education needs and to develop programs to satisfy these needs. Much of this concern and activity have been a direct result of involvement in the ARA and MDTA programs.

The programs have also had another effect. There has developed in Michigan a core of administrators and instructors who have had first-hand experience with the problems of mass retraining. It is doubtful whether it would have been possible to develop this cadre without the experiences in the federal programs. It is possible that in the long-run development of a comprehensive training program, this reservoir of experience and personnel will prove to be one of the most fruitful results of the federal training program.

## THE FUTURE OF RETRAINING IN MICHIGAN

It is obvious from the above presentation that the major retraining efforts in Michigan, both private and public, have affected the utilization of the state's manpower resources only to a minor degree. The early hopes that training and retraining programs would solve Michigan's dilemma of persistent unemployment were not realized, and have turned to cautious optimism.

State officials, manpower specialists, and educators did not initially understand the complexity of the unemployment problem in Michigan and the relationship of retraining to that problem. It was felt that the unemployment problem could be solved simply by giving the unemployed worker new skills which were more adaptable to the labor market. Very little attention was paid to the need for literacy training or training in social skills as a prerequisite for participation in the labor market. This realization has come only recently when the unemployment problem persisted even after the ARA and MDTA programs had "skimmed the cream" of the unemployed and provided technical training for them. An assessment of the training needs of unemployed youth and hard-core unemployed was late in coming. Only now is some serious thought being given to these problems.

Another drawback to retraining in Michigan was the inadequacy of educational resources in some of the local communities where the unemployment problems were severe. The lack of a strong, well-developed state system of vocational education proved to be a serious handicap.[22] In some cases, there was resistance on the local level by school districts to retraining programs since the demands would strain already overtaxed and inadequate facilities. In Detroit, retraining made demands on the school system at a time when the facilities and the educational staff were faced by an unprecedented increase in general school enrollment and a reduction in the tax revenue for school budgets. Any evaluation of job retraining in Michigan must be made against this background.

What are the future prospects for retraining in Michigan? There seems to be consensus on the part of state and local officials that a well-organized, permanent retraining program is needed.

There is still considerable discussion, however, on how to organize such a program. To what extent should on-the-job training as against institutional instruction be used? Should there be a concentration of training programs in centralized skill centers, or should the training programs be dispersed in available facilities? To what extent can some of the public school facilities be adapted to such a program as against the development of totally new facilities? The answer to these questions as well as the possibility for a comprehensive training program will depend on two factors: (1) the availability of federal and state funds, and (2) the willingness of local and state officials to commit community resources to a retraining program. There is no doubt that local and state experience with the ARA and MDTA programs have stimulated considerable thought and discussion about the availability and allocation of community resources to a retraining program.[23]

### NEW DIRECTIONS IN RETRAINING

It is quite clear that future efforts in retraining will need to be more integrated and oriented toward the long run than they have been in the past. An attempt will need to be made at greater coordination and utilization of training resources in a given land area. The establishment of area training schools with little regard for political boundaries seems to be a definite possibility.[24] Staff and facilities will need to be concentrated in these schools in continuous programs to service the many training and retraining needs of the area. These schools must be concerned not only with retraining for the unemployed, but also with training for youth who are entering the labor market and upgrading for workers who are currently employed.

Training for the hard-core unemployed, especially in Detroit, will present special problems. It is becoming increasingly apparent that technical training alone will not suffice as a solution to the problem. The more basic needs in this group are literacy training, education in social skills, guidance in formulation of long-range goals, and guidance in job-seeking. Training must be placed in the broader context of family and community rehabilitation. This suggests an integrated attack on the problems of poverty, slum areas, delinquency, and school dropouts. Any approach which is centered around a narrowly conceived, single-course training will do these people little good. It is unfortunate that both of the federal retraining programs have emphasized training geared to a single job opportunity. This emphasis has missed the major needs of the hard-core unemployed.

It should be noted that the privately sponsored training programs for Michigan have been more responsive to the training needs of the hard-core unemployed. These programs have recognized the importance of providing a social environment where the worker will be motivated to participate in the labor force and to try to maximize his potential. In addition, these programs have a strong preventative emphasis, working with potential high-school dropouts and trying to give the worker new skills to fall back on before unemployment occurs. These privately sponsored training programs, of course, have some limitations. They restrict their operations to specific geographical areas and have small budgets. The need for these programs is great. Whether they will be extended depends on the extent to which financial support can be mobilized from the community.

There is some indication that unions may come to play a greater part in retraining in Michigan.[25] We have already mentioned that all of the craft unions operate apprenticeship programs to meet normal job mobility needs. Several unions have established temporary programs in the past to serve their members who were affected by job displacement. The Typographical Workers' Union in Detroit gave special instruction on automatic typesetter machines to permit some of their members to qualify for new jobs. The Communication Workers' Union provided special retraining to displaced linemen. These programs are mainly geared to the special problems of union members and are not concerned with the unemployment problem directly. They do, however, have the indirect effect of preventing unemployment.

In October, 1963, the federal government approved an MDTA training grant to the United Automobile Workers' Local 412 in Detroit. It was only the second time in the history of the act that a training grant was given to a labor union. The course was designed to train sixty people for jobs in each of three engineering skills. The actual operation of the course was the responsibility of the local, although the administration of the course was shared with the International Union. Trainees were drawn from three groups of applicants: (1) workers presently employed but due to be replaced by automation, (2) workers presently employed but in lower skilled jobs, and (3) workers presently unemployed due to lack of technical skills. Whether this program will become a model of future union services to its members and the community cannot be predicted at this time. The program, however, does open up new possibilities for union services.

Training and retraining under the ARA and MDTA programs have emphasized the need to give to a selected group of the unemployed preparation for a specific occupational specialty. In the auto repair courses, one group of candidates was selected and trained for auto transmission jobs, while another group was selected and trained for general auto repair. This emphasis on training for a narrow specialty was a consequence of the programs' legal requirements, which made it necessary to train candidates for immediate jobs available in the labor market. The result is that some workers were trained for specialties that will be obsolete in the near future. One way of avoiding this difficulty was incorporated into a retraining plan which was proposed jointly by the Michigan Employment Security Commission and the State Vocational Educational Service. The logic of the plan is quite simple. Instead of training candidates for a single occupational specialty, a course of instruction is given for a number of related skills in a given sector of the economy. There may be a demand for clerks, typists, clerk-typists, business machine operators, bookkeepers, and stenographers. The trainees in the course are all given the same curriculum in business skills for the first four weeks of the course. As the student moves through the course, he receives successive training in a number of business office operations. The graduate of the course has a knowledge of a wide number of business skills, which can act as a buffer against the obsolescence of any one skill and possible job displacement. Using this strategy, it is also possible to terminate the course for a candidate with limited abilities and still have given him a completed unit of vocational training.[26] This approach could be tried in a business skills sequence and, if successful, could be applied in principle to other areas of training.

Three other trends should be briefly noted. First, there will undoubtedly be more training for unemployed youth. A retraining program under the Manpower Development and Training Act for 400 youths, unemployed high-school graduates and high-school dropouts, has already been established in Detroit. The youths are given both classroom instruction and on-the-job training. The trainees are concentrated in sales and clerical courses with additional emphasis on the development of social skills for the labor market. Second, more attention will be given to on-the-job training for the unemployed. Although this provision was prominent in the Manpower Development and Training Act, it has not been used extensively in Michigan. Finally, we will probably see a greater concentration of retraining efforts in the Detroit metropolitan area where the retraining needs of the unemployed are particularly critical. It is here that considerable effort will be brought to bear to aid the most disadvantaged workers—the Negro, the unemployed youth, and the older displaced worker.

### SUMMING UP

Some of Michigan's problems in retraining were common to the problems found in any state which has taken part in the two retraining programs under the federal government. Given the lack of background and facilities in public retraining, the first two years were necessarily a trial-and-error period in retraining. There has been steady improvement in the organization, administration, and operation of the ARA and MDTA programs, and it is apparent that in the future training and retraining programs will be an integral part of the state's manpower utilization program.

It is necessary, however, to be realistic in any appraisal of retraining as a panacea to the state's manpower problems. A comprehensive program of manpower training and retraining can keep the Michigan labor force adaptable to technological change, and it can also make possible a better utilization of manpower resources. But retraining is only meaningful if linked to other policies of economic security. Toward this end, an adequate manpower policy must assure the worker against sudden and arbitrary job displacement. It must eliminate racial, ethnic, and educational barriers to his employment opportunities. It must also soften the shock of job displacement and unemployment through adequate financial assistance. Finally, there must be intensive efforts at economic development where new job opportunities are forthcoming. Only in this context can training and retraining function effectively as a manpower utilization catalyst and help to promote a sound state economy.

### EPILOGUE, 1967

The passage of time since this study was completed does not invalidate the basic insights that were recorded about the training of workers in the Michigan labor market. We have reached a point in job training where we must analyze and evaluate our early experiences—successes and failures—in order to plan for the future. The training experiences with workers cannot be viewed in any snapshot fashion; they must be viewed as a moving series of images where the past becomes prologue to the future. It would require another report to record the extensive march of events that has taken place since the completion of the study that has been recorded above.

New problems have come into focus; not simply because the old ones have been solved. It may be a mark of professional maturity and an increased social responsibility that there is an increased concern with the non-technical aspects of training, particularly among disadvantaged workers. The earlier view that vocational placement must utilize only the skills that were brought to the employment office has been successively replaced by two new perspectives: (1) the worker must be given added skills if he is to compete and (2) in some cases the opportunity structure must be modified through job development if he is to function in the world of work. These are dramatic changes in perspectives and signal a new intervention pattern in the impersonal forces of the labor market.

In the mid-1960's more and more effort is being concentrated on manpower development programs for the disadvantaged in the urban ghettos. The Human Resource Development Program and the Concentrated Employment Program of the U.S. Department of Labor are primarily designed to develop and intensify manpower resources for the residents of ghetto areas. These programs, part of the "new look" in manpower development, view the job problems of ghetto residents as interrelated with other social and economic issues and require the cooperation of the widest range of resources, public and private, for a solution. We are also viewing an intensive effort to involve the business community in the solution of these problems, sometimes on humanitarian grounds but more frequently as an on-the-job contractor and as a training-for-profit business enterprise.

But by far the most important emphasis has been on the coordination of manpower resources. The ARA and MDTA programs required coordinated efforts of two agencies—the state employment service and the state vocational education department. Manpower programs have grown in number and thirty-two different agencies and programs are now in existence. The wisdom of coordination and the nature of it are still hotly debated, but most new programs posit as a central assumption the coordination of agency resources.

It should be noted that these new emphases are not unique to training in Michigan but reflect national trends and problems. The new directions in Michigan training have been dictated less by local problems than by national programs and trends. This is certainly to continue for the indefinite future.

## REFERENCES

1. The Trade Expansion Act passed in 1963 also includes training provisions, but had not become operative in Michigan as of this writing. There are also a number

of training efforts by private organizations, but these are specific to given areas and designed to deal with particular problems in those areas. Evaluation data on the effectiveness of these programs are almost nonexistent.

2. The data and sample have several limitations which should be noted. The data were obtained from MT forms 101 and 102; no personal interviews were conducted with the trainees. The first form reports on the characteristics of the trainee —sex, age, education, previous labor market experience, etc. The second form contains information on the trainee's progress in the course and some post-training labor market experiences. It was necessary, then, to confine our observations to the reported data and, in many cases, the information was quite sketchy.

Observations were limited to a six-month experience with MDTA courses and a year of experience with ARA courses. Our sample was, therefore, weighted in the direction of ARA retraining programs—955 ARA retrainees in contrast to 318 MDTA retrainees. There is another serious limitation to the sample as a fair representation of the Michigan experience with federal retraining programs. Many of the early courses under both programs suffered from poor planning, problems of coordination, and inadequate facilities. In later courses, these problems were overcome with the result that both administrative and trainee performance improved. It was also in the later courses in MDTA that new experimental approaches were introduced. The present sample will not reflect these improvements in training or course design, but is limited, instead, to the early experiences of the two programs.

3. Michigan Employment Security Commission, *Manpower in Michigan: A Look at the Sixties* (2nd ed., January, 1962), pp. 6–7.

4. Michigan Employment Security Commission, *Michigan Labor Market Letter,* Vol. 18 (July, 1963), 4.

5. One of the direct correlates of this volatility is a variation in the size of the hard-core unemployed of Detroit. In a high automobile demand period, many of the traditionally hard-core unemployed become employed and are not in immediate need of training. In such a period, retraining the hard-core may offer greater problems since the workers who cannot be absorbed represent the most difficult employment problems in the labor market.

6. "The Future of the Detroit Metropolitan Area," in *Michigan in the 1970's,* eds. William Haber, W. Allen Spivey, and Martin R. Warshaw (Bureau of Business Research, The University of Michigan, 1965), pp. 203–40.

7. Unemployment had to be 6 per cent or more of the labor force, discounting seasonal or other factors. The average annual unemployment rate must have been: (1) at least 50 per cent above the national average of unemployment for three out of the last four years; (2) at least 75 per cent above the national average of unemployment for two out of the last three years; and (3) at least 100 per cent above national average of unemployment in one of the last two years.

8. Eight hundred and three trainees were either enrolled or graduated by June 1, 1965.

9. The observations in this section are based on special tabulations prepared by the Office of Manpower, Automation and Training. The tabulations cover all ARA trainees as of September 1, 1965, but MDTA trainees are under-represented because only MDTA institutional courses are included in the tabulations. MDTA trainees in on-the-job training courses or special programs were not included in the tabulations.

10. Comparable data were not available for the ARA trainees.

11. The current surge in blue-collar employment does not invalidate this long-term trend.

12. It should be noted that the Michigan state law on unemployment insurance does extend the possibility of retraining for the unemployed. Section 28e states that an unemployed individual is eligible for benefits if: "He has, when directed by the Commission, attended a vocational retraining program maintained by the Commission or by any public agency designated by the Commission." Very little use has been made of this provision.

13. Michigan Employment Security Commission, *Michigan Labor Market Letter,* Vol. 18 (July, 1963), 14–15.
14. The Michigan Employment Security Commission maintained records on the reasons for which the trainees left the course before completion. Of the 157 trainees who did not complete the course, 102 left voluntarily; 28 trainees were dropped for cause (e.g., chronic absenteeism, lack of discipline, lack of aptitude), 19 trainees came under the 52-week disqualification clause of the programs, and no data were available for 8 trainees.

    These data should be considered with a note of caution. The reason for leaving the course was largely the judgment of the instructor. Frequently, the instructor recorded that a trainee left voluntarily even if his dismissal was imminent. There was a tendency to give trainees the benefit of the doubt since those who were dismissed from the course for cause were not eligible for any other training for one year. Some of the trainees could see dismissal from the course as imminent and decided to leave voluntarily. Finally, a number of trainees found that the course did not live up to their expectations and decided to quit. Trainees in this latter group were reticent about giving "dissatisfaction with the training course" as a reason and often gave some fictitious reason.
15. Age of the trainee was not significantly related to course completion.
16. Certain limitations of the data must be mentioned. As we have already noted, only trainees from the early MDTA courses were included in the sample, weighting the sample in the direction of ARA trainees. In addition, Michigan Employment Security Commission procedures provide for follow-up of trainees only for a two-month period. Three reports on post-training employment are filed: one at course completion, a second after the first month, and a final report after the second month. If a trainee is reported employed in the first report, he is not followed up in subsequent reports. These reports, then, are confined to whether the trainee became employed, the nature of the employment, his wages, and whether the employment was training-related. No data were available on how many jobs a trainee had and how long he held a job. Conversations with a number of trainees indicate that they were financially pressured to take temporary employment if a full-time job were not available. The data on re-employment experiences are confined to a two-month period and, thus, fail to answer a crucial question: what is the impact of training on the long-run adjustment of the trainee in the labor market?
17. The U.S. Department of Labor reports that 70.1 per cent of the MDTA trainees in the nation were placed in jobs at the end of training as of December 31, 1962. U.S. Department of Labor, *Report of the Secretary of Labor on Research and Training Activities Under the Manpower Development and Training Act* (February, 1963), p. 46. The Department of Labor reported 70 per cent placement for ARA trainees. Bureau of Employment Security, U.S. Department of Labor, *Manpower Training Operations Under the ARA* (April, 1963). Information obtained from the research division of the Michigan Employment Security Commission indicates that by November 30, 1963, about 79 per cent of the ARA trainees and about 83 per cent of the MDTA trainees in Michigan had been placed. The discrepancy between our findings and the MESC data may be explained partly by (1) the changing composition of the trainees—more courses in mechanical arts and business skills provided later trainees with a better chance for placement—and (2) job finding became more efficient and produced better results after lengthy experience with the programs.
18. Whether this was the result of training alone remains a question. An adequate research design would need a matched control group of nontrainees to make meaningful statements about the effects of training on full-time job opportunities.
19. Any set of skill categories will pose this problem.
20. For a detailed discussion of the NORC rating system, see Albert J. Reiss, Jr., *Occupations and Social Status* (New York: The Free Press of Glencoe, Inc., 1962), chs. II, IV, and V.
21. Sar A. Levitan, *Federal Manpower Policies and Programs to Combat Unemployment*

(Kalamazoo, Michigan: The W. E. Upjohn Institute for Employment Research, February, 1964), p. 26.

22. It should be noted that states with strong systems of vocational education were able to develop "crash programs" in retraining with little difficulty. Wisconsin and Connecticut are two examples. In these two cases, state officials grafted the retraining programs to existing vocational education facilities. The previous experience with vocational education together with the immediate availability of organized teaching staffs, curricula, and building space gave these states a great advantage in retraining workers. In contrast, Michigan and Indiana were forced to spend considerable time in assembling staff, planning curricula, and seeking building facilities.

23. This is most evident in Detroit where there has been considerable experience with the ARA and MDTA retraining programs in dealing with the unemployment problem. Two local committees have been established under the sponsorship of the mayor's office. The first committee is pursuing plans for the development of a skill center where a variety of training courses and facilities will be centralized. The second committee is charged with the tasks of assessing, mobilizing, and coordinating community resources for an ongoing retraining program.

24. One such school has already been established on the campus of Northern Michigan University in Marquette and has been quite successful. A wide variety of courses is available, and the trainees are housed on the campus. The program is financed by MDTA funds. Trainees come from all counties of the Upper Peninsula and from a number of counties in western Michigan. They receive the regular MDTA training allowance for their families plus an additional allowance for the personal needs on campus.

25. The state and Detroit area advisory boards of the MDTA program have labor representatives who play an active part in approving the courses to be offered and as liaison between the program and their organizations. There has been, however, criticism of the program by labor organizations. One repeated criticism by union officials, especially in the skilled crafts, is that the training poses a potential threat to the apprenticeship training system, performance standards, and worker seniority status. It is argued that the programs bring newly trained workers into direct competition with union members of considerable experience and long seniority. There is also criticism of the legal restrictions which do not permit public training to upgrade union members who are employed. This upgrading would result in some benefits to the unemployed, since the vacated jobs, not requiring considerable training, could be realistically filled by unemployed workers.

26. As the MDTA program is operated at the present time, candidates who are dismissed before completion of the courses do not have anything to show for their time and effort. The candidate is also required to wait one year before applying for any other training under the MDTA program. Through use of the open-ended program approach, the candidates who desire to become stenographers and fail will at least have some clerical or typing skills to show for their efforts.

## VIII

ARNOLD R. WEBER

■

# EXPERIMENTS IN RETRAINING: A COMPARATIVE STUDY

Retraining the unemployed is clearly a growth industry. Since 1960 a concern over persistent unemployment and the disadvantaged has been translated into action along many fronts. One of the most promising responses to this problem has been the proliferation of retraining programs, an endeavor whose economic logic is impeccable. In a rapidly changing economy, some proportion of unemployment is attributable to the fact that displaced workers do not have the skills necessary to obtain new jobs. By equipping the unemployed with the required skills, they may be returned to productive and remunerative employment to the benefit of both the individual and the community.

As with any growth industry, however, retraining programs have come in all sizes and shapes. Some of the most ambitious efforts have been initiated under the provisions of the Manpower Training and Development Act. Other public programs have been developed at the state and local levels. In addition, private measures have been taken within the framework of union-management agreements to retrain displaced workers. These programs often differ substantially with respect to the constituency they purport to serve, the content of the training, the financial support extended to the retrainees, and the expectation of employment upon completion of the program. Each of these factors will affect the administration and ultimate success of the retraining effort.

In this respect, there are obvious advantages to a comparative study of the different approaches to retraining the unemployed. First, it is necessary to select and describe the various "models" of retraining. Second, the results of these different projects will be examined in terms of the performance of the trainees in the program and their subsequent experience in the labor market. And third, cross-sectional analysis may provide the basis for broader inferences about public and private efforts to retrain the unemployed.

## THE ORGANIZATION AND ADMINISTRATION OF RETRAINING

Five retraining projects have been investigated which, together, encompass a variety of administrative, financial, and labor market considerations. The specific cases studied include private efforts to retrain displaced meatpacking workers in Omaha, Nebraska, and Forth Worth, Texas; two programs initiated under the auspices of the Area Redevelopment Administration in Carbondale and Murphysboro, Illinois; and the vocational training activities of the Welfare Rehabilitation Service of the Cook County (Chicago) Department of Public Aid.

The Fort Worth project was initiated under the provisions of the labor agreement between Armour and Company and the United Packinghouse, Food and Allied Workers Unions (UPWA) and the Amalgamated Meatcutters and Butcher Workmen of North America. During the summer and autumn of 1962, the company proceeded to close down a large meatpacking plant in Fort Worth, displacing approximately 1,000 employees. When the impending shutdown was announced, the parties agreed to launch a program to aid the displaced workers through the offices of the Automation Fund Committee. The Committee had been established by the terms of the collective bargaining agreement and is comprised of union, management, and "public" members. It is generally concerned with the problems of technological change and worker displacement.[1]

As the Forth Worth project developed, it had two major objectives. First, it involved efforts to facilitate the direct placement of former Armour employees in new jobs. Second, the displaced employees were offered the opportunity for retraining in different occupational skills for which there appeared to be some demand in the local labor market and contiguous areas. Ultimately, 167 former Armour employees entered a wide variety of training programs. Data for all 167 retrainees were collected for the period July, 1962, to February, 1964.

A similar set of circumstances surrounded the establishment of the Omaha, Nebraska, program. In 1961 the Cudahy Meatpacking Company constructed a new plant in Omaha to replace its existing, obsolete facility in the same city. Whereas the old plant had a complement of 3,000 workers, the new unit required only 2,100 production and maintenance employees. Consequently, there were approximately 900 "surplus" employees involved in the changeover. As in the Armour situation, an

Automation Fund had been created by Cudahy and the UPWA to finance ameliorative programs for workers affected by technological change. Similarly, the parties offered the displaced employees the option of training for new occupations aimed at possible jobs outside the company. Unlike the Armour case, however, the Cudahy program was largely administered by officials of the State Employment Service rather than a representative retained by the Automation Committee. The project enlisted 65 persons and was maintained on a formal basis for a twenty-month period ending in mid-1963. This study incorporates data dealing with 59 of the 65 retrainees.

The Carbondale and Murphysboro retraining activities were part of an overall program to improve economic conditions in a chronically depressed area in southern Illinois. With support from the Area Redevelopment Administration, two new firms were attracted to these adjacent communities in 1962. The Technical Tape Corporation, a manufacturer of commercial and industrial tapes, was located in Carbondale, while McNair Metals, an aluminum fabricator, commenced operations in a new plant in Murphysboro. Initial statements indicated that approximately 700 persons would be employed by Technical Tape and 100 by McNair Metals. Both these estimates proved to be overly optimistic. Recruitment was carried forth at a slow pace so that by May, 1963, barely 100 workers had been hired at Technical Tape and approximately 60 at McNair. In February, 1964, these totals had increased to 265 and 81, respectively. Prospective employees were screened by the local office of the Illinois State Employment Service and, if accepted by the employer, entered training programs aimed at specific jobs in the companies. Data were obtained for the first 33 retrainees at McNair and the first 31 at Technical Tape. The experience of these retrainees was recorded for a ten-month period between July, 1962, and May, 1963.

The Chicago retraining program is conducted exclusively by government agencies at the local level. For several years the Welfare Rehabilitation Service (WRS) of the Cook County Department of Public Aid has extended a variety of social and vocational services to unemployed recipients of public aid. The WRS training activities were originally aimed at persons who suffered from physical, social, and psychological handicaps. "Therapy shops" were established to help prepare public aid recipients for gainful employment in the labor market. Training in light industrial occupations was linked to intensive counseling and other personal services. In 1958, the scope of the Rehabilitation Services' activities was expanded to include a wider range of clients and training programs. Although handicapped persons still comprise a significant part of the trainees, the focus has been shifted to unemployed persons in general. The courses offered include rudimentary industrial occupation, nurse's aide, licensed practical nurse, food handler, domestic servant, and clerk-typists. Information was available from WRS records for 330 persons who entered the program in 1961 and 1962. Of this total, 277 had been enrolled in the Industrial Training Course (ITC) and 53 in the nurse's aide course.

Aside from the fact that all of the projects investigated are broadly concerned with training unemployed workers, substantial differences exist in the orientation and administration of the individual programs. These differences highlight the choices available to policy makers and may help to reveal the shortcomings and potential benefits associated with the alternative approaches.

First, as indicated above, the five programs were sponsored by different types of organizations. The Fort Worth and Omaha projects were initiated by private groups within the framework of a union-management agreement. On the other hand, the Carbondale and Murphysboro programs were public efforts stimulated by federal legislation. In Chicago, the inspiration for the program came from local agencies.

These differences in sponsorship were further reflected in different administrative arrangements for the implementation of the projects. The Fort Worth project was administered exclusively by a private agency, although technical aid was provided by the local office of the State Employment Service. In Omaha, company and union officials limited their activities to the approval of expenditures for particular training courses. Otherwise, the day-to-day administration of the program was handled by staff members of the Nebraska State Employment Service who were assigned the task as a special "demonstration project" of the U.S. Department of Labor.

Responsibility was also shared in Carbondale and Murphysboro. There, the selection of the trainees was delegated to the local Employment Service office, the formal training was supervised by the Vocational Training Institute of Southern Illinois University under a contract with the government, and the employer determined the specific content of the courses, made the final decision on the selection of the trainees, and carried out most of the actual instruction. In Chicago, both responsibility and authority for the training activities were lodged in the WRS.

The unique orientation of the individual programs also meant that retrainees were recruited from different categories of unemployed workers who were subjected to disparate criteria of acceptance. Thus, the Fort Worth and Omaha retrainees were drawn from unemployed workers who generally had a long-time attachment to a specific job in a particular industry and who were now forced to make an immediate transition to new occupational and industrial sectors of the labor market. In Fort Worth, no applicant was peremptorily denied the opportunity for retraining. Instead, every effort was made by the Automation Committee to find a suitable training course in the light of the applicant's background and aptitudes. Somewhat more stringent standards of acceptability were used in Omaha. Admission to a training course was determined by both a union-management committee and officials of the State Employment Service. The acquiescence of the Employment Service was necessary to qualify the retrainee for unemployment compensation while he was in training.

The ARA programs drew on unemployed workers in the local labor market at large. Consequently, the applicants were comprised of some persons who had had no labor force attachment at all, those who had withdrawn from the labor market some time in the past, and active job seekers who had experienced varying periods of unemployment. Similarly, there was a wide diversity in the occupational and industrial background of the applicants. The selection of retrainees was carried out by the State Employment Service. Unlike Forth Worth and Omaha, absolute qualitative standards were used in the light of the specific job requirements in Technical Tape and McNair Metals. On occasion, the Employment Service would approve an applicant whom, for various reasons, the company found unacceptable. Such disagreements over the acceptance of trainees would then be "worked out" in discussion between the Employment Service and company representatives.

The Chicago project was the only case in which an element of coercion was introduced into the recruitment of trainees. That is, if a Public Aid case worker determined that a welfare recipient was "employable," the latter was directed to report to the WRS. Following a counseling interview, the unemployed person might then be enrolled in one of the training courses conducted by the Rehabilitation Service. Refusal to enter training might result in a penalty—the loss of welfare benefits. As might be expected, many of the referrals had been unemployed for prolonged periods of time and had a tenuous labor force attachment. Similarly, a large number of the potential trainees had migrated to Chicago in the past decade from a southern-rural environment.

Considerable diversity existed in the occupational scope of the five retraining projects. No formal limitations on choice were established in Fort Worth and Omaha. Training was approved for any course for which the applicant was qualified, provided that the training had some realistic connection with local labor market conditions. The courses included cosmetology, machinist, welding, food service, electronics, clerk-typist, data processing, automobile mechanic, and barber, among others. A full listing of the courses approved in Omaha and Fort Worth, as well as in the other cases, is presented in Appendix A.

A narrower range of choice was available to the trainees in Carbondale and Murphysboro. Obviously, the alternatives were constrained by the job requirements in each plant. In fact, the trainees were more or less placed in particular jobs based upon an assessment of the individuals' aptitudes and the companies' needs. Most of the jobs involved semiskilled machine operations with little direct transferability in the labor market. The trainees in Technical Tape were instructed in the operation of coating, slitting, and rewind machines and other equipment indigenous to the manufacture of tape. The McNair Metals trainees were assigned to extruders, die presses, cutting saws, and related metal-processing machines. In each case, the training was carried out on the job, although the trainees at McNair did receive one week of classroom instruction in the fundamentals of metallurgy.

The Chicago project had a shifting occupational orientation to training. Indeed, the content of the Industrial Training Course can scarcely be considered occupational training in the formal sense. First, a substantial part of the support for the training activities was obtained from local firms with whom the WRS contracted to carry out certain manufacturing and finishing operations. Thus, the character of the training at any given time is determined by the work contracts negotiated by the WRS. During the period of the study, the enrollees in ITC were engaged in putting magnets in plastic letters for children's alphabet sets, simple soldering, power riveting, and grinding. The majority of the trainees, however, assembled, counted and packaged various products. Second, the training capabilities of the WRS were limited by the available equipment and the volume of the work orders. Thus, drill presses, power riveters, and power sewing machines were the most advanced pieces of equipment on hand. Moreover, these machines and tools might remain idle at any given time because of the lack of appropriate work contracts.

Although the Industrial Training Course often does provide the enrollees with simple manual skills, it is clear that one of the primary objectives of the program is to develop or preserve effective work habits. By requiring regular attendance and providing close supervision, it is hoped that those persons without any industrial background at all, or those who have experienced prolonged unemployment, will maintain some contact with useful economic activity and the labor market. This judgment is modified in the case of the nurse's aid course and other WRS programs with a relatively well-defined occupational focus. Although the training may serve the purpose of work habituation, it also aims at equipping the trainees with specific, marketable skills.

Because of the different administrative arrangements and occupational choices, considerable variation existed in the duration of the training courses in the cases studied. In Fort Worth and Omaha, the length of training varied from four weeks to eighteen months, depending upon the course in question. In addition, the actual elapsed time was affected by whether the trainees attended the course on a part-time or full-time basis. The Carbondale and Murphysboro programs, on the other hand, were fixed at six and eight weeks for different jobs with explicit starting and termination dates. The Chicago Industrial Training Course project had a recognized time limit, but no mandatory period of instruction. That is, as soon as a person entered the program, an effort was made to place the trainee on a job. If the trainee was hired, he was immediately dropped from the program. Where no placement was made, enrollment in the program was continued for six months. In practice, some trainees were kept in ITC for as long as nine months, pending placement in a job. Thus, ITC was also a "staging area" for labor market activity by the WRS on behalf of the trainees. The employment of the trainee, of course, meant the reduction or elimination of public aid payments. Again, the nurse's aide course may be distinguished from ITC. Here, the course lasted four weeks, and each trainee was expected to remain enrolled until completion.

There were also significant differences among the cases studied in the nature and magnitude of the financial support provided to the retrainees. No direct financial aid, except the full payment of training expenses, was given to the trainees in Fort Worth and Omaha. In Omaha, however, an administrative ruling by state officials made it possible for persons enrolled full-time in "approved" training courses to receive unemployment compensation benefits to which they were otherwise entitled even though they were not "available for employment." Approval was made by the demonstration project staff in the Omaha office of the State Employment Service. In fact, almost all of the Cudahy retrainees benefitted from this provision. Texas law did not permit a similar arrangement. Therefore, most of the trainees attended school in the evening either because they had found some temporary job, or in order to remain "available for employment" and preserve their rights to unemployment benefits.

The provisions of the Area Redevelopment Act assumed the financial support of the Carbondale and Murphysboro retrainees during the course of the program. In Murphysboro each trainee received an allowance of $36 per week, supplemented, in the case of the Carbondale trainees, by $18 in wages. The extra income arose from the fact that the Technical Tape program involved the production of goods for commerce. Under these circumstances, the law required the payment of wages for the time spent engaged in such production activities.

The financial arrangements in Chicago were coercive rather than supplementary. Unwillingness to participate in a training program might be penalized by the loss of welfare benefits. The amount of the benefits varied with the number of dependents in the trainee's family, but ranged from $63 to approximately $350 per month. The probability of being cut off from public aid is diminished somewhat by the character of bureaucratic relations between the WRS counselors and the Public Aid case workers. The case workers generally have a great distaste for the coercive aspects of enrollment in the WRS program. Therefore, when the Rehabilitation Service counselor recommends revocation of aid for unwillingness to participate in a designated training program, the case workers may seek to continue the welfare payments by demonstrating that nonparticipation was justified by cause. In fact, many of the potential retrainees cannot enter or continue in a course because of personal and domestic difficulties. In this manner, the possible financial penalties associated with a failure to undergo training may be the basis for a subtle process of negotiation.

The origins and administration of the different programs meant that there were considerable differences in the expectation of employment following the completion of training. At Technical Tape in Carbondale, the trainees were assured that the successful completion of the course would result in full-time employment with the company. The fact that the trainees received wages during the period of instruction helped to confirm the expectation. In Murphysboro, on the other hand, employment prospects were ambiguous. That is, the trainees knew that specific jobs were available, but they were further informed that the screening process for employment would be continued through the training period and that not all of the trainees would be hired, even if they finished the course without mishap.

The Omaha, Fort Worth, and Chicago programs generally lacked any connection with specific jobs. Instead, they were broadly related to the labor market. Of these three cases, the greatest implicit expectation of employment prevailed in Omaha, largely as a reflection of labor market conditions. Omaha is a sizable labor market with total employment of approximately 100,000. In addition, unemployment rates in the area have been consistently low and have seldom exceeded 3.5 per cent in the past five years. While the Cudahy project was under way, unemployment ranged between 2.7 and 3.2 per cent of the labor force. Because of the relatively small number of trainees and the nature of the skills involved, there was a high expectation that those who completed their courses would find suitable employment.

In Fort Worth, labor market conditions would not support any strong optimism. Although total employment in Forth Worth exceeded 200,000, unemployment was over 5 per cent when the program was initiated. Moreover, additional pressure on the labor market was expected to develop because of major layoffs at General Dynamics, the largest employer in the city. A quick survey was conducted to pinpoint occupations for which there might be a substantial demand, but the results had only a limited reliability. For some occupations, such as practical nurse, there was a perceptible demand; however, the prospect for persons trained in other occupations was less certain.

The Chicago program had the most tenuous connection to the labor market and any specific expectations of employment on the part of the trainee. First, in most cases, the skills involved in the ITC program in particular were extremely general in nature. Of the courses studied, only the nurse's aide program had a specific relationship to a known demand in the labor market. Second, the character of the training changed as different work orders were contracted for by the WRS. Third, the constituents served by the program generally had experienced prolonged periods of unemployment and to a considerable extent had lost contact with the labor market. Indeed, the WRS program was distinguished by its efforts to restore the effective work habits and the idea of useful economic activity in the minds of the participants. The Chicago project was supported by intensive measures to achieve the placement of the trainees, but only within the broad labor market context described above.

## CHARACTERISTICS OF THE RETRAINEES

The immediate objective of most retraining programs is to improve the economic condition of the unemployed. However, an analysis of the characteristics of the trainees enrolled in the five programs included in this study underscores the contention that the "unemployed" is comprised of differentiated subgroups. As shown in Tables VIII.1, VIII.2, and VIII.3, significant differences existed in the personal and labor mar-

TABLE VIII.1

CHARACTERISTICS OF RETRAINEES BY SEX AND RACE

| Project | No. | Sex | | Race | | |
|---------|-----|------|--------|-------|-------|----------------|
| | | Male | Female | White | Negro | Latin American |
| Chicago | 330 | 47.8% | 52.1% | 8.4% | 91.2% | 0.3% |
| Murphysboro | 31 | 59.3 | 40.6 | 53.4 | 44.8 | 1.7 |
| Carbondale | 33 | 100.0 | 0.0 | 96.9 | 3.0 | 0.0 |
| Omaha | 59 | 38.7 | 61.2 | 74.1 | 25.8 | 0.0 |
| Fort Worth | 167 | 60.4 | 39.5 | 46.1 | 35.9 | 17.9 |
| Total no. | 620 | | | | | |

ket characteristics of the particular trainee groups. In Chicago, Omaha, and Fort Worth, the composition of retrainee groups largely reflected

## TABLE VIII.2

CHARACTERISTICS OF RETRAINEES BY AGE AND MARITAL STATUS[a]

| Project | Age | | | | | | Marital status | | |
|---|---|---|---|---|---|---|---|---|---|
| | Under 20 | 20-29 | 30-39 | 40-49 | 50-59 | 60+ | Single | Married | Divorced |
| Chicago | 2% | 23% | 40% | 23% | 12% | 0% | 44% | 56% | 0% |
| Murphysboro | 15 | 46 | 18 | 12 | 9 | 0 | 36 | 64 | 0 |
| Carbondale | 19 | 48 | 16 | 10 | 7 | 0 | 48 | 52 | 0 |
| Omaha | 0 | 24 | 49 | 20 | 7 | 0 | 12 | 88 | 0 |
| Fort Worth | 0 | 0 | 32 | 40 | 24 | 4 | 16 | 83 | 1 |

[a] No. = 620.

## TABLE VIII.3

CHARACTERISTICS OF RETRAINEES BY EDUCATION AND PREVIOUS OCCUPATIONAL ATTACHMENT[a]

| Project | Education (in yrs.) | | | | Occupational category | | | | Skill level | | |
|---|---|---|---|---|---|---|---|---|---|---|---|
| | 0-6 | 7-9 | 10-12 | 13+ | Blue-collar | Service | White-collar | None | Unskilled | Semi-skilled | Skilled |
| Chicago | 23% | 35% | 41% | 1% | 70% | 21% | 3% | 6% | 79% | 12% | 3% |
| Murphysboro | 0 | 21 | 73 | 6 | 72 | 10 | 3 | 15 | 33 | 42 | 10 |
| Carbondale | 0 | 16 | 65 | 19 | 58 | 16 | 13 | 13 | 29 | 52 | 6 |
| Omaha | 2 | 24 | 64 | 10 | 100 | 0 | 0 | 0 | 59 | 36 | 5 |
| Fort Worth | 13 | 41 | 40 | 6 | 100 | 0 | 0 | 0 | 58 | 32 | 10 |

[a] No. = 620; not ascertained = 6. Tabulations based on sample of 614.

the qualities of the specific constituencies served by the agencies providing the training opportunities. In Carbondale and Murphysboro, the dominant consideration was the criteria for selection applied by the local Employment Service office and the employer.

The same general pattern describes the characteristics of the Carbondale and Murphysboro trainees. In both cases, the emphasis was on the younger, better educated workers. Over 60 per cent of the trainees were under 30 years of age and over 80 per cent were less than 40. Similarly, all of the trainees had more than seven years of education, while approximately 80 per cent had been in school for ten years or more. In Carbondale, in particular, nearly 20 per cent of the trainees in the sample had attempted college. In fact, two of the trainees had been attending college immediately before their entrance into the program and had been attracted to the opportunity by the prospect of summer employment.

Consistent with the younger average age of the group, a relatively high proportion of the Carbondale and Murphysboro trainees were unmarried. In addition, 13 to 15 per cent did not have any work history or occupational attachment and therefore, could be classified as new entrants into the labor force. Those who had worked in the past generally had been employed in blue-collar, semiskilled occupations. In Carbondale, however, where women comprised a majority of the trainees, 13 per cent had been in white-collar jobs, primarily as telephone operators.

Some bias is undoubtedly present in this sample of ARA trainees. That is, the study was limited to the first group of trainees selected at Technical Tape and McNair. As the number of persons selected increased, it might be expected that there would be a greater representation of older, less educated, and relatively unskilled workers. Nonetheless, the evidence indicates that the selection agencies tended to accept higher-quality workers as long as they had a choice—even where it was not clear that the technical level of the training required such standards.

A different picture is presented by the Omaha and Fort Worth trainees, who were selected exclusively from the ranks of displaced meatpacking workers. In both situations more than 75 per cent of the retrainees were 30 years of age or older. Indeed, none of the Fort Worth trainees was under 30, while approximately 70 per cent were over 40 and 28 per cent were 50 or more. Similarly, a substantial proportion of these groups had less than ten years of formal education. All of the Cudahy and Armour retrainees had, of course, some identifiable occupational attachment, primarily in unskilled blue-collar categories. Moreover, the labor market prospects for these groups were also affected by the substantial representation of minority groups such as Negroes and Latin Americans. Further, limitations on the selection of training courses and subsequent labor market activity were imposed by the fact that in both cities, 40 per cent of the trainees were women. In Fort Worth, in particular, over half of the women were also Negroes.

The trainees in the Chicago group might also be expected to have a relatively bleak view of the labor market. First, an overwhelming proportion of the trainees were Negroes. Second, many of the trainees had extremely limited educational backgrounds; 22.6 per cent of the trainees had less than seven years of education and 58 per cent less than ten years, much of which was obtained in southern rural schools. Third, the previous work experience of most of the trainees had been in unskilled blue-collar and service occupations. And fourth, about 35 per cent of the participants were 40 years of age or older.

The characteristics of the trainees are of considerable significance when related to the general occupational orientation of the particular training programs. Thus, the quality of the trainees in terms of age, education, and previous work history tended to be highest in Carbondale and Murphysboro where almost all the jobs were semiskilled in nature and some were actually unskilled by the usual standards. Conversely, training in several skilled occupations was provided in Omaha and Fort Worth, where the overall quality of the participants was low. In Chicago, low-level training was associated with limited education and work experience.

The relationship between the skill level of the training and that of any previous job held by the trainee is presented in Table VIII.4. The

TABLE VIII.4

RELATIONSHIP OF SKILL LEVEL OF TRAINING TO SKILL LEVEL
OF ANY PREVIOUS JOB

| | | Skill level | | | |
|---|---|---|---|---|---|
| | | Higher | | Lower | |
| Project[a] | Same | 1 level | 2 levels | 1 level | 2 levels |
| Chicago | 79 | 12 | —[b] | 9 | — |
| Murphysboro | 60 | 33 | — | 7 | — |
| Carbondale | 52 | 11 | — | 37 | — |
| Omaha | 32 | 47 | 21 | — | — |
| Fort Worth | 25 | 52 | 21 | 2 | — |

[a] Sixty-five persons in the total sample of 620 had had no previous job; data were not available on six persons, leaving a sample of 549 as the basis for these tabulations.

[b] Less than 1 per cent.

table was constructed by rating the occupation for which the person was being trained and the most skilled job he or she had held in the past. All jobs were rated on a three-point scale of "unskilled," "semiskilled" and "skilled." Reference was made to the *Dictionary of Occupational Titles* wherever possible. In Fort Worth, 72 per cent of the trainees enrolled in courses in which the occupational skill content was one or two levels above that of any previous job. An equivalent relationship is noted in the Omaha case. On the other hand, a majority of the Carbondale and Murphysboro trainees remained at the same skill level. In addition, 37 per cent of those enrolled in the Carbondale program and 6.6 per cent of those in the Murphysboro program actually moved down the occupational ladder. In Chicago, most of the trainees held the same occupational level, while relatively small groups moved up or down in the hierarchy. It is apparent that the five programs represent significant differences in the degree to which they attempted to upgrade the skills of the unemployed workers.

### EXPERIENCE IN TRAINING

In view of the differences in the nature of the five programs, considerable variation might be expected in the subsequent training experience of the participants. In each case, the trainees were confronted with a different set of financial incentives, expectations, and training demands. Moreover, the trainees themselves were heterogeneous in terms of both demographic characteristics and labor market background.

The experience in training under the five programs is shown in Table VIII.5. All of the categories are self-explanatory except "partial com-

TABLE VIII.5

EXPERIENCE IN TRAINING[a]

| Project | Complete | Partial complete | Dropout | Still in training |
|---------|----------|------------------|---------|-------------------|
| Chicago | 79% | 5% | 15% | 0% |
| Murphysboro | 66 | 15 | 18 | 0 |
| Carbondale | 87 | 0 | 13 | 0 |
| Omaha | 44 | 3 | 39 | 14 |
| Fort Worth | 68 | 9 | 18 | 6 |

[a] No. = 620; data not ascertained = 4. Tabulations based on sample of 616.

plete." This designation refers to those cases in which the trainee was judged to have attained sufficient competence in the occupation for which he was being trained before the formal completion of the course. In each instance, he left the course to take an actual job that was directly or indirectly related to the training. Such a "partial complete" designation is important in distinguishing people in this category from those who dropped out of training without achieving the occupational objectives of the course.

Several observations may be made from these data. First, with the exception of Omaha, there is surprisingly little variation among the dropout rates for the different cases. Thus, the dropout rates for Carbondale, Murphysboro, and Fort Worth ranged from 13.3 to 18.8 per cent, while in Omaha the proportion of dropouts was 38.9 per cent, or more than double the rate in the next highest case. Second, limited but significant margins of persons were still in training in Omaha and Fort Worth twenty months after these programs had been initiated. Third, "partial completes" were found in each city except Carbondale. In contrast, the proportion falling in this category was highest in Murphysboro, the other ARA project.

This comparative experience undoubtedly reflects a complex of interdependent factors. The relatively high dropout rate in Omaha probably stemmed from labor market considerations and the intrinsic qualities of the program. On the one hand, the Omaha labor market enjoyed a high level of employment so that most of the trainees were aware that the prospects for a job, albeit an unskilled job, were relatively good without retraining. In economic terms, this meant that the imputed opportunity cost of the training was substantial. The temptation of alternative employment became especially great when the union and management at Cudahy worked out an arrangement whereby employees who had been severed from the company could return on a short-term, irregular basis as "replacement workers" at the new plant. If a former employee worked as a replacement for one day, he retained recall rights for another two years. This arrangement clearly nurtured the hope that by "hanging on," a displaced worker might ultimately gain permanent employee status with Cudahy once again. Despite concerted efforts by the program administrators to persuade the participants that, in any case, the training was insurance against the future, a sizable proportion succumbed to the enticement and dropped out.

The Omaha training program, as noted previously, also attempted to upgrade substantially the skill level of the trainees. This meant that the training courses were long and often difficult. Moreover, the longer the course, the more likely that a trainee would exhaust his unemployment benefits and be left without income. Consequently, about one-third of the dropouts withdrew because of this pressure on the cerebrum or the purse.

In Fort Worth, the enticement of remunerative employment was generally lacking. The displaced workers had no expectation of re-employment with Armour and the unemployment rate, although not severe by national standards, was nearly double what it was in Omaha. The jobs that were available were, for the greater part, in unskilled, low-paying positions. The availability of these jobs, therefore, did not create a strong disincentive for continuation in training. On the contrary, their availability appeared to reduce the dropout rate as compared to Omaha. That is, because persons enrolled in training on a full-time basis during normal working hours did not qualify for unemployment benefits, most of the former Armour employees attended evening classes. This arrangement had two salutary consequences. First, it permitted those trainees without jobs to draw unemployment benefits to the full extent of their eligibility. Second, as the benefits were exhausted, those who were still in training could still seek and accept a temporary job without dropping from the program. Ultimately, about 50 per cent of the trainees had some employment while enrolled in an evening program. One of the striking features of the Fort Worth project was the willingness of the trainees to expend considerable effort to see their courses through to completion. As a result, the dropout rate was substantially lower than in Omaha, notwithstanding important similarities in the organization of the programs.

Conditions were propitious for a high rate of completion in Carbondale and Murphysboro. In both cases, the duration of the course was relatively brief, financial allowances were paid while in training, there was a high expectation of employment immediately following the completion of the program, and the trainees were generally young and relatively well educated. In fact, Carbondale had the lowest dropout rate while Murphysboro was under 20 per cent, but slightly higher than Fort Worth. All of the dropouts in Carbondale were women who withdrew voluntarily because the work "made them nervous" or because they otherwise found the job content unsuitable. In Murphysboro, half of the dropouts left voluntarily while the other half were asked to drop because of lack of interest or aptitude. It is significant to recall that the trainees' income in Carbondale included both wages and a training allowance as compared to Murphysboro, where only an allowance was given.

The training experience in Chicago also revealed a low dropout rate notwithstanding the limited expectation of employment and the variable occupational content of the instruction. Undoubtedly, this result reflected the powerful influence of the financial conditions associated with participation in the program. That is, no trainee dropped from the program voluntarily without jeopardizing his or her welfare benefits. The dropout group was thus composed of persons who the WRS counselors ruled would not benefit from the training or those who, for certified personal reasons, could not continue in training without undue hardship.

Of the five programs, only Omaha and Fort Worth still had people in training nine months or more after the projects had commenced. In some instances, this was attributable to the length of the course. For example, one Fort Worth trainee had entered college with the ultimate objective of becoming a teacher, while some of the trainees in Omaha were engaged in advanced electronic courses. In other cases, the trainee had temporarily dropped out of the program for financial or domestic reasons and had re-enrolled when circumstances permitted. The administrators of the Omaha and Fort Worth projects adopted a flexible policy in such cases to encourage the completion of the courses, even though it might take considerable time.

The incidence of "partial completes" also highlights significant differences in the five programs. Murphysboro boasted the largest proportion of "partial completes" because the employer was expanding operations and anxious to put those trainees who made rapid progress on a regular employee status as soon as possible. In Fort Worth, the nighttime scheduling of the courses permitted the trainees to seek regular employment while financial pressures often created an incentive for rapid completion of the program. In Chicago, efforts to place the trainees were carried out at every stage of the course, although the success of these efforts was limited. Only Carbondale had no persons identified as "partial completes." This development is probably attributable to the fact that Technical Tape was slow to get into production, and management had no incentive to accelerate the progress of the more able trainees.

Gross differences in the size of the various training groups and the relatively small number of persons involved in three of the cases make it inadvisable to engage in highly refined comparative analysis of the five programs. However, some insights into the factors influencing the experience in training may be obtained by aggregating the trainees in all of the groups.

Most of the conventional demographic variables, by themselves, are of limited significance in distinguishing the experience of the trainees in the programs. The differences in completion rates with respect to race, sex, age, and education were small and do not give rise to any clear inferences. The lack of a relationship between education and experience in training stems from the fact that in most cases there was a conscious effort to match the content of the course to the qualifications of the trainee. Indeed, the only significant difference was between the trainees who had been to college and those with lesser education. The dropout rate for trainees with some college education was 24 per cent while it ranged from 14 to 18 per cent for the trainees in the lower educational classifications.[2] This development was attributable in a large measure to the fact that three of the four college students enrolled in the Carbondale and Murphysboro programs withdrew to return to school.

There was a major difference in the training experience of single and married persons. As shown in Table VIII.6, 20 per cent of the married

TABLE VIII.6

TRAINING EXPERIENCE BY MARITAL STATUS[a]

| Training | Single | Married |
|---|---|---|
| Completed | 82% | 68% |
| Partial | 6 | 7 |
| Dropout | 12 | 20 |
| Still in training | 0 | 5 |

[a] No. = 620; data not ascertained = 4. Tabulations based on sample of 616.

trainees dropped out of their courses while only 12 per cent of the single persons withdrew.[3] Although the Chicago results exercised a dominant influence on the aggregate data, the dropout rate was also lower in all the other cases but Carbondale. In Fort Worth and Murphysboro, in particular, the dropout rates for married persons were more than double the rate for single persons. The married persons may be expected to be under the greater financial pressure to meet family obligations which, in turn, may create a need for immediate employment and an income level higher than that provided by a training allowance or unemployment benefits. This is especially true where the married person is a male. Even in the case of women, it may be assumed that they would not enter training unless they played an important economic role in the household. In this sense, the same factors that apparently contribute to a low unemployment rate for married job seekers may also contribute to a relatively high dropout rate in training for this group.

All things considered, the demographic variables do not seem as important in determining experience in training as the relationship between the participant's previous work history and the skill level of the occupation for which he was being trained. Table VIII.7 shows the experience in training for all five cities with respect to the relationship between the skill level in any previous job held by the trainees and the skill level of the training. The results strongly indicate that those who attempted to jump two skills in the course of their training were more likely to withdraw from the program than those persons who remained at the same skill level or who moved up only one notch on the scale. Thus, the dropout rate for those attempting to move two levels was more than twice the rate for those at the same level or only one level higher than their previous occupational experience. At the same time, there was no significant difference between the trainees who remained at the

TABLE VIII.7

Experience in Training by Relationship of Skill Level
of Training to Skill Level of Any Previous Job[a]

| Training experience | Skill level | | | | |
|---|---|---|---|---|---|
| | | Higher | | Lower | |
| | Same | 1 level | 2 levels | 1 level | 2 levels[b] |
| Completed | 79% | 79% | 48% | 84% | 0% |
| Partial complete | 9 | 5 | 6 | 3 | 0 |
| Dropout | 12 | 12 | 27 | 14 | 0 |
| Still in training | 0 | 4 | 19 | 0 | 0 |

[a] Sixty-five persons in the total sample of 620 had had no previous job, and data were not available on six persons, leaving a sample of 549 as the basis for these tabulations.
[b] Only one case in this category.

same level and those who jumped one level. This relationship between success in training and the upgrading of skills is further supported by data dealing with the skill level alone. That is, the dropout rates for those enrolled in courses involving training in unskilled,[4] semiskilled, and skilled occupations were 11, 14, and 23 per cent, respectively.

Additional analysis was carried out to determine if the dropout rate was different for those persons whose training involved interindustry shifts at the same time that they sought to upgrade their skills.[5] Although the data are limited, there was no systematic variation in the experience of the trainees who made interindustry shifts as contrasted to those whose previous work history was in the same industrial sector as the training course in which they were enrolled. Apparently a person who was a janitor or materials handler in a factory finds it as difficult to become a machinist as a person who was a construction laborer. If industrial experience contributes to successful occupational retraining, this salutary influence will probably be realized only under narrow circumstances.

Within the framework of this study, experience in training appears to be determined in a large measure by a combination of factors relating to the financial conditions associated with the program, and the relationship of the trainee's work history to the skill level of the occupation for which he is being trained. Thus, the chances for successful completion of training are improved when the real or imputed costs of the program to the individual are low or negative. This implies that the level of income while in training is relatively high and that there are negligible opportunity costs arising from possible foregone employment. In addition, the impact of any given level of costs will be diminished where family obligations are limited and the anticipated benefits of training are substantial in terms of the expectation of employment following training. As an independent variable, the likelihood of the successful completion of training is also improved when the trainee moves up only one major rung in the occupational ladder.

This specification of optimal conditions for training poses no real surprise. Unemployed workers should be no less astute than their employed brethren in assessing their economic interests. It is unreasonable to expect workers to maintain a personal commitment to retraining when the net costs appear to be substantial or the training process puts too great a demand on their existing stock of skills and aptitudes. One of the important problems of retraining the unemployed is to develop programs that are responsive to the economic perceptions and qualifications of the jobless.

## THE EMPLOYMENT RECORD

One direct measure of the effectiveness of retraining is, of course, the employment record of those who participated in the programs. Data concerning the employment experience of those who completed training in the five cities are presented in Table VIII.8. In each case, 75 per cent or

TABLE VIII.8

EMPLOYMENT EXPERIENCE OF TRAINEES: COMPLETE AND PARTIAL COMPLETE, ALL CITIES[a]

| Employment experience | Chicago (n = 278) | Omaha (n = 30) | Murphys- boro (n = 27) | Carbon- dale (n = 26) | Fort Worth (n = 126) |
|---|---|---|---|---|---|
| Never employed | 21% | 24% | 7% | 4% | 4% |
| Employed at some time, but presently unemployed | 0 | 0 | 4 | 4 | 16 |
| Presently employed | 79 | 75 | 89 | 92 | 80 |

[a] Total number = 487; data not ascertained = 3. Tabulations based on sample of 484.

more of these successful retrainees were employed. As might be expected, the best employment experience was registered in Carbondale and Murphysboro, where 92 and 89 per cent the trainees, respectively, were working. They were followed by Fort Worth with 80 per cent, Chicago with 79 per cent, and Omaha with 75 per cent.

These results should be interpreted in the light of differences in the time elapsed since the completion of training. In Murphysboro and Carbondale, data on employment experience were collected six to eight months after the course was completed. The employment status of the

Omaha and Fort Worth trainees generally was verified from six months to a year following the conclusion of instruction in individual cases. Thus, there was some time in which to determine the labor market activity of these trainees.

In Chicago, on the other hand, the WRS records extended for only a brief period after training. If a trainee was placed on a job, the counselors usually did not make any follow-up unless particular individuals were referred back to them for some reason. This happened in about one-third of the cases. Consequently, the employment data do not provide information on the economic fate of many of the trainees after they started their first jobs. Because these jobs frequently were with small, marginal firms, a significant number of the trainees may have reverted to an unemployed status over time. Nonetheless, the immediate employment record of the Chicago trainees is striking in view of the character of the program and the background of the participants. As a result of minimal training linked to intensive counseling and placement efforts, three out of four of those completing the program were moved from a situation of complete dependency to one of useful economic activity.

Several other dimensions of the trainees' employment record may be enumerated. First, those employed were working full-time, or more than thirty hours per week, in the overwhelming majority of cases. Part-time work was a significant consideration only in Fort Worth, where 12 per cent of the employed persons were known to be working less than thirty hours per week. This group was comprised almost exclusively of Negro women.

Second, most of those who had never been employed since completing training were not actively seeking work. In Omaha, six out of the seven persons who had never been employed were women who had finished a ten-month course in cosmetology (beauty operator) but showed little disposition to use their new skills immediately in the labor market. Most of the women were married and apparently viewed the skills as an insurance policy to fall back upon in the event that there was some pressing need for extra income in the household. In a like manner, the never-employed groups in Carbondale, Murphysboro, and Fort Worth were largely comprised of persons who had withdrawn from the labor market or who were only seeking work sporadically. Because there were no follow-up interviews in Chicago, any judgment on the labor force attachment of the trainees who were never employed will be conjectural. It may be noted, however, that about one-third of this group had designated physical handicaps.[6] In addition, in a purely economic sense, the continued receipt of welfare benefits reduced the direct pressure to seek employment.

Third, even in the relatively short period following the completion of training, there was a substantial amount of job changing. In Chicago, 35 per cent of those who were employed were known to have held at least two jobs since they finished training at the WRS. The proportion of job changers in Fort Worth was somewhat lower, but still constituted about one-quarter of those who were or had been employed. At the other end of the scale, in Murphysboro, Carbondale, and Omaha, less than 15 per cent of those who completed training had had more than one job in the period covered.

The incidence of job changing reflected both demand and supply factors. In Chicago and Forth Worth, about half of the job changers were laid off involuntarily, while an equal number quit because of dissatisfaction with the work, the wages, or the distance they had to travel to the job. Consistent with the full-employment condition of the Omaha labor market, almost all the job changers quit their initial jobs to take more favorable employment. The limited amount of turnover in Carbondale and Murphysboro is consistent with the organization of these programs. That is, if the trainees or the employer were dissatisfied with each other, such attitudes would have been manifested in the dropout rate while the course was still under way.

The employment record of those who completed training may be further evaluated by a comparison with the labor market experience of those who had dropped out of training. The small number of people involved in the dropout group permits only the most tentative judgments. As shown in Table VIII.9, however, the dropouts generally did

TABLE VIII.9

EMPLOYMENT EXPERIENCE OF TRAINEES (DROPOUTS) BY CITY[a]

| Employment experience | Chicago (n = 48) | Omaha (n = 16) | Murphysboro (n = 6) | Carbondale (n = 4) | Fort Worth (n = 27) |
|---|---|---|---|---|---|
| Never employed | 80% | 29% | 16% | 50% | 14% |
| Employed at some time, but presently unemployed | 0 | 0 | 0 | 0 | 14 |
| Presently employed | 20 | 71 | 84 | 50 | 72 |

[a] Total number = 108; data not ascertained = 7. Tabulation based on sample of 101.

not fare as well in the labor market as those who completed training. The 75 per cent unemployment rate among Chicago trainees reflects the fact that most of the dropouts were really "force-outs" who withdrew from the program because of personal difficulties or their inability to profit from the training. On the other hand, the higher level of employment of the dropouts in Fort Worth and Omaha may be related to the financial arrangements associated with these programs. A trainee was likely to drop out to seek employment as other sources of income while in training, particularly unemployment compensation benefits, dried up. If it is assumed that half of the Omaha dropouts for whom no information is available were working, the proportion of those employed to the entire group is equivalent to that of Fort Worth. The difference between the status of the Murphysboro and Carbondale dropouts, in turn, probably arises from differences in the labor force attachment of men and women. All of the dropouts in the former case were men while in the latter program, they all were women.

A consideration of the aggregate data for all five cases permits additional inferences concerning the factors that helped to determine the employment record of those persons who completed training. Again, demographic variables have limited usefulness in distinguishing between the labor market experience of the trainees. First, there is no significant difference in employment status with respect to race. The employment rate for both Negroes and whites was approximately 80 per cent. Over 90 per cent of the Latin American trainees, most of whom were located in Fort Worth, were employed, but there are too few observations in this group to make any firm judgments.

Second, there was only a slight difference in the employment status of married and unmarried persons. The employment rate for the married trainees was 77 per cent and for the unmarried group, 82 per cent. The same general relationship prevails when the data for Chicago and the other four cities are considered separately. As indicated previously, the effect of marital status seems to be most significant when assessing the experience in training. Once the married trainees managed to complete the program, they faced the same prospects in the labor market as their unmarried counterparts.

TABLE VIII.10

EMPLOYMENT STATUS BY SEX: ALL CITIES[a]

| Employment experience | Male | Female |
|---|---|---|
| Never employed | 15% | 16% |
| Employed at some time, but presently unemployed | 81 | 79 |
| Presently employed | 4 | 5 |
| *Chicago* | | |
| Never employed | 25 | 17 |
| Presently employed | 75 | 83 |

[a] No. = 486; data not ascertained = 3. Tabulations based on sample of 483. Chicago number = 278.

Third, there is no substantial difference in the overall record of men as compared to women. Table VIII.10 indicates that the aggregate employment rate for males was 81 per cent and 79 per cent for females. In Chicago alone, however, the experience of women was measurably better than that of the men. The validity of this difference was corroborated by the placement counselors at the WRS who declared that the nature of the demand for labor in the segment of the market that they served made it easier to place Negro women than Negro men. Many of the women were hired for service or light assembly and packaging jobs.

Beyond these demographic factors, the skill level and industry orientation of the training appear to have influenced the aggregate employment record of the completed trainees. As shown in Table VIII.11, the em-

TABLE VIII.11

EMPLOYMENT EXPERIENCE BY SKILL LEVEL OF TRAINING: ALL CITIES[a]

| Employment experience | Unskilled | Semiskilled | Skilled |
|---|---|---|---|
| Never employed | 22% | 8% | 12% |
| Employed at some time, but presently unemployed | 0 | 7 | 12 |
| Presently employed | 78 | 85 | 76 |

[a] No. = 486; data not available or skill-level designation inappropriate = 20. Tabulations based on sample of 466.

ployment rate for those who engaged in training at a semiskilled level was somewhat better than those whose instruction was focused on unskilled and skilled occupations. This difference is accentuated when examining the experience of the Chicago group alone, where the comparison is between trainees in unskilled and semiskilled areas. In the other cases, however, the employment record of the unskilled trainees was superior to the semiskilled trainees, but both were better than the skilled group. The happy ending for those in the unskilled category outside of Chicago stemmed from the fact that they were enrolled primarily in the Carbondale and Murphysboro programs where the likelihood of employment was high.

The observation that persons trained for skilled occupations have a less impressive employment record than those who are trained for unskilled or semiskilled jobs runs counter to most common-sense evaluations of the current state of the labor market. In view of the overall shift in demand to skilled occupations, the trainees equipping themselves for jobs in these areas may be expected to benefit accordingly. As indicated in cases studied, several factors may moderate this optimism. First, those who are trained for skilled occupations may become only marginally competent in these jobs as a result of formal instruction. At any rate, they lack the on-the-job experience that is often demanded by employers in hiring for skilled positions. This appears to be particularly true for jobs like automobile mechanic, welder, machinist, air conditioning and refrigeration mechanic, and beautician, which constituted a large proportion of the skilled training courses.

Second, some of the skills involved were associated with the service industries in which utilization of the skills frequently means becoming self-employed. A few of the beauticians in Omaha and Fort Worth, for example, did set up their own businesses, but employed workers cannot be expected to have the capital or the disposition to take this leap.

Third, the ascension to the ranks of the skilled may often require a shift from one industrial sector to another, especially if the skills fall in the service trades. Under these circumstances, the failure to obtain employment may reflect the fact that the newly groomed skilled worker has very limited information about the appropriate labor market. The relationship between employment status and interindustry shifts associated with occupational training is shown in Table VIII.12. Clearly those

TABLE VIII.12

EMPLOYMENT EXPERIENCE BY INDUSTRY RELATIONSHIP
OF TRAINING TO WORK HISTORY: ALL CITIES[a]

| Employment experience | Same industry | Different industry |
|---|---|---|
| Never employed | 8% | 17% |
| Employed at some time, but presently unemployed | 4 | 5 |
| Presently employed | 88 | 78 |

[a] No. = 486; data not appropriate (no previous job or industry designation) = 46. Tabulations based on sample of 440.

whose training called for an interindustry shift in terms of their previous work history had a poorer employment record. The same relationship prevails when Chicago and non-Chicago cases are treated separately.

Accordingly, training in general and the acquisition of specific skills in particular are not always broad pathways to employment. Where the acquisition of skills carried with it a movement to a heretofore strange sector of the labor market, parallel steps must be taken to provide information and guidance to help the trainee adapt to his new economic environment.

## JOB CONTENT AND TRAINING

Up to this point, the relative effectiveness of retraining has been analyzed in terms of completion rates and the general employment record of the trainees. An additional basis for evaluation may be provided by a comparison of the content of the jobs held with that of the training. Presumably, a training program has come closer to realizing its objectives when subsequent employment is training-related.

The problems of obtaining the appropriate data are formidable. In many cases, not enough was known about the job content even to venture an educated guess. In other instances, an assessment of the content relationship of employment to training may be arbitrary. The difficulties were magnified in Chicago where there was a complete reliance on written records, some of which contained full descriptions of the training content and employment while others were spotty. The data rest on a firmer foundation in Carbondale, Murphysboro, and Fort Worth where most of the trainees were interviewed. In Omaha, on the other hand, the data were obtained from records and extensive interviews with the program administrators. As a result of these problems of evaluation, a little over 20 per cent of the cases were discarded at this stage of the analysis. There is no prima facie reason for believing that there are significant differences in the discards as compared with the overall sample.

With these caveats in mind, some general insights may be offered. The relationship between the content of the trainees' last job and the occupational subject matter of the training for the five programs is presented in Table VIII.13. The categories "directly related" and "unrelated" are

TABLE VIII.13

RELATIONSHIP OF EMPLOYMENT TO CONTENT OF TRAINING, BY CITY[a]

| Relationship of employment to training | Chicago (n = 199) | Omaha (n = 21) | Murphysboro (n = 25) | Carbondale (n = 25) | Fort Worth (n = 119) |
|---|---|---|---|---|---|
| Unrelated | 3% | 5% | 12% | 8% | 38% |
| Indirectly related | 16 | 10 | 64 | 20 | 10 |
| Directly related | 81 | 85 | 24 | 72 | 52 |

[a] $n$ = No. Total no. = 389.

self-explanatory. The "indirectly related" classification includes those cases in which the trainee used his specific skills some of the time on the job, or in which his training gave general support to his employment activities. For example, this category included a person who had taken a combination welding course and who used this skill frequently, but not exclusively, in his job as a millwright. Similarly, a salesman who used his newly acquired skills in bookkeeping and typing to keep records and hence improve his efficiency was also classified as "indirectly related."

The highest proportion of persons in training-related jobs was found in Omaha and Chicago. In these cities, over 90 per cent of the trainees who were or had been employed were engaged in jobs directly or indirectly related to their training. The overwhelming number were in the directly-related category. The Omaha experience doubtless reflects the salutary influence of full employment in the local labor market. In this context, there was a greater possibility that skills and jobs could be matched, even allowing for imperfect information on the part of the job seekers.

The picture presented by the Chicago data requires a more subtle explanation. In view of the nature of the training and the orientation of the WRS program, it might be expected that most of the jobs would have only a limited connection with the training content. Several factors, however, pushed in the opposite direction. First, about fifty of the trainees were included in the nurse's aide course, and all were placed in directly related jobs. Second, the training was built around work contracts from outside firms where manpower requirements were probably similar to those of other firms that were likely to recruit from this segment of the labor market. Thus, there was a built-in transferability of skills. In fact, most of the trainees who worked at assembly and packing tasks or a power sewing machine at the WRS ended up doing the same thing when they were hired. And third, consciously or otherwise, the ITC program adopted a "broad band" approach to training so that most of the participants had sampled a variety of light industrial activities.

The Fort Worth data indicate approximately that 38 per cent of the trainees were in jobs completely unrelated to their training. Again, the labor market appeared to have a powerful effect. That is, the existence of a 5 per cent unemployment rate probably meant that it was often difficult for the older worker, as was often the case in Fort Worth, to find a job in a specific occupation of his choice. In addition, some of the jobs, such as clothes presser and cashier-checkout clerk, proved to be very low-paying, and many of the trainees sought alternative employment opportunities. These overtly rational decisions were augmented by other cases where, for no ostensible reason, the trainees had turned down relatively well-paying jobs in the occupations for which they were trained.

The Murphysboro results reveal a pattern different from that of all the other cases. Here, the majority of the trainees ended up in jobs only indirectly related to their formal training. This result is consistent with the observation that the management at McNair Metals used the training program primarily as a device to screen applicants for permanent employment. Once a trainee completed the formal course of instruction, he was usually moved to another job in the plant that often had only an indirect relationship to his training. Thus, a metals handler on a furnace could be moved to a die casting or extrusion machine. Those who were in unrelated jobs generally were persons who found employment outside the firm. As shown in Table VIII.13, there was less shifting around among the Carbondale trainees because of the equal division of the group between men and women. Members of each sex were limited to particular jobs in the plant.

Several of the points noted in examining the individual cases are underscored by a cross-sectional analysis. Thus, Table VIII.14 shows that

TABLE VIII.14

RELATIONSHIP OF EMPLOYMENT TO CONTENT OF TRAINING BY AGE,
ALL CITIES[a]

| Relationship of employment to training | <29 | 30–39 | 40–49 | 50+ |
|---|---|---|---|---|
| Unrelated | 3% | 16% | 21% | 22% |
| Indirectly related | 29 | 10 | 16 | 17 |
| Directly related | 68 | 74 | 63 | 61 |

[a] No. = 389.

the older trainees are considerably more likely to be employed in jobs completely unrelated to their training, probably as a consequence of age barriers to entry into new occupations. Moreover, Table VIII.15 indicates

TABLE VIII.15

RELATIONSHIP OF EMPLOYMENT TO CONTENT OF TRAINING
BY SEX, ALL CITIES[a]

| Relationship of employment to training | Male | Female |
|---|---|---|
| Unrelated | 18% | 11% |
| Indirectly related | 26 | 8 |
| Directly related | 56 | 81 |

[a] No. = 389.

that women enjoyed greater success than men in utilizing their newly acquired skills. The superior record of women reflects the fact that many of them were able to move into the service positions for which they were trained, such as nurse's aide and practical nurse. Chronic shortages usually exist in these occupations; however, as will be shown subsequently, these "shortages" are usually associated with low wages.

The skill level of the program also seemed to have some influence on the relationship of the job content to the training. Thus, Table VIII.16

TABLE VIII.16

RELATIONSHIP OF EMPLOYMENT TO CONTENT OF TRAINING,
BY SKILL LEVEL OF TRAINING, ALL CITIES[a]

| Relationship of employment to training | Unskilled | Semiskilled | Skilled |
|---|---|---|---|
| Unrelated | 5% | 17% | 26% |
| Indirectly related | 18 | 20 | 11 |
| Directly related | 77 | 63 | 63 |

[a] No. = 389.

reveals that those who received instruction in relatively unskilled tasks were more likely to apply their training in subsequent jobs than persons who had received instruction in semiskilled and skilled occupations. These data largely reflect the Chicago and Carbondale experiences. More significantly, the trainees in the skilled category showed the highest proportion employed in jobs completely unrelated to their training. Approximately 26 per cent of this group did not use their skills at all. Although age was probably a contributing factor, the inherent characteristics of the occupations were also an important consideration. That is, higher skills tend to be more specific in nature. An assembler may use his skills, albeit rudimentary, in a variety of industrial situations, but an automobile mechanic cannot tune engines on a factory floor. In this manner, training for specialized, skilled occupations may hold the greater risk that it will never be utilized or add to the job seekers' versatility in the market.

Achieving a close relationship between job content and training can be overemphasized as a desideratum of retraining programs. To be sure, it is desirable to link training to specific productive activities wherever possible. However, a collateral but important objective of such programs is to reorient unemployed workers to the labor market. The instilling of a new "sense of mobility" in the market may turn out to be one of the most beneficial consequences of retraining in the long run. This goal is at least partially achieved when the training promotes labor market activity and employment, even though the job is not fully congruent with the formal training.

RETRAINING AND GEOGRAPHICAL MOBILITY

It is sometimes suggested that occupational retraining will increase geographical mobility. The reasoning is direct and intrinsically plausible. Once an unemployed worker acquires new skills, he has considerable incentive to use the skills in gainful employment. Therefore, if he does not obtain a job in his local labor market, he is likely to move to other areas in search of employment opportunities. In addition, the retrained job seeker may now feel that he has a marketable skill to offer so that the expectation of employment will be enhanced if he moves.

In fact, geographical mobility was virtually nonexistent in the five cases examined here. Only three persons in the entire sample of 620 persons were known to have moved more than fifty miles following the completion of training. One woman moved from Carbondale to another city in Illinois, and two men left Omaha. None of the trainees left the Fort Worth area or Murphysboro, and available information does not indicate that any of the people in the Chicago project moved out of the city. Even if it is assumed that all those persons for whom no post-training data is available moved from the project city, the amount of geographical mobility would still be negligible.

This observation becomes partly explicable by reference to the nature of three of the programs. The objective of the ARA projects in Carbondale and Murphysboro was expressly to bring jobs to the unemployed rather than workers to jobs elsewhere. In addition, the skills involved were highly specific and aimed at the requirements of the two firms that ultimately did employ most of the trainees. In Chicago, the trainees were indigent and could scarcely be expected to assume the costs of relocation. Similarly, the receipt of welfare benefits probably had a holding effect on the dropouts and unemployed trainees.

No ready explanations may be made for the lack of mobility on the part of the Omaha and Fort Worth trainees. It may be noted, however, that both cities encompass large market areas, and although Fort Worth had about a 5 per cent unemployment rate, it was not by any definition a "depressed area." The Forth Worth trainees also had refused the opportunity to transfer to other, distant Armour plants under the terms of the union-management agreement. If they had wanted to move from Fort Worth, presumably they would have availed themselves of this option. Omaha, as previously indicated, generally enjoyed a low unemployment rate, and job prospects locally were good. In any case, the observed experience demonstrates that if geographical mobility is increased by retraining, such a relationship only develops under circumstances not encompassed by these five cases.

## THE WAGE EXPERIENCE

The wage experience of the employed trainees obviously constitutes an important criterion in assessing the effectiveness of different programs aimed at jobless workers. Whether or not a job is training-related, most commentators will agree that such programs should help the trainee to earn an adequate income. Data concerning the wage experience of the trainees have been collected wherever possible. These data are incomplete, and, in one case, fragmentary, for two reasons. First, in many instances, wage information was not available for particular individuals. This was especially the case in Chicago where data was lacking for ninety-three individuals, or about one-third of the total number employed in the Chicago sample. Eighty-six of those for whom information was missing were women, and from the available data concerning the wage experience of the women trainees in that city, it may be assumed that most of them received between $1.00 and $1.25 per hour. Information was also missing in several cases in Omaha because the program administrators had lost track of many of the trainees once they were placed on jobs. This problem was negligible in Carbondale, Murphysboro, and Fort Worth.

Second, some of the trainees either took jobs where compensation was on a commission basis or went into business for themselves. In either case, there was considerable variation in earnings or acute problems of calculating net wages. For these reasons such cases were generally omitted from the calculations. This omission had the most substantial effect in Omaha and to a lesser extent in Fort Worth. Overall, reasonably complete data were available for Fort Worth, Carbondale, and Murphysboro. Chicago had a large number of observations even without the large group of women, but wage information was collected for only eight of the completed and employed Omaha trainees. The aggregate data covers 355 persons in all cities. The wages noted are for the trainees' last jobs.

The distribution of wages for each city is shown in Table VIII.17. The

TABLE VIII.17

WAGE EXPERIENCE OF COMPLETED TRAINEES, BY CITY[a]

| Wages per hour | Chicago (n = 183) | Omaha (n = 8) | Murphysboro (n = 25) | Carbondale (n = 25) | Fort Worth (n = 114) |
|---|---|---|---|---|---|
| <$1.00 | 9% | 0% | 0% | 0% | 16% |
| 1–1.24 | 50 | 12 | 0 | 0 | 30 |
| 1.25–1.49 | 26 | 0 | 44 | 60 | 27 |
| 1.50–1.74 | 7 | 25 | 52 | 20 | 10 |
| 1.75–1.99 | 4 | 12 | 0 | 0 | 8 |
| 2.00+ | 4 | 50 | 4 | 20 | 9 |

[a] n = No. Total number = 355.

lowest wages were earned in Chicago where 60 per cent of the employed trainees received less than $1.25 per hour and only 15 per cent had hourly wages of $1.50 or more. Clearly, the employment of the Chicago trainees was concentrated in low-wage firms, many of which drew on the reservoir of unskilled and semiskilled Negroes.

The wage experience in Forth Worth also indicated that retraining might not pave the way to the good life. That is, as many as 46 per cent of the employed trainees were earning less than $1.25 per hour. For the greater part, this group was comprised of women. The lowest category, in particular, was made up exclusively of Negro women who were employed in service and trade occupations. At the other end of the distribution, 25 per cent of the trainees, mostly white men in semiskilled and skilled jobs, received over $1.50 per hour. Outside of Armour and a few other large, unionized firms in the area, the Fort Worth labor market was characterized by sharp competition on the supply side and heavy pressure on wage levels.

The concentration of earnings in Murphysboro and Carbondale mirrored the wage structure of the Technical Tape Company and McNair Metals. As the trainees moved into a regular employment status, they were generally slotted into the $1.25–1.49 and $1.59–1.74 brackets. The attainment of regular employment status was a mixed blessing to the women trainees in Carbondale. While they were in training, their wages and government allowance equalled $54.00 per week; when they completed training, their income dropped to $52.00 per week. As might be expected this decline in earnings after they had "proven themselves" in training was the cause of considerable anguish among the women. Meanwhile, a few of the other trainees in Murphysboro and Carbondale earned more than $2.00 per hour after they were either promoted to supervisory positions or left the firms to seek employment elsewhere.

The Omaha data, as previously specified, are extremely limited. Nonetheless, they do hint that the Cudahy trainees did relatively well in the labor market. Such a result might be expected in view of the full-employment conditions and high wage levels that prevailed in the area.

The cross-sectional analysis of the wage experience of all the trainees for whom data are available generally conforms to expectations. Tables VIII.18, VIII.19, and VIII.20 reveal that lower wages were earned by

TABLE VIII.18

WAGE EXPERIENCE BY SEX, ALL CITIES[a]

| Wages per hour | Male | Female |
|---|---|---|
| <$1.00 | 4% | 17% |
| 1–1.24 | 21 | 51 |
| 1.25–1.49 | 29 | 25 |
| 1.50–1.74 | 22 | 3 |
| 1.75–1.99 | 8 | 2 |
| 2.00+ | 16 | 2 |

[a] No. = 355.

TABLE VIII.19

Wage Experience by Race, All Cities[a]

| Wages per hour | White | Negro | Latin American |
|:---:|:---:|:---:|:---:|
| <$1.00 | 5% | 13% | 5% |
| 1–1.24 | 13 | 48 | 26 |
| 1.25–1.49 | 37 | 24 | 26 |
| 1.50–1.74 | 23 | 7 | 11 |
| 1.75–1.99 | 5 | 4 | 11 |
| 2.00+ | 17 | 4 | 21 |

[a] No. = 355.

women and Negroes and that the economic fortunes of the trainees tended to diminish when they were over 40 years of age. The impact of these three factors combined is manifested in Table VIII.18 since many of the women trainees were also over 40 and Negroes. In addition, both

TABLE VIII.20

Wage Experience by Age, All Cities[a]

| Wages per hour | <29 | 30–39 | 40–49 | 50+ |
|:---:|:---:|:---:|:---:|:---:|
| <$1.00 | 6% | 7% | 14% | 19% |
| 1.00–1.24 | 33 | 37 | 40 | 32 |
| 1.25–1.49 | 32 | 31 | 25 | 30 |
| 1.50–1.74 | 19 | 8 | 12 | 11 |
| 1.75–1.99 | 2 | 8 | 3 | 4 |
| 2.00+ | 8 | 9 | 6 | 4 |

[a] No. = 355.

the educational level of this group and skill content of the training were low. Among these women, over 65 per cent of those who were employed received less than $1.25 per hour.

This dour picture is relieved somewhat by Tables VIII.21 and VIII.22, relating wages to the skill level of the training and the jobs held. In the top wage classifications, those who underwent training in skilled occupations and/or were employed in a skilled job, clearly did better than those in the semiskilled and unskilled categories. The lower end of the wage distribution for the skilled trainees and job holders was primarily composed of barbers and beauticians who, after eight to ten months of full-time training, found themselves in a glutted, low-wage market. Again, the problem was accentuated among the Negro women, many of whom could find jobs only in shops catering to white clientele where customs prevented them from using the full range of their skills. These cases

TABLE VIII.21

WAGE EXPERIENCE BY SKILL LEVEL OF TRAINING, ALL CITIES[a]

| Wages per hour | Unskilled | Semiskilled | Skilled |
|---|---|---|---|
| <$1.00 | 10% | 13% | 5% |
| 1.00–1.24 | 42 | 34 | 27 |
| 1.25–1.49 | 30 | 31 | 21 |
| 1.50–1.74 | 9 | 14 | 13 |
| 1.75–1.99 | 4 | 1 | 14 |
| 2.00+ | 5 | 7 | 20 |

[a] No. = 355; data not ascertained = 3. Tabulations based on sample of 352.

aside, there does seem to be some evidence that when those trained for skilled jobs can be oriented to the new sector of the labor market in which they must operate, the economic rewards will be relatively generous.

TABLE VIII.22

WAGE EXPERIENCE BY SKILL LEVEL OF JOB, ALL CITIES[a]

| Wages per hour | Unskilled | Semiskilled | Skilled |
|---|---|---|---|
| <$1.00 | 13% | 6% | 4% |
| 1.00–1.24 | 53 | 20 | 19 |
| 1.25–1.49 | 26 | 36 | 10 |
| 1.50–1.74 | 4 | 24 | 19 |
| 1.75–1.99 | 2 | 7 | 11 |
| 2.00+ | 2 | 7 | 37 |

[a] No. = 355.

## RETRAINING: PROBLEMS AND PROSPECTS

One of the first lessons to be learned from an evaluation of programs of retraining the unemployed is that short-term evaluations may be risky and misleading. The effects of retraining, like those of investment in any form of education, are revealed over a relatively long period of time. Thus any profound evaluation of retraining must await the efforts of further researchers who patiently record the economic fate of those who have participated in what still must be called a noble experiment. Nonetheless, even within the relatively short time horizon afforded by the cases in this study, some summary observations may be made about the character and the impact of the various approaches to retraining. So many statements have been made about the promise or alleged futility of retraining that Pope's admonition about the dangers of limited knowledge may be disregarded in this case.

The evidence presented in this study indicates that there is something approaching a "sure thing" in retraining. That is, as shown in the Murphysboro and Carbondale cases, retraining programs can be expected to be highly "successful" in terms of completion and employment rates if the trainees are young and relatively well educated, if reasonably generous allowances are provided during the period of training, if the course is of relatively short duration, and if the occupational training is directly linked to a set of specific employment opportunities. In both ARA cases, unemployed persons were channeled into the labor market and were, for the greater part, placed successfully on jobs. Of course, objections may be raised that such programs merely skim the cream off the unemployed and neglect the really hard cases which should be the primary focus of public efforts. The fact that young college students were recruited for training programs built around uncomplicated skills does not lend comfort to those who are interested in thwarting the emergence of an economically stagnant "underclass." Such recriminations may be countered, however, by the claim that it is equally important to use retraining to insure that those with the highest long-run potential are not left to future economic inactivity.

The Chicago project raises a glimmer of hope for those who have an optimistic view of the ability of retraining to ameliorate the lot of the acutely disadvantaged groups among the unemployed. By most standards, the WRS program dealt with the hardest cases. Its constituency was comprised largely of poorly educated members of a minority group who were in a position of formal dependence on the public for their economic wellbeing. In addition, the training provided had a minimal vocational content, and its main objective was to revive some connection between the unemployed worker and useful economic activity. At the same time, the immediate financial inducements to participate were punitive rather than supplementary.

Despite doubts concerning the quality of the training and the protestations of social workers, the evidence indicates that the program enjoyed a fair amount of success in achieving its limited objective of lifting the impoverished unemployed back into the labor market. It is true that the immediate economic rewards to the trainees were relatively meager. Also the available data did not make it possible to trace the subsequent employment experience of the trainees. However, by offering a minimal amount of training within an institutional setting and linking this training to assiduous efforts at placement, some movement was generated where inertia had prevailed in the past.

If the Chicago project might be criticized because its sights were set too low, the Fort Worth and Omaha programs established goals that were, perhaps, overly-ambitious. The persons served by these programs had been recently engaged in productive activity, but their skills were generally nontransferable and they suffered from deficiencies in formal education and a working knowledge of the labor market. Moreover, the Fort Worth trainees in particular had the additional disadvantage of a high average age. Training was offered in a wide range of occupations, many of them in the skilled categories. While these programs were marked by some success, the dropout rate in Omaha and the earnings record in Fort Worth revealed that these efforts did not include adequate financial support for the trainees or a sufficiently realistic attitude toward the problems of placement in the labor market. The Omaha and Fort Worth experiences did demonstrate that through intensive administrative measures, it is possible to develop a broad-gauged program catering to persons of different abilities and including a wide variety of skills. It also revealed that the price of such flexibility may be some disappointment, at least in the short run. These disappointments do not necessarily mean that such flexible programs involving a substantial degree of occupational upgrading are ineffective. Rather, the experiences indicate that ambitious programs must be bolstered by equally far-ranging support of the trainees in the classroom and the labor market. In any case, the private projects have shown a much greater willingness to experiment, and they offer useful lessons to the administrators of public programs who have been disposed to concentrate on the "sure things."

Beyond these broad comparisons of the five programs, the study suggests certain general observations concerning the organization and implementation of retraining, whether under private or public auspices. A basic requirement of effective retraining is the establishment of realistic financial conditions. The financial elements involve a balancing of income and costs and may be both direct and indirect. First, there is the income obtained while in training. This income may be in the form of direct grants from a public or private agency, or it may be self-generated through supplementary employment. The direct payments should be sufficient to permit the trainee to participate in the course without great personal sacrifice or pressure. This seems to be especially true for married persons with family responsibilities. Thus any program of direct financial aid should clearly take into account the different obligations of the trainees.

Public attitudes toward financial aid to unemployed persons who are taking training is cloaked with the same puritanical notions that are associated with most programs for public aid. There is often the presumption that such aid will promote malingering and subsidize the idle. This judgment is as misleading when applied to retraining programs as it is in many other areas. Training is generally an arduous experience for the unemployed worker and can scarcely be considered institutionalized malingering. Moreover, the hard economic facts indicate that the price of maintaining support levels below the amount necessary to sustain the trainee during the course of the program would be a relatively high dropout rate which, in turn, implies the waste of those resources that have been invested in the dropouts. The amendments of the MDTA affording supplementary financial support to persons who are in training for a relatively long period of time and who have a number of dependents is clearly a step in the right direction and should help to improve the completion rate in these federal programs.

The problem of maintaining an adequate level of income may also be mitigated by encouraging trainees to work while they are enrolled in training. The idea of permitting "unemployed" trainees to work, at first glance, might seem inherently contradictory. If the trainees could find jobs, presumably they would not be in training. Such a statement obscures significant differences among the unemployed. Some of the unemployed, as in Omaha and Fort Worth, are in a transitional state where the usefulness of their previous skills has been destroyed because of radical changes in the location of industry or other factors. In many cases, they can find a job, but these jobs will have very limited economic potential. In addition, in any labor market there is a margin of part-time employment or otherwise undesirable positions that may be taken on a short-term basis. These jobs can provide the income that is necessary to carry the would-be or actual trainee over a period of financial deprivation. Without such arrangements for increasing income, many potential retrainees will fail to enter an appropriate course or drop out once the course is in progress. The relatively good completion record of the Fort Worth program stems from the fact that many of the trainees could engage in this form of self-help. Again, the amendment of the MDTA program permitting trainees to work up to twenty hours a week without deducting the income from their training allowance is obviously a step in the right direction.

A second financial consideration affecting the unemployed person's decision to enter and remain in training is the expected present value of the training. Clearly, if the training is associated with a high expectation of employment upon completion of the course, the trainee is more likely to see the program through to fruition. The Murphysboro and Carbondale programs indicated that the anticipated flow of benefits does not have to be too high to reinforce the commitment to training. In both these situations, the rates of pay were moderate, but the high expectation of employment resulted in high completion and employment rates of the trainees. At the same time, the receipt of a subsistence allowance helped to relieve any immediate financial pressure on the trainees.

In situations where retraining is not linked to specific employment opportunities, as in the ARA programs, the state of the labor market obviously will influence the expectations of the trainees. In this regard, labor market conditions play a somewhat ambiguous role in determining the ultimate success of retraining programs. Obviously, an active and diverse demand for labor is a necessary condition for a happy conclusion to any retraining program. The answer to that oft-stated refrain, "Retraining for what?" must be retraining for jobs that are presently available in the market or in occupational areas in which the demand for labor is expected to increase in the immediate future. At the same time, a full-employment labor market may mean that those persons who are presently unemployed and who might profit from retraining and the upgrading of skills will not enter training. The immediate attractions of a $1.75 per hour job as a janitor may outweight the inducements of a $2.50 per hour job as a machine operator following an eight- to twelve-month training program.

Some of these factors appeared to be at work in Omaha. Out of 1,000 displaced workers who were eligible for training, only 6 per cent availed themselves of this opportunity. And once the training programs were under way, four out of every ten trainees dropped out before the courses were completed. The fact that many of the courses were of relatively long duration increased the opportunity cost of training to the job seeker. Conversely, the fragmentary data available indicates that those who did complete their training in Omaha were likely to obtain jobs in the skills for which they were trained and at a reasonably high wage rate. In this manner, local labor market conditions may have a "twist" effect on the conduct of retraining programs: a strong demand for labor is a prerequisite for the long-run success of retraining, but it also dampens the enthusiasm of the potential retrainees for vocational self-improvement.

Within a broader labor market content, retraining has also been viewed as a device to equip the unemployed with the high level skills demanded by the modern economy. On this count, the results of this study are mixed. The Chicago project, and to some extent, Carbondale and Murphysboro, showed that it is possible for retraining to successfully move the people laterally among occupational classes or vertically a short distance up the occupational ladder with some success. Similarly, the implicit "broad band approach" adopted in the Chicago project for semiskilled jobs seemed to give these programs a greater effectiveness than they otherwise would have had. Where substantial upgrading was attempted, however, as in Omaha and Fort Worth, the results were not as encouraging. Those persons attempting to move up two skill levels were less likely to complete training than those who were involved in more modest programs.

In part, this dropout rate probably reflected to some extent the additional opportunity costs incurred in the longer programs. But in many cases the programs were beyond the immediate reach of the trainees. Thus if substantial upgrading is to be attempted, these movements probably cannot be achieved through "crash programs" with the success that might be desired. To usher the unemployed into the skilled sectors of the labor market, it will probably be necessary to adopt more demanding qualifications in terms of formal education and aptitude, or a more intensive program over a longer period of time involving preliminary investment in improving the basic educational level of the trainees. This does not mean that there should be a slavish adherence to rigid criteria for acceptance in programs involving substantial skills. The Fort Worth and Omaha experiences were encouraging enough to indicate that many people have a potential that has not been realized. Instead, the relevant conclusion is that rigid, "canned" programs are not likely to succeed. When substantial upgrading is attempted, greater attention must be given to adapting the structure and content of the program to the particular characteristics of the trainees.

The problems of retraining unemployed workers also extend to post-training efforts at placement. As the Chicago project revealed, intensive placement efforts can be a powerful supplementary factor in retraining. If the problem of the unemployed is their inability to operate effectively in the labor market, equipping them with new skills is obviously only part of the job. These new skills must be augmented with information about the availability of appropriate employment opportunities and guidance in the techniques of job seeking. Most labor market studies have shown that job seekers have a great dependence upon information informally provided by friends and relatives. As the unemployed lapse into a chronic state of idleness, these sources are likely to dry up. That is, given the nature of socio-economic residential patterns, unemployed persons are likely to know other unemployed persons. This "external diseconomy" of labor market information of the unemployed was a factor in Chicago, and, to some extent, in Fort Worth.[7]

The necessity for intensive placement assistance acquires a new importance where the training has involved an upgrading of skills. Here, it may be necessary for the retrainee to enter a heretofore alien sector of the labor market to seek a job with specific attributes. Thus the need for supplementary services in connection with retraining is most urgent to the success of the program. Some efforts along this line were taken in Fort Worth and Omaha, but because the programs were private in orientation, the resources were allocated on a limited or sporadic basis. Those persons who were trained for skilled occupations and who did find jobs in these occupations enjoyed the greatest economic returns, but the proportion which managed to find an appropriate niche in the labor market was lower than for the less skilled trainees.

The problems of occupational mobility were accentuated by the lack of geographical mobility on the part of the trainees. As indicated previously, there was almost no geographical mobility at all in each of the five cities. In three of the cases, a certain amount of immobility was built into the programs, while in Fort Worth the propensity to move might have been diminished by the age level of the trainees. In addition, insufficient time might have elapsed. Nevertheless, any presumption that occupational retraining will lead to increased geographical mobility is not verified in these studies. In fact, it may be hypothesized that geographical mobility and occupational retraining are substitutes in the preferences of the unemployed workers. Those who are likely to move will do so without the lure of new economic horizons presented by retraining. On the other hand, those who remain in an unemployed status in a particular labor market comprise the prime prospects for retraining.

Finally, the experience of the trainees in this study does not support any expectation that retraining will result in the immediate enrichment of the trainees. As a matter of fact, the retrainees generally earned only modest wages. However, additional data dealing with nonretrainees from the same group of displaced Armour workers in Fort Worth showed that the economic performance of the trainees, as marginal as it might have been, was still superior to that of the nontrainees both in terms of employment and earnings.[8] In addition, it may be misleading to emphasize earnings in a short-term analysis of the results of retraining. Retraining in the short run is best viewed as a device to give the unemployed worker a new foothold in the labor market. It may not offer the unemployed worker immediate economic bounties, but it does facilitate a movement toward economic autonomy and productive activity. If it is conceded that social and economic problems are solved in small increments, then programs for retraining the unemployed constitute a significant advance.

## REFERENCES

1. For a description of the activities of the Armour Automation Committee, see George P. Shultz and Arnold R. Weber, *Strategies for the Displaced Worker* (New York: Harper & Row, 1966).
2. The dropout rates for the different educational classifications were as follows: 0–6 years = 14 per cent; 7–9 years = 15 per cent; 10–12 years = 18 per cent; 13 and above = 24 per cent.
3. The distinction between "married" and "single" sometimes became blurred, especially in Chicago. Some of the trainees had been part of a family unit in the past, but at the time that they were enrolled in the WRS program, they apparently were

living as individuals and according to WRS records had no dependents other than themselves.

4. The notion of "training" for unskilled jobs may, at first glance, seem inherently contradictory. However, almost every job requires some skills in the sense of personal organization and adaptation to a work environment. In this manner, bagging letters for children's alphabet toys or placing a roll of tape on a winding machine cannot be considered a "skill" but it does involve a pattern of work habits and systematic physical movements for which some measure of "training" may be necessary. If the trainee has never been subjected to the discipline of a work process of this nature, the training may be a significant improvement in his capabilities. Most of the "unskilled" trainees were found in Chicago with an additional few in Carbondale and Fort Worth.

5. Work histories were collected for most of the trainees. These histories were then analyzed in terms of the individual's experience in particular industrial sectors such as manufacturing, service, construction, trade, communications, etc. Wherever possible each training course was given an equivalent industrial identification. In this manner, a female trainee in Carbondale who had been employed as a telephone operator and who was now being trained as a rewind operator at Technical Tape was classified as making an interindustry shift from communications to manufacturing. Similarly, a former construction laborer or agricultural worker in training at Murphysboro also made an interindustry shift. Such classifications were not possible where the trainee had no work history or where the training course had obvious interindustry applications.

6. The term "physical handicap" was used very broadly in Chicago. Moderate obesity was classed as a handicap, for example.

7. I am indebted to David P. Taylor for this point.

8. See "Progress Report on the Fort Worth Project of the Armour Automation Fund Committee," *Monthly Labor Review*, Vol. 87 (January, 1964), 53–57.

# Appendix A

▰▰▰▰▰

## Occupations and Skills for Which Retraining Was Provided

### CARBONDALE

Coremaking machine operator
Rewind machine operator
Slitting machine operator

Slitting machine helper
Compound weigher

### MURPHYSBORO

Conduit threader
Dusenberry machine operator
Die casting machine operator
Extrusion machine operator
Extrusion handler
Milling machine operator

Melting furnace
Press saw operator
Saw operator
Material handler
Brake press operator

### CHICAGO

Assembler (individual)
Assembler (chain)
Packer
Nurse's aide
Paint spray
Power stitching
Power stapling
Punch press
Riveting
Shipping clerk
Sorting

Spot welding
Stock clerk
Power sewing machine operator
Inspector
Materials handler
Heat sealing
General job skills
Clerk-typist
Typist-stenographer
IBM machines operator
Licensed practical nurse

## Fort Worth

Auto body and fender repair
Auto mechanic
Bookkeeping
College-teaching
Practical nurse
Electronics
Cosmetology-beauty operator
Barber
Air conditioning and refrigeration
    installation and repair
Clerk-typist
Typist-stenographer
Welding: combination gas and electric
Welding: heliarc
Machinist
Retail meatcutting
Warehouseman-stock clerk

Food service
Clothes presser
Cashier-checkout clerk
Music-piano teacher
Landscaping
Sales
Florist
Power sewing machine
College-ministerial
General education
Diesel engine mechanic
Animal care
Real estate broker
Heavy equipment operator
Radio and TV repair
Cook-chef

## Omaha

Auto body and fender repair
Auto mechanic
Air conditioning and refrigeration
    installation and repair
Welding-combination gas and electric
Stationary engineer

Retail meatcutting
Cosmetology-beauty operator
Barber
Electronics technician
College-teacher

# IX

## GLEN G. CAIN
## AND
## ERNST W. STROMSDORFER

■

# AN ECONOMIC EVALUATION OF GOVERNMENT RETRAINING

# PROGRAMS IN WEST VIRGINIA

## INTRODUCTION AND SUMMARY

Thirty-five years ago a major change in public attitudes toward unemployed workers was demonstrated in federal legislation that dealt with the widespread and prolonged unemployment of the Great Depression.* This concern was climaxed by the Employment Act of 1946, which emphasized the use of monetary and fiscal measures to combat general unemployment. But within the last decade there has been a second significant revision of public attitudes toward unemployed workers. Recognition is now being given to the particular (nongeneral) unemployment resulting from severe labor market handicaps (on the supply side) or from structural change (on the demand side) which occurs unevenly throughout the economy. Such unemployment is often concentrated in a particular area, industry, occupation, or group in the population, and the revision in attitudes has led to government action to attack the problem by such direct measures as retraining unemployed workers.

Government investment in the retraining of unemployed workers is, however, only one approach to the problem of facilitating labor force adjustments to structural change. The use of monetary and fiscal measures

* Glen G. Cain is currently (1967) at the University of Wisconsin, Ernst Stromsdorfer at Pennsylvania State University. The authors are grateful to Professors Gerald G. Somers, Benjamin Bridges, and Robinson G. Hollister for helpful comments.

to expand the level of aggregate demand is not ruled out and is, indeed, an essential part of any program to achieve full employment. But since the focus of retraining is on different aspects of the problem, and since large amounts of resources have already been committed to retraining, it is important to evaluate the results of this investment effort—even though all the evidence is not yet in.

This chapter reports an economic evaluation of a program, sponsored by the federal and state governments, to retrain underemployed and unemployed workers in West Virginia. We emphasize from the outset that we are analyzing the results from only one segment of time from one particular program among a great many.

The underlying basis for an evaluation is a simple one. We have information on the labor market experiences (employment and earnings) of a group of workers who received retraining, as well as a monetary measure of the costs of retraining. We have data on the labor market experience over a similar period for a control group—workers who did not receive retraining. The two groups are matched on the basis of some broad socio-demographic characteristics. It is then determined on the basis of several sets of *monetary* criteria whether the retraining has "paid off."

An important feature of this study, we feel, is the data we present on earnings. Many past evaluations of the retraining programs have been limited (necessarily so by the data available) to comparisons of employment records among those taking and those not taking retraining. It is true that a comparison of the employment experience is a basis of evaluation that is consistent with the goal of reducing unemployment that is emphasized in the legislation authorizing retraining.[1] However, there are several reasons why the relative improvement in earnings that results from retraining is a preferred basis for evaluating the program. One advantage is that earnings improvement not only incorporates the gains from obtaining employment but in addition provides a more comprehensive measure of the quality of jobs obtained. Another reason for looking at earnings instead of jobs, as such, is that even in the context of "full employment" we could still evaluate the program by observing earnings.

Our results show that in the large majority of cases the unemployed who underwent retraining had larger earnings in the post-training period than their counterparts in the control group. This fact alone obviously does not establish an economic justification for the program. We need to know what the costs of the program were and whether the increase in earnings—our measure of the benefits—was sufficient to "cover" these costs. Armed with these data on costs and earnings differences and given the critical assumption that the control group provides a valid comparison for the study group, we are able to make an economic evaluation of the training program.

There are two broad generalizations, each with an important qualification, that summarize our findings. The first is that there are sizable differences in the measured benefits of the training program among the several socio-demographic subgroups. The earnings of men appear to have been increased considerably more than the earnings of women, and younger men have benefitted more than older men, in this respect. The lower-educated groups benefitted more than the higher-educated groups— a result which may be surprising to some readers. However, small sample sizes and attendant problems of statistical unreliability make the comparisons very tentative. The second generalization is that, despite the heterogeneity among groups, the overall result is a considerable excess of benefits over costs, implying that the program has paid substantial dividends. Here the reservation is that our basis for measuring how the program paid off, a basis which appears to us to be the best available, still unfortunately contains biases which tend to overstate the benefits.

Both generalizations are demonstrated by several measures of earnings and costs which we show in tabular form in the section, "The Tabulations of Costs and Earnings." These tables constitute the core product of our empirical work and the basis for the evaluation of retraining among the sample groups of our study.

An indication of the order of magnitude of costs and benefits of the program is given by the following average figures for males in our sample: the costs per trainee were about $900—the sum of our estimates of his foregone earnings, of the direct costs to the government of the training program, and of the subsistence and other payments made to the trainee by the government. (The costs borne solely by the trainee, after accounting for the various subsidies he received, were only $230.) The average increase in annual earnings realized by the trainee after completion of the course was estimated to be about $900 also. In other words, the training program for these workers paid for itself in one year. Such a rapid pay-back period indicates very high capital values of this investment in training and very high (internal) rates of return on the investment.[2] Indeed, we do utilize these latter measures of evaluating investments and show rates of return and capital values that are in general quite high. However, these constitute nothing more than the mechanical results of computations based on the estimates of earnings and costs we use, and it is the *estimates* and the assumptions underlying *their* calculation that are critical in our evaluation of the program. We will, therefore, give heavy emphasis to the methodology of our procedures.

## A DESCRIPTION OF THE DATA AND
## A DISCUSSION OF CONCEPTS

### THE DATA

The basic data source for this study is a set of extensive interviews conducted for 1,379 workers in West Virginia during the summer of 1962. Most of the workers who took retraining had completed their retraining courses at this time. A follow-up survey was conducted in the spring of 1964. Thus, for some workers we have employment data extending over two years beyond the date when they completed training. For all workers we have a minimum of eighteen months post-retraining labor market experience.

Five different types of workers were interviewed in the original study. There were 501 workers who completed some specified retraining course; 233 who dropped out of some retraining course before its completion; 65 who did not report for retraining after acceptance into a course; 127 who were rejected after applying for retraining; and 453 workers who had no contact with retraining and who had very recent unemployment experience immediately prior to the time when most retraining was occurring in West Virginia.

This study is limited to two of these groups—those who completed a course of retraining and those who had no contact with the retraining program. We will refer to these two groups as "trainees" and "nontrainees." The sample of workers who completed training were all those enrolled in certain specified retraining courses that were selected on a judgment basis. Efforts were made to select courses which differed as to type of skill, length of instruction, course sponsor, and area of the state in which the instruction was given. However, in one area, McDowell county, *all* those who had completed training were included in the study provided they could be located and would consent to be interviewed. No efforts were made to select courses on the basis of their potential success or failure. (See Chapter II in this volume, by Gibbard and Somers, for a more complete discussion of the sample design.)

The nontrainees were selected on an essentially random basis—every tenth person was chosen—from the files of the unemployed in the local Employment Service Offices. The trainees are our study group and the nontrainees are our control group.

The training was sponsored by the Area Redevelopment Act (ARA) of the federal government or by the Area Vocational Training Program (AVP) of the state government of West Virginia. The courses sponsored by ARA tended to be of short duration, sixteen weeks or less, with a full day of instruction, and were geared to immediate employment opportunities in semiskilled and service occupations within the specific locality in which the retraining occurred. The AVP-sponsored courses tended to be longer, up to six months or a year, but with only a few hours of instruction per week. They included construction trade skills as well as semiskilled and service occupations. These courses were often, but not necessarily, geared to immediate employment opportunities in the training locality. Total class hours devoted to any given course was about the same for both ARA- and AVP-sponsored training.

In attempting to assess the net impact of retraining it is necessary to control for other factors that would exert an important influence on the criteria variables of the study. To this end individuals in the two samples were grouped on the basis of age (two groups), education (two groups), sex, and race (whites only).[3] Table IX.1 identifies the eight categories based on these groups and gives the number of observations in each.

General business and employment conditions were undoubtedly changing during the time period covered by our study—both because of the business cycle and seasonal factors. We use two means to help control for these potential influences. First, we show costs and earnings data for different durations of time in the post-training period—in each case, of course, using the same duration and period for both trainees and nontrainees. Secondly, the trainees were divided on the basis of the quarter in which their training ended. These periods ranged from the last quarter in 1961 to the July-to-September quarter in 1962. The labor market experiences of the control group were somewhat different depending on the quarter, and these differences were taken into account in comparing, for example, the earnings foregone by the trainees. We present our empirical results for the trainees according to the classifications in Table IX.1 which combine all those completing a course of training during the twelve-month period over 1961 and 1962, but it should be remembered that the costs and earnings are based on the quarter-by-quarter calculation. The nontrainees were matched against these groups on the basis of the socio-demographic characteristics shown in the table, and the employment and earnings experiences of the two groups were compared.

## CONCEPTS OF COSTS AND EARNINGS

The appropriate definitions of costs and earnings will depend on the purposes for which they are to be used. We present alternative measures to account, principally, for the different perspectives of the individual trainee and of society as a whole.

1. *Wage earnings and the treatment of taxes.*—The individual will consider taxes as a reduction in his income, and his definition of earnings would be net of taxes. The appropriate concept for society includes taxes,

## TABLE IX.1
### DISTRIBUTION OF TRAINEES AND NONTRAINEES BY SEX, AGE, AND EDUCATION

| Sample | Male | | | | Female | | | |
|---|---|---|---|---|---|---|---|---|
| | <35 yrs. of age | | 35–54 yrs. of age | | <35 yrs. of age | | 35–54 yrs. of age | |
| | <12 yrs. educ. | 12+ yrs. educ. | <12 yrs. educ. | 12+ yrs. educ. | <12 yrs. educ. | 12+ yrs. educ. | <12 yrs. educ. | 12+ yrs. educ. |
| Trainees[a] (n = 341) | 37 | 132 | 33 | 24 | 19 | 30 | 28 | 38 |
| Nontrainees[b] (n = 284) | 61 | 34 | 103 | 17 | 11 | 23 | 21 | 14 |

[a] Of the original 501 workers in our sample who completed a course of training, 160 were excluded, for the following reasons: 33 were nonwhite; 13 were white, but over 55 years of age; 47 did not return a usable 1964 questionnaire; 8 were out of the labor force for health reasons; 59 whose training ended *before* the last quarter of 1961 or *after* the last quarter of 1962.

[b] Of the original 453 nontrainees, 169 were excluded for the following reasons: 55 were nonwhite; 44 were white, but over 55 years of age; 56 did not return a usable 1964 questionnaire; 14 were out of the labor force for health reasons.

since it is his full earnings that measures the value of his labor and not just the "take-home" pay. Thus, our evaluations will be calculated on the basis of net market wages for the individual (where in practice we exclude only income taxes) and gross market wages for society.

2. *Voluntary status of "not in the labor force."*—An adult may be in or out of the civilian labor force and if in, either employed or unemployed. When an individual voluntarily chooses to leave the labor force, we might assume that he or she receives as much imputed or "psychic" income as the earnings available in the market. In fact, this is the assumption we make for our estimate of the private measure involving individual perceptions of costs and earnings.[4] The market wages earned in the individual's most recent job prior to leaving the labor force are used to measure the imputed income. This interpretation of voluntary departure from the labor force may be appropriate for measuring the increment to the stock of human capital resulting from the program, but is not appropriate for measuring the increment in the current output of goods and services. In any case this interpretation probably sets an upper limit on the measure of earnings foregone. We also present what amounts to a lower limit by assigning zero earnings to the period when a person is voluntarily out of the labor force. This lower limit is used in the calculations of the social measure—a procedure that has the convenience (but not necessarily the justification) of tying in with the customary accounting of national income. Undoubtedly, the "true" measures, both private and social, lie somewhere in between our two extremes.

3. *Transfer payments.*—We again consider both "private" and "social" measures for the two types of transfer payments involved—transfer payments and training allowances. Transfer payments is the term we will use for the following types of payments: general relief, aid to dependent children, unemployment compensation, workmen's compensation, and social security. Income-in-kind received from the surplus commodities and food stamp programs is not included since we had little information about the amount and distribution that was involved.

Training allowances were often merely a new name given to the continued payments of unemployment compensation, which the worker had been receiving before he began the course. In any case, training allowances were intended to provide a subsistence allowance for the workers during the training period and are clearly a transfer payment. The reason for distinguishing this from other payments is that training allowances are a type of cost of the program that is specifically paid for by the legislative appropriations for the training program.

It is important to note, however, that, from the standpoint of the measurement of "real resources" used in the nation as a whole, transfer payments in general are approximately costless. The cost to one person (the "taxpayer") is almost entirely offset by the gain to the recipient and, except for the administrative costs and possible distortions imposed by the structure of taxes employed to finance the payments, no net change in the level of real resources results. (However, the composition of resources used may differ if the expenditure patterns of those who pay the taxes and those who receive the payments are dissimilar.)

We assume that the transfer payments are considered as "ordinary" income by the recipient, not to be distinguished from income from other sources.[5] However, since the individual trainee was likely to have been receiving some transfer payments if he had not enrolled in the course, we should consider only the additional income he gets as his gain. The transfer payments received by a comparable group of nontrainees serve as a basis for determining what the trainees would have received.

We suggest on the basis of the foregoing considerations, that transfer payments should constitute neither a cost nor a benefit to society as a whole, but that they are income to the individual and should be taken into account in the calculation of the private return on the investment. This is our best suggestion as economists, but it is, perhaps, unrealistic to overlook the political considerations surrounding transfer payments. The majority of the tax-paying public, it will be objected, will look upon any increase in transfer payments as costs to them, and they will view any reduction in these payments as a real benefit of a successful retraining program. In order to accommodate this widely prevailing viewpoint (however dubious we believe it to be from the point of view of economics), we treat an increase in transfer payments as a cost to "society" and thus impose on the retraining program the requirement that it pay back benefits (i.e., increased earnings) that, in principle, could be used to compensate the "taxpayers" for any additional expenditures they make in the form of transfer payments involved in the execution of the program. The basis for calculating the net increase in transfer payments is as follows: the payments made to the nontrainees (the control group) during the training period represent what society would have been paying to the trainees had they not enrolled. These are subtracted from the sum of training allowances and other welfare payments given to the trainees, and it is only the difference which is considered as a cost of the retraining program to "society." The corollary to this procedure is that any net savings in transfer payments as a result of the training program are to be counted as benefits for all future periods. However, we will not count these "savings," because the post-training period we are observing is one of exceptional economic hardship in West Virginia, and the amount of transfer payments is not representative of what future periods would entail.

4. *The costs of the training program.*—We look upon the costs of

the program as being conceptually divided into two categories. The first category is that which we have already discussed under the heading, "Transfer Payments." These are expenditures of the program, such as the training allowances, or expenditures incidental to the program, such as increased welfare payments, that we assume are used by the trainees for consumption—for food, clothing, rent, etc. The second type of costs is those that provide for the investment part of the program— the retraining itself. "Direct costs" and "opportunity costs" make up this second type of costs category. Direct costs include expenditures for teachers' salaries, materials used in the training courses, the user cost of the building, and other administrative costs. The individual trainee could be assumed to ignore the direct costs, since any increase in his current or future taxes to pay for them would be negligible. For the societal point of view, however, these expenses are considered costs—real resources that are used in making the investment.

Parenthetically, we might note that the direct costs we have defined are assumed to have no consumption value to the trainee—otherwise we would have categorized the amount of such consumption as a transfer payment. (As a hypothetical example, there might be free lunches given during the training program.) To be sure, nonconsumption direct costs do represent in part the transfer of investment expenditure to the trainee: "income-in-kind" in the form of instruction and training. But we consider these as benefits that will show up as future earnings (and future consumption). In other types of programs the distinction between consumption-value expenditures, considered as transfer payments, and investment-value expenditures, considered as direct, resource-using costs, may be more ambiguous than we believe it is in the case of the retraining program.[6]

The largest cost of retraining that is borne by the individual, and one that is also important to society, is the opportunity cost of his time spent while taking the retraining course. Properly representing this opportunity cost is one of the most difficult problems we encounter. Ideally, we would like to know what earnings (direct market earnings or imputed nonmarket earnings) the individual would have earned had he not enrolled in and attended the training course. The previous earnings of the trainees appear to us to be an inaccurate measure since their past wages apply to that more fortunate time when they were more fully employed (as coal miners, for example) and before they were hit by the structural changes that reduced their earnings opportunities and, in this case study, made their economic environment a depressed area. Such earnings would greatly overstate the opportunity costs relevant during the time of the retraining projects. We have used instead the amount of wages earned during the training period by the comparable group of workers who took no retraining, which is to represent what income the trainees would have earned in the market, given their age, sex, race, and education. (See below for a discussion of the assumption of comparability.)

The amount earned by the trainee during the program need not be zero, of course. Some were able to hold down a job, usually part-time, while training. Any net differences between these earnings and those obtained by the comparable group of nontrainee workers is then treated as the opportunity cost.

5. *The time period of the observations.*—We can choose among several time periods as a basis for making our measurements. Monthly earnings data for trainees and control groups are available for 18 months to 27 months after the end of retraining. For those persons who first completed their course of training we have data covering 27 months; for those finishing next, 24 months; for the next group 21 months; and for the final group of graduates who finished in the third quarter of 1962, 18 months. For one choice of a time period, we use the first 18 months after retraining, and this provides us with our maximum sample size, since all our subjects have earnings data for this time period. A second choice of the time period, which maximizes the length of time in which the effects of training could show up for all trainees, covers only the trainees for whom we have data for 27 months.

Finally, we show a comparison of the earnings reported for the last available quarter of the study—January through March, 1964. Here we are allowing the greatest length of time to elapse after the end of retraining, and we will be able to observe the labor force experiences after the occurrence of transitions, readjustments, and, in some cases, migrations of the trainees. On these grounds this measure may reveal a truer picture of what future earnings will look like. Other things equal (like the state of the labor market), we expect the earnings to be higher after the trainees have had some on-the-job experience and time to shop around in the market. On the other hand, note that the quarter involved is customarily the most sluggish in economic activity, and earnings would tend to be lower for this reason. As a final comment, we should note that since our measures utilize differences between costs and earnings of our study group and control group, the alternative time periods and concepts are critical only insofar as they apply differentially to the two groups.

### THE CRUCIAL ASSUMPTION: THE COMPARABILITY OF THE TRAINEES AND NONTRAINEES

We have noted that the largest component of the private costs of the training program are the opportunity costs—the earnings foregone while taking the training courses, and we have explained that our measure of this cost is the earnings of the comparable group within the sample of nontrainees. Further, the measure of benefits we employ is the earnings differential of those who have taken the training versus those in our sample who have not. It is clear, therefore, that the assumption that the labor force experience of the nontrainees represents how the trainees would have fared had they not undertaken training is enormously important. Several comments are in order.

1. At the outset we note that among men, the *overall* labor quality of the trainees is higher than that of the nontrainees by the customary indexes of educational attainment and age levels. As pointed out in the Introduction, the "cream of the unemployed" were selected for retraining. However, our controls for age, sex, education, and race narrow considerably the range of incomparability. Unfortunately, we run into marked sample size differences between the experimental and control groups within these sub-classifications. That is, we have more trainees than nontrainees in a given sex-age cell with twelve years of education and over, and more nontrainees than trainees in the same sex-age group with less than twelve years of education. (See Table IX.1.) This is, of course, the consequence of the original favorable selectivity of the group to be retrained.

Now, the problem of maintaining sufficiently large numbers in the cells of our tables inhibits us from using finer measures of education and age, or such additional factors as the individual's previous occupations and employment experiences, or other variables that could contribute to a more precise estimate of the net impact of retraining. In the case of women, for example, marital status and family composition are likely to be especially important.[7] The evidence we have, however, suggests that finer classifications would show that the trainees possess slightly more favorable labor force characteristics than their counterparts among males. For example, among males under 35 years of age with less than twelve years of education, the trainees average 9.8 years of schooling and the nontrainees 8.5; among males over 35 years of age with less than twelve years of education, the averages are 8.7 for the trainees and 7.4 for the nontrainees.

2. What about the unmeasured but important aspects of "attitudes" and "personality" differences between the two groups? Consider the following two types of individuals who are likely to be excluded from the trainees and included among the nontrainees: first is the group of workers who lack the ambition, intelligence, or temperament to seek out the opportunity to take a retraining course or, perhaps, to be selected for a course had they applied. The omission of this type from the sample of trainees implies that an earnings differential in their favor cannot be

attributed solely to training but must in part be attributed to the personal characteristics. Similarly, opportunity costs are understated by using the nontrainees' earnings, since the actual foregone earnings would have been higher if the "higher quality" trainees had been working.

A second group excluded from the trainees, however, has the opposite effect. This group is made up of those who are so likely to regain employment quickly that the courses of retraining have little appeal. By this interpretation the more "desperate" among the unemployed tended to seek retraining. And since we might assume that they were "desperate" in part because their labor skills were not in demand, the overall labor quality of the nontrainees may be higher than that of the trainees, with corresponding effects on our interpretation of earnings differentials and opportunity costs.

Which of the two "omission effects" is the more important? Our judgment is that among men the effect of favorable selectivity outweighs that of unfavorable selectivity for the retraining programs. On balance, then, it is likely that the males who underwent retraining are of somewhat higher labor quality than the nontrainees, even within comparison groups that control for certain measurable factors. Among women, however, we suggest that the nontrainees, who were in fact already on the files of the Employment Service Office, had a stronger commitment to the labor force than the female trainees. This fact may well imply that among women the nontrainees are the more willing workers—or of higher quality—than the trainees. (These points are taken up again in the discussion of our empirical findings in the third section.)

3. A third point of incomparability lies in the special placement efforts made for some of the retrained workers—principally the male trainees. In extreme cases, the trainees had practically guaranteed jobs in some established plants in the area. In some instances the companies had been awarded defense contracts on a preferential basis in accordance with our national policy to encourage industrial activity in distressed areas such as West Virginia. In such cases the successful placement of the workers who completed a retraining course is, to some extent, owing to the policy which created new jobs rather than to the training program as such. In part, of course, the decision to place the contract in West Virginia was motivated by the supply of trained workers which the program promised. The important point from the standpoint of our analysis is that the benefits accruing to the workers who completed some of the courses in retraining reflect a mixture of policies, and the net impact of retraining cannot be isolated.

4. Finally, we assume that the incidence of unemployment among the nontrainees, both during the training period and in the post-training

period, was not related to the labor market experiences of the trainees. The issue here is whether or not the worker who completed a retraining course "took a job away from" one who had no contact with retraining —with the result that (in this study) a nontrainee becomes or stays unemployed. If this in fact happened, we would be comparing the earnings of the *employed* trainee, presumably measuring the value of his productivity, to the *unemployed* nontrainee's zero earnings, which are obviously less than the worth of his labor. The comparison would give a grossly exaggerated measure of the improvement in the productivity of the trainee that is attributable to his retraining course.

Under conditions of full employment (or "normal-full employment"), investments in improving the productivity of people may be and are measured in just this way—by observing the extra earnings of the recipient of the investment. This is what is done in the studies of the returns to investments in education or to on-the-job training.[8] We do not worry about a college graduate (or a journeyman) taking a job away from a high-school graduate (or an unskilled worker) and leaving the latter unemployed—if we do in fact have normal-full employment. West Virginia, however, is far from a full-employment economy, and this raises a tough methodological problem for our research.

An important question that relates to this problem is the extent to which a program of retraining creates new jobs, in which case employment of the trainees need not be at the expense of employment of nontrainees. This issue is analyzed in greater detail in the Appendix, and at this point we should like to state briefly the conclusions of that discussion. The general case for a net expansion of employment as a result of a program of retraining has some theoretical support, but the same *a priori* arguments suggest that the quantitative magnitude of the expansion is likely to be minuscule. Only a relatively small increase in government expenditures has been generated by these programs, and it is the increases in expenditures (or, in other words, increases in aggregate demand) that provide the really significant force for employment expansion.

As we have noted in point 3 above, however, there are increased expenditures pumped into the West Virginia economy that are related, directly or indirectly, to the retraining program. These are likely to have expansionary multiplier effects, given the pervasive unemployment. The net result for the specific case of West Virginia (as distinct from the nation as a whole) may well be one in which more new jobs are created than are foregone by making the expenditures in West Virginia rather than in another part of the country. A final justification for the assumption that the unemployment experiences of the nontrainees are not affected by what happened to the trainees is simply that the number of trainees is small (a few thousand) compared to tens of thousands of males and females of these age and skill groups in West Virginia.

### SOME FINAL LIMITATIONS

No effort has been made to ascertain whether a worker does, in fact, get a job in the general area for which he has been retrained. However, we should recognize that the improvement of worker-quality may take other forms than the narrowly defined skill acquisition. For example, the enhancement of the individual's commitment to the labor force, to work-group cooperation, to his aspirations or incentives, or to other factors which make the worker generally more productive—all will contribute to his earnings capacity.

We again emphasize that only money returns are being calculated. Some of the benefits described above are likely to contribute to non-pecuniary returns, which will escape our measure. Also, to the extent that the programs successfully enable the worker to become self-sustaining, they reduce hardships of unemployment and low income on secondary parties such as his children. Finally, by improving the worker's education and his own and his family's morale, the successful program benefits society in general in its effects on political and civic participation. To an unknown extent these factors offset the upward bias in our results based on the selectivity of the trainees and the sometimes special arrangements made to assure them job placement after retraining.

## THE TABULATIONS OF COSTS AND EARNINGS

### COSTS

An overall picture of the costs of retraining is shown in Table IX.2. The average costs to society for the retraining of a male are $918; for retraining a female, $527. The average private costs to males and females are much less, $233 and $30, respectively. For social costs we add columns (7), (8), and (9) to the social measure of wages lost, (5). Private costs are the sum of columns (1) and (3) and the negative of column (9). Supporting details and comparisons among subgroups are contained in Table IX.3. The categories of costs were discussed in the previous section, and the figures in these tables require little comment. Recall that the private and social measures of wages will differ because of the differences in the treatment of taxes and of being voluntarily not-in-the-labor-force. Clearly, the costs to the individual trainee are quite small, and this might be expected when it is remembered that he is unemployed at the time the training course begins and that the economic environment is as depressed as West Virginia was during these years.

## TABLE IX.2

### Average Costs per Trainee During Training by Type of Cost, Private and Societal Estimation

| | Private | | | | Society | | | | | |
|---|---|---|---|---|---|---|---|---|---|---|
| | Opportunity costs | | | | Opportunity costs | | | | | |
| | Total wages[a] (1) | Monthly wages (2) | Transfer payments[b] (3) | Total private costs[c] (4) | Total wages[a] (5) | Monthly wages (6) | Transfer payments[b] (7) | Direct training costs (8) | Training or subsistence allowance for entire training period (9) | Total social costs[d] (10) |
| Male (n = 226) | $362 | $113 | $ −49 | $233 | $355 | $111 | $ 49 | $434 | $ 80 | $918 |
| Female (n = 115) | 156 | 71 | 13 | 30 | 103 | 47 | −13 | 298 | 139 | 527 |

[a] The total figures apply to the entire training period. The average durations of training courses were 3.2 months for males and 2.2 months for females.

[b] Transfer payments, which do not include the training allowance reported in the last column of the table, is computed as the net average difference between the welfare payments received by the trainee group and the comparable group of nontrainees. A negative figure under the heading of private costs (as is the case for males) denotes a larger payment made to the trainees than to the nontrainees so that a subsidy was involved. A negative figure under the heading of transfer payments (as is the case for females) shows that larger payments were made to the nontrainees than to the trainees so that net savings were involved. The "savings" disappear, of course, with the inclusion of the training allowances.

[c] Columns 1 + 3 − 9.

[d] Columns 5 + 7 + 8 + 9.

## TABLE IX.3

### Average Monthly Wages and Transfer Payments, Including Training Allowances, Received During the Training Period for Trainees and Nontrainees: Social and Private Estimates[a]

| Type of income received | Male | | | | Female | | | |
|---|---|---|---|---|---|---|---|---|
| | <35 yrs. of age | | 35–54 yrs. of age | | <35 yrs. of age | | 35–54 yrs. of age | |
| | <12 yrs. educ. | 12+ yrs. educ. | <12 yrs. educ. | 12+ yrs. educ. | <12 yrs. educ. | 12+ yrs. educ. | <12 yrs. educ. | 12+ yrs. educ. |
| *Market wages (monthly)* | | | | | | | | |
| Trainee | $ 30 | $ 78 | $155[b] | $ 70 | $38 | $ 5 | $36 | $17 |
| | (30) | (78) | (153) | (66) | (37) | (5) | (36) | (16) |
| Nontrainee | 153[c] | 196[c] | 159 | 271 | 63 | 44 | 70 | 90 |
| | (160) | (200) | (159) | (252) | (77) | (92) | (91) | (103) |
| *Social income (monthly)* | | | | | | | | |
| Trainee | 33 | 39 | 59 | 40 | 0 | 7 | 0 | 6 |
| Nontrainee | 39 | 17 | 48 | 24 | 11 | 16 | 8 | 6 |
| *Training or subsistence allowance* | | | | | | | | |
| Trainee | 34 | 28 | 8 | 19 | 82 | 72 | 53 | 53 |
| *No. of observations* | | | | | | | | |
| Trainee | 37 | 132 | 33 | 24 | 19 | 30 | 28 | 38 |
| Nontrainee | 61 | 34 | 103 | 17 | 11 | 23 | 21 | 14 |

[a] Private measures are given in parentheses. The two principal differences in social and private measures of income are that the latter is "take-home" pay (excluding income tax deductions) and that it includes imputed income for a period of voluntary withdrawal from the labor force. (See text for a fuller discussion.)

[b] The relatively high earnings made during the training period for this group are attributable to two peculiar cases of trainees who earned an average of $516 a month for the 10–12 months of their training period. It might be pointed out that such examples indicate that some of the trainees were highly ambitious and persevering.

[c] The lower social measure (which is pre-tax earnings) for males in this cell is, of course, unusual. It primarily reflects school attendance and some short-term illness for part of the time of five of the nontrainees. These uses of time are given zero worth in the social measure but are credited as imputed income for the private measure.

The retraining subsistence payments and the direct or overhead costs of the training program are included in the costs to society.[9] More male than female trainees held part-time jobs during training, and this is one reason for the higher average subsistence payment to females. Another is that more males were enrolled in the initial state training program (AVP), which did not provide training or subsistence allowances. The principal reason for the higher direct costs of training courses for males was the longer average duration of the courses and the typically higher cost of training equipment and materials.

As we would expect, average wages earned during the entire training period (our measure of opportunity costs) are greater for the nontrainees; the men in this category earned, on the average, about $110 more a month than the trainees.

In Table IX.2 the pre-tax earnings of the trainees were subtracted from the pre-tax earnings of the nontrainees for the social measure of opportunity costs. The after-tax earnings are used in the private measure along with imputed earnings for the nontrainees who were voluntarily out of the labor force.[10] No imputed earnings were attributed to any trainees during the duration of the course, and among the nontrainees this was important only for women.

For males the private measure of earnings exceeds the social measure by only 2 per cent ($365 compared to $355), whereas for females the private measure is one-third larger ($156 compared to $108). The greater relative importance of imputed earnings among female nontrainees when they were voluntarily out of the labor force accounts for the larger size of the private measure of earnings foregone for females.

The differential amounts of transfer payments received by the two samples were not large. Trainees received slightly more than nontrainees among men (only $49 over the entire training period) and slightly less ($13) among females. Many of the female trainees were not eligible to receive any transfer payment (see Table IX.3). As we have noted previously, the positive cost of transfer payments to society is a negative cost (or income) to the individual recipient.

## EARNINGS AND BENEFITS

The most important of our measures of the benefits of the training program is the earnings differential between trainees and nontrainees during the post-training period. We calculated the earnings difference over three time periods. An overall view is given in Table IX.4, and comparisons among the specific subgroups are shown in Table IX.5.

Depending on the time period used to calculate the earnings differential, the male trainees show increases of $61 to $67 per month on an individual estimation basis, $83 to $84 on a societal basis; and the female

TABLE IX.4

AVERAGE MONTHLY EARNINGS DIFFERENTIALS (NONTRAINEES' EARNINGS SUBTRACTED
FROM TRAINEES') FOR SELECTED TIME PERIODS AFTER THE END OF TRAINING,
PRIVATE AND SOCIETAL ESTIMATION[a]

| | (1) | | (2) Maximum time period after training ended[b] | | (3) 1st quarter 1964 only | |
| | First 18 mo. after training ended | | | | | |
| Sex | Private[c] | Social[d] | Private | Social | Private | Social |
|---|---|---|---|---|---|---|
| Male (No.: 226 trainees 215 nontrainees) | $67 | $84 | $66 | $85 | $61 | $83 |
| Female (No.: 115 trainees 69 nontrainees) | 9 | 16 | 7 | 14 | −1 | 15 |

[a] The differentials reported in this table are the weighted average of the differentials computed separately for each of the comparison groups. (See Table IX.5 for the tabulation of post-training earnings by comparison group of trainees and nontrainees.) As averages, these earnings differentials may be subjected to a statistical test (the t-test) of the differences of means. All the differentials reported for males are statistically significant (that is, different from zero) at the 1 per cent level; all those reported for females are insignificant at any level less than 20 per cent. As an example of confidence limits for the earnings differentials for males, the social measures have a 95 per cent probability of being between $56 and $112, $58 and $112, and $51 and $115 for columns (1), (2), and (3) respectively.

[b] This figure is a weighted average for 4 groups having a maximum of 18, 21, 24, and 27 months of post-training labor market experience.

[c] The private measure is net of taxes and assumes that the workers who voluntarily leave the labor force earn an imputed income equal to what they earned in the job they held immediately preceding the time when they left the labor force.

[d] The social measure includes federal income taxes but no state taxes or social security. Zero earnings are imputed for that time when a worker is voluntarily out of the civilian labor force.

trainees show a differential of private earnings from $1 to $8 and increased social earnings from $11 to $15 per month. The earnings differentials for males are highly significant in a statistical sense, whereas the differentials for females are not statistically significant. In this chapter we will work with and discuss the differentials as given (their most likely values), but the statistical unreliability of the estimates for females should be kept in mind when interpreting the data. We will use only the two periods, eighteen months (column 1 of Table IX.4) and first quarter

TABLE IX.5

AVERAGE MONTHLY WAGES AND TRANSFER PAYMENTS RECEIVED PER PERSON FOR TWO POST-TRAINING TIME PERIODS FOR COMPARISON GROUPS OF TRAINEES AND NONTRAINEES: PRIVATE AND SOCIAL ESTIMATES[a]

| Type of income received and period | Male | | | | Female | | | |
|---|---|---|---|---|---|---|---|---|
| | <35 yrs. of age | | 35–54 yrs. of age | | <35 yrs. of age | | 35–54 yrs. of age | |
| | <12 yrs. educ. | 12+ yrs. educ. | <12 yrs. educ. | 12+ yrs. educ. | <12 yrs. educ. | 12+ yrs. educ. | <12 yrs. educ. | 12+ yrs. educ. |
| *Monthly market wages (18-month post-training period)* | | | | | | | | |
| Trainee | $240 | $332 | $256 | $276 | $81 | $80 | $111 | $114 |
| | (231) | (300) | (251) | (268) | (111) | (115) | (122) | (118) |
| Nontrainee | 141 | 240 | 158 | 281 | 73 | 80 | 63 | 105 |
| | (148) | (232) | (160) | (261) | (107) | (117) | (103) | (104) |
| *Monthly market wages (first quarter, 1964)* | | | | | | | | |
| Trainee | 283 | 368 | 306 | 307 | 93 | 84 | 107 | 137 |
| | (268) | (329) | (293) | (296) | (127) | (131) | (113) | (138) |
| Nontrainee | 167 | 277 | 189 | 365 | 94 | 112 | 49 | 113 |
| | (168) | (269) | (193) | (341) | (126) | (154) | (99) | (135) |
| *Monthly transfer payments (18-month post-training period)*[b] | | | | | | | | |
| Trainee | 10 | 5 | 27 | 11 | 1 | 3 | 0 | 2 |
| Nontrainee | 32 | 13 | 46 | 17 | 5 | 7 | 4 | 4 |
| T − N | −22 | −8 | −19 | −6 | −4 | −4 | −4 | −2 |
| *Number of observations* | | | | | | | | |
| Trainee | 37 | 132 | 33 | 24 | 19 | 30 | 28 | 38 |
| Nontrainee | 61 | 34 | 103 | 17 | 11 | 23 | 21 | 14 |

[a] Private measures are given in parentheses.

[b] These figures for the 18-month post-training period differ only slightly from those of the other two periods used.

1964 (column 3), in succeeding tables since these for the most part illustrate the upper and lower values of our estimates.

There is little variation in the earnings differential of the trainees relative to the nontrainees among the different time periods. In particular, we failed to find support for our expectation that those completing training will experience more favorable employment and earnings after an interval of a few months, a period of searching for jobs and adjustment.

The earnings differential for females shows greater relative variation among time periods and between social and private measures. Job turnover and movements in and out of the labor force are, it is well known, much more prevalent among females, and this adds to the random variability in the data for females—added variability which is accentuated by the smaller sample size of females. The substantially lower earnings margin of female trainees is probably attributable to the attrition in employment brought on by two causes: (1) the jobs for which the women were trained are characterized by high attrition rates (e.g., nurse's aides; see Chapter II of this volume for a discussion of training courses for women); (2) the women enrolled in the training courses were, themselves, less committed to the work force because of their personal disposition and larger family responsibilities. This point is discussed further below.

A second measure of the benefits of the training program is the decrease in welfare payments made to unemployed workers after they have been trained and are re-employed. Adhering to our strictly monetary calculations, these reduced social payments show up as benefits to society but as decreased earnings (or costs) to the individual.[11] The differences in transfer payments going to the trainees relative to the nontrainees are included in Table IX.5. The savings to society implied by these figures are not large, but the consistency of smaller payments to each group of those who have completed a training course is impressive.

Table IX.5 shows the earnings and transfer payments received by the two samples for the more narrowly classified comparison groups. Although the generalization that the earnings differential is in favor of those who have completed a course in retraining holds up, there are exceptions and some interesting contrasts among the groups.

Note first of all that the measures of earnings based on the point of view of society are larger among men and smaller among women than are the private measures, which are given in parentheses. This reflects the importance of the tax bite from the earnings of men (which makes the net earnings of the individual less than the pre-tax figure) and the unimportance of any imputed earnings attributed to men who voluntarily leave the labor force. For women the reverse is true: taxes are not a major deduction from their low wages, but imputed earnings for non-market work are far from negligible.

Look secondly at the earnings differential between trainees and nontrainees. The extra earnings of the trainees are greater on a social estimation basis than on a private basis for men; no clear pattern shows up for women. Again, we note that taxes deducted will be relatively larger from the (generally) higher salaries of the trainees, and thus their pre-tax earnings are relatively larger than the post-tax earnings, compared with the nontrainees.

Two observations that may be made on the differential impact of retraining among our socio-demographic groups are similar to the findings of other studies of training programs. These are that retraining appears to benefit men more than women; and younger men more than older men. Over the eighteen-month period of post-training experience, the trainees show a positive earnings differential over the nontrainees for three of four groups for both men and women, but the social estimates of the differences are substantially greater for men—$99, $92, $98, and $5—than for women, where the differences are $8, $0, $48, and $9 reading across the page from left to right, beginning with the lower educated and younger groups.

Several factors help explain the overall poorer performance of the female trainees. Before training, fewer women among the trainees claimed a regular occupation (only 50 per cent), while among the nontrainees about 80 per cent reported a regular occupation. A related point is that women in the sample of nontrainees on average had more extensive employment experience prior to retraining, which also implies a firmer attachment to the labor force. Among groups of women under 35 years of age, where the comparative performance of the trainees was poorest, the percentage of this group with children under six years of age was greater than for the nontrainees. For reasons of home work responsibilities, then, we might expect the trainees to be in the labor force less, with obvious consequences for their employment and earnings experience. Finally, we stress the fact that the numbers of observations for females under 35 years of age are quite small.

This bit of *ad hoc* rationalization of our "deviant cases" is not meant to refute the conclusion that women gained less from training programs than the men in our study. Rather, we suggest that the characteristically high labor force turnover rates among women and competing responsibilities for their time do make generalizations quite hazardous when we cannot control for many more variables and do not have many more observations.

Among adult men we should not expect peculiarities of results because of differences in labor force participation. So, this certainly would not explain the "deviant case" of the negative earnings differential of male trainees, aged 35–54, with twelve years of education or more. The greater earnings of the nontrainee group here constitute a puzzle. They may reflect an especially productive sample of nontrainees, an unproductive sample of trainees, a failure of these specific courses of retraining, etc. But perhaps one should not be excessively concerned about this result, since the size of the sample is by far the smallest (28 trainees and 17 nontrainees) of any of the male comparison groups and represents less than 10 per cent of the observations.

## THE TRAINING PROGRAM AS AN INVESTMENT

An attempt to analyze the results of the previous section in terms of investment theory clearly seems appropriate. There is a need for a summary judgment that simultaneously takes into account the data on costs and benefits. We use three common techniques of evaluation: payback periods, rates of return, and capital values. These techniques involve slightly different perspectives and give different measures of performance, but in the context of this chapter there is no need to choose one among them as the correct measure. For, although there are many subtle, technical, even esoteric issues involved in investment analysis, such issues are not important in our study, where the results presented in the previous section lead to a one-sided conclusion in favor of the training program as a profitable investment. Questions do surround this latter conclusion, and we review them again in the next and final section of this paper, but these questions do not involve the mathematical techniques of measurement that we have adopted. In this section we will tentatively accept as valid the empirical results of the preceding section.

### THE PAY-BACK PERIOD

We begin with the concept of a pay-back period—a simple but sufficient device to indicate emphatically the general profitability of the retraining project we have studied. From Table IX.2 we obtain an estimate of the average cost per trainee of the program. These costs are shown in Table IX.6 on a private and social estimation basis for men, women, and the total. The average duration of the training courses was 3.2 months for men and 2.2 months for women—a sufficiently short period of time that an interest rate can be ignored. Next, we restrict our measure of benefits to the market earnings differential enjoyed by the trainees during the post-training period. (See Table IX.4.) This ignores the small savings to society (or small "costs" to the individual) of reduced social payments made to the trainees during the post-training period we examined.

TABLE IX.6

Average Costs of the Training Program per Person and the Average Number of Months Required for the (Positive) Earnings Differential of the Trainees to Pay Back (Equal) These Costs

| | Basis for estimating costs and earnings[a] | | | | | | | |
| | Private | | | | Society | | | |
| | | Pay-back period in mo. | | | | Pay-back period in mo. | | |
| Sex | Av. costs | 18-mo. post-training | Max. post-training | 1st quarter 1964 | Av. costs | 18-mo. post-training | Max. post-training | 1st quarter 1964 |
|---|---|---|---|---|---|---|---|---|
| Male | $233 | 3.5 | 3.5 | 3.8 | $918 | 10.9 | 10.8 | 11.1 |
| Female | $ 30 | 3.3 | 4.3 | ∞ [b] | $527 | 32.9 | 37.6 | 35.1 |
| Both sexes (weighted) | $165 | 3.5 | 3.6 | 4.1 | $787 | 12.8 | 12.8 | 13.1 |

[a] Private costs include wages foregone minus transfer payments and training or subsistence allowances. Social costs include wages foregone, direct costs, and subsistence allowances. We assume no savings to society in the post-training period because of reduced transfer payments to those who complete training (relative to what they would receive had they not taken in training).

[b] Zero earnings benefits in this cell, which implies that the investment would never be paid back.

Source: Tables IX.2 and IX.4.

Table IX.6 shows the number of months required to pay back the costs of the program according to the different time periods used to compute the earnings differential. All three periods show approximately the same pay-back period, however, the really important difference is between private and social measures, especially as they involve "costs." Smaller private costs make the pay-back period considerably shorter for the individual than for society for each time period. Among women, where the opportunity cost (of wages foregone) is low and where the training allowance was relatively large, the costs are almost zero (only $30). In principle they could be negative—which would indeed make retraining a very profitable venture for the trainee!

Of greater policy and theoretical interest is the pay-off of the investment to society as a whole. The shortest pay-back periods for males and females together are around 13 months. For male trainees the period is about 11 months. This is prior to the end of the post-training period (18 to 27 months) for which we have earnings data. Thus, in all future periods any earnings advantage enjoyed by the trainees will represent "clear profits," and we could expect ten to forty years of additional labor force participation by these workers.

The length of time necessary to pay back the costs of training is by far the longest for the female trainees, especially from society's point of view. The private earnings advantage of the female trainees is quite small (falling to zero for the first quarter, 1964 period), but so are the private costs of their training. The pay-back period for society stretches up to three years for women. For those lengths that exceed the 18 to 27 months for which we have data, we make the assumption that the earnings differential during the observed post-training period remains constant during the next year.

## RATES OF RETURN

The determination of a pay-back period for the male training program was made with earnings data we actually collected. There was no need to project into future periods where we have no data, since the accumulated earnings differential in favor of the trainees during the eighteen-month post-training period was sufficient to establish a pay-back period within the range of our known experience.

This advantage is absent when we turn to the computation of rates of return and capital values of the investment in training, since here we need estimates of the total benefits of the program, which involve the earnings differential over all future years worked. We seek the rate of return which equates the present value of the costs of the program to the present value of the benefits, where the costs are incurred over several months of training and the earnings differential of the post-training period extends until permanent retirement from the labor force. A heroic assumption made to simplify the computations and at the same time to achieve realistic (and perhaps conservative) results is that the earnings differential between comparison groups of trainees and nontrainees declines linearly at the rate given by the average for the first eighteen months after retraining and the slightly lower average for the last three months (first quarter, 1964).[12]

Although we had suggested earlier that the earnings differential between trainees and nontrainees might widen as time elapsed after the completion of training, the evidence we have suggests the opposite result —nontrainees began narrowing the gap in the labor market performance measures of employment rates and earnings. Perhaps the severely depressed economy in West Virginia placed the lesser skilled nontrainees at a particular disadvantage during the period 1962–63. When the state's business conditions improved in 1964, the relative disadvantages of the nontrainees may have had a lesser effect. Another reason the trainees may have fared particularly well, compared to nontrainees, early in the post-training period is that job placement efforts in their behalf may have given them a head start, the effect of which was likely to have diminished over time.

For purposes of calculating annual rates of return, the monthly earnings differential (trainees' — nontrainees') shown in Table IX.4 are translated into annual equivalent dollar amounts. The annual amount of the differential is computed on the basis of two time periods, an "early" period based on the first eighteen months after retraining and a "late" period based on the first quarter in 1964, and these amounts are entered in Table IX.7 to indicate the differentials for the first and second years after retraining. The absolute difference between the first and second years is extended year by year into the future until either the trainee reaches retirement age or the differential vanishes. The absolute difference between the "early" period and the "late" period is $1 per month or $12 per year, as shown in Table IX.4. Given the initial costs of the program (shown in column 1 of Table IX.7) and the expected working lifetimes of the trainees (based on columns 4 and 5), we can use the estimated lifetime pattern of differential earnings to compute a rate of return. The general formula for a rate of return is:

$$f(r) = \sum_{t=1}^{n} \left\{ \frac{C_t - B_t}{(1 + r)^t} \right\} = 0$$

where $C_t$ and $B_t$ are the costs and benefits per time period, $t$, and $r$ is the rate of return which equalizes the present values of the costs and benefits.

The assumptions underlying Table IX.7 permit a simpler formula:

$$C_0 = \sum_{t=1}^{n} \frac{B_1 - 12(t - 1)}{(1 + r)^t}$$

where $n$ is the number of years to retirement age.

Three rates of return are shown in the final column of Table IX.7: for all trainees, 92 per cent; for male trainees, 109 per cent; for female trainees, 29 per cent. We report only the rates of return to society, which were much lower than the private rates. The largest part of the costs of the program, direct costs and subsistence allowances, were borne entirely by the government, so the critical test will concern the social rate of return. As an example of why we do not consider the private rate of return as a critical variable for policy analysis, consider the case of female trainees. The private costs for female trainees were only $30 (see Table IX.6), and even though the earnings differential for the first year was only $108 (twelve times the $9 shown in column 1 in Table IX.4) and then vanished by the second year (see column 3 in Table IX.4), the rate of return is 260 per cent! (We have $30 = \dfrac{\$108}{(1 + r)}$. Thus, r = 2.60.)

TABLE IX.7

SOCIAL RATES OF RETURN ON THE INVESTMENT IN RETRAINING

| Group | Costs per trainee | Benefits: Earnings differential | | Average age during training | Years in working life[c] | Rates of return |
|---|---|---|---|---|---|---|
| | | 1st year[a] | 2nd year[b] | | | |
| Total | $787 | $ 736 | $724 | 33 | 33 | 92 |
| (males and females) | | | | | | |
| All males | 918 | 1,008 | 996 | 30 | 36 | 109 |
| All females | 572 | 192 | 180 | 39 | 27 | 28 |

[a] Annual equivalents of the monthly figures reported in Table IX.4 for the first 18 months after the training had ended.

[b] Annual equivalents of the monthly figures reported in Table IX.4 for the last three months in the post-training period for which we have data (first quarter, 1964). The annual earnings differential (trainees' − nontrainees') for all subsequent years is based on a linear extrapolation of the first-to-second year trend.

[c] Retirement age assumed to be 65.

All the rates, except perhaps for women, are extraordinarily high. Had we included a growth rate in earnings, say 2 per cent, along with the assumption that the same rate applies to the earnings of both trainees and nontrainees, then the absolute spread of earnings would widen and the rate of return would be even higher. We will comment on the large sizes of the rates of return after presenting capital values of the program in the next section.

For the separate age and education groups we computed social rates of return on the assumption that the dollar differential in earnings was constant for the entire future working lives of the trainees. This assumption was required because the two-year trends given by our data were too erratic among the small sub-groups. With this assumption the rates of return for the sub-groups were, of course, generally higher, but what is interesting is the relative ranking among the groups. Reading from highest to lowest, we have:

Males, aged 35–54, less than 12 years of schooling
Females, aged 35–54, less than 12 years of schooling
Males, less than 35, less than 12 years of schooling
Males, less than 35, 12 or more years of schooling
Females, aged 35–54, 12 or more years of schooling
Females, less than 35, less than 12 years of schooling
Males, aged 35–54, 12 or more years of schooling
Females, less than 35, 12 or more years of schooling

For the last two groups listed the earnings differential was in favor of the nontrainees, implying a negative rate of return.

Among males there is a slight tendency for the younger group (under 35) to benefit more from the program than the older group. The reverse is true for women. The reason may be that both older males and younger females have a weaker attachment to the labor force. Both male and female groups with less than a high-school education show higher rates of return than the better educated groups.

## NET EXPECTED CAPITAL VALUES

For our final measure of the benefits to retraining we calculate the capital value (or present value) of the discounted stream of net earnings-benefits that accrue to the trainee and society over time. The fact that the costs of the program are subtracted from the benefits is implied in the use of the term, "*net* earnings-benefits." The capital value, then, gives a dollar amount for the "worth" of the retraining program, and any positive amount indicates that the program has "paid off." Negative values imply that the costs (given the discount factor) exceed the returns. The formula used to estimate the capital value is as follows:

$$V = \sum_{t=a}^{66} \frac{E_t}{(1+r)^{(t+1-a)}}$$

where $V$ is the capital value of the returns to a given group of trainees; $a$ the average age of the group of trainees; $E$ the net earnings differential of the trainees over the nontrainees (this will be negative during the training period and will generally be a positive, but declining, amount for all periods in the post-training period. The rate of decline is the same as that used in the calculation of rates of return—see Table IX.7). $r$ represents the selected rate of discount.

The discount factor is preselected by the investigator. In an investment like the retraining program, a higher interest rate will lend more weight to the initial costs and less weight to the benefits, which are delayed. We show calculations involving two discount rates, 5 per cent and 10 per cent. The former is somewhat above the government's "borrowing rate," which is sometimes used as the lowest reasonable discount factor in benefit-cost analyses of government projects. A rate of 10 per cent represents a second standard of the opportunity costs of the money used for the training program and corresponds to a pre-tax rate of return obtainable in the private sector of the economy.

The results of the capital value computations are presented in Table IX.8. The capital values are higher for the social than for the private estimation concepts, whereas the reverse was true for the rates of return. There are two reason for the relatively small sizes of the private capital values. One is that the earnings differential in favor of the trainees by the private measure declined more sharply in the last three months of

TABLE IX.8

NET EXPECTED CAPITAL VALUES OF THE RETRAINING PROGRAM, 3, 5, 8, AND
10 PER CENT DISCOUNT RATES, PRIVATE AND SOCIAL ESTIMATION[a]

| | Discount rate | | | |
|---|---|---|---|---|
| Group | 3% | 5% | 8% | 10% |
| *All trainees* | | | | |
| Private[b] | $ 2,006 | $ 1,990 | $ 1,758 | $1,638 |
| Social | 13,013 | 10,336 | 7,725 | 6,553 |
| *Male trainees* | | | | |
| Private | 4,313 | 3,985 | 3,565 | 3,325 |
| Social | 18,243 | 14,200 | 10,391 | 8,732 |
| *Female trainees* | | | | |
| Private | 82 | 80 | 78 | 76 |
| Social | 1,376 | 1,239 | 1,072 | 981 |

[a] The lifetime pattern of earnings-benefits from the training program is based on the extrapolation of the annual earnings differential (trainees' − nontrainees') observed in the first and second year after the end of retraining. See Table IX.7.

[b] The private measure of earnings is net of taxes, and the trend (based on Table IX.6) showed a sharper decline from the "early" period after retraining to the "late" period. The extrapolation of this trend is largely responsible for the much smaller private capital values than social capital values.

our post-training data, and the extrapolation of this trend into subsequent years reduced the summed values. A second reason is that the computational procedure for capital values gives, in effect, less weight to the small initial costs of the private measure and more weight to the larger, pre-tax earnings which increase the social measure.[13] This second reason is not trivial, for even if we assumed a constant dollar differential for all subsequent years in the trainees' working life, the private measure of the capital value would exceed the social measure.

The capital value of the net earnings benefits per male trainee is $3,985, given a 5 per cent discount factor and the private concept of measurement. Under societal concepts, the corresponding figure is $14,200 per male. The capital value per female trainee of the program is $80 or $1239 for private and social measures, respectively, at a 5 per cent discount rate. The use of a 10 per cent discount rate reduces the largest benefits to about 40 per cent of what they are at 5 per cent.

If we assume that the earnings of both trainees and nontrainees would grow at a constant rate in the future, then the annual growth rate could be added to the discount rate for all the capital values shown in Table IX.8. If, for example, the growth rate equals 2 per cent, the figures in Table IX.8 would be the capital values for discount rates of 7 and 12 per cent, instead of 5 and 10 per cent. Alternatively, by assuming a growth rate, say, of 2 per cent, the capital values of the earnings differential for 5 and 10 per cent would be the same as if we used a 3 per cent and 8 per cent rate *and no growth rate,* and using these latter rates raises the capital values, as is shown in Table IX.8.

These lump-sum monetary benefits of retraining, like the rates of return, appear to be large. On a per capita basis for the white males in our sample the upper and lower amounts are $14,200 and $3,325. These capital values may be compared with those computed by Gary Becker for the earnings improvement attributable to a college education. For white males, using data for 1949, Becker shows capital values of a college education to be $30,000 when a 4 per cent discount factor is used and $4,000 with a 10 per cent factor.[14]

## CONCLUSIONS

### A Summary of the Results of This Study

This economic evaluation of government-sponsored retraining has consisted of a study of participants and nonparticipants in the training programs in West Virginia in 1961 and 1962. The courses selected for analysis were representative of the types of courses which are being offered on a large scale throughout the country under the Manpower Development and Training Act. The depressed economic conditions of West Virginia were and are precisely the kind that the Area Redevelopment Act and the Manpower Development and Training Act are designed to alleviate. It is reasonable to suppose, then, that information from studies of the training program in West Virginia will apply to programs in other areas. Our general but tentative conclusion from this study is that the training program has been highly successful.[15]

As a basis for weighing the benefits of the program against its costs, we compared the experiences of a study group of workers who completed courses of training and a control group of workers who had no contact with the courses. The measurement of costs was relatively straightforward. The benefits consisted of the additional wages earned by the trainees over and above the earnings of the control group—a measure based on the assumption that the earnings of the latter represent what those who completed training would have earned, on average, had they not taken training. The factors of time and area (or, in other words, the "economic environment") were the same for both sample groups. We controlled also for the race, sex, age, and broad educational level of both groups.

The earnings advantage gained by the trainees was presented in the third section, and overall it appeared to be substantial. In the fourth section we offered an operational definition of the term "substantial" by using three common techniques of investment analysis to evaluate the earnings benefits.

(1) First, the pay-back period of the investment in training was shown to be quite short. An advantage of this measure was that there was little or no need to project the earnings data into the future, since for most groups, including the trainees as a whole, the pay-back period was less than the number of months of post-training experience for which we had data.

(2) Second, we computed rates of return—a concise and comprehensive technique of evaluation, but one which required the hazardous estimation of future earnings. The rates were exceedingly high even though we assumed no growth rate, confined our measure to the lower social rates, and counted transfer payments as costs (even though we did not project reduced social payments and include these as savings or benefits to society).

(3) Finally, the capital-value technique was used. With this measure society showed larger gains than did individuals (reversing the ranking of the other two techniques), but in both instances the capital values were large.

The foregoing discussion has dealt with the overall result of the training program. Also of interest are the wide variations in results among the different subgroups of our sample. These may be summarized briefly. Men gained much more than women from training, mainly because of the poor (even negative) returns on the part of the younger female trainees. Among older women, who are past the ages when child-bearing is very likely, the benefits of training were consistently large, although smaller than for men. In general, younger men did better than older men, but this was entirely due to the poor (again, negative) comparative performance of the small group of older men with twelve years of schooling or more. Among younger men, on the other hand, the better educated group had the higher return on investment in training.

## An Assessment of the Results of This Study

The validity of our investment analyses depends principally on the validity of the underlying data. Let us review the important issues concerning the data which make our findings tentative rather than final. First is the relatively small number of observations, particularly in the case of women. Note, however, that this problem is most serious in precisely the two comparisons that are unfavorable to the finding that the training program substantially benefits the trainees—in the cases, that is, of women and of older men with twelve years of schooling or more. A second problem is errors in the data, particularly reporting errors since many of the data are based on mailed questionnaires and on the respondent's memory of events in the months past. To some extent we expect that the use of group averages minimizes the importance of errors found among the individual observations. Finally, there remain the questionable assumptions of the comparability of the study group (trainees) and the control group (nontrainees). Despite our controls, this is indeed a problem, particularly in the context of unemployment and the special placement efforts that were sometimes made on behalf of the trainees. However, the returns on the investment were high, and they could be reduced substantially to take account of "incomparability" without falling to levels that would be considered "low" by customary standards.

The monetary returns on the investment, however, were extremely high—so high that one (perhaps an economist) might ask whether or not the retraining would take place in the absence of governmental programs—and, if not, why not? Why, for example, does not the market provide retraining for workers like those in our sample when the pay-off is so great? Formal and informal opportunities for training among adult workers actually are quite widespread,[16] but there are compelling reasons (due to market imperfections) why these opportunities may not be utilized to an economically optimal extent. The reader may doubt (as do the authors) that such astonishingly high rates of return could be attributable to "imperfections," and may suspect (as do the authors) that the trainees were of higher labor quality or got preferred treatment in the job market. Nevertheless, the imperfections in the market for human resources and human capital may be pronounced, especially among the disadvantaged groups like those to whom the retraining programs are directed.

Evidence of imperfections is demonstrated by the existence of high levels of involuntary unemployment. In general, the conventional methods for improving one's earnings, like retraining or even migration, as a practical matter require a normal level of unsatisfied demands for jobs—in other words, full employment. Without full employment private voluntary efforts at training and mobility—particularly among disadvantaged and currently unemployed workers—cannot be expected to yield high returns, on the average. But since conditions of unemployment are well within the means of governmental policymakers to rectify, although not within the means of the private business sector, this type of imperfection can be overcome so that what would otherwise be an unprofitable training program can become profitable.

A second type of market imperfection is more subtle; it is also more pervasive since it extends to periods of full employment as well as recessions. The generic type of imperfection in the market for and of human resources lies in the capital market. On the one hand, those for whom retraining programs are intended are too poor to finance the costs of the investment; and on the other, the capital market is relatively inaccessible to them, and they cannot borrow the funds to finance the investment. One variant of this type of imperfection is the absence of an "insurance fund" that would cover safely a large number of cases, which for individuals might entail intolerably high risks. The underlying basis for the inability of the capital market to function at an optimum level in this market of the relatively poor and the hard-core unemployed is the quasi-illegality of using one's own person as collateral.[17]

Despite the high pay-off shown in this study, or perhaps because of it, we should emphasize again that we do not claim that the worth of the retraining programs depends solely on efficiency grounds. Considerations of equity should weigh heavily where alternative types of assistance, like relief, do not hold out the hope of self-support and independence to the long-term unemployed and underemployed. An analysis of the retraining programs should go a step beyond determining whether the subsidy results in employment, however. As part of our consideration of equity, we should also ask whether the new job is at someone else's expense. If the answer is affirmative, then the resulting reshuffle of unemployment itself must be justified, and the question of what groups among the unemployed are selected for retraining takes on greater importance.

Retraining programs are becoming an increasingly important instrument of public economic policy, largely because they promise to further the goals of both efficiency and equity. They deserve attention and study in order that we might determine the manner and extent of their implementation. In this chapter we have evaluated one such program, and for the sample as a whole, we conclude that the training program is a sound investment.

## REFERENCES

1. For example, the stated purpose of the most important legislation on training, the Manpower Development and Training Act, is to "deal with the problem of unemployment resulting from automation and technological change and other types of persistent unemployment."
2. The internal rate of return is calculated by equating the present value of the investment cost outlays with the present value of the additional income flows. Capital values are the present values of future income streams obtained by capitalizing the stream of net expected earnings with some chosen rate of discount. Both methods provide a standard for judging alternative investments and establishing priorities.
3. There were too few nonwhite individuals in the sample to permit their inclusion without an inordinate amount of special attention, so no comparisons involving nonwhites are made. After our work was completed Winston Tillery, currently with the U.S. Department of Labor, conducted a separate analysis of nonwhites in the West Virginia training program. His results support the general favorable verdict we reach on the training program. Tillery's full study will be available as a Master's thesis in industrial relations at the University of Wisconsin. A brief discussion of these results is given in Glen G. Cain and Gerald G. Somers, "Retraining the

Disadvantaged Worker," in *Research in Vocational and Technical Education,* proceedings of a conference on research in vocational education (Madison: Center for Studies in Vocational and Technical Education, University of Wisconsin, 1967).

4. This is most reasonable for females who leave the labor force to assume the responsibilities of homework, especially child care. The cases of voluntary departure from the labor force among males in the prime working ages are very rare and usually involve entry into the armed forces. Persons who are involuntarily out of the labor force—most often the disabled—are excluded from this study. About 3 per cent of the eligible nontrainees and about 1.5 per cent of the trainees were excluded for this reason.

5. The assumption is, in other words, that transfer payments and training allowances are not viewed as "tainted money" by the recipients. Rather, it is "ordinary" income which the individual receives because of (1) a previous investment (insurance); (2) for services rendered (caring for children) or (3) because of the social consensus (relief).

6. We are grateful to W. Lee Hansen and Burton Weisbrod for helpful discussions of these issues.

7. One of the authors is currently employing a multiple regression framework to control simultaneously for a large number of variables. Our impression is that the lack of refinement in the methods used in this paper is not serious. Some preliminary results are reported in Chapter II in this volume and in the paper by Gerald G. Somers and Ernst W. Stromsdorfer, "A Benefit-Cost Analysis of Manpower Retraining," in *Proceedings of the Seventeenth Annual Meeting,* Industrial Relations Research Association, December, 1964 (Madison, Wisconsin: IRRA, 1965).

8. See, for example, Gary S. Becker, *Human Capital* (New York: Columbia University Press, 1964), and Jacob Mincer, "On-the-Job Training: Costs, Returns, and Some Implications," *Journal of Political Economy,* Supplement, Vol. 70, No. 5, Part 2 (October, 1962), 50–79.

9. The total overhead costs of a given course of instruction were divided among those who completed the course to obtain the average direct costs of the program. No attempt was made to pro-rate some of the costs to workers who dropped out of a given course before its completion. The direct training costs attributed to the trainees are, therefore, slightly overstated.

10. Our technique for determining the amount of taxes deducted was quite crude, but it had the virtue of computational simplicity. For each cell group we computed the average weekly earnings and average family size of members in the group. With this information we used the 1963 tax table to determine the average tax applicable to the group. Social Security payments, state and local taxes, and other deductions were ignored. The tax cut of 1964 affected only the earnings for the first quarter of 1964, and no adjustment in our procedure was made for this. Bear in mind that we do not find sharp differences in tax rates among the workers of our sample who all receive relatively low salaries.

11. This is not to say that the individual worker is unhappy with the substitution of market earnings for welfare payments. He is probably glad to be earning a wage, but in measuring the dollar returns and losses of training, we consider a reduction in welfare payments, by itself, as a loss in income.

12. In a draft of this chapter circulated earlier, we assumed that the observed earnings differentials between trainees and nontrainees remained constant over the remaining years of their expected working careers. We now believe that it is preferable to use the evidence at hand, which shows the trend of narrowing differentials. This is consistent with the data reported by Gibbard and Somers in Chapter II, which show a decline in the difference in unemployment rates among nontrainees relative to trainees. As brought out in that chapter, unemployment rates in West Virginia were generally declining in the post-training period.

13. To see this, consider the simple example in which a $2 return in one year on a $1 investment has a capital value of slightly less than $1 but a rate of return of 100 per cent, whereas a $10 return on $8 invested yields only a 25 per cent rate of return but has a capital value of slightly less than $2.

14. Becker, *Human Capital,* p. 115.
15. Throughout this study we make no distinction between average and marginal costs and benefits and, in fact, use only the average return of the program as the relevant concept for evaluation purposes. To answer questions pertaining to the extension of the program and its future pay-offs, the marginal concept is, of course, desired. However, the average and marginal benefits should not differ greatly in such relatively small-scale programs as retraining where considerable expansion could be effected without running into diminishing returns. Furthermore, it is likely that the marginal costs of these types of new and experimental programs would not rise, and might even fall, as the levels of the programs were expanded. Some of the fixed costs have been made, and there ought to be a great deal of increased efficiency in the operation of the program as the administrators learn from experience.
16. See Mincer, "On-the-Job Training . . . ."; also the report on the extent and sources of formal training among adult workers in U.S. Department of Labor, *Manpower Report of the President, 1964* (GPO, 1964), pp. 66–76.
17. Becker makes this point in the following terms: "Since human capital is a very illiquid asset—it cannot be sold and is rather poor collateral on loans—a positive liquidity premium, perhaps a sizable one, would be associated with such capital. . . ." *Human Capital,* p. 55.

# Appendix A

# Can Retraining Create Jobs and Reduce Unemployment?

The issue of whether retraining can or is likely to reduce the existing unemployment rate lies in the background of several parts of the evaluation of the retraining program we present, and it deserves some extended comments. Our opinion is that the best short answer is "no." * But this should be qualified, both in principle—i.e., on theoretical grounds—and in practice in the case of West Virginia where increased spending is part and parcel of the retraining program.

Perhaps the first point to make is why the negative to the question posed is so emphatic. The answer is simply that the motive for hiring workers is their production of goods that people will buy: no purchases, no hirings. Since retraining, by itself, does not generate more income in the hands of consumers, it will not generate more jobs. Consider that even when a retrained worker is hired and turns out a product that is sold, the expenditure made here is not made somewhere else. Again, no net increase in expenditures, no net increase in jobs.

But there are some theoretical qualifications to this stark conclusion.

(1) The decrease in expenditures made "elsewhere"—i.e., other than on the products turned out by retrained workers—may be in a sector that is capital-intensive. Thus, the decrease in spending in the capital-intensive sector will not decrease employment as much as the increase in employment in the sector where the retrained workers have been hired. Mentioning this possibility amounts to more than an idle exercise in taxonomy. Retraining does operate to lower the real costs of labor and to induce the hiring of more labor by employers and the utilizing of less of other factors of production, which we can lump together under the classification "capital." This phenomenon is most clearly seen where the program involves a governmental subsidy to on-the-job training, or when

* The authors wish to acknowledge the stimulating comments of Professor John Culbertson on the subject matter of this appendix, although he is not responsible for our interpretation and conclusions.

the government bears part of the employers' costs of search for labor. In the more common institutional retraining program, we can view the results as raising the productivity of the workers to the point where employers are willing to hire them at their acceptance wage. We have a higher quality of labor at old prices.

The greater utilization of labor is nothing more than the conventional "price effect" in the firm's decision about how to produce its desired output. Thus, even with constant output and constant expenditures, we could expect more labor to be employed. The only requirement for this effect is the possibility of substituting "labor" for "capital" in production process. (Quotation marks are used because we intend to include the cases where "labor" means employees and "capital" could refer to the time and efforts of the owners or the managerial staff.)

(2) A second way in which employment of retrained workers may not be offset by less employment elsewhere and thereby permit a net expansion of jobs is when the "new" expenditures are made at the expense of savings. The motivating force behind this fortunate change in spending habits is also quite conventional. Greater spending (on consumption) is stimulated by lower prices. Lower prices, in turn, have been the result of the "output effect" of the lower cost of labor. When the price of a factor of production is lowered, we expect, in general, not only a substitution of that factor for other factors, but also such lower overall costs of production that prices may be lowered to stimulate the sale in the market of a greater volume of the output. The prerequisite here is some degree of price flexibility. Even if there is no increase in consumers' incomes, we could expect a shift from savings goods to consumption goods and some increase in employment.

(3) In the first two points we have called for some flexibility in the production process or some downward price flexibility in the market for consumer goods. We have not assumed downward wage flexibility; indeed, complete wage flexibility would eliminate all involuntary unemployment. In a context of unemployment, we must adhere to some wage rigidity. Since all wages, however, are not equally rigid, we might ask which ones are likely to be more or less flexible and see what implications this has for employment expansion.

Perhaps the ultimate in wage rigidity is illustrated by the "social minimum wage." Indeed, wages are in some cases so rigid at these levels that "unemployment" may persist for years. We should expect a greater degree of wage flexibility among workers earning something more than these minima. Given some job placements for retrained workers, cutbacks in employment elsewhere would be restrained by downward wage flexibility. Again, this would all show up finally in lower labor costs, greater output, lower prices, more sales, and more employment.

Two points should be made immediately. First, any wage flexibility among the employed workers is likely to come about by cutting labor costs in ways other than reducing money wages—by raising work loads or cutting expenditures for the comfort of employees, for example.

Second, we would certainly hope and expect that the government would seek to expand aggregate demand (increase the money supply or cut taxes, for example) to ease the enlargement of our labor force and to ease the financing of greater expenditures by consumers. It is difficult to place much faith in the power of the employment expansion effects of retraining without increasing aggregate demand.

In this connection, it is interesting to note that precisely such a mixture of policies is followed by the government in its depressed area programs. Retraining programs are supported by subsidies to industries and the relocation of firms in the area. Unemployment benefits and other relief measures are usually expanded. Almost all the money comes from outside the depressed area, and in such a context of widespread unemployment, multiplier effects of the spending assume a real importance. Net increases in employment are quite likely, and within the area job placements gained by graduates of retraining programs need not come at the expense of those who were not part of the programs.

REFERENCE MATTER

# Bibliographical Appendix

## Other Publications Stemming from the Ford Foundation Project on Retraining the Unemployed

By Gerald G. Somers

*Book Chapters*

"Retraining the Unemployed: A Preliminary Survey," *Hearings Before the Subcommittee on Employment and Manpower of the Committee on Labor and Public Welfare,* United States Senate, Eighty-Eighth Congress, First Session, June 7, 1963, and published as a chapter in *Men Without Work: The Economics of Unemployment,* ed. Stanley Lebergott. New York: Prentice-Hall, 1964.

"Retraining and Labor Market Policy," a discussion at the 1963 University of California Conference on Unemployment, published as a chapter in *Unemployment and the American Economy,* ed. Arthur M. Ross. New York: John Wiley and Sons, 1964.

"Training the Unemployed," chapter for *In Aid of the Unemployed,* ed. Joseph Becker, S.J. Baltimore, Md.: Johns Hopkins Press, 1964.

"Research Methodology in the Evaluation of Retraining Programs," published as a chapter in *Labour and Automation, Bulletin No. 1, Automation: A Discussion of Research Methods.* Geneva: International Labour Office, 1964.

"Retraining: An Evaluation of Gains and Costs," a paper presented at the University of California Conference on Unemployment Research in Boulder, Colorado, June, 1964, and published as a chapter in *Employment Policy and the Labor Market,* ed. Arthur M. Ross. Berkeley, Cal.: University of California Press, 1965.

"The Experience with Retraining and Relocation," presented at the Conferences on Manpower Policy, Berkeley Unemployment Project, New York City, June 20–22, 1966. Published as a chapter in *Toward a Manpower Policy,* ed. R. A. Gordon (New York: John Wiley and Sons, 1967), pp. 215–48.

"Evaluation of Manpower Development Programs," in *Human Resources Development,* eds. E. B. Jakubawskas and C. P. Baumel (Ames: University of Iowa Press, 1967), 143–52.

*Other Papers*

"Area Redevelopment Policies and the Older Workers," presented at the International Gerontological Research Seminar, Markaryd, Sweden, August, 1963, and Sixth International Congress of Gerontology, Copenhagen, August, 1963. Published in the Proceedings, *Age With a Future,* ed. P. From Hansen. Copenhagen: Munksgaard, 1964.

"Training and Retraining: Research as a Guide to Policy," presented at the Training and Retraining Conference sponsored by the Brookings Institution and the American Foundation on Automation and Employment, Williamsburg, Virginia, January, 1964. Published in the "Conference Report" (Washington: Brookings Institution, 1965), App. C, Sect. 8, pp. 1–35.

"A Benefit-Cost Analysis of Manpower Retraining" (with Ernst Stromsdorfer), *Proceedings of the Seventeenth Annual Meeting,* Industrial Relations Research Association, December, 1964 (Madison, Wis.: IRRA, 1965), 1–14.

"An Evaluation of Retraining Programs for Unemployed Older Workers," presented in a conference sponsored by the National Council on the Aging, Washington, D.C., October, 1965. Published in *Technology, Manpower, and Retirement Policy,* ed. Juanita Kreps (Cleveland, Ohio: World Publishing Co., 1966), pp. 109–25.

"An Evaluation of Government Retraining Programs for Older Unemployed Workers in the U.S.A.," *Proceedings of the Seventh International Congress of Gerontology,* Vienna, Austria, June 27–July 2, 1966, pp. 221–24.

"Retraining the Disadvantaged Worker" (with Glen Cain). Published in *Research in Vocational Education,* proceedings of a conference on research in vocational education (Center for Studies in Vocational and Technical Education, University of Wisconsin, 1967), pp. 27–44.

"Job Vacancies and Occupational Statistics: Discussion," presented at the Annual Meeting of the American Statistical Association, Philadelphia, Pa., September 11, 1965. Published in *ASA Proceedings,* January, 1966.

*Articles*

"Research on Manpower Implications of Technological Change: A Discussion," *Labor Law Journal,* Vol. 14, No. 8 (August, 1963), 669–76.

"Automation, Retraining and Public Welfare," *Automation and Public Welfare,* supplement to *Public Welfare* (journal of the American Public Welfare Association) (April, 1964), 18–26.

"Une programme de recherche sur la formation professionelle des adultes aux Etats-Unis," *Sociologie du Travail* (Janvier–Mars, 1965), 60–70.

*Reports*

"Government-Subsidized On-the-Job Training: Surveys of Employer Attitudes," in *Hearings Before the Subcommittee on Employment and Manpower of the*

*Committee on Labor and Public Welfare,* Sept., 1965. U.S. Senate, 89 Cong., I & II Sess. (Washington: GPO, 1966), 23–29.

"Retraining and Migration as Factors in Regional Economic Development" (with G. H. McKechnie and M. Tucker), report prepared for the Office of Regional Economic Development, September, 1966.

PUBLICATIONS AND REPORTS BY CO-OPERATING SCHOLARS
ON THE RETRAINING PROJECT

*Borus, Michael E., Assistant Professor, Michigan State University*

"The Effects of Retraining the Unemployed in Connecticut," unpublished doctoral dissertation, Yale University, 1964.

*The Economic Effectiveness of Retraining the Unemployed.* Boston: Federal Reserve Bank of Boston, 1966.

"A Benefit-Cost Analysis of Retraining the Unemployed," *Yale Economic Essays,* Vol. 4, No. 2 (Fall, 1964), 371–430.

"The Cost of Retraining the Hard-Core Unemployed: An Economic Evaluation of the 1963 and 1965 Amendments to the Manpower Development and Training Act," *Labor Law Journal,* Vol. 16, No. 9 (September, 1965), 574–83.

"Response Error in Survey Reports of Earnings Information," *Journal of the American Statistical Association,* Vol. 61, No. 315 (September, 1966).

"Time Trends in the Benefits from Retraining in Connecticut," *Proceedings of the Twentieth Annual Meeting,* Industrial Relations Research Association, December, 1967 (Madison: IRRA, May, 1968).

*Cain, Glen G., Associate Professor, University of Wisconsin*

"Retraining the Disadvantaged Worker" (with G. Somers), published in *Research in Vocational Education,* proceedings of a conference on research in vocational education. Center for Studies in Vocational and Technical Education, University of Wisconsin, 1967.

*Chesler, Herbert E., Assistant Professor, University of Pittsburgh*

"Worker Retraining Under the Area Redevelopment Act: A Massachusetts Study," unpublished doctoral dissertation, based on research supported by the grant, completed at Massachusetts Institute of Technology, 1963.

*Gibbard, Harold A., Chairman, Department of Sociology, West Virginia University*

"Factors Affecting Retraining in West Virginia," *Labor Law Journal,* Vol. 15 (July, 1964), 424–30. Extracted as "Retraining in West Virginia," *Monthly Labor Review,* Vol. 87 (June, 1964), 661–62.

"The Upgrading of Human Resources in Appalachia," presented at the annual meeting of the Society for Applied Anthropology, April 30, 1965, Lexington, Kentucky.

*Hausman, Leonard J., Assistant Professor, Indiana University*

"Using Monetary Incentives to Mobilize and Stabilize the Employment of Welfare Recipients," unpublished doctoral dissertation, University of Wisconsin, 1967.

*E. C. and K. S. Koziara, Assistant Professors at Drexel Institute and Temple University, respectively*

E. C. Koziara, "Employer Evaluations of Federal Retraining," *Training Directors' Journal,* Vol. 9, No. 10 (October, 1965).

E. C. and K. S. Koziara, "What Form Should Government Retraining Take?" *Personnel,* Vol. 42, No. 6 (November–December, 1965).

E. C. and K. S. Koziara, "Tax Cut and Retraining: Relative Merits in Combatting Unemployment (Employer Views)," *Atlanta Economic Review,* Vol. 16, No. 5 (May 1966).

E. C. Koziara, "Government Retraining of the Unemployed," paper presented to Plans for Progress, December 13, 1965, Washington, D.C.

E. C. and K. S. Koziara, "An Appraisal of the Strength and Weaknesses of Federal Retraining Programs," paper presented to American Petroleum Institute's Division of Refining, May 10, 1966, Houston, Texas.

E. C. Koziara, "Employer Evaluations of Federal Retraining," paper presented to California Counseling and Guidance Association, February 13, 1967, San Diego, California.

*Levine, Marvin, Assistant Professor, Ohio State University*

"An Evaluation of Retraining Programs for Unemployed Workers in the United States," unpublished doctoral dissertation, University of Wisconsin, 1964.

"Union Retraining Programs and the Role of Collective Bargaining in Combating Chronic Unemployment," *Labor Law Journal,* Vol. 15, No. 6 (June, 1964), 368–85.

"Training and Retraining in American Industry: An Appraisal of the Evidence as an Ameliorative for Unemployment," *Labor Law Journal,* Vol. 15, No. 10 (October, 1964), 634–47.

"State and Local Retraining Programs and Legislation: A Case for Federal Action," *Labor Law Journal,* Vol. 16, No. 1 (January, 1965), 27–43.

"The Failure of Apprenticeship Training in Skilled Manpower Development," *Labor Law Journal,* Vol. 16, No. 10 (October, 1965), 635–42.

"The Evolution of Vocational Education and Training in Employment Stabilization," *Labor Law Journal,* Vol. 16, No. 12 (December, 1965), 778–89.

*McKechnie, Graeme H., Assistant Professor, York University*

"Retraining and Geographic Mobility: An Evaluation," unpublished doctoral dissertation, University of Wisconsin, 1966.

"The Older Worker and Retraining—A Survey of MDTA Experience," in *Proceedings of a National Conference on Manpower Training and the Older Worker,* sponsored by the National Council on the Aging, Washington, D.C., January 17–19, 1966, pp. 68–77

"Vocational Retraining of the Unemployed" (with Gerald G. Somers), *Proceedings of the Twentieth Annual Meeting*, Industrial Relations Research Association, December, 1967 (Madison: IRRA, May, 1968).

*Moser, Collette, Assistant Professor, Rutgers University*

"An Evaluation of Area Skill Surveys as a Basis for Manpower Policy," doctoral dissertation in process, University of Wisconsin.

*Pichler, Joseph, Assistant Professor, University of Kansas*

"The Influence of Shutdown Provisions upon the Adjustment Patterns of Displaced Workers," unpublished doctoral dissertation, University of Chicago, 1965.

*Schaefer, Carl, Department of Vocational-Technical Education, Rutgers University*

*Pennsylvania Meets the Challenge of Retraining: Case Studies of a Three-Pronged Attack* (with John Shemick). Pennsylvania State University Press, 1965.

*Smith, Wilbur J., Research Associate, University of West Virginia*

"The Cost and Benefits of Retraining and Relocation in an Economically Depressed Area: A Case Study of Five Counties in West Virginia," doctoral dissertation in process, University of Wisconsin.

*Solie, Richard J., Associate Professor, University of North Dakota*

"Job Retraining Under the Area Redevelopment Act: The Campbell-Claiborne Counties (Tennessee) Case," unpublished doctoral dissertation, University of Tennessee, August, 1965.
"The Employment Effects of Retraining the Unemployed," *Industrial and Labor Relations Review*, Vol. 21 (January, 1968).

*Stromsdorfer, Ernst W., Associate Professor, Pennsylvania State University*

"A Benefit-Cost Analysis of Manpower Retraining" (with G. Somers), in *Proceedings of the Seventeenth Annual Meeting*, Industrial Relations Research Association, December, 1964 (Madison: IRRA, 1965).
"The Determinants of Economic Success in Retraining the Unemployed," *Journal of Human Resources*, Vol. 3, No. 1 (Winter, 1968).

*Weber, Arnold, Professor of Industrial Relations, University of Chicago*

*Strategies for the Displaced Worker* (with George Shultz). New York: Harper and Row, 1966.

# INDEX